Economic Aspects of New Deal Diplomacy

Economic Aspects of New Deal Diplomacy

LLOYD C. GARDNER

BEACON PRESS   BOSTON

To William Appleman Williams

The distinction between factors that are "economic" and those that are "non-economic" is, indeed, a useless and nonsensical device from the point of view of logic, and should be replaced by a distinction between "relevant" and "irrelevant" factors, or "more relevant" and "less relevant."

Gunnar Myrdal, *Economic Theory and Under-Developed Regions*, 1957

Preface

There have been few works on American economic diplomacy in the twentieth century; there have been only one or two specialized books on New Deal economic diplomacy, and these deal with postwar planning. That fact in itself is sufficient justification for undertaking this study. It began several years ago as an investigation of the nature of American anti-colonialism, but it soon became apparent that United States policy towards the colonial empires could not be separated from the complete corpus of New Deal diplomacy. Beyond that understanding came another: New Deal foreign policy had to be understood as a result of policies from earlier years and traditions, and it had to be understood for its influence upon the present. Gradually I was led deeper into economic materials until I decided that they would be the medium of the the study.

By the mid-1950's the New Deal had become a legend. Whether it was a good or bad influence depended upon one's politics. Liberals yearned for a return of the kind of leadership the country had experienced under Franklin D. Roosevelt; Conservatives pinched liberals' nerves with a counter-claim that Roosevelt had sold out the country at a series of war-time conferences with the British and the Russians.

The argument that developed from this clash distorted the past and made it serve purposes not warranted by the evidence. And it clouded the achievements of New Deal diplomacy just as much as it exaggerated its shortcomings.

The greatest distortion resulted from the dual assumption many historians have made about the New Deal and its foreign policy. There is, first, the insistence that the New Deal brought forth the finest elements of the American nonideological, pragmatic tradition. But at the same time a case is built, perhaps unconsciously, for a kind of exceptionalism by stressing Franklin Roosevelt's personal impact upon New Deal foreign policy—almost it would appear, to the exclusion of all other forces and factors. Such an assumption tears those twelve years out of American tradition and history and pins them up for exhibit on a totally blank background. No wonder, then, that exaggerations are made about the New Deal and Roosevelt!

The evidence presented in this study, on the contrary, indicates that the New Deal's approach to foreign policy was as much shaped by older principles and traditions as by any initiated by Franklin Roosevelt, who after all, had also grown up believing in such important American policies as that of the Asian Open Door.

It is contended here that, after a momentary pause, New Deal foreign policy rejoined the mainstream in 1934 with the adoption of the Reciprocal Trade Agreements Act. We are still in that mainstream. The major change which came out of World War II was that this current now runs through political alliances—both general and vague, such as the United Nations, and specific and pointed, such as NATO.

The present book falls roughly into four parts. The first describes the 1933–34 interregnum, when the New Deal, primarily concerned with domestic troubles, nevertheless perfected the means for restarting trade expansion efforts. From 1933 to 1937 New Deal foreign policies felt their way in Latin America, Asia, and Europe. From 1937 to 1941 the commitments in each area became firm and the understanding of the Axis challenge well implanted in the minds of American leaders. During the war the scope of American foreign policy widened until it included commitments all over the world. Postwar planning closely integrated economic, political, and ideological concepts into a well-developed overview. And not a few American leaders believed it was just high noon of the American Century.

I owe a great deal to many friends and teachers. Professors Walter LaFeber of Cornell University and Thomas McCormick of Ohio University have provided me with broad insights into other periods of American history as they relate to the New Deal, and sustained me with their friendship and encouragement.

President Fred Harvey Harrington of the University of Wisconsin first encouraged my interest in the New Deal and gave guidance and badly needed criticism of my work at a crucial stage of what eventually became this study.

Professor William Appleman Williams of the University of Wisconsin listened to my ideas for this book and has been a penetrating critic and an unceasing friend. My wife, Nancy, acted as an uncomplaining and unpaid secretary so that important research could be completed during the summer of 1961. I want also to thank the staffs of all the research libraries where the basic materials for this book were found and put together.

For all errors, of course, I am solely responsible.

L.C.G.

New Brunswick, N.J.
September, 1963

Introduction

It is now more than a quarter of a century since Franklin Delano Roosevelt's death. So much has been compressed into that time period that we find it hard to believe that the New Deal ended twenty-five years ago. Despite this phenomenon, American foreign policy is still being made by men who formed their deepest convictions about this country's place in the world during the 1930's and the Second World War. Every President since 1945 has declaimed against returning to negative "Isolationism," and each Secretary of State has given us a new corollary to the "Munich Analogy." Dean Rusk asserted in 1968 that the ultimate issue in Vietnam was nothing less than a new form of the challenge first posed by Hitler's Germany. To fail thirty years after Munich, he warned, would surely bring on a repetition of those events in Europe—with even more disastrous consequences for the world.

If I were setting out to re-write *Economic Aspects of New Deal Diplomacy* today, I would feel compelled to say much more about Franklin Roosevelt's struggle with his own "Isolationist" impulse, and endeavor to relate that conflict to a general statement of the importance of historical consciousness in the determination of all policies, including economic foreign policy. I would certainly wish to comment at length on the problem of rationality in decision-making, and the force of irrational motives in distorting all manner of well-laid plans. Added perspective reduces some images, and seems to magnify others. Yet the Great Depression still stands out in my mind as the necessary beginning point for any serious discussion of New Deal foreign policy. To the policymaker of that day, the depression was much more than a memory or an analogy: it was everyday reality. Franklin Roosevelt's generation had been shaped by the First World War and the failure of peacemaking at Versailles, but the 1929 crash and what came after impressed upon them the weakness of political structures caught in the path of economic calamity. Moreover, it offered them an economic interpretation of current world events which they projected both forwards and backwards. Congressmen investigated the "Munitions-makers" and the bankers in an effort to locate their influence on the decision to go to war in 1917. They did not ascribe Woodrow Wilson's choice for a declaration of war to economic causes, but their findings led to a demand for neutrality legislation, and a general resolve to stay out of any economic entanglements which might involve the United States in a new war. If there had been an economic motive, the bankers rightly insisted, it was far more pervasive than a simple desire on Wall Street's part for a big share of war loans. As one banker told the investigating committee in 1936, a newspaper dispatch in October, 1914, revealed that "there were 100,000 steel men idle in the Pittsburgh district. That gives a picture of our industrial situation at that time. There was a large amount of idleness. There was great dullness in our industries with an export business if we could."

Lawmakers in that decade of the National Recovery Administration and the Agricultural Adjustment Act understood the way such conditions influenced decision-making—even though they found themselves unable to legislate effectively against future economic involvements—better than historians in the 1950's, who, in Robert Freeman Smith's phrase, "view the period from 1920 to 1942 through the smoke-filled air of the Pearl Harbor attack." The very recent Congressional debate over government financing of the proposed supersonic transport project (SST), which took place in an atmosphere of economic instability, brought to mind memories of the "unemployment" issue of the 1930's. By the end of the debate, SST proponents had all but conceded the argument on the merits of the proposed aircraft, and turned to the employment issue as a last resort. If Congress voted down the project, it was asserted, 15,000 workers would be out of a job the next day, with thousands more to come in the future. The advocates lost in two crucial votes in the House and Senate, but the debate illustrated the way in which economic conditions intrude into policy questions. More often, these economic forces are implicit in Congressional deliberations. In 1930, for example, Congress did not set out to ruin the post-Versailles international economy with the Smoot-Hawley Tariff; nor were many of its members fully conscious of the delicate balance that had been struck between economic and political security among nations since the war.

The point is that we are talking about a way of seeing the world, and how general economic conditions of that world shape the parameters of decision-making. In some instances, quite obviously, the concern is reduced to the protection of a local market; in others it centers on the question of restoring access to world markets. These efforts often conflict and produce arguments. Various other factors then intrude on the consciousness of the policy-maker, sometimes diverting his decision into unanticipated directions. But the thrust of policy usually comes back to the main channel.

Projected forwards, American policymakers saw the post-World War II economic issue as the task of restoring the world economy to pre-depression foundations: non-discrimination and multilateralism. The lesson that had been learned in the depression was that the United States would have to accept political responsibility this time. The nation would have to accept responsibility for seeing to it that the war-torn economies of Western Europe had markets available to them in Europe, as well as in Asia, Africa and Latin America. It was not, therefore, that the United States "needed" Eastern European markets after World War II; the issue was far more serious than a few oil wells in Rumania or the return of the properties of the Singer Sewing Machine Company. It was a political question in that what was at stake was an environment conducive to the survival and expansion of American—and American style—institutions. For a decade before the outbreak of war, the dominant influence on American political life had been the depression. During the war several economists predicted a return to prosperity—at least in the short-run —but I have yet to find a single high-level policymaker who felt there was more than a fifty-fifty chance to avoid a new economic debacle. And they all agreed that if it were to be avoided, the United States would have to take the lead. That meant, when it came to Eastern Europe, that Washington would have to take the lead in demanding an Open Door policy.

When the peace treaties with Germany's former satellites in Central and Eastern Europe were presented to the Senate for ratification in 1947, former Secretary of State James F. Byrnes was asked:

> Yesterday the *New York Times* issued a very dramatic series of reports from its correspondents all over the world. These reports pointed out the fact that state-controlled economies have appeared everywhere, and that only here in the United States and in Canada, actually, are we still devoted to a belief in so-called private enterprise.
> I should like to ask the Secretary if any of these treaties give us reason to believe that they lay the present foundation for the defense of individual enterprise in a world in which state-controlled economy has become so dominant.

Byrnes's assurance that they did proved meaningless in the context of the Truman Doctrine and the Marshall Plan. Whatever promise the treaties had held for meaningful East-West diplomacy had to be abandoned in the face of rising world tensions. In that crisis countries like Czechoslovakia which had hoped to bridge the gulf between East and West, and which could have become the focal point for patient economic diplomacy, were sacrificed to ideological necessity.

* *

Many of the issues discussed in *Economic Aspects of New Deal Diplomacy* have since become subjects of excellent monographs. I would have profited greatly from these studies in the writing of my own book; they would have saved me from a great many errors of fact and interpretation of specific events. In re-writing the book, I would have dealt in much greater detail on certain other subjects, e.g., the conflicts between interests within the United States: raw materials producers and manufacturers, extractors and investors, entrepreneurs and corporations. I would certainly have devoted chapters to Anglo-Japanese-American competition in Asia, to the problem of state-controlled competition (whether Fascist or Communist) and its repercussions on domestic policy debates, and to special issues such as air planning and world resources questions. And when it was done, it would have been a different book. As it now reads, *Economic Aspects of New Deal Diplomacy*, represents an effort to understand the place of the New Deal in the history of American foreign policy, not a full development of all the economic factors pertaining to its operation. I have discussed some of these problems in other places; others remain suggestions for further study. Finally, I am grateful to Beacon Press for making this book available to a wider audience in a new decade. It may offer these readers an introduction to some of the substantive stuff behind diplomatic rhetoric.

L.C.G.

East Brunswick, N.J.
March 29, 1971

Contents

Economic Aspects of New Deal Diplomacy

1· The Crisis of the New Order

A society struggling neck-deep and still sinking in a modern Slough of Despond confronted Franklin D. Roosevelt and the New Dealers in 1933. Hoping to save their country, these men could themselves but dimly discern where the alternative paths towards solid ground would finally end. Vaguely they led towards two areas, internationalism and self-containment.

How to make a choice between the two was the crisis of the new order. Although the basic elements in each alternative had been at least partially understood since their first well-reasoned presentation by Jeffersonian laissez-faire landed expansionists and Hamiltonian mercantilists, much of the difficulty facing Roosevelt as he attempted to find the right way came from the very ambiguity of, and also within, each of these legacies as they had fallen to each new era and new generation of political leaders. For Jefferson learned from Madison and Gallatin the necessity of manufactures, and Hamilton had seen the need for westward expansion. Only in their earliest explication then, had Jefferson stood for agrarian expansion alone, and Hamilton for a more contained society. Each had changed his views before the end of his career.

Modern internationalists had followed that way of the pilgrim and pioneer across the country and on to the Pacific Ocean. New frontiers still existed, they said; on them the American could restore himself and his nation. "Even America, with all her magnificent resources," declared one national economic leader who had already spent much time on world frontiers and who would be called upon by the New Deal, "can never be wholly self-contained. . . . We are now on the threshhold of a new stage of progress and . . . America must lead the way." [1] So expansion and manufacturing had been linked throughout American history even during Jefferson's and Hamilton's time, and was at its peak in the twentieth century.

But how? asked others. America still remained trapped in depression

3

quicksands for month after month following the crash in 1929. Perhaps the answer could be found by proffering new incentives to the worried heirs of those earlier frontiersmen. Nineteenth-century settlers had become cotton growers and then cotton exporters; railroad builders had reached the Pacific and then tried to build in China and Manchuria; miners had dug in the Northwest and then searched for new mines through Latin America; and businessmen had sold to capacity and then looked everywhere for new markets. Further incentives could be given these men to go out into the world only if Washington could restore at least a modicum of international cooperation in a world that sought salvation in extreme nationalism.

Those who urged the nation towards self-containment stressed the impossibility of fulfilling this condition. If for no other reason, then, the nation could best be restored by policies based on national planning. Recovery having been achieved, there would still be plenty of opportunity to see if America perpetually needed new frontiers. They were confident that the nation would come to see that it did not, and that prosperity through internationalism was only an illusion. How could the panacea of free trade (by which actually was meant increased exports) heal the country's ills, for example, when it already enjoyed the largest free-trade market in the world? These men were planners who had grown up on the editorials of the *New Republic,* come to maturity during World War I, and been given, perhaps, a final molding by the dramatic suggestions and formulas of the British economist, John Maynard Keynes.[2]

Only a few of these men continued all the way to isolationism. Most granted that the frontier had played a key role in maintaining American democracy, and they had become planners only when their fright at continued conflicts, and even wars, on the frontier overcame earlier ways of thinking. A few were even disillusioned by such purely domestic frontier problems as the dust bowl, and what it led to—corporation farming. The brilliant Progressive editor William Allen White spoke of this last development, but his recognition of the need to control "great aggregates of capital" on the still semifrontier land in and around Kansas was not unlike the mood that made many Progressives prefer nationalism to internationalism. "These chain farmers propose to wipe out the home and country town, buy their machinery directly from the manufacturer, (or make it) combine of course in one or two marketing units and do for our wheat country exactly what Bolshevism is doing for the wheat country of Russia. It is a curious parallel." [3]

If White was correct, the original frontier thesis—that democracy was a product of and sustained by the existence of a frontier where class differences melted away—could not be maintained any longer. On the other hand, as the father of the thesis, Frederick Jackson Turner, wrote in 1896, the internationalists had developed their own corollary which stated that the Far West, having been linked to the other sections of the country, might stimulate a "drastic assertion of national government and imperial expansion under a popular hero." Turner correctly predicted that Theodore Roosevelt would become such a hero.[4] But they hardly identified the search for new frontiers in such blunt terms as Turner had set forth in his work. For most internationalists were more circumspect.

The second Roosevelt, still uncommitted to either path at the time of his first inaugural address, demanded "direct, vigorous action" and pledged himself to use his executive power to pull the country out of the depths. But as he finished this speech, there remained little more than a vague halo of Progressivism hanging over the Capitol.

Anxiously, Congress assembled in special session to hear how the New Deal proposed to transform this ethereal stuff into something solid. It obediently enacted a spate of emergency legislation, heard plans for a National Recovery Administration and an Agricultural Adjustment Administration, and, amid some clamorings for more radical action, left Washington, having designated the NRA and the AAA the primary guides and means to recovery.

But within the year it became evident that these experiments in cooperative regulation just could not free large segments of the economy from the stubborn muck. Improvement there was, but millions of unemployed received little comfort from watching the Blue Eagle NRA banners on parade. Farm prices rose, but agricultural problems like the sharecropper's perennial dilemma were scarcely diminished. Worse, there was a growing uneasiness that these programs actually consolidated more and more power in the already dominant forces and groups within industry and agriculture. John Dewey, the American philosopher who best expressed his country's faith in such experimentalism, had dramatically warned that an entirely new framework had to be found. Capitalism was no longer sufficient: "We have permitted business and financial autocracy to reach such a point that its logical political counterpart is a Mussolini: unless a violent revolution brings forth a Lenin." [5]

Neither catastrophe befell the nation: a measure of recovery ensured the political success of the New Deal, and it appeared, therefore, that

Dewey had underestimated the enduring viability of his and the New Deal's pragmatism.

Or so the story went. It gained as much strength as a legend as the years passed. Authors first described the New Deal as a revolution, then defined it as evolution—but as either it had been democracy's answer to its severest domestic crisis. And in the general prosperity that followed World War II, the question seemed irrelevant to most Americans. Yet there remained doubts. How many of the society's fundamental problems had really been corrected, or even attacked? How real had the recovery been? How dangerous the path taken? Such questions raised a particularly difficult one concerning the development of New Deal foreign policy. Explaining the mood of the nation at the time of the NRA and the AAA, historians suggested that Roosevelt's early foreign policy of isolation, big-navyism, and extreme nationalism had been forced upon him by the isolationists. In this view the nation finally realized its folly only just in time to allow Roosevelt to lead the Allies against the Axis menace.

In 1945, however, Henry Steele Commager presented a counterview to this interpretation: "In the 1890's we aggressively assumed a position as a world power, and the roots of our present involvement trace back to that decade." [6] This interpretation minimized tactical maneuvers and stressed the continuity in American foreign policy from the closing of the frontier through the New Deal years.

Few New Dealers, even among the Administration's intellectual leaders, took time in 1933 to formulate their assumptions so exactly. Some were in fact pure pragmatists; on the other hand, many had the frontier motif deeply ingrained in their experience and shifted back to it just as soon as nationalistic planning proved insufficient to restore the country—first as a supplement, then almost as a substitute.*

One of the clearest explanations of the alternatives before the New Deal came from the outgoing president, Herbert Hoover, who described not two, but three paths out of the Depression.

---

* It often goes unnoticed that a shift from nationalistic planning to internationalism was quite possible for even the most dedicated Keynesian thinker. Among many such interpretations of Lord Keynes's thought, a recent one in *Business Week* (March 9, 1963, p. 160) was striking. It warned that Keynes must be interpreted properly to the 1960's. Keynes had called for policies to increase liquidity and total demand during a depression. But, said *Business Week*, he also believed that wage rates must be held in check if the other policies were to work and ensure productivity gains which would then "be translated into lower prices in international markets, thereby helping the nation's balance of payments position."

HOOVER EXPLAINS THE ALTERNATIVES

On the evening of February 13, 1933, the National Republican Club of New York City heard the President's informal farewell address. His theme was the direct relationship between America's depression and the world situation. In drafting this speech, Hoover had called upon his Secretary of State and other Department officers to submit their ideas and to help him with its organization. This speech was the Hoover Administration's final plea for a policy of international cooperation. In this last fortnight of his stewardship, however, the President stood alone against the inevitable like a deserted chess king. As he spoke, financial castles crumbled in Memphis, St. Louis, Kansas City, New Orleans, and Detroit. Secretary of State Henry L. Stimson noted gravely that Hoover had "hoped to get through the last two weeks of his term without a collapse. But now it had come in Detroit, and the Lord only knows how far it will go." [7]

The banking crisis convinced Hoover all the more that he must get his views across to the nation before the New Deal assumed power. In happier days, he had personified the successful American pioneer. Starting from California he had ranged across Asian and Middle Eastern lands, bringing wealth to himself and honor to the nation. He had then helped Woodrow Wilson make the world safe for American democracy, and had stayed on for the no less exacting work during "normalcy" of guiding American businessmen into world markets. He had summarized his faith in *American Individualism* (1922) as follows: So long as the American retains the spirit of the pioneer, there would remain frontiers of "human welfare" waiting always to be developed. "The pioneer spirit is the response to the challenge of opportunity, to the challenge of nature, to the challenge of life, to the call of the frontier." [8]

In this, the fourth winter of the Great Depression, Hoover sought a new way to rephrase that challenge. He decided to present it as a three-pronged choice before the nation:

"The American people will soon be at the fork of three roads. The first is the highway of cooperation among nations, thereby to remove the obstructions to world consumption and rising prices. This road leads to real stability, to expanding standards of living, to a resumption of the march of progress by all peoples. It is today the immediate road to relief of agriculture and unemployment, not alone for us but for the entire world." [9]

Now it was true that Herbert Hoover had come to the presidency as the candidate of the party which had once rejected internationalism by staying out of the League of Nations. It is also true that he had signed the nationalistic Smoot-Hawley Tariff Act of 1930. But the Republican party's Charles Evans Hughes had actively encouraged international cooperation among world naval powers by calling the 1921 Washington Naval Conference; the Warren Harding Administration had adopted the unconditional most-favored-nation trade agreement policy; and its internationally oriented Commerce Secretary Herbert Hoover had led American industry to all the far reaches of the globe. So great was this drive that one Commerce Department official who served under Hoover pointed out that from 1923 to 1929 commercial attachés or trade commissioners were sent into "practically every foreign country." Foreign trade soared to all-time highs.[10] There was a striking parallel between British foreign policy after the Napoleonic Wars and American foreign policy in the 1920's. In each instance the nation had to supply money and loans to its allies, and even its enemies. In each instance the nation involved wanted to follow a policy of political isolation, yet enjoy commercial advantages. But no one ever treats British foreign policy in this period as big I Isolationism.

From Woodrow Wilson on, suggests Max Lerner in *America as a Civilization,* various groups felt they had a "stake in the emergence of an active American responsibility in the world: in the case of business groups, the stake was the maintenance of open world markets, in the case of liberals the maintenance of a world climate hospitable to the basic freedoms." [11]

President Hoover and Secretary Stimson, like most American policy makers, integrated these drives and interests into a comprehensive world outlook. But in the closing world of 1933 America's rivals, and even its friends, challenged and denied Washington's ability to keep the world open. Japan had started to fence off Manchuria, Great Britain to build preference barriers around the Commonwealth, and Germany to undertake the reconstruction of a past empire in Central Europe.

A few years earlier, at the end of World War I, America's best-known frontier writer, Hamlin Garland, had foreseen this development and feared for his country's future: "What will come after this destruction ends? For forty years America has enjoyed a steady advance. It cannot expect to have another forty years of like tranquillity. We are getting the habit of war." [12]

Garland preferred to "back-trail" from the Middle Border and the frontier. Hoover insisted, however, that the challenge need not mean war if the nation could take the lead in the search for world cooperation. There were still some nations that might be persuaded to maintain international morality and international material standards, such as the gold standard, and America had certain levers to pull, such as the Allied war-debts, to hold England and France at least momentarily to policies of cooperation. Or so Hoover believed. But he reluctantly admitted that Garland might be right and that the United States might have to take the second path if cooperation proved impossible: "The second road is to rely upon our high degree of national self-containment, to increase our tariffs, to create quotas and discriminations, and to engage in definite methods of curtailment of production of agricultural and other products and thus to secure a larger measure of economic isolation from world influences. It would be a long road of readjustments into unknown and uncertain fields. But it may be necessary if the first way out is closed to us." [13]

Indeed, the Hoover Administration had ventured out a little way on this path. By 1933 the President declined to go any farther, but several conservatives, such as Bernard Baruch, Gerard Swope, and Henry I. Harriman, pondered the possibilities of going beyond the Reconstruction Finance Corporation, the Federal Farm Board, or the Administration's small public works program. They agreed with Columbia University's Nicholas Murray Butler: "The man with a plan, however much we dislike it, has a vast advantage over the group sauntering down the road of life complaining of the economic weather and wondering when the rain is going to stop." [14]

Far across the political continuum stood other advocates of national planning, such as John Dewey and Charles Beard. There were also growing numbers of socialists and communists "of the heart" in America at this time, but Dewey and Beard best combined American traditions with a new political program. The latter's *Open Door at Home* (1934) contained the most dramatic suggestions for a new foreign and domestic policy. He began by attacking the historic Open Door policy in the Far East as a dangerous illusion—illusory in that the markets of China could never absorb the surpluses from an unbalanced economy at home, dangerous in that the pursuit of such markets led to foreign wars. Using the Open Door as a symbol, Beard turned it inward and called for a revitalization of the American economy through "continuous control over the processes of production and consumption."

He hoped that the United States would progress towards democratic socialism.[15]

These antipodal segments of American opinion thus shared a belief that national policies grounded in national planning might offer the best, if not the only, way out of the depression. Conservatives thought it a distasteful alternative; Progressives welcomed it.

There remained still a third alternative, said Hoover: "The third road is that we inflate our currency, consequently abandoning the gold standard, and with our depreciated currency attempt to enter a world economic war; with the certainty that it leads to complete destruction, both at home and abroad." [16]

From recent contacts Hoover gloomily expected that Roosevelt would choose either the second or the still more dangerous third path. But the Republican President also knew that inflationist opinion was not limited to the Democratic party. Montana silver miners and Iowa farmers, Chicago salesmen, and even some New York bankers were asserting that a cheap dollar could raise domestic prices and stimulate exports. Most disturbing, these inflationists advocated the very actions that Washington had condemned in others, such as Japan and Great Britain, two nations which had left the gold standard and devalued their currencies.[17]

Hoover could see no end to this kind of global economic aggression but war. Japan's combined military and economic attack on American interests was the prime case in point. Washington tried to dissuade Tokyo from its course; and although Secretary Stimson occasionally advocated a more bellicose response, his main emphasis was on logic and reason. In January, 1933, he told the Japanese ambassador about "our theories of what the movement against war meant and [how] we were trying to protect our civilization, and if Japan wanted to live on a different basis than the one we had chosen with these peace treaties she had better get out of the peace treaties and not break them. We should consider ourselves living in two different worlds." [18]

Stimson thus censured Japan's forward movement in Manchuria, but he was equally upset by Japan's economic warfare. For American leaders drew no distinction between the economic and political worlds: they were the same. Hence the Secretary admonished the French ambassador concerning his country's war debts to the United States that "cooperation in the re-establishment of world prosperity is uppermost in the mind of my government. In this connection, however, it should not be forgotten that the integrity of agreements is one of the principal supports upon which the stability of society rests." [19]

To the Republican leadership, Japanese and French actions represented grave challenges to the interlocking parts that made up world order and stability. Those nations who were dissatisfied should seek an agreed upon amendment to their commitments, but they had absolutely no right to abrogate them unilaterally. That was Washington's view, but to the rest of the world such an order was an unreal jigsaw puzzle, which Americans cursed when it would not stay together.

And despite his best efforts, Stimson forlornly admitted that the pieces were sliding apart. The problem confronted him everywhere. The United States could not recognize the Soviet Union in 1932, for example, as he wrote Senator William Borah, because the Japanese would claim that Washington's determined stand on not recognizing Tokyo's puppet rulers in Manchuria was only opportunism, masking "force or political alliances." [20]

Elsewhere multiple Latin American revolutions wrecked the Hoover-Stimson vision: "If we try to take the lead for them, at once there is a cry against American domination and imperialism. But in Leticia the action of Peru has been so unprovoked and so without any defense, that we may have to intervene to protect the treaties which are being smashed. It is Manchuria once again on a small scale." [21]

Across the Atlantic Ocean in the African country of Liberia there was another cruel dilemma developing. A Government unfriendly to the vast Firestone rubber interests gained power at this time, and Washington suspected that London was trying to replace United States influence there. Both Hoover and Stimson were determined to protect American interests, even though international cooperation would suffer if gunboats had to be sent to Liberian ports. Stimson especially feared the "howl this would produce in Europe and among our blacks in this country, and the ease with which it could be made to appear inconsistent with our Manchurian policy." [22]

In Europe, Hoover compromised his principles even more by allowing arms sales to Yugoslavia, though they cut against his over-all policy. The President admitted to Stimson that he was an "opportunist in this matter, trying to earn a dollar by foreign sales wherever possible." But these two later stood against the rest of the President's advisers when the question of an arms embargo came before the Cabinet. The State Department had drafted a proposal for presidential authority to impose such an embargo whenever the executive determined such shipments would aid warring countries. The remainder of the Cabinet Secretaries insisted, as did several powerful economic interests, that nothing should be done during a depression which would hinder foreign sales.[23]

"The trouble today," concluded Norman Davis, a foreign policy adviser to both Hoover and Roosevelt, "is that all nations are threatened with continuing losses in trade and investments because none of them are willing to give up anything, no[t] even armaments, in order to save everything." This outlook led Hoover to press his arguments upon President-elect Franklin Roosevelt. He hoped to persuade the New York Governor to support the outgoing Administration's plans for international debt negotiations, disarmament talks, and a proposed world economic conference to be held at London.[24]

Roosevelt was skeptical of these pleas; he was more than half-convinced they were no more than political maneuvers. In addition he had come to doubt that further efforts at international planning in the world of 1933 would bring much success. "Just how Great Britain can take the hint of President Hoover," agreed the *New York Times* on January 1 of that year, "and give more trade to the United States as compensation for war-debts reduction is beyond the comprehension of both protectionists and free traders." In the previous twelve months, concluded the *Times* article, Britain had absorbed four times as much from the United States as it had sold here.

Roosevelt's campaign, when it touched on foreign policy, had pinpointed just such weaknesses in Republican internationalism. At Columbus, Ohio, he had charged that Hoover was all wrong in saying that the depression had come to America from other countries. True enough, American foreign loans had collapsed when foreign nations could no longer sell to the United States because of the high tariff, but that was not the same thing Hoover had been arguing.[25]

This exposé of Republican selfishness at home and abroad did not, however, explain how the Democratic candidate's program would be any more effective. In fact, most critical observers wondered if he had any program at all, much less a logical and consistent alternative. At San Francisco, Roosevelt told the Commonwealth Club that the days of frontier individualism were over and the nation needed centralized planning, but in Butte, Montana, he assured silverites that he believed in American initiative in all "important matters of world-wide concern. You and I know the manner in which different parts of the United

States are interdependent, and you and I are coming to realize the inter-dependence of all nations in the world in such matters." [26] Although the Brains Trust (later called Brain Trust) was said to be "national-istic," Roosevelt was known to have internationalist advisers as well. And Herbert Hoover might just as easily have authored the Butte, Montana, speech.

In short, despite his repudiation of the Hoover thesis, Roosevelt had not chosen either of the other two alternative paths the Republican had described on February 13, 1933.

ROOSEVELT LISTENS TO THE BRAINS TRUST
AND OTHERS

In the 1932 campaign the members of the Brains Trust were the strongest proponents of national planning. Raymond Moley of Columbia had brought these men to Roosevelt's attention when the latter was still Governor of New York. Moley once defined the causes of the depression as the Brains Trust saw them as follows: "We agreed that the heart of our difficulty was the anarchy of concentrated economic power." Beyond that starting point, though, the Brains Trust members sharply divided. Moley envisaged a partnership between big business and the body of the citizenry acting through the Government, and later when it came into being the NRA most nearly approximated his out-look. Rexford Tugwell offered a different view. He believed that the Government ought to be the focal point for reconciling differences between particularist interests and controlling their natural selfishness. He differed from Moley primarily on the character of big business. Tugwell thought that any partnership would have to be forced by the Government—on the Government's terms. Seventeenth- and eighteenth-century mercantilistic language and logic dotted his philosophy. "Under this plan," he said of the AAA, "it will pay farmers, for the first time, to be social-minded, to do something for all instead of for himself alone. We thus succeed, we think, in harnessing a selfish motive for the social good." [27]

Public virtues from private vices—here, indeed, was an updated mercantilism. Tugwell's thoughts on the westward movement of the past century also seemed mercantilistic in origin. The drive west had resulted in the "occupation of our Empire. It was a source of raw materials and a market for goods. So far as raw materials were con-cerned, Idaho and Colorado, for example, were treated exactly like

Mexico or Peru." Recognizing these past successes, Tugwell now insisted that America had to rationalize its Empire rather than search vainly for new adjuncts.[28]

Adolf A. Berle brought the Brains Trust his ideas on the role of modern industrial corporations in the breakdown of traditional relationships between personality and property. He felt that this development needed to be understood if a comprehensive view of the Great Depression—and the path to recovery were to be successfully mastered. "Liquid property is, in form and legal theory substantially the same as was the old farm, or the tapestry weaving shop in France," wrote Berle. "But the substance of it has been bled white—white of personality, white of satisfaction, of creative desire, white of that quality of property which Mussolini, in one of his more inspired moments called the 'extension of personality.' " [29]

Berle had several recommendations for returning personal responsibility to modern society. "I am imagining also," he told another presidential adviser, "that a considerable part of the relief program might be handled by means of loans to individuals, so that their name would appear on the note; the individual notes gathered in by relief or other similar agencies and thus consolidated; and guaranteed entering into the banking structure, This might take care of the 'white collar' and intelligentsia classes of relief." [30]

As Moley later remarked, the Brains Trust thus opposed traditional internationalism as the solution to the problems of the American economy. But while they provided inspiration and substance for the attack on the immediate domestic crisis, they occasionally looked beyond to American participation in world affairs. And even in the first days of the New Deal, some of them modified their theories more towards alternative solutions. "It was not that tariff reduction was *per se* incompatible with the economics of the New Deal that was taking shape," observed Moley. "But that there was a crucial question of timing and method." Within a few months this adviser would himself advocate cooperation at the London Economic Conference; still later he defended Hoover's darkest path, unilateral inflation, "in order that Oriental and South American countries may again be able to purchase American goods." [31]

Tugwell, too (still imbibing good mercantilist thoughts), did not shut out speculations about the future course of empire. "Across that sea [the Pacific] lies the underdeveloped Orient, and in it lie comparatively unexhausted riches." One of his memoranda to Roosevelt, "International Economic and Financial Policies," suggested reciprocal trade agreements as a way to stimulate exports to benefit both the consumer and the farmer. Adolf Berle wrote another calling attention to the vast underdeveloped markets of Russia as a possible outlet for farm surpluses. Moreover, he noted elsewhere, European war debts made a good bargaining point for tariff reductions. President Hoover, it will be remembered, thought exactly the same thing.[32]

Berle believed that new frontiers in science and technology had to be explored if America were to overcome the depression. In presenting this truism, the adviser incidentally posed the critical question about the American frontier thesis as it had been amended by 1933: "It is not easy to think of a civilization which is not constantly pushing out its frontiers in terms of goods and services, though geography is beginning to be a restricted field." [33]

Geography was restricted, and even within that possibility, other barriers to foreign expansion were growing all over the world. Yet those closest to foreign policy problems in the New Deal urged a continued thrust into new areas. As Ernest K. Lindley put it," Mr. Hull's program aimed at the revival of international laissez-faire capitalism." [34]

While a United States senator, Cordell Hull was known to be one of the few members of Congress who regularly studied foreign periodicals. This Tennessee Democrat appeared to be the natural choice for Secretary of State, though many wondered if Hull's internationalism would survive among Brains Trust ideas. Historic low-tariff politics in the Democratic party may have made his choice an essential one for Roosevelt, but to stop there misses another crucial point: Hull's freer trade pleas appealed to many groups besides the Southern Democrats. Meditating upon the causes of World War I, Hull had decided that "unhampered trade dovetailed with peace; high tariffs, trade barriers, and unfair economic competition with war." In 1929 he had sternly warned fellow legislators, "conditions soon will compel America to recognize that these ever increasing surpluses are her key economic problems, and that our neglect to develop foreign markets for surpluses is the one outstanding cause of unemployment." That year was the last prosperous one for a decade, and Hull's analysis seemed even more valid during those ten years after the "bust." [35]

Franklin Roosevelt did not believe that Cordell Hull had the answer to America's problems; but he did not shut him out even in the early New Deal, and he moved closer to Hull's position each year. Roosevelt's personal friend Sumner Welles, who shared Hull's views on the importance of foreign trade, was soon named Undersecretary of State. A career diplomat "with a cold eye and a forbidding appearance," Welles saw the folly of American Big Stick diplomacy in Latin America. If the clouds of suspicion could be pushed aside, however, something like an economic commonwealth might appear in the Western Hemisphere. Wishing to emphasize these possibilities, Welles sent Roosevelt a memorandum on inter-American relations: "We cannot expect to preserve the sincere friendship of our neighbors on this Continent if we close our markets to them. We cannot enjoy the markets of the American continent, which have as vast a potential as any in the world, unless we permit the citizens of our sister nations to trade with us." [36]

Though the Good Neighbor Policy did not actually originate with this memo or with the New Deal, it has justly been associated with it from the inaugural address. Remembering that, it is also necessary to recall that the Policy was never intended to be a philanthropic gesture. As Welles informed a colleague, a million dollar Public Works Administration appropriation had been secured for the construction of a Pan American highway which all concerned believed would promote inter-American commerce and cooperation.[37]

Besides Cordell Hull and Sumner Welles, other State Department policy makers—such as Herbert Feis, William Phillips, and Stanley K. Hornbeck—provided day-to-day guidance under Hoover and stayed on in key positions when the New Deal came to power. These men all wanted active participation in world political and economic affairs. "Can you spell out the elements of what would be a joint international program to raise world prices?" Feis asked a prominent economist. "Events will certainly force policy in the direction of expansion; I am in hopes that men will guide events that way before events force them." [38]

Stanley Hornbeck's circle of vision focused on the Far East, but he soon broadened it to include the rest of Asia and the world. In the 1920's he had supported government aid to exporters to help gain world markets: "It will be necessary to adopt in some respects at least, the tactics of competitors . . . . Is it not both reasonable and expedient that this government should use every fair means to prevent the denial by other governments of opportunities to American companies to which they are entitled?" [39]

These problems filled Hornbeck's mind as he addressed the American Conference on the Causes of War in the 1930's: "Having made of their country a world power, and having during the last 3 decades overcome or been deprived of their natural aloofness, the American people have been brought up against certain age-old problems in international relations." This nation's solution had been the Open Door Policy, which was, he added in an official policy memorandum, merely a particular application of certain principles "which are general as regards our foreign policy." The principles were equality of trade opportunity and territorial integrity. [40]

With all of this advice—Hoover's three alternatives, Brains Trust nationalism (whether temporary or permanent), and the internationalist ideas of the State Department—Roosevelt was well informed. But his final decision would no doubt be shaped also by his own ideas and experience.

THE EARLY EDUCATION OF A PROGRESSIVE

"He probably would not go as far as I would go," wrote Senator Burton K. Wheeler to another liberal in June, 1932, "but we cannot always get as candidates, people who entirely agree with our views." [41] Liberals who supported Roosevelt's candidacy in 1932 generally shared Wheeler's opinion and the pragmatic conclusion that the New York Governor was possibly the best choice for them. They knew that Roosevelt had gathered a group of "thinkers" around him at Albany and Hyde Park, but had they been as aware of the doubts even within this circle of advisers, their alarm would have been much greater. Rexford Tugwell once described the advisers' role as that of detail suppliers for Roosevelt's mental notebook. The pages were already headed on many issues, and the candidate was apparently looking for new means rather than a new set of ends.

It was, to begin with, the notebook of a Progressive. After a short apprenticeship in the New York State Legislature, Roosevelt's enthusiastic support for Woodrow Wilson at the 1912 Democratic Convention brought him a position of power in the new Administration. Like his cousin Theodore, Franklin Roosevelt started a national career as Assistant Secretary of the Navy. He served in that position from 1913 to

1920, and became a strong champion of naval power. Speaking of the navy's role near the end of this service, Secretary Roosevelt declared: "Our national defense must extend all over the Western Hemisphere, must go out a thousand miles to sea, must embrace the Philippines wherever our commerce may be . . . ." [42]

In 1920 he reaffirmed the importance of protecting our "commerce, no matter on what sea . . . . I think it can fairly be said that our navy shall be equal to the greatest." In that year Roosevelt helped lead the fight for the League of Nations as his party's vice-presidential candidate, but political defeat and then physical illness shortly thereafter removed him from any sort of political office. As he recovered, he maintained his contacts within the party. Equally important, Roosevelt kept his views before the nation. Observing the growing hostility between the United States and Japan, he called for cooperation between the two nations to complete the upbuilding of the Orient. "It is true that we shall continue to overlap and perhaps to clash in the development of the commerce of the Pacific, but when we consider the potential trade of the vast territories and huge populations bordering the North Pacific and South Pacific Oceans," he wrote in a 1923 issue of *Far East Review,* "there would seem to be enough commercial room and to spare for both Japan and us well into the indefinite future . . . ." [43]

Chiding Republican Latin American policies before a Georgia audience in 1928, he insisted that the United States had to regain "its position of moral leadership." "The nineteen or twenty republics to the south of us in Latin America . . . have seen what they call our imperialism . . . . It is an announced Democratic doctrine not to interfere in the internal affairs of our neighboring sister republics . . . ." [44]

Though much of the assertiveness had mellowed since his days as Assistant Secretary of the Navy and his campaign for the vice-presidency when he had boasted of writing Haiti's constitution, Roosevelt always preserved his interest in an expanding foreign trade and in America's world role. In 1928, for example, he not only spoke of assuming moral leadership but undertook as one of his many business ventures the formation of the Federal International Investment Trust to stimulate foreign trade. Upon election to the Governorship of New York, he requested his friend, the financier and diplomat Norman Davis, to complete the work. The Investment Trust, he explained to Davis, would "adequately fill an urgent need for expanded facilities in our international financial relations." In this letter, Roosevelt enclosed the organizing committee's prospectus, which called the reader's attention to the lack of adequate credit facilities available to the American exporter—a situation that presented a "stonewall handicap to manufacturers, miners, and farmers who must look beyond domestic demands for markets to consume their production. For 150 years we have been primarily concerned with the domestic market. Now the situation has changed." A classic example of the pervasive, yet seemingly unconscious, and therefore all the more interesting, influence of the frontier thesis on foreign policy assumptions, this prospectus might have been made a part of the wording of the New Deal Export-Import Bank Act a few years later.[45]

Ironically, expedients like the Federal International Investment Trust drew Roosevelt's sharpest criticism during the 1932 campaign.

By 1930 most Americans would have been happy enough just to see the domestic market restored. "There is no question," Governor Roosevelt said in answer to an inquiry, "that there will be a gain throughout our country of communist thought unless we can keep democracy up to its old ideals and its original purposes." In New York he tried to do this through conservation, electrification, and public works.[46]

For the nation, though, Roosevelt was less affirmative about that kind of planning. He advocated a balanced budget, equivocated on the burning farm-surpluses issue, and presented a generally conservative appearance in 1932. "Mr. Roosevelt's mind," Tugwell suggested, "was struggling all those months, evidently, to crystallize some program which would be more than the re-establishment of old institutions and their reform. We did not supply it for him; and he would not put it together from what he had available or what anyone else should supply . . . ." [47]

Although other advisers—who would have disagreed with Tugwell on that point—were contending that the proposed NRA and AAA constituted a genuine social and political revolution, it seems unlikely that Roosevelt considered them to be any more than the culmination of Progressive thought, stemming from World War I regulatory schemes or Trade Association planning of the 1920's. It is even more unlikely that Roosevelt would have approved them had he thought that they were revolutionary. In later years he quite often backed into reform measures as self-protection against more drastic measures. The Emergency Banking Act of 1933 and the Wagner Labor Relations Act were good examples. By means of the former, the President prevented nationalization of the banking system; by the latter, he avoided much more radical labor demands. He seemed not to question the fundamental structure of the economy until the 1937 recession forced him to consider the gloomy possibility that "many TVA's" might be the only answer to the riddle of poverty in the midst of plenty. The World War II rearmament program allowed him to put aside a final judgment on that question.[48]

Roosevelt felt surer of himself and his country on international questions. The domestic pragmatism of the New Deal was not repeated in foreign policy matters, though there were tactical shifts from time to time. The journalist and close observer of the New Deal who wrote that through "Secretary Stimson and Norman H. Davis, he accepted the major tenets of Mr. Hoover's foreign policy," may have been off the mark, at least as far as timing is concerned, but those two did provide Roosevelt with advice which fitted his own background and proved more durable than the NRA and the AAA.[49]

After Hoover failed to convert Roosevelt to his ideas for managing the war debts and economic conference questions, there was little communication between the two men. Hoover had wanted Roosevelt to declare his support for the international gold standard and to accept his proposal for a joint commission to deal with both the disarmament and the war debts problems. The president-elect was willing for preparations for the London economic conference to go forward, and he was willing to see one or two British delegates to discuss economic matters. "This difference is more the result of misunderstanding than anything else," Norman Davis insisted in a letter to Stimson, "and a reconciliation of views would most probably result from free and frank conversations." [50]

Stimson did want to see Roosevelt, if only to save a little for the Hoover Administration's point of view. And Roosevelt readily agreed to invite the Secretary to Hyde Park for a general discussion which would commit no one and which would serve as a final briefing on foreign policy.

The Secretary went to Hyde Park on January 9, 1933, to talk about European problems, but also to discuss his policy towards Japan's forward movement in Manchuria. Indeed, it was on this latter subject that the two reached the greatest measure of agreement. Stimson came to Roosevelt bringing both moral and practical arguments against recognizing Japan's puppet state in Manchuria. From the beginning of America's existence as a nation, he had just recently told the Union League Club of Philadelphia, the country had been linked in policy and in commercial interest to the development of China and Japan. For that reason, Washington had originally sponsored the Open Door Policy. "Our foreign trade has now become an indispensable cog in the economic machinery of our country," he asserted. "It is essential to the successful and profitable functioning of our whole nation." [51]

American protection of the Philippines, Stimson confided to his diary on another occasion, centered in America's need for Oriental markets. "I told him," he wrote, referring to a conversation with a Philippine leader, "that the landmarks which were settled had to do with the steady westward progress of this country towards Pacific trade and good relations with China, with whom I expected to see commerce develop more and more." [52]

The Secretary may have communicated none of these thoughts to Governor Roosevelt; that was probably unnecessary, since they were the same as those Roosevelt had expressed many times. Now the President-elect complimented Stimson on the nonrecognition of Japan's actions in Manchuria, commenting that he had felt that this "Stimson Doctrine" should have been announced even sooner. "He said that it was his belief that Japan would ultimately fail through the economic pressure against the job she had undertaken in Manchuria . . . ." The Secretary advised keeping the Navy at Hawaii, anyhow, to prevent the possibility of an attack on the Philippines or the American west coast, and Roosevelt followed this suggestion.

Returning to the war debts matter, Roosevelt explained shortly that his opposition to Hoover's joint commission plan came from his belief that it would have been politically unwise—the nation was tired of Hoover's commissions. He repeated his desire to talk with individual representatives from England and France. Their discussion ended with some references to Caribbean matters, which would become of some interest in a few weeks, but as the conference broke up, newspaper reporters wanted to hear about the debt situation and the London Conference. [53]

Governor Roosevelt gave them vague replies that could have referred to either European or Far Eastern questions: "I am willing . . . to make it clear that American foreign policies must uphold the sanctity of international treaties," he declared. To Tugwell and Moley this statement seemed to repudiate their counsel against foreign adventures. Moley, the more concerned, remarked: "It endorsed a policy that invited a major war in the Far East." [54]

Hoover was upset about what he decided was Roosevelt's failure to comprehend the international economic crisis. "The question which we have to meet is: Will the United States take a courageous part in the stabilization of the world economic situation? The British debt question is but a small segment of this problem. It should not be discussed except where there is to be a full quid pro quo in effort on the part of Great Britain to bring economic remedy to the world which would alter the course of economic degeneration in the United States." The meeting of a single delegate or two with Roosevelt would simply not suffice, for full-scale discussions were required. "No concession should be given to the British until that project is complete and then only if it shows results to the United States." [55]

Davis's contention that the differences between Hoover and his successor were only a question of method was strengthened from Roosevelt's attitude that discussions with the British Government must include "world economic problems in which the two Governments are mutually interested." Roosevelt defined these on February 3, 1933, as the tariff, the gold standard, exchange control, and disarmament. At the same time he insisted upon talking with European representatives before the London Economic Conference; when he did, these bilateral conversations pulled him back from the path of immediate international cooperation.[56]

Franklin Roosevelt had a well-filled notebook when he delivered his inaugural address. At that time it was opened to the NRA and AAA pages, but there were bookmarks sticking out of other pages which would soon be used. Even while the Senate was debating the AAA, Senate Democratic leader Joe Robinson speculated sadly, "How slowly the law of supply and demand works in the face of multitudinous trade barriers!" Across the aisle, Republican Senator Arthur H. Vandenberg urged his colleagues to enact legislation to construct the St. Lawrence Seaway so that Michigan exporters might compete in world markets. "Is that not an economic aspiration to which the nation is prayerfully committed?" [57]

When New Deal domestic planning failed to bring immediate recovery, the Administration turned to other remedies. Reform measures were continued, and there was a renewed attempt at rationalization in the "Second New Deal," but more and more these were pushed into the background by a series of expedients like the unilateral inflation Hoover had so dreaded. Soon, too, the Reciprocal Trade Agreements

Act would guide the country back onto an internationalist path, and at length the Administration would complete a second shift from unilateral competition to international cooperation in the face of the Axis threat.

Roosevelt had unintentionally predicted the course of New Deal foreign policy in a speech to the New York Grange in February, 1932. After denying that he was still interested in American participation in the League of Nations, the candidate assured the assembled farmers that he well understood their need for "additional outlets." "The highest ideals of America demand, that, with strict adherence to the principles of Washington, we maintain our international freedom and at the same time offer leadership to a sorely tried humanity." [58]

He fell short only in not predicting that eventually the United States would have to take on political responsibilities if it were to gain markets and offer leadership to the world. The problem in 1933 was to find a way out of the economic crisis. When straddling all three paths proved impossible, the New Deal settled on international cooperation, but not until some years had passed, with many difficulties unresolved.

A little over a year after the Roosevelt Administration assumed power, Congress enacted the Reciprocal Trade Agreements Act. Significantly, State Department arguments for this trade policy sounded very much like Roosevelt's 1932 speech before the New York Grange: each promised greater foreign trade and leadership "to a sorely tried humanity." This act was the basis of New Deal foreign economic policy. We need to consider now the processes of thought and the pattern of events that led to its adoption.

I suppose it is conceivable that by the force of law
we might be squeezed back into our territorial frontiers. But, as a matter of fact, our economic frontiers
are far out to sea and in foreign countries. . . . Our
foreign trade, our shipping, and our overseas investments—these are just as much a part of American
prosperity and American economic life as trading
out in the Middle West or between the states.

William S. Culbertson, *Reciprocity*, 1937

2 · To the Reciprocal Trade Agreements Act

"Two years ago," Cordell Hull congratulated the President in 1935, "the
American people were overwhelmingly in a state of mind to try almost
anything in the way of governmental plans or devices or expedients to
deal with the horribly dislocated financial and economic conditions."
Hull was convinced that the Administration's "comprehensive economic program" had barely prevented a socialist or fascist revolution.
"It is about time for New Yorkers to see that if Roosevelt fails, the
popular swing will not be back to the Ogden Mills and the Wadsworths
of this world (at least for 5 or 6 years to come) but in the direction
of greater radicalism," added another State Department officer.[1]

Believing the New Deal to be the only realistic alternative to extreme
centralization, the Secretary of State and his aides could accept its
reformism, but there were many who believed that the Administration
was heading straight towards disaster. George N. Peek was one:
as the first director of the AAA, he discovered "no end of intense young
men" in his and in other executive offices who were out "gunning for
the profit system as though it were some rapacious wolf . . ." Mr.
Peek stood with the more conservative faction in the early New Deal
coalition; yet he also opposed Cordell Hull's trade liberalism, believing
that it would be just as destructive of American agriculture as New
Deal liberalism. The resounding Peek-Hull clash over the Reciprocal
Trade Agreements Act filled State Department halls with its angry
sound and penetrated into the White House. And when it finally sub-
sided, the United States had adopted a foreign economic policy which
put it back in the mainstream of American foreign policy.[2]

24

Each side in the debate agreed upon one thing. The scarcity economics of the NRA and the AAA was not the solution to America's sickness. Peek had special interests behind him, but as a 1936 booklet distributed by the General Motors Export Company's vice-president affirmed, Hull's more numerous supporters were encouraged by "what the present Administration has done and is doing for America's foreign trade . . ." The automobile executive added that this praise was "very sincerely intended even by those sponsors of the booklet who may not agree with some of the other national policies." This was reason enough, he ended, for voting for Roosevelt in 1936.[3]

And former Secretary Stimson, who had failed to bring Roosevelt over to the Hoover Administration's views on tactics, replied "somewhat jocularly" to a question on New Deal foreign policies that he would change his politics and become a Democrat if Republican politicians shifted their attacks from domestic matters to New Deal foreign policies.[4]

So while some conservative leaders and political opponents shared Secretary Hull's uneasiness and discontent about power centralization in quasi-legislative, quasi-judicial, quasi-executive agencies like the NRA and the AAA, they also joined with him in believing that it was not the exercise of power *per se* that was so dreadful, but the direction in which these agencies might push the country. Many conservatives welcomed Hull's fight to give the President and the State Department much greater power in handling foreign policy, especially through the Reciprocal Trade Agerements Act. Opposition came from some agricultural areas, those who produced solely for the home market, and a loose grouping of those calling themselves isolationists.

The ability to raise or lower tariffs without Congressional approval in each and every instance was central to the success of Hull's whole system. Secretaries of State had always complained, with good reason, that the American Congress's near-veto power on treaties threatened always to make the conduct of foreign policy impossible. Hull's success in obtaining the Act in 1934 explains his rising confidence in Roosevelt and the New Deal; but as late as 1938 he described himself as hardly able to keep silent before the many New Deal domestic schemes. That he was able to survive extreme New Dealism may have been a surprise to himself even in that year. Certainly he had doubted it back in 1933, when Roosevelt completely undercut him at the London World Economic Conference, when, months later, he unsuccessfully argued against the manner in which Russia was granted diplomatic recognition, and finally when, still later, his archantagonist, George Peek, seemed to be winning the inner struggle over trade policy.

This struggle divided the Administration, and although Roosevelt stayed aloof for a time and actually seemed only slightly interested, it brought out the intense concern over developing a satisfactory economic foreign policy and restoring foreign markets. Roosevelt's stance was deceiving and was no doubt determined by political considerations, for he too felt keenly about foreign trade.

Writing in the sophisticated internationalist-minded (and capitalist-minded) American periodical *Foreign Affairs,* exiled Bolshevik intellectual Leon Trotsky presented a Marxist interpretation of American policy: "Sooner or later American capitalism must open up ways for itself throughout the length and breadth of our entire planet. By what methods? By *all* methods. A high coefficient of productivity denotes also a high coefficient of destructive force." From a more friendly point of view came this judgment a few years later: "The Roosevelt Administration's international economic policy may be called the taproot of the political and military united front which the peaceful nations organized too late to prevent the Second World War but in time to win it and make their victory a victory for collective security and the United Nations." [5]

Of this much there is little doubt: though the New Deal refused to accept political commitments until 1941, its economic foreign policy never contemplated self-containment and moved towards greater participation in the world economy only a few months after the London Economic Conference.

ROOSEVELT AND THE LONDON ECONOMIC CONFERENCE

The Brain Trust wanted President Roosevelt to turn his back on the World Economic Conference to be held in June, 1933. He refused to indicate, however, that he had changed his mind about favoring some sort of international action to raise prices.[6]

England and France hoped that a favorable settlement of the World War I war debts owed the United States might be forthcoming at the Conference—or at least negotiations begun. President Hoover had promised nothing, but he and his representatives at preliminary talks long before the Conference had dropped hints and stressed Washington's desire for a general settlement which would not deal merely with the "question of debts and reparations, nor tariff rates as distinguished from a general tariff policy." Any sort of settlement depended upon England and France coming around to the American point of view.[7] Consequently, Economic Adviser Herbert Feis warned in January, 1933, that the country was putting too much stress upon the war debts and international stabilization programs. The United States and Great Britain should be more concerned about preventing new trade barriers and reaching agreements "precluding discrimination against each other's trade and making for common defense against discriminations inaugurated by third parties. . . ."[8]

In another memo Feis suggested how this might be done. London should be induced to "grant greater access in its markets for some of [America's] agricultural products by lessening the trade barriers to which they are now subject." On January 15 Stimson brought up some of these points in a telephone conversation with Roosevelt. He urged the President-elect to secure assurances from the British that they "would stabilize sterling as a means of raising world prices. . . ." Of course, if the United States wanted to "join the race for national inflation which is now going on among the nations," Stimson went on, that was a different matter. Roosevelt replied quickly that he did not want to enter such a race. At this point Roosevelt's policy towards the London Conference was still unsettled. In line with his comment to Stimson, Roosevelt later spoke favorably of international stabilization to French Premier Eduard Herriot, noting that "such a device to help revive world trade might help revive the United States."[9]

But at the conclusion of these conversations with Herriot and other world leaders in the spring of 1933, whatever past ideas he may have had gave way to the conviction that a firm dollar-pound-franc ratio would be disadvantageous to the United States. He was not so afraid as Hoover had been about abandoning the international gold standard. Secondly, there was no denying that England had gained a breathing space domestically and internationally by leaving gold, and some key figures inside the Administration held the point of view that the United States should at least threaten to leave the gold standard, in order to persuade other nations to cooperate.[10]

In addition, the NRA-AAA programs were based upon strict regulations. These might be swept away before a flood of European goods if a weakened United States opened its gates too soon. Talking from the President's elbow, Raymond Moley bespoke a changing mood in the White House: "The people of the United States must recognize that world trade is, after all, only a small percentage of the entire trade of the United States." [11]

Few in the State Department welcomed such words—or Moley's titular position among them as Assistant Secretary of State. At the same time, the President encouraged Hull by allowing him to suggest an international tariff truce for the duration of the London Conference. And from the way Norman Davis, who had earlier met with Prime Minister Ramsay MacDonald, had been talking in support of the kind of agreement the Hoover Administration had suggested, European leaders may well have been uncertain about American policy. Could not England and the United States join in a program to overcome the international depression? Davis importuned. "An improvement in conditions would increase the ability and the willingness of the debtors to pay and would also affect the attitudes of the creditor as regards demand for payment." A few hours later Davis elaborated on his plea in another conversation with the British Prime Minister. If the United States, Great Britain, and Canada drew up a draft trade treaty, "it might serve as a model which other countries could adopt and thus become a step toward the general breaking down of trade restrictions." [12]

By May, 1933, however, Davis reported from London that the English were still busy with "trade agreements containing quota and preferential clauses." One of the most objectionable of these was being negotiated with Argentina. Nor could MacDonald's Government agree to an economic truce without a prior understanding on the debt question. "There is great discouragement in certain quarters here despite a stiff upper lip," one State Department officer said, noting reaction in Washington.[13]

Davis had one final suggestion to make. The American delegation at the forthcoming conference could confront the British with the prospect of a "race with us for international trade . . . ," unless they agreed to cooperate "with us on broad lines through mutual stabilization." But the President saw little chance that the situation could be changed much by any kind of bargain or pressure. "A summer holiday with the world in its present tragic condition," he told MacDonald, "would be regarded by the people of the United States as indefensible." When he selected the American delegation, it became evident that he had come to see the Conference as not much more than a way of fulfilling domestic political commitments. Inflationists and orthodox gold-

bugs were juxtaposed, making agreement within the delegation unlikely, and making their impact on other delegations little short of
traumatic, especially since there had been continuing indications that
America seriously wanted an international solution to the depression.[14]

Roosevelt's actions as the conference time approached confirmed
the fears of those who suspected a turn towards isolationism. He took
the United States off the gold standard, decided to reserve tariff legislation until a later session of Congress, and, after the Conference met,
repudiated his own delegation when it negotiated a loose stabilization
agreement with Britain and France. "England would like to have us
go back on gold," he explained some months later, "but would not
follow herself, thereby keeping her favorable trading position absolutely liquid." [15]

In London, Secretary Hull had not been so much concerned with the
stabilization proposals as he had about other trade barriers, such as
high tariffs, preferential arrangements, and regional blocs. These were
far more stagnating in international commerce, he thought, and he
hoped that just as Charles Evans Hughes had broken up the naval arms
race at the 1921 Washington Naval Conference, he might free trade
in 1933. But he learned that Roosevelt had decided not to press tariff
legislation and had agreed to submit any tariff arrangements made at
London to Congressional review at the next session.

But to go back to Hull's opening speech to the Conference on June
12, before he was thus disappointed the Secretary had outlined the
progress of civilization as the result of the achievements of the great
trading nations of the past: "All past experience teaches that the power
and influence of a nation are judged more by the extent and character
of its commerce than by any other standard." The western nations
had better realize, and quickly, Hull warned, that their future depended
upon the adoption of liberal trade policies to meet this crisis.[16]

President Roosevelt sent his famous bombshell repudiation of the stabilization proposal on July 2, 1933. A "sound internal economic system"
in each nation, he asserted, would contribute far more to world recovery. World trade was "an important partner" in recovery efforts but
"here also temporary exchange fixing is not the true answer. We must
rather mitigate existing embargoes to make easier the exchange of
products which one nation has and the other nation has not." The day
before, he had privately informed Hull that the United States needed
a sufficient interval to allow price-lifting efforts to work. These reasons

and Roosevelt's growing disillusionment with England and France determined United States policy at London.[17]

These policy pronouncements jolted Hull and completely demolished Moley, who had come to London to save the Conference and who was primarily responsible for the stabilization draft. Recovering as best he could, Hull called Washington by trans-Atlantic telephone to find out if Roosevelt had turned permanently to self-containment. "I cannot believe long range interests lie in this direction," he wired earlier. Could he make any promises, he asked, on trade matters "with all that this implies with regard to later concrete action on the American side?" Roosevelt answered obliquely that the Secretary could offer to discuss reciprocal trade agreements after his return to Washington.[18]

Hull fretted in London, but the President enjoyed the impact of the explosion he had caused, telling a State Department official that it would give the country a psychological lift by countering the general impression that America always lost out at international conferences.[19]

Free now to combat low prices by unilateral inflation, the President invited some new advisers, Professors George F. Warren and James Harvey Rogers, and his friend Henry Morgenthau, Jr., to meet with him and discuss their ideas on the price of gold in relation to America's depression.

Warren argued convincingly that overproduction was not the main problem, but rather a shortage of gold. Mankind had long since chosen the metal for the keystone in the arch of politics and economics, therefore all commodities depended upon its price level. Before World War I prices had held stable and satisfactory, but since then the unceasing demand for more and more manufactures had widened unfavorably the ratio between gold and other products. Nations which used it to back their currencies had suffered the worst. No wonder the dollar had appreciated so far. And by 1933 it was simply too scarce and too valuable to reduce the ever-rising mountain of goods. A way out, concluded Warren, was to make government purchases of gold at prices well above the world market level. This would depreciate the dollar and make it more plentiful.[20]

James Harvey Rogers agreed with Warren, but felt other points had to be made. Gold purchases might not suffice, for how would the expanded currency which would result, and the expanded credit which would then follow, be put to productive use? State capitalism or socialism would inevitably take over unless private enterprise responded quickly enough. "Meanwhile," cautioned Rogers, "the ever more clogged conditions of trade and ever more drastic reductions in our exports throw a continually darkening pall over the prospects of sustained recovery." [21]

Hence, said Rogers, the gold shortage was not only a domestic problem, but also a threat to world trade. Unable to trade freely, nations might retreat behind "walled estates not unlike those of the Dark Ages." Quite correctly, students of this episode in American economic history have placed the greatest emphasis upon these economists' influence on domestic inflation schemes, but they have unwisely ignored their long-range interest in foreign trade and thus distorted their ideas. Professor Rogers actively participated in the quest for foreign markets: on planning committees to reduce tariffs, as a member of an abortive research group to analyze Russian markets, and as an adviser on economic policy towards the Far East. These men wanted to follow Hoover's third path, not his second one. Hull was annoyed that their ideas disrupted his plans at London, but a measure of domestic recovery had to precede trade planning in order to overcome the continually falling prices in the fall of 1933.[22]

In the harvest months of 1933 corn, wheat, and cotton prices fell to new lows. Southern planters warned Agriculture Secretary Henry A. Wallace that they could not survive another winter of five-cent cotton; midwestern hog-growers even suggested that they should slaughter ten million of their own pigs to create scarcity price increases; dairy farmers acted: they poured gallons of milk into mud ditches rather than accept further price reductions. Roosevelt felt sure that if he waited much longer, the nation would harvest a revolution. There remained "one more remedy," he confided to a Cabinet official, "and that was the purchase of gold." [23]

Combined with other New Deal tonics (and bad weather which reduced crops), the gold purchase program halted the downward plunge and "got us off the hot spot for a time," as Secretary Wallace later quipped. Currency depreciation also gave the United States a small temporary advantage in world markets and stimulated exports. Secretary Wallace agreed that this second effect was worth while too, but he disliked thinking about continually applying palliatives or permanent restrictions of the AAA type. As he told a meeting of the Council on Foreign Relations in late October, 1933, some way had to be found to accept a billion dollars a year in imports in order to pay for agricultural exports, or the crops of forty million acres of good land would have to be plowed up each season.[24]

Legislators from silver-producing states had another answer, they thought, which went hand in hand with the gold purchase program. By raising the price of their favorite commodity, the United States Government could increase as well "the exchange value of the money of China, India, Mexico and South American countries 60 percent in relation to our currency. . . . There is no doubt," said one, "it will enormously increase our export trade to those on a silver currency." Key Pittman had been arguing since 1931, and probably earlier, that the silver issue was an integral part of the China Question, which in turn was the most important consideration relative to the relief of "our surplus production." The head of the United States Chamber of Commerce, Julius H. Barnes, agreed with Pittman that low silver prices "could not but harm the business situation of the world." This proved to be a mistaken notion, at least to the extent that silver purchases could bring about a world-wide revival of trade, but from 1930 to 1935 it conjured up dreams once again of the Great China Market.[25]

When Raymond Moley somewhat surprisingly picked up this theme and now declared that he supported silver purchases because "a large part of the world's population" based their currencies upon it and could then use the dollars they received to "increase their purchases of American goods," his situation paralleled one in the Depression of 1893. In each instance orthodox bankers and a few conservative intellectuals polished their assumptions and found they could include silver as well as gold. Brooks and Henry Adams had influenced Senator Henry Cabot Lodge towards that point of view in the 1890's. "Loving paradox," Henry wrote of his brother in his autobiography, *The Education of Henry Adams* that "Brooks, with the advantage of ten years' study, had swept away much rubbish in the effort to build up a new line of thought for himself, but he found that no paradox compared with that of daily events." Brooks was a leader in the Bi-metallist Club of Boston, which advocated coinage of silver to secure Asian and Latin American trade. If this were done, contended Brooks Adams, "we may win this round and that will pull us through. The crash will then come upon the next generation." [26]

Brooks's prophecy was accurate, but in neither case was his remedy sufficient. Roosevelt did order silver purchases, but mostly for domestic political reasons. He also realized that experimentation with inflation had definite limits; in early 1934, therefore, the Administration sent to Congress the Gold Reserve Act, which fixed the price of gold at about $35 per ounce. "Our objective has been to get rid of the surpluses," the President remarked to newsmen. "We got rid of a great deal of cotton and we got rid of a great deal of copper." [27]

Government gold purchases continued right down to World War II— first, because the program did aid exports in various ways, and, secondly, after 1936 they became part of America's opposition to Axis expansion. Silver purchases had a more checkered career, though Secretary Morgenthau managed to turn an encumberance into an advantage in both Asia and Latin America. In the latter area, the silver program became tied to the Good Neighbor Policy—and its vicissitudes.

DIPLOMATIC RECOGNITION OF RUSSIA

The Gold Reserve Act gave Roosevelt flexibility by allowing him to increase or decrease the dollar's gold content, and this overcame any other nation's attempts to subvert the dollar in international trade. But both he and Morgenthau knew that currency wars were futile except in self-protection; hence the Secretary scanned world frontiers for likely markets which could be improved through more positive financial diplomacy.[28]

Morgenthau's ventures into international affairs often upset Secretary Hull, and this occurred for the first time over the question of diplomatic recognition of the Soviet Union. Having persuaded the President to extend a credit to China so that cotton could be exported there, Morgenthau then wanted to extend a similar credit to Moscow. The idea appealed to President Roosevelt, who already considered the fifteen-year-old nonrecognition policy futile, especially since Russia offered a natural counterweight to Japan and Germany. Ironically, Secretary Stimson's opposition to Japanese advances led him, for consistency's sake, to reject Russian recognition; he had told Roosevelt that Russia had fallen down in "her willingness to behave according to the fundamental principle of the family of nations . . . ." [29]

Not a few business leaders had decided that Soviet morality, or the lack of it, could be overlooked in a depression-glutted economy. Recognition would provide a bridge to Russia over which goods and services would flow and relieve the American surplus. In 1930 United States exporters had enjoyed 26 per cent of Russia's foreign trade; but within two years Germany, Italy, and Great Britain had captured all but a small part of that market. Distraught Americans, unaware of political considerations in Europe which might have caused such shifts, thought that the State Department should respond by extending diplomatic recognition—and credits—to match European competitors.[30]

The Hoover Administration had said no—other nations had gained Russian markets, but the principal cause of declining American sales there was a lack of purchasing power in the Soviet Union, which had not developed "as a result of the indifference of the Government to the interests of its nationals engaged in manufactures and commerce." Recognition would not help the situation and would undercut Washington's over-all foreign policy.[31]

Even so, the campaign among businessmen for recognition went on. The General Motors Export Corporation's Graeme K. Howard, for example, suggested to James Harvey Rogers in May, 1932, that a small group of businessmen and experts should examine conditions first hand in Russia "with a view to making a fair and unbiased appraisal" of the situation. Taken together, a series of reports would carry great weight with the Administration. But the trip was called off when those involved decided it was best to "stay close to the fireside during this critical period." [32]

Pressure was growing for recognition: "I would vote for recognition," declared Senator Robert Wagner, "purely for trade relations purposes." Public relations expert Ivy Lee, the creator of the new Rockefeller image, was among the leading proponents of recognition. Lee even shocked the liberal William E. Dodd with his exaggerated claim that he alone had brought it off a few months later. "His sole aim was to increase American business profits," marveled Dodd, Roosevelt's new Ambassador to Germany.[33]

Russian Foreign Minister Maxim Litvinov had magnified potential markets in his country at the London Economic Conference, dangling a billion-dollar bait before American representatives. This great market could be realized if conditions were right. Both Professor Moley and William C. Bullitt, a foreign policy adviser to Wilson and a friend of the President, struck at this lure and took it back to Washington. There followed almost immediately a multimillion dollar credit from the Reconstruction Finance Corporation for cotton purchases. Business hopes soared! In a few weeks over forty applications from businessmen who wanted such exports came before the RFC. But Bullitt was not at all satisfied by this piecemeal approach to the Soviet Union. He viewed these private deals between "various subsidiary organizations" and Russia as reaching "alarming proportions." Bullitt urged the Administration to formalize its relations with Russia first, for this would be the only real way to protect the United States against sceret clauses of a Russo-German trade agreement, or others like it, or to secure a final settlement of the Russian war debt.[34]

Opponents of recognition realized they had to overcome the alluring prospects of Russian markets: thus Indiana's Senator Arthur Robinson contended that recognition could not in the "slightest degree remedy our economic situation. . . . But propaganda is afloat on all sides, perhaps never more insistent than now . . . ." Secretary Wallace was also skeptical, thinking that the Soviets might become competitors rather than customers, and his colleague, Secretary Hull, had several additional objections. What about the Soviet repudiation of Russian war debts? What about the Comintern's agitation for world-wide revolution? And how would the United States be able to deal with a nation which traded only through state monopolies? [35]

Despite the objections of his Secretary of State, Roosevelt opened negotiations with Litvinov in the fall of 1933, and the latter made proposals on each of these matters which satisfied the President that recognition would serve the best interests of the United States. "Generally speaking," he remarked to James Farley, "I feel I have driven a good bargain, not only for this country, but for the world, and that it will go a long way toward preserving the future peace of the world." [36]

Almost immediately the Administration matched the ante put up by other countries to play for Russian markets: it created the Export-Import Bank, to facilitate credits to the Soviet Union. The international corporation lawyer John Foster Dulles discussed New Deal economic policy in *Foreign Affairs*. Private foreign loans had failed to maintain markets, he wrote: therefore the "risk would be placed upon the taxpayers as a whole rather than upon individual investors. . . ." The Government would henceforth supply dollars for "foreigners to acquire goods for which domestic consumers would otherwise have to be found." [37]

"At all times," President Roosevelt accordingly wrote the State Department, "it should be made very clear . . . that the credits we extend will result in immediate orders for American goods and thus put American workmen to work." [38]

Secretary Hull, however, distrusted the New Dealers, let alone the revolutionists in Moscow, and demanded the settlement of the debt issue before any credits would be granted. Upon his return from the Montevideo Conference, he was angered to discover that no trade commitment had been obtained from Litvinov but "only a memorandum with some figures scribbled on it." The Russian foreign minister upset Hull even more in the next few months by expressing opinions at variance with the State Department's understanding of the recognition negotiations. When the Soviet official told Ambassador Bullitt that Russia had expected a loan which could be spent anywhere, Bullitt replied that Roosevelt had never contemplated a direct loan but only "a commercial credit to be expended in the United States." [39]

The two disagreed also over the total amount Russia had accepted as its war debt to the United States. Litvinov argued that the amount Washington claimed and the way in which the claim had been made would raise all the old debt questions with Great Britain and France, and then he snapped that Russia would not have to deal with Washington at all on these questions and could buy all it needed from Great Britain and France. "I replied," Bullitt reported, "that such a course would not lead to the development of the sort of relations between our countries which we both hoped might develop." [40]

As postrecognition relations deteriorated, the United States almost decided not to open consulates in Russia. And by 1936 Ambassador Bullitt was thoroughly disillusioned with his mission. Inability to reach agreement on the broad sweep of Russian-American problems left him fearful about the future, and of Russian competition in economic matters. "The Soviet Government," he warned, "has not the slightest intention of abandoning its monopoly of foreign trade." [41]

Recognition served another policy aim, for Roosevelt thereby set the Japanese on notice and safely moved the fleet from the Pacific to the Atlantic. Businessmen were disappointed, but they were "somewhat calmed" by the shortly concluded (January, 1935) Trade Agreements Act, under which the Soviet Union agreed to "purchase goods to the value of $30,000,000." When this was later boosted to $86,000,000, even the State Department's attitude was sweetened. [42]

Foreign Minister Litvinov had his complaints, too. He was chagrined that Russia could not involve the United States in an alliance system either in Europe or in the Far East. Ambassador Bullitt readily agreed with him on this point at least: "The basis of our foreign policy from

1936 to 1940 may be summed up in the homely phrase: we wanted to have our cake and eat it too." [43]

REBUILDING THE GREAT WHITE FLEET

Bullitt's reference was to the idea that America could enjoy economic advantages without political responsibilities. One way to do this, thought many, was to keep the navy strong. The idea of the Export-Import Bank demonstrated the sanguine belief that America could take part in economic affairs without bothering with world political commitments. The Export-Managers Club urged the creation of a second bank, and in response to this and many similar pleas it was accomplished. The establishing order from the President's office read: "Our Government must continue to cooperate with foreign traders if foreign markets are to be maintained in the face of many obstacles which have grown up in recent years against foreign trade." [44]

Secretary of Commerce Dan Roper came back from a European tour in 1936 convinced that American policy should be to exchange commodities and stay free from European squabbles. Yet the constant expansion of American-owned branch plants posed the question of their protection, and one of the crucial questions to be decided before diplomatic recognition was given to General Francisco Franco's government a few years later was to be his attitude towards the American-owned Spanish Telephone and Telegraph Company and other American properties.[45]

Though the navy could not do much about protecting American interests in Spain—or perhaps in Australia, Germany, Sweden, England, France, India, and Italy, where industries strong enough to seek better profits had established new plants since the beginning of the depression —it symbolized American power, and the great prewar crisis in the Orient—the Japanese attack on the gunboat, *Panay*—was occasioned by the habitual naval protection given nationals in China. The navy had been the main arm of United States expansion from the Spanish-American War both in Cuba and in the Philippines, through the years when control of the Caribbean was established, and extending into the period when the *Panay* was challenged by Japanese usurpers.[46]

Naval strategists in the 1930's were faithful students of Captain Alfred Thayer Mahan, America's most eloquent spokesman for naval power. The imperialist movement had avidly consumed his books and articles dealing with the influence of sea power on the course of history. Mahan's central axiom was that nations aspiring to political and economic leadership must secure open communications lines and coaling stations to feed their flotillas. This naval thinker predicted that the great battleground of the future would be in the Pacific Ocean: "Coincidentally with our own extension to the Pacific Ocean, which for so long had a good international claim to its name, that sea has become more and more the scene of political development, of commercial activities and rivalries, in which all the great powers, ourselves included, have a share." [47]

President Theodore Roosevelt took Mahan at his word and built the Great White Fleet; in the Navy Department, staff officers began positing the way in which the battles might take place. Warplan ORANGE was their best analysis of how a conflict with Japan would evolve, increasingly the most probable enemy in the Pacific.

During the first years of the second Roosevelt's presidency, the Navy Department sent several memoranda to the White House re-emphasizing its mission and pointing out that with a strong navy the country would not have to resort to entangling alliances to protect its interests. Roosevelt jocularly expressed a similar view to Navy Secretary Claude Swanson when the two discussed using Public Works Administration funds for shipbuilding. "Well, Claude," the President smiled, "building up the Navy is certainly building worthwhile public works." Cordell Hull was more to the point: as a relief measure, he recalled in his *Memoirs,* new construction might have provided employment in coastal cities, but it was necessitated by German and Japanese expansion. "But we had to be careful neither to antagonize the isolationists at home nor to discourage those nations abroad which still strove for disarmament." "The Administration and the country," one of Hull's aides added to the Italian chargé, "now realized that this policy of disarmament was not destined to bear fruit." [48]

Japan's decision not to accept an inferior position, such as the Washington Naval Conference's 5:5:3 ratio, was the main factor behind naval rearmament. The Chief of Naval Operations, Admiral William H. Standley, advised State Department officials that unless the Administration wanted to back off and "throw over the rights of trade" in the Orient, the American delegates at preliminary naval discussions at London in the fall of 1934 must oppose Tokyo's demands for equality.[49]

The diplomats agreed with Standley. Not only would a weak naval policy encourage Japanese expansionists—it might also throw England and Japan together "to a point where they might join forces in attempting to exclude the United States from the Asiatic market." [50]

When Chief Delegate Norman Davis addressed the meetings, he explained that the United States could not support absolute naval equality for Japan without doing violence to the "equilibrium of political and economic rights" which had been established in 1921. Japan replied by renouncing the Washington Treaties, pressing its forward movement in China, and finally striking at Pearl Harbor. The United States started rebuilding its navy in 1934 and completed the job after 1938.[51]

THE GENESIS OF THE RECIPROCAL TRADE AGREEMENTS ACT

Currency depreciation, the Export-Import Bank, rebuilding a powerful navy—all were good supports for a yet uncompleted trade program. Until the Administration worked out such a plan, Secretary Hull could not but remain disturbed. Others felt the same way. The American Automobile Manufacturers Association had supported Governor Roosevelt in 1932 because they had believed he would pursue a tariff policy that would bring "compensatory liberalizations from those countries which offered potential outlets." [52]

The International Chamber of Commerce advised Roosevelt that it was pleased at learning that he had quoted from one of its resolutions on foreign trade. Wilson's special adviser, Edward M. House, wrote in *Foreign Affairs* that the basic tariff problem confronting the New Deal was to find out "how to enable foreigners to earn enough dollars here to pay their debts and to take our exports, without the necessity of foreign loans." Secretary Wallace, always interested in foreign trade, was pleased by a quickening interest in world trade "in our great eastern seaports." Adolf Berle advised Roosevelt that the promotion of advantageous foreign trade through reciprocal trade agreements and the Export-Import Bank could become a major means of recovery.[53]

This growing pile of reports jibed with Secretary Hull's basic overview. To provide a "Brain Trust" for his program, Hull brought Professor Francis Sayre, Woodrow Wilson's son-in-law, to Washington. Sayre traveled from university platforms to business gatherings, speaking on foreign trade as the alternative to greater government regulation, socialism, and the loss of individual freedom. In scholarly books he contended with supporting statistics that "American domestic recovery lies through world recovery." "Ever since the industrial revolution . . . trade has been the principal index of a nation's prosperity." Former Secretary Stimson aided Sayre and all of Hull's efforts with a 1934 radio address on behalf of the Reciprocal Trade Agreements Act. Expanding exports, he said, were indeed the sole alternative to the "suppression of our hereditary initiative and the love of freedom." [54]

With such strong currents behind him, Secretary Hull seems to have been headed straight to success. But there were obstacles set before him by powerful opponents who reiterated over and over the infant industries argument, the claim that cheap foreign goods would drive American farmers and workers from the fields and factories, and the plea that special industries could not survive increased foreign trade.

No sensible policy maker, therefore, could advocate anything like free trade or even a general tariff reduction. Hull and his aides reached for the next best thing (in truth, in some ways it was the *best*)—reciprocal trade agreements with the unconditional most-favored-nation principle. This plan needs some explanation. First, it is always proposed by a strong industrial nation which wants to secure markets for a broad sweep of its manufactures. Only a great power can afford to risk injury to some industries in order to obtain these larger markets. Paradoxically, this risk often must be taken to provide a "safety valve" to high production. In a typical example under the most-favored-nation principle, the United States might offer Brazil concessions on coffee in return for lower rates on sewing machines and other manufactures. If a third nation should then happen to receive a better concession from Brazil, the most-favored-nation clause of the prior agreement would automatically ensure that the United States would receive an equal reduction in the Brazilian tariff.

The United States first felt strong enough (and troubled enough) to advocate the unconditional most-favored-nation principle in the 1920's, when Secretary of State Charles Evans Hughes instructed his diplomatic officers around the world: "It is now considered to be in the interest of the trade of the United States, in competing with the trade of other countries in the markets of the world, to endeavor to extend the acceptance of that principle. The enlarged productive capacity of the United States developed during the World War has increased the need for assured equality of treatment in foreign markets." The sources for this message went back some years and William S. Culbertson, of the

United States Tariff Commission, later remarked that the State Department had originally drawn these conclusions from one of his Commission's reports and embodied the most-favored-nation policy from then on.[55]

But as Culbertson pointed out so well in a major work on American trade policy, *Reciprocity* (1937), American concern for this kind of approach went back to the previous century and actually had intellectual beginnings coincidental with the birth of the nation.

The Tariff acts of 1890 and 1897 both included provisions allowing the President to negotiate for reciprocal trade agreements. And if he could not persuade a foreign country to grant American products a reciprocal concession, he had the power to raise tariff rates on that nation's exports. In 1896 the Republican party platform advocated reciprocity, and President William McKinley later avowed: "Reciprocity is the natural outgrowth of our wonderful industrial development under the domestic policy now firmly established. . . ."[56]

But trade treaties always encountered difficulties in Congress. In 1922 Culbertson wrote Secretary Hughes to urge adoption of trade policies complementary to Hughes's approach at the Washington Naval Conference. The United States, he insisted, must have the "open door in economically backward areas of the earth, including colonies." Discrimination in such areas must be broken down. There were two ways to achieve this goal. One was the unconditional most-favored-nation trade policy, which would facilitate access to such markets. Secondly, the United States must engage in "investments in banks, shipping, railroads, and factories, and [obtain] contracts for public works and government supplies." Hughes and President Warren Harding agreed with Culbertson on both counts.[57]

Hoping to sidestep domestic criticism, the State Department wanted to negotiate the first such agreements with nations producing raw materials, who could absorb manufactures. But this attitude alarmed George Peek, who saw in it one more sacrifice the American farmer would be called upon to make for the industrialist. As the farm program's administrator, he had a direct line to the White House, and he used it to express his fears. A midwestern farm machinery manufacturer who saw life as a conflict of functions rather than of classes or regions, Peek charged that high tariffs on foreign manufactures had protected the industrialist, but low tariffs on farm products and raw materials had forced the farmer to compete with the world. This unhappy fact "prevented a free exchange of goods and services within the United States between the two great groups." Rex Tugwell had been making the same point: Eastern industrialists had exploited the farming West as their continental empire; it was their raw materials source and their market for overpriced goods. Now they wanted to continue that exploitation, Peek argued, by sacrificing the farmer to the trade agreements program of Cordell Hull.[58]

Peek, abhorring AAA scarcity economics, tried to substitute his own trade policies as an alternative. He wanted to subsidize dumping and to engage in direct barter practices. "I am in politics for agriculture— not in agriculture for politics," was his declaration. For a time, during the farm crisis of 1933, this attitude gave him stature in the Administration; but when prices rose, Hull's broader outlook prevailed.[59]

Peek managed to interest the President in a detailed study of past American trade policies, to be conducted by him, designed to strike a balance-sheet analysis. Believing that he could show Hull was dead wrong, Peek presented the completed study to the President, who looked it over while Hull was in South America resuming his pleas for liberal trade. The Secretary had enjoyed a personal triumph at the Montevideo Conference by "surrendering" America's claim to intervention rights under the Roosevelt Corollary to the Monroe Doctrine. The Conference had then responded favorably to his trade resolutions in favor of reciprocal trade agreements,[60] introduced on December 12, 1933.

When Hull then wired the President asking for a free hand, Roosevelt expressed sympathetic concern but warned that current NRA and AAA readjustments still made the time inauspicious. The Secretary also learned that Peek had been named chairman of an interdepartmental committee to find foreign markets for agricultural goods through *either* reciprocal trade agreements *or* barter arrangements. Peek's challenge had crested; State Department officials predicted a "repetition of the Moley situation." [61]

During the impasse, Congress passed the Reciprocal Trade Agreements Amendment to the Smoot-Hawley Act in order to expand "foreign markets . . . as a means of assisting in the present emergency in restoring the American standard of living." Since the legislators did not specify the exact means to be used, the debate between Peek and Hull was only partially resolved. Peek now took a stand against the most-favored-nation principle.[62]

But Hull's leverage was constantly increasing. The American Manufacturers Export Association wrote Roosevelt that it approved the American position at Montevideo. Charles Taussig, long a tariff and foreign policy adviser, notified Hull that the National Foreign Trade Council's reaction was "splendid; in fact the whole atmosphere of the Conference was indicative of the rapidly changing sentiment of the country in regard to foreign trade." [63]

Peek countered by suggesting instances where unwanted imports had followed the adoption of a reciprocal trade agreement. Perhaps exasperated by this conflict within the Administration, Roosevelt told the two to sit down and work out a compromise. Hull tried, but he and Sayre knew that such a thing was impossible and marshaled support from the other executive departments to bolster their view. Their real offensive, however, was contained in several memos to the President.

In the first of these, Hull asserted that the most-favored-nation clause would "maintain the position of American commerce in many countries which now buy more from us than we buy from them, particularly the chief European countries." [64]

"It is manifest," continued the second, "that the United States never faced a more outstanding responsibility to furnish the world both a program that is sound and leadership that is alert and aggressive than at this crucial stage while there is yet a chance to save and finally restore a normal economic situation." [65]

Two more memos refuted Peek's dumping warning. "The answer to this view," wrote Francis Sayre, "is that those in charge of the trade agreement program are most carefully conferring the concessions accorded to each country to those commodities of which each country is the chief or at least an important source of supply." He cited as proof British generalizations of concessions to the United States which allowed only minor advantages to be gained by the American exporter. "The same would also be the case for the most part with respect to the generalizations which other countries would gain from the trade agreements which we make." [66]

Always an advocate of greater national planning, Tugwell later noted somewhat unhappily that the internationalists had their "victories too—notably in preserving the 'most-favored-nation policy' . . . ." Yet in losing the contest, George Peek kicked up an issue around which the dust still has not settled. Slighted as a bombastic agrarian conservative who soon fell out with his fellow New Dealers, Peek nevertheless uncovered some of the difficulties in the Hull program. He realized that the United States probably could not maintain its previous near monopoly in the production of several manufactures and commodities and that raw materials producing nations had acquired their own Manifest Destiny visions: "Coffee has taught the Brazilians the great lesson that nations which depend upon the export of raw materials can never be free." Moreover: "We have an immense free trade area of our own and our primary problem is to see that within our own borders the returns for productive effort by various groups are maintained upon levels which will permit the free exchange of products between the groups. Our problem is to maintain free trade at home within a balanced economy." [67]

"It is curious that the internationalists base their views on trade, world peace and what not on the conception of a static world . . . . When they talk about restoring international trade, they have in mind going back to some period when this or that country had a supremacy. They do not seem to realize that the world is always moving and that trade is never 'restored.' " [68]

Peek's alternative was not a satisfactory solution, but his criticism hit close to the mark. State Department publicists constantly affirmed that trade agreements among industrial nations were of primary interest; even so, the majority of trade agreements before 1940 were with underdeveloped countries. If Peek's assertions were not a valid argument against the expansion of world trade, they were a legitimate complaint about these Hull treaties. The Secretary did want very badly to complete negotiations with Great Britain for an agreement, not alone for trade advantages but also to build a united front among friendly industrial powers. Thus he told the Japanese ambassador on one occasion that the United States and Japan had to work together in the Far East, where Asian peoples lived "chiefly in a very primitive condition." The "rehabilitation of all those peoples involved vast needs of capital and of other phases of national cooperation." No one country could supply these needs within a number of generations. The Foreign Office should understand, he told the British ambassador another time, that if London and Washington remained at odds, "nothing in the future can be more certain than that food and raw-material producing countries would be driven to the establishment of their own crude manufacturing plants as a permanent policy." [69]

The British ambassador may have smiled to himself at this reminder of the Foreign Office's nineteenth-century outlook. However that may be, the British Empire's outstanding historian Sir Keith Hancock has observed that "The growth of the 'open door' principle projected itself beyond national and imperial decision into international convention. The European powers by agreement with each other began to limit their sovereign rights of discrimination. Among themselves . . . they built up a network of most-favored-nation agreements which committed them, not indeed to low tariffs, but to impartial tariffs. In the management of their colonial dependencies they accepted more extensive limitations upon their sovereign powers—limitations which 'created a measure of European solidarity in the colonial world.' " [70]

Intentionally or not, this came close to the views of American policy makers in the twentieth century. Culbertson had expressed it directly in his letter to Secretary Hughes; Stimson and Hoover had tried to achieve it; and Hull carried on the attempt in the 1930's. These leaders continually linked the Open Door Policy and the most-favored-nation principle, and we shall see how insistent this became in World War II.

Several intellectual, political and economic leaders met at Nicholas Murray Butler's home about this time and came up with the same answer to America's quest in the modern world. There was, they concluded, an "inevitable relationship" between the United States and the underdeveloped countries. It was characterized by the differences between the two kinds of economies. This relationship must be put "upon a safe foundation; it is to the interest of the United States that there be financial and economic stability in all parts of the world and that there be restored that confidence in the integrity and safety of international relations without which peaceful and profitable commerce is impossible." [71]

Henry Wallace put forth similar views in *New Frontiers* (1934), and his quotation of Illinois Governor Frank Lowden climaxed his own arguments and is worthy of full repetition. In 1922 Lowden had stated that isolation could be achieved in only one way: "The way is to let, say thirty per cent of our wheat fields go back into prairies, and fifty per cent of our cotton fields go back into forests, and to close half of our copper mines and curtail our production along many other lines. We can live within ourselves better perhaps than any other nation in the world if we are willing to pay the price, but we must readjust our whole life from one end to the other. I find no one who is willing to pay that price and therefore we have got to concern ourselves in the affairs of the world." [72]

Lowden had well summed up the impossibility of seeking economic gains and refusing to participate politically. The political responsibilities of the early Good Neighbor Policy were not great, though they became more so; in the Far East the United States could not confine Japanese ambitions within the Open Door Policy; and in Europe, political neutrality proved unavailing.

Like Henry James's American woman abroad who, "with her freedoms, her immunity from traditions . . . represents the conservative element among a cluster of persons," the Hull trade program seemed conservative not only to antidemocratic governments but also to the British Empire and other friends.

In the past we, too, stationed some soldiers in Central America and left them there as long as ten years, but the results were bad, and we brought them out. Since then we have found it more profitable to practice the "Good Neighbor Policy."

Cordell Hull to the Japanese Ambassador, 1941

3 · The Good Neighbor Policy

By 1933 the Latin America portfolio which President James Monroe had started with his Doctrine over a hundred years earlier bulged with additional doctrines, pronouncements, and corollaries. Long before President Franklin Roosevelt announced his Good Neighbor Policy, American leaders had begun the task of culling out the still valuable portions of the Latin American portfolio. Their predecessors had tried all ways to fit the Big Stick into this briefcase; but no matter how they strained, it always disarranged and crumpled their other policy papers.

Roosevelt's election further facilitated such reviews, but it was hardly the only cause or even the primary factor in stimulating this second look. And the Good Neighbor Policy was the logical result. In the early 1800's the United States had extended a welcoming hand to Latin American countries as they broke away from European rulers. As the North American nation rapidly assumed hemispheric leadership, it put aside such young enthusiasms for revolution and behaved more like the maturing industrial power it was. Washington treated Latin American nations sometimes as equals, sometimes as wards to be guided and corrected. So great did American predominance become that by the end of the century a Secretary of State could rightly claim that Washington's decisions were practically fiat in the whole Western Hemisphere.

To make Secretary Richard Olney's assertion stick, the United States inevitably intervened in Latin America—directly, but also indirectly, against European claims activities. The Good Neighbor Policy was partly an admission that the United States should act more tactfully in its relations with weaker neighbors, and partly a realization that military intervention actually hindered the effective employment of American economic and political power. Nor was it morally consistent to condemn Japan's forward movement while continuing and initiating military intervention in equally doubtful circumstances.

47

This last consideration influenced Secertary Stimson, who was deeply concerned with trying to preserve the world of the Washington Treaties; it also affected many other career officers in the State Department who had been striving for many years to modify the harsher aspects of dollar diplomacy.[1]

Of the men who were then most closely associated with working out this Good Neighbor approach in the Roosevelt years, Cordell Hull, in an analysis of an early crisis, best represented their thinking. "I am telling people who have property there," he explained concerning the Cuban revolution of 1933, "to let it be injured a little, while the Cubans are establishing a government themselves, because should the Cubans themselves establish a government, the outbreaks will gradually cease, business will return to Normalcy, and the Americans will recover their losses." [2]

Breaking the habit of intervention, as Hull well knew in this circumstance, was not so easily done. The United States had rejected formal colonialism or imperialism; interventionism had also proven unsatisfactory. But the question remained: How rationalize the existing tensions between a powerful metropolitan center and the semideveloped areas around it?

The kind of Good Neighbor Policy practiced from 1933 to 1937 was the culmination of past thinking on this problem. In rebuilding inter-American trade, the cessation of military intervention had become an absolute prerequisite, even to conservative thinkers. Some wanted to go on from there and plan for a Commonwealth of the Americas, but aside from the 1936 Buenos Aires Conference, which opened the way to collective defense programs in the Hemisphere, not much was accomplished positively towards that goal.

After a very shaky start in Cuba, the Good Neighbor Policy managed to dissipate many suspicions, yet preserve the substance of American power and authority. There was the unofficial support the Roosevelt Administration gave to the formation of the Foreign Bondholders Council, for example, or, better yet, the very positive support it gave to the extension of Pan American Airways' network all through Latin America. But after 1937 it required much more than these things and the recall of American marines to keep the Good Neighbors from rocking the boat.

HOW THE GOOD NEIGHBOR POLICY EVOLVED

"I am getting quite blue over the way in which all Latin America is showing up," Secretary Stimson lamented in his diary for November 11, 1932. "It seems as if there is nothing we could count on so far as their having any courage and independence is concerned . . . ." Thus did this dilemma of America's great power versus its responsibility and self-restraint puzzle Stimson. From all over South America, Central America, and the Caribbean, reports of conflict and revolution piled onto the desks of the State Department. From Chile came descriptions of American property-owners' fears that the government there intended to seize their holdings, perhaps even to demand cash, in order to satisfy angry insurgents. Peru asked Washington for the loan of Pan American Airways pilots to supplement national forces in suppressing a revolt. Stimson's gloomy mood did not lead him astray here, but within weeks he and President Hoover were backed into the position of considering seriously the possibility of dispatching a "war vessel" to Lima to "give a feeling of security" against unrestrained mobs.[3]

They both knew what the outcome would be if that were done: All the efforts to reverse the trend towards permanent military interventionism would have gone for nothing. Stimson had already promised to pull American marines out of Haiti and Nicaragua, though he wanted to reserve the right to intervene in Central America. Moreover, he had also announced that Washington would henceforth recognize Latin American governments upon their *"de facto* capacity to fulfill obligations" as members of the family of nations. Blatant intervention to restore or initiate a new government under the pretense of *de jure* recognition policies was to come to an end. It was ironic that this first Stimson Doctrine, the *de facto* recognition policy for Latin America, was forgotten because of the second Stimson Doctrine, the *de jure* recognition policy applied to Manchukuo.[4]

Hoover and Stimson disliked military intervention as a means of compelling stability. Liberals, of course, had been prodding the State Department for some time on this question, but many others whose primary concern was far less idealistic had also been pointing out its bad effects. In 1931 an American planter in Central America complained that the marines only stirred up hatred because they "hunt down and kill Nicarauguans in their own country." Some critics justly remarked that American marines were also being killed! And Congress was asserting itself against the continued costs of military occupations and election supervision. Under these pressures, and that of his own convictions, President Hoover appointed an investigating commission to look into the situation in Haiti. At the completion of its mission, one of its members reported dismally: "Because we have power, brute force, guns, economic advantage, prestige and what not, and these are in fact if not truth subject people, we rule over them as our inferiors and they hate us and we suspect them and regard them as amusing creatures." [5]

Something had to be done: Secretary Stimson chose to provide these countries with the means to ensure their own domestic security (and that of American interests) through an American trained militia. Some businessmen were skeptical, but Stimson pushed aside their objections, as the following State Department notes indicate: "Lives and property in the interior of Nicaragua are to be protected by the Guardia, and if the company is not satisfied with that protection it has two alternatives; either to provide for its own protection—the Secretary understood that the company had two machine guns already—or to withdraw, and he hoped they would not do that." As it turned out, of course, there was no need to withdraw, since a Nicaraguan dictator effectively used the Guardia (even up to 1956) to gain power and maintain order. It was, as Laurence Duggan later remarked, somewhat sanguine to hope that the Guardia would have stayed out of politics.[6]

When Chilean creditors appeared at the Department asking for military intervention, they found the Secretary equally unresponsive. "Japan is using that argument," he admonished them, "to justify the absorption of Manchuria and . . . the invasion by an army of nearly 100,000 men of Shanghai and we were the one country which had stoutly opposed Japan's argument." Debt collecting by military force "would be more misrepresented and more dangerous than ever before." [7]

Though there were other dissenters, most American economic and political leaders accepted the Secretary of State's assumptions. Congress, for example, had actually laid the foundations for the Nicaraguan plan in acts passed in 1922 and 1926 permitting United States officers to serve in South American armies and navies; in the famous J. Reuben Clark Memorandum the State Department had downgraded the Roosevelt Corollary to the Monroe Doctrine; and the Coolidge Administration sent New York banker Dwight Morrow—whom the critic Edmund Wilson characterized once as the small man with the big voice of

American capitalism—to Mexico as a good will ambassador to strike a compromise between Mexico City's revolutionary demands and the security demands of American investors.[8]

Thomas P. Lamont, Morrow's partner at J. P. Morgan and Company, summed it up neatly: "The theory of collecting debts by gunboats is unrighteous, unworkable, and obsolete. While I have, of course, no mandate to speak for my colleagues of the investment banking community, I think I may safely say that they share this view with Mr. Morrow and myself." [9]

By 1933, then, the future course of inter-American relations had been pretty well set. The Good Neighbor Policy had been poured like hot liquid metal into this mold and then dumped out all shiny and new in Roosevelt's inaugural speech. Secretary Stimson minted some of the coins in a speech to the Union League Club. Latin America countries, he said, "are producers of raw products suitable for our consumption and offer potential markets for great varieties of our manufactures." [10]

Sumner Welles had long ago made the same point in one of his 1922 policy papers: These nations are "looking to the United States for money, and the United States is looking to them for profitable commercial and investment opportunities." Ten years later, in a key memo to Franklin Roosevelt, Welles added some political advice on how this could be done. "I favor the principle of consultation between the governments of the American republics wherever there arises in this Continent any question which threatens the peace and well being of the American world." [11]

Roosevelt liked this advice: he had already approved Hoover's plan to remove the marines from the Caribbean, and he gradually completed the task. He had told former Secretary Stimson very candidly that "Latin Americans would always be jealous of us," but "it was very important to remove any legitimate grounds of their criticism." [12]

How to do this and yet secure what Latin American expert Carleton Beals was calling the joint goal of the business community—namely, as Secretary Stimson and Sumner Welles defined it, "a common bloc for the purpose of furthering trade and stimulating recovery"—was a tough proposition. Already unrest and revolution prompted by the depression's bad effects on exports and prices threatened property and investments. Indeed, some said the depression had begun with South Americans defaulting on their loans from the United States. If the political structure in these countries were to be turned upside down, the future would be clouded for American interests. As one experienced American diplomat advised a newly assigned colleague, "We are vitally interested in our trade with those countries and in seeing that the peace is kept there." Or, as Cordell Hull bluntly remarked to newsmen at the Montevideo Conference, "We must sell abroad more of these surpluses." [13]

By 1935 Latin America was absorbing 54 per cent of America's manufactured cotton exports; 55 per cent of steel-mill exports; 33 per cent of leather and rubber, silk, paper, electrical, and industrial exports; and 22 per cent of automobile exports. Investments had risen from $1,125,000,000 in 1919 to $5,000,000,000 in 1934. "We are entrepreneurs in Latin America," exclaimed a Commerce Department official, "but are mere creditors in Europe." [14]

From its beginning the New Deal might have tried to channel Latin American unrest towards a Commonwealth of the Americas. It did make that kind of an effort after 1937 and during World War II (but never completed it), but in 1933 these policy makers were still a long way from undertaking such a far-reaching program.

Revolutions were difficult to control; a commonwealth of the Americas would necessitate an industrial, political, and social revolution. There would have to be a very great tolerance, and a willingness to forego important advantages for a doubtful long-range possibility. On the other hand, when these revolutions did come in the 1960's, they were just that much more violent and, in some cases, that much more anti-American.

"The foreign ownership of natural resources," Adolf Berle once explained, "operates as a net deduction from the proceeds of Latin American products which can be used to satisfy Latin American needs." This meant that when Chile exported five dollars' worth of raw copper, it never brought near that amount to the Chilean economy after the foreign owners' profits were skimmed off; even worse, this copper came back to Chile reshaped into a twenty-five dollar lamp.[15]

Though Berle saw the implications of such problems, the Good Neighbor Policy from 1933 to 1937 only improved the quality of the thread used in sewing the pattern of inter-American relations. Many Latin American leaders were satisfied then, but what is now called the "Revolution of Rising Expectations" was just beginning.

Even so, New Deal leaders continued to see Latin America as one new frontier, to be opened to ever more trade and investment. Hence they sought stability and opposed tendencies which might constrict free access to those countries, be it through regional groupings or barter deals with Germany or other European powers. As Roosevelt wrote a friend in 1941: "The policy of the Government during the past eight and a half years has been directed consistently towards the strengthening of the inter-American concept on the broadest basis and has been opposed to regional groupings within the Western Hemisphere either political or economic." [16]

THE NEW DEAL "FIELDS" A REVOLUTION IN CUBA

The first crisis of the Good Neighbor Policy came in the 1933 Cuban Revolution. Washington's resolve not to use military force wavered, and its rigid economic solutions for promoting stability poked through the soft rhetoric of the Policy. Ironically, it fell upon Adolf Berle and Sumner Welles to deal with this crisis of the First Hundred Days of New Deal diplomacy.[17]

Like Woodrow Wilson's Mexican problem in 1913, which led unhappily to military intervention at Vera Cruz, the Cuban debacle came to the next Democratic President as the immediate legacy of the Republican years, though in fact it had been coming since the Spanish-American War. Roosevelt was understandably vexed about it, since Hoover had reassured him at their meeting in November, 1932, that Cuba remained "perfectly safe." This assurance was based upon the supposed ability of President Gerardo Machado to sustain his regime in power. Supported by both the Administration and American financial and business interests, Machado had weathered several political storms, but the depression was something different, bringing drastically lowered sugar prices and rising unrest on the back streets of Havana and on foreign-owned sugar *centrales*. Machado could respond only by tightening security restrictions. Stimson, though worried, preferred to allow the "bankers who have a big stake in Cuba" to pull the Cuban leader out of the mess, but even they had become weary of such undertakings.[18]

Besides, as Stimson understood so well, what could be done about the depression without much broader cooperation in the world? The hope that Machado could somehow recover was forlorn; yet, interestingly enough, Stimson told a Roosevelt aide in January, 1933, that although Machado might be less than desirable, he probably could "hold the country safe and suppress revolutions." And he told the

President-elect that there seemed little necessity for intervention. Still, he said less confidently, Cuba was a Pandora's box better left unopened.[19]

Unsatisfied, Roosevelt lifted the lid by sending Adolf Berle and Charles Taussig to Havana to seek a way to steady the island republic. They reported to Roosevelt just before he left Warm Springs, Georgia, to assume office. They had a double-barreled solution: raise Cuba's sugar quota in the United States market and simultaneously impress upon Machado the need for social and political reform. Roosevelt approved the suggestions and sent Sumner Welles to carry them out.[20]

After studying the situation in Havana, Welles reported confidently that "a fair commercial agreement" with Cuba would indeed serve the dual purpose of "distracting the attention of the public from politics" and assuring the United States "practical control of a market it has been steadily losing for the past ten years . . . ." Machado could be persuaded to grant the reforms, continued the special ambassador, since he knew that he "could not remain in power for long" if the United States withdrew its support. Welles opposed direct action against Machado, fearing, as had others, that a chaotic revolution might follow with its obvious threat to stability and American property.[21]

A few days later, he added that the dictator might be pressured to hold elections if conditions grew worse, but "nothing more prejudicial to our whole Latin American policy" could be imagined than military intervention—or even forceful diplomatic action.[22]

In the United States those closely concerned with Cuban affairs voiced their approval of this approach. "Your conception of reciprocity treaties," the Cuban Chamber of Commerce in the United States wrote to Roosevelt, "as effecting the best means of restoring our lost trade and safeguarding American interests abroad is particularly accurate with respect to Cuban-American relations."[23]

So far so good: The Administration and the business community had reached similar conclusions as to the best way out of a bad situation. "The prospect of a more profitable share in the American sugar market," Laurence Duggan informed Charles Taussig, "is a plum which Ambassador Welles intends to withold until definite progress towards a solution of the political unrest has been made."[24]

As Welles neared his goal, a sudden general strike undercut him and completely washed away Machado's power. To save what remained, the Ambassador quickly decided that he must retire the dictator before further erosion destroyed any basis for agreement. In Washington the President had a hard time with newsmen, disavowing any interference "with the internal affairs of another nation." At first it seemed fortunate, then, when Machado was overthrown from within, but unhappily the moderates who accomplished his rout were soon overthrown themselves by a more radical group led by intellectuals and "army sergeants." [25]

This new regime was headed by Ramón Grau San Martín, who talked as though he meant to change Cuba's economy in ways displeasing to most Americans. Welles, already disappointed by his failure to pull off the whole thing quietly, became more and more alarmed at what he was seeing in Havana. Finally, and in direct contradiction to his earlier position, he requested a limited intervention in September, 1933, asking three times for troop landings. Roosevelt and Hull recoiled at this request, but dispatched ships and airplanes to the Caribbean to protect American lives. Welles managed to make political use of the navy force, however, by instructing the ships to proceed to a "wide distribution . . . in Cuban ports for moral effect" and to fire no salutes to the Cuban flag so long as the present leaders remained in control of the government. The idea backfired, however; apparently the ships lent strength to the Grau government, and Welles had to request their withdrawal! [26]

Embarrassing questions popped up in presidential news conferences. "Lay off this intervention stuff," Roosevelt pled, but in Cabinet meetings he searched hard for a satisfactory alternative. He directed Agriculture Secretary Wallace to publicize Administration hints that the 1934 Cuban sugar allotment would be stepped up from 1.7 million to 2 million tons. Secret Service reports warned that such pacification attempts had come too late, for "American sugar companies have been subjected to all kinds of abusive impositions . . . with present exactions by the Communists with the connivance of the Government they will have to close down." [27]

Adolf Berle rushed off to be the Administration's Man in Havana for the second time. He was to explain the financial and economic situation to Grau. American business "could not and would not" deal with his government. Welles, too, tried but failed to convince Grau to give up. He did, however, plant seeds of ambition in one of Grau's army sergeants, Fulgencio Batista. This occurred shortly after Batista had put down an uprising against Grau. Welles flattered him with the comment that he was "the only individual in Cuba today who represented authority." [28]

Welles then returned to Washington, but before departing Havana he punctuated his earlier statements by ordering a flight of four airplanes to sweep across Cuba.[29] Admittedly there was a "bad situation" developing in Cuba, as Roosevelt told former Secretary Stimson, but he fully supported Welles. Latin American leaders were not so sure of this American Ambassador's good neighborliness. Mutterings of interventionism and the Big Stick could be heard all the way up to the State Department and the White House. Roosevelt had made it plain that American ships had been sent only to protect lives, but Latin American objections led him to the further promise that any intervention would be a multilateral undertaking and not by United States fiat. Welles and Undersecretary William Phillips drafted an additional policy statement, which, in effect, turned the Cuban situation into a Gilbert and Sullivan paradox. They asserted that since Grau lacked the support of any major political faction in Cuba, United States diplomatic recognition of his regime would actually amount to political intervention! Only if Grau could be kept supplied with large quantities of material and moral aid could he stay in power; therefore, the United States would "welcome any provisional government in Cuba in which the Cuban people demonstrate their confidence." [30] This weird logic in reverse was employed by Welles's successor to explain why a new government in Havana did not yet have popular support. Jefferson Caffery maintained that Grau had had support only from the ignorant masses, not from any key political faction; but when the new government took over, its difficulties came only from the large number of ignorant Cubans.[31]

Colonel Batista had in fact taken the hint and turned on Grau, overthrowing him and forming a government under the nominal direction of Carlos Mendieta. This new government's haste to provide assurances to Cuban conservatives and Americans was matched only by the speed with which Washington moved to extend Batista the diplomatic recognition the State Department had denied Grau.[32]

Once more negotiators sat down to work out the fair "commercial agreement" Welles had promised. But Mendieta's government received even more. Though Washington had claimed, when Grau was in power, that such succor was intervention, the Administration now granted an Export-Import Bank loan to Cuba. In asking for the loan, the Cuban secretary of the treasury pointed out that the increased sugar allotment would not supply Cubans for at least a year with enough dollars to buy very much from the United States, but a loan would "determine an expansion of the Cuban market for American goods" almost immediately.[33]

"With a view to enabling the Cuban Government to maintain peace and tranquillity in that country," Hull explained, the United States was placing an embargo on arms to Cuba. Satisfied that the fire had "burned itself out," the Administration formally renounced the Platt Amendment and the right of intervention. But an economic adviser in the State Department pinpointed what had taken place both in the narrow sense of his words and through their general import. Speaking of the Cuban trade agreement, this official noted that "in return for concessions on our part in respect to sugar and a very few other things, we receive concessions all along the line." [34]

This sort of sugar deal continued all through the 1930's, culminating with a 25 million dollar loan to Havana just before World War II— again to maintain stability in the face of possible revolutionary activity. The American Ambassador in these later days reported that he saw more corruption in Havana and Cuba in general than anywhere else he had been except Nazi Germany. If the Cubans would not let the United States guide them in this treacherous circumstance, he added, then "all sorts of things are possible here." The Good Neighbor Policy seemed only to be putting off the inevitable.[35]

Elsewhere in the Caribbean, the New Deal moved to make its participation less apparent, and in 1934 Sumner Welles could tell the American Minister in Nicaragua that the end of constant hectoring and meddling in a public manner had indeed produced good results. But in the fall of 1933 deep shadows from Cuba overfell the Montevideo Foreign Ministers Conference, where Secretary Hull hoped to restart his trade program after having been stalled at London. Disturbed by reports that Mexico planned to force the issue of "intervention and other questions," the Secretary even considered canceling the meeting.[36]

A QUID PRO QUO AT MONTEVIDEO

Latin American experts in the State Department complained that Mexico had "let us down badly" in announcing its desire for a resolution forbidding United States intervention in Latin American internal affairs. Some American liberals were reluctant to serve on the United States delegation to the Montevideo Conference because of the Cuban situation. Steeling himself against these setbacks, Hull departed for the Conference with the delegation, warning them not to bring up the Monroe Doctrine or any of its corollaries. Once in Montevideo, he adopted the manner of a Tennessee politician greeting local voters or maneuvering in the halls of Congress. He popped in on other delegations in their hotel rooms, saying "Howdy-do" and, with extended hand, announcing that he was "Hull of the United States" come to get acquainted.[37]

When the formal meetings began, the Secretary continued to speak softly and allowed other nations to answer attacks on the Cuban policy. When the Mexican resolution freed pent-up emotions of past years in a tremendous demonstration, Hull calmly walked to the front of the hall and signed away the rights of the Roosevelt Corollary.[38]

But the Montevideo Conference did not end at that dramatic moment. Hull secured in exchange many new Roosevelt Corollaries, for the other resolutions on economic and political cooperation were interpreted by him to mean acceptance of his trade program. "Every trade arrangement under this program," he reported happily to the President, contemplated "an increase of production and trade for the United States . . . ." Moreover, these resolutions presaged the enactment of protective laws for foreign investments which industrial nations need to make when they produce more than they can consume and "engage in investments deemed sound from every business standpoint." [39]

Although never formally titled so, this "Montevideo Program" was the first blooming of the Good Neighbor Policy. It was much like the Open Door Policy in China; and Assistant Secretary Sayre wanted Department officers to call it to the attention of all European nations as well. Yet most of the trade agreements which were to come under the Montevideo Program, like the Cuban one, provided for the broad acceptance of American manufactures for concessions on raw materials and only indirectly fitted the realities of European-American relations in the sense of a movement towards lower trade barriers.[40]

Indeed, the State Department spent a great deal of time in the 1930's fending off European challenges to the Montevideo Program. It was particularly distressed by the growth of discriminatory exchange agreements and barter trade deals—two mechanisms which some Latin American nations claimed were needed by them to protect short supplies of dollars and yet obtain sufficient supplies for their economies.

"In view of the injurious consequences . . . of the spread of such agreements," asserted one official, "it remains sound policy for us to abstain from them as far as possible and to seek to discourage their use." The State Department stuck by this, even repudiating an advantageous barter arrangement that George Peek had worked out early in the New Deal. Suitably enough, Peek's resistance to Hull's growing power in foreign economic matters ended here.[41]

More positively, United States policy makers came up with a substitute for discriminatory exchange policies, which they admitted were symptomatic: they used the Export-Import Bank to supply dollars which could be spent in the United States, or to make arrangements so that a Latin American country could feel free to enter into a trade agreement with the United States. In fact, the Administration finally decided to advise the Bank every time trade negotiations were initiated, so that "concurrent conversations might be opened with representatives of that country by the Export-Import Bank or by the private holders of blocked balances." This plan had the additional advantage of spreading out the risks of the American exporter, assumed in the 1920's by private bankers, to the citizenry as a whole. No less a public works project than any PWA undertaking, no less a subsidy than AAA supports, this use of the Export-Import Bank nationalized, at least in spirit, the foreign trader—and his problems.[42]

In many instances this idea worked well: Brazil's situation demonstrated the need to combine trade agreements, loans, and anti-German pressures to make the Good Neighbor Policy work effectively. The New Deal negotiated one of its first trade agreements with Brazil; it was understood that Rio would unfreeze blocked dollars so that the trade agreement would have a greater chance of increasing American exports to Brazil. The American Chamber of Commerce in Brazil had been warning that Rio de Janeiro's exchange policies and its tendency to favor restrictive dealings with Germany would destroy the trade agreement, but it was assured by Washington that the most-favored-nation clause would end the problem.[43]

These hopes were premature. Throughout 1936 Secretary Hull had to keep repeating Washington's opposition to Brazilian flirtations with Germany. Finally Rio cut free from this infatuation in exchange for a sixty-million dollar loan from the United States. It came just in time, for the American Chamber of Commerce there had denounced a proposed barter deal with Germany as the "greatest single obstacle to free trade in South America." This jibed with State Department opinions that it was not so much the amount but the method Berlin had tried to use which threatened to cut into American trade outlets. And that was the reason the United States had responded so quickly and vigorously.[44]

German and Japanese competition worried Americans, first of all because it was effective, secondly because it directly opposed United States plans, and finally because it came from aggressive national governments. From Peru, for example, the American Embassy reported its detailing of an attaché to look into rapidly growing Japanese trade advances. Roosevelt was interested enough to direct James Harvey Rogers to carry out a currency survey of all South America aimed at "minimizing German and Italian influence on this side of the Atlantic." The nation's exporters, as represented in the National Foreign Trade Council, passed resolutions against German trade methods and discussed stronger ways of combating the competition.[45]

In 1936, against this backdrop of trade rivalry in an unsettled world and political opposition to German and Japanese expansion, President Roosevelt took the initiative by calling for a special meeting at Buenos Aires. He came to the Argentine city and received the acclaim of its citizenry as the author of the Good Neighbor Policy. At the Conference he called for inter-American solidarity not only against foreign military attack but also against inroads cut into the Western Hemisphere by economic and cultural activities. "They trust you," Josephus Daniels congratulated him, "because you have shown your faith" by ending military intervention in the Caribbean.[46]

"It cannot be denied," admitted the German Minister at Montevideo in a cable to Berlin, "that Roosevelt has achieved extraordinary results in South America" with the Good Neighbor Policy, juxtaposing this comment with another about how the United States was "exerting very strong pressure against Germany commercially." Similar reports were reaching Berlin from Chile and Brazil. German diplomats were impressed by the "extended" field of American action, which had gone from "economic and commercial" opposition to driving "Germany out of the Brazilian market" and over-all political opposition. Political Commentator Percy Bidwell analyzed German-American trade rivalries in a not unsimilar fashion: "The traditional interpretation given to the Monroe Doctrine makes it difficult to divorce economic from political considerations." [47]

THE GOOD NEIGHBOR POLICY BY 1937

By 1937 the Good Neighbor Policy had achieved permanence. No one wanted to revert to military intervention. Trade had improved by 236 per cent from 1933, although it was not to regain its predepression heights until World War II. Business conditions in Latin America were relatively prosperous. The United States was more highly regarded there than it had been for many years. Yet no Latin American nation believed that increased trade with the United States or a greater number of foreign investments would automatically bring it prosperity. At best such a situation produced subservience; at worst it made the nation like a fish bobbing up and down on a line cast from the North.

Mexico's reforming president, Lázaro Cárdenas, dramatized the feelings of many Latin American leaders in 1935 when he insisted that his country had to get out of the "colonial stage of exploitation which has prevailed and has brought such paltry returns . . . ." Three years later his notions brought him into sharp conflict with Washington over the expropriation of foreign-owned Mexican oil fields.[48]

Attempting to lay the ghost of past American policies, Adolf Berle spoke to this very problem in 1941, in explanation of nineteenth-century imperialism. "When you said 'economic interests,' you meant that you wanted markets. You proposed to sell your goods in certain areas, and, if you had imperialistic ambitions, you intended to back up your selling plans with as much political pressure as might be needed."[49]

Liberals like Berle hated imperialism. He had grown up fighting it in the Caribbean; but the foreign policy of a dominating metropolis, like the United States, demonstrated that past definitions of colonialism or imperialism needed revision. It might well have been that the Good Neighbor Policy was all that could have been achieved given the milieu and the character of the personalities involved; but to say this was more than a tactical change in past policies is a mistaken formulation and expression about the recent past.

The decision not to use gunboats to collect private debts did not mean an end to all attempts to collect them or—more importantly—an end to using dollar diplomacy to further American interests. The private loans were replaced by public ones, and after 1938 this idea was further extended to developmental loans. In 1933 American financial leaders formed the American Council of Foreign Bondholders, numbering among their members J. Reuben Clark and Norman Davis. Both Secretary Stimson and his successor, Hull, gave the Council their blessing. The former believed that it should have "the encouragement of the Government" in an unofficial way, while Hull regarded the formation of the Council as a "matter of obvious common sense," and implied that his Department would "always be willing" to cooperate with it "within the limits of appropriateness and wisdom." [50]

Norman Davis replied for the Council by suggesting that it would always seek to reconcile any conflicts between private interests and official action. The Council set forth its aims clearly in its *Bulletin:* "Competent observers agree that foreign loans should perform one of two functions. They should result in commercial advantages to the lender, or in political gains. If they accomplish both, so much the better." The degree of support from the State Department was never great, although in 1936 Sumner Welles told Ambassador Daniels that the United States would not finance the second section of the Pan American Highway until a settlement had been reached with the bond-holders committee on Mexican indebtedness. Daniels was never ordered to deliver this as a formal message, but it demonstrated how thin-skinned the Good Neighbor could be.[51]

The New Deal continued official support to Pan American Airways' private empire in South America. Since the 1920's this company had been the chosen instrument of American foreign policy on commercial air matters. In 1928 Congress passed the Kelly Foreign Air Mail Act, which gave Pan American a powerful annual subsidy of over 2.5 million dollars, in the face of expected European competition. The State Department had helped the company achieve its goals in Central America by supporting the famous "Form B" contracts which the airline used to gain monopoly privileges on mail and passenger cargoes.[52]

New Deal Postmaster General James Farley advocated continuance of these subsidies, writing to Roosevelt in 1935 that they were necessary to United States "trade relations with these countries." And Pan American's president, Juan Trippe, defined his company as the "aerial ambassador of American industry." After 1938 Pan American was employed to help oust German and Italian competitors in South America. It also gained federal funds to build bases in South America and Africa and even on Pacific islands. In some ways Pan-American, too, became a government agency like the Export-Import Bank, though the airline pulled at the limiting reins this development placed on it.[53]

Viewed as a way to develop an informal empire, or sphere of influence, the Good Neighbor Policy was an advance over anything that had gone before. Competition with Germany and Japan was as keen as in any other area of the world, and growing more so. If the United States wanted to maintain pleasant relations with Brazil, wrote a director of the Export-Import Bank, "still an undeveloped empire, with everything that common phrase connotes," then some way had to be found to overcome all other rivals.[54]

A way had to be found also to meet the swelling tide of Latin American nationalism. "The belief that the capitalistic technique is inevitably and inextricably enmeshed with the great principles of democracy," argued America's friend and critic Luis Muñoz Marín, is "a barrier to understanding in areas where experience with the backward forms of that technique has not left happy memories." After 1937 this consideration, Axis competition, and a recession at home led Washington to provide a greater measure of substance to the rhetoric of the Good Neighbor Policy.[55]

Our traditional China policy resulted partly from attitudes of mind created in us by our westward expansion across the open spaces of the American continent . . . . In the 1890's after the passing of the frontier at home, we established a new theoretical frontier in the Open Door doctrine in China; we were continuing the same process.

John King Fairbank, *The United States and China*, 1958

My hope and prayer was that all the civilized nations, including Japan, should work together . . . so as to promote to the fullest extent the welfare of their respective peoples and at the same time meet their duties to civilization and the more backward populations of the world.

Cordell Hull to the Japanese Ambassador, 1934

4 · Asian Dilemmas

Though the Roosevelt Administration never made John Hay's demands for "equality of opportunity" in China and for the "territorial integrity" of that country, as phrased in the Open Door notes, the specific *casus belli* for war with Japan, these ideas were the basis of American Far Eastern policy, and they conflicted with Japan's forward movement in Asia. Tokyo's ambitions began in Manchuria in 1931, spread into North China, and finally swelled into a dream of a Co-prosperity Sphere for the whole area. America's great difficulty in defending its policy was to find a way to meet these specific challenges, for while statesmen from Hay to Cordell Hull excelled in the construction of fine phrases, the Open Door Policy was actually full of contradictions.

"None of us can tell what the next phase of this almost insane tide of events will do to anyone here," lamented Adolf Berle to Henry Stimson in 1940. "If the issue had been squarely faced, as you proposed to face it, in Manchukuo, neither we nor the world would have been in the present mess." [1]

Ah, but—not only was Secretary Stimson's strong stand in 1931 not supported by President Hoover, but Stimson himself was ambiguous about the Far Eastern policy he professed, and not at all so sure as Berle implied a decade later. "The statement of our intention not to

64

recognize the fruits of that aggression," he had written Walter Lippmann, "was merely a forcible way of bringing forward that principle and insuring that it should be considered by the family of nations. This end has been highly successful, both in the Assembly of the League and among the nations of South America." In other words, the Stimson policy on the Far East was a part of that world view which the Secretary and President Hoover shared and which seemed to sustain them even when it was no longer relevant to the world about them. The New Deal inherited both the policy and the dilemma.[2]

So long as Japan's ambitions appeared compatible with at least the spirit of the Open Door Policy, Washington had been tolerant. The forward movement in Manchuria which had led to the Stimson Doctrine forced some to consider a final break with Japan, but only a few were then willing to risk a war in 1931–32 to keep the door open in that single area. For one thing, other relations with Japan remained better than satisfactory. Stimson himself pointed out a few days before leaving office that "in the relations between the United States and Japan, economic factors are of outstanding importance. The protection of the 3,600 American citizens who reside in Japan and of the $466,000,000 of American capital invested in the Empire occasions little difficulty. Our trade with Japan is the greatest single element in our trade with the Far East." [3] In some ways America had encouraged Japan's ambitions, for, as Ambassador Joseph Grew explained, it was highly in "our own interest that Japan should remain a strong, prosperous and productive country under conditions of peace, justice, stability and security, and that our mutual trade and other relations should flourish in the future as they had in the past." [4]

Relations with Japan were a proven quality (and quantity), but the China policy had seemingly turned out to be only a Great Illusion. There were two very good reasons: The Great China Market had never materialized, and China had remained divided and unstable despite the aegis of the Open Door Policy. China's multiple weaknesses made for indecision from 1931 to 1937 (and even after). Another handicap policy makers had to overcome in trying to come up with a plan to stop Japan was that the Open Door Policy was meant not to foment wars but to prevent them—and that was the main reason Washington clung to it.

After 1933 heavier weights than before pulled the balance down on the other side. Japan did not stop with Manchuria, but moved on into

North China, launching a full-scale effort in 1937. Secondly, as an observer for the Institute of Pacific Relations noted, it began to look as if China stood on the verge of solving some of its problems, so much so that many foreign nations sent trade missions to see if the Nationalist government actually was stabilizing the country, and to lay plans for participating in a possible Chinese revitalization. The United States, Germany, and Great Britain all sent such missions in 1935. Washington, with Secretary Morgenthau eager to do more, was turning its silver purchase program into a continuing foreign aid scheme for China, having learned that the original idea of the silver purchase plan was backfiring in China. "Morgenthau wanted to help China," wrote a student of this policy, "if American interests could also be protected." [5]

China's survival as an independent nation was only part of the problem. As Ambassador Nelson T. Johnson wrote: "The Japanese want so much. They want to drive every vestige of occidental influence out of China, Indo-China, Siam, Straits Settlements, India, Burma, Dutch East Indies and the Philippines. Also Siberia. They must go on. Nothing will stop them except a collapse at home or a decisive defeat in the field of their operations." [6]

Washington did not want to make a choice between those alternatives, so from 1933 to 1937 the State Department searched for some way to contain Japan's aspirations within the framework of the Open Door Policy. It was not willing to confront Japan with a final showdown, but on the other hand it was not willing to give up the Policy. Thus it opposed granting Japan naval equality in 1934 and 1936, half-heartedly tried to resurrect the Second China Consortium, and, after the Japanese invasion of China in the summer of 1937, organized the Brussels Nine Power Conference. This last was especially futile, since anything acceptable to Japan would have compromised the Open Door Policy, and American attempts to find a compromise between Japan and China, on Washington's terms, were unacceptable to Tokyo.

Late in 1941—too late—came a report from Ambassador Grew concerning a conversation with Shigenori Togo, the Japanese foreign minister. After studying all the relevant documents, Minister Togo explained, he had concluded that the United States simply did not understand the realities of the Far Eastern situation. The American Secretary of State, continued Togo, had at least twice informed Japanese representatives that America regarded their country as the stabilizer of Asia, yet the Secretary had not then been able to understand Japan's need for raw materials and its deep commitment to a satisfactory solution in China.[7]

Of course the realities Togo mentioned were largely the result of Japanese militarism in the Far East, but that does not invalidate his analysis of America's Far Eastern policy, for he had hit upon the central dilemma of the Open Door.

OPENING THE DOOR

"The way was clear to me," mused Austin Tappan Wright's fictional American consul to *Islandia*, "still quite a young man, to open vast new fields for the glory and good of my countrymen and of world commerce, and to reap my reward in power and consciousness of pioneer work ably done in the face of able rivals."

Wright had caught the spirit of America's young diplomats as they sallied into the Pacific to confront able rivals in China and Asia.[8]

Japan was first among these competitors; having adopted western technology for self-protection, the Japanese also learned how to speak about and act from ideas of Manifest Destiny.

The United States had had but little difficulty in usurping Spain's hold on the Philippines in 1898; Japan had won a less certain victory in the Russo-Japanese War a few years later. Consequently, Tokyo's position in Manchuria and Korea was less secure than the firm territorial grasp which the United States had on the Philippines. But from 1900 on, America was less and less interested in formal colonial empire and became dedicated to the expansion of the Open Door Policy instead. Washington believed that this approach would yield the United States all the advantages an empire might bring yet force upon it no binding responsibilities or dangerous political involvements. Admittedly this was a risky way to look at Asian policy, but with his large industrial base the American was sure that he could compete anywhere so long as he had equality of opportunity, and he was so sure that he desired all of China for an open market. For a time Japan accepted these terms in exchange for American recognition of some of Tokyo's claims. Several diplomatic notes and verbal exchanges formalized the tacit understanding.

By the end of World War I it was clear that Japan had been merely biding its time. Tokyo's Twenty-One Demands on China, its eagerness to replace German interests on the Shantung Peninsula, and its boldness in the Siberian intervention alarmed American leaders. Some way had to be found to strengthen the Open Door Policy in order to curb these ambitions. The first decision Washington made was to reverse its earlier rejection of a banking consortium among the powers which would require China to borrow from them all rather than causing dissension by borrowing only from one.

United States policy makers were not happy at having their hand thus forced. "In my judgment," emphatically declared one American negotiator, banker Thomas Lamont, Japanese leaders "ought to be down on their knees in gratitude to the American, British and French groups for inviting the Japanese group to become a partner and for being so patient in the matter." [9]

Lamont's anger and pugnacity arose from his experiences in the Far East, where he had seen the Japanese effort in Siberia. Upon returning to his own country, Lamont had serious words for the State Department to consider: "If the Japanese General staff is permitted to continue its present policy in Siberia we shall see that great region west of the Ural mountains in the economic grip of Japan and the most valuable market in the world closed to American manufacture and export." Japan could be brought into line "and learn table manners from Western groups" only through the steady application of persuasion and pressure.[10]

Charles Evans Hughes used persuasion at the Washington Naval Conference of 1921–22. Torn by revolution and foreign intrigues, China was reduced to being an onlooker while the United States proposed to settle Far Eastern relations. This Conference provided several opportunities for Washington to increase its power in Asia. The 1905 Anglo-Japanese Alliance had given Tokyo a good counterweight to American pressures; Hughes wanted to replace it with multilateral conventions equally binding upon all. Of course, the successful negotiation of treaties limiting naval armaments received the most publicity, but as Hughes pointed out: "In this country the prospect of the continuance of the Alliance had caused no little uneasiness." If American policies were successful, Hughes added, there would seem "to be no exigency requiring the continuance of the Agreement." And the United States did manage to replace the Anglo-Japanese Alliance with the Five Power, the Four Power, and the Nine Power Treaties.[11]

Some years later, in the face of increasing tensions with Japan, Far Eastern Adviser Stanley K. Hornbeck recalled the purpose of the Washington Conference and those treaties: "The Nine-Power Treaty was made not alone, not even primarily, for the protection of China. It was made for the purpose of defining various rights and safeguarding various interests of all the parties concerned. Its purpose was to stabilize a situation, to ensure each and all of the Contracting Parties against aggression or encroachment on the part of any, and thus to promote the cause of harmony and peace." [12]

Feeling optimistic at the results of the Conference, Secretary Hughes then told the members of the American Historical Association: "The Open Door policy is not limited to China. It voices, whenever, and wherever there may be occasion, the American principle of fair treatment and freedom from unjust and injurious discrimination." Satisfied with these broad commitments, Hughes decided that the latest of the special arrangements with Japan, the 1917 Lansing-Ishii Agreement should be of "no further force or effect." [13]

A BREACH OF CONTRACT

For a decade the Washington Conference's multilateral conventions sufficed. The United States fulfilled its obligations by discouraging Chinese attempts to set America and Japan at odds. Thus when the Chinese tried to force the American and Foreign Power Company to stay clear of the Consortium in purchasing a Shanghai concern, Secretary Stimson probed the matter carefully. He was not unsympathetic, he said, towards the efforts of Americans to "extend their business in China," but he suspected the "motives of the Chinese in this matter . . ." [14]

The depression acted as a spur to more militant elements in Japan. On September 18, 1931, Japanese army units began a forward movement in Manchuria that Tokyo could not or would not reverse. "There was a feeling in Japan," said a member of the America-Japan Society, "that the country had to have an economic outlet, but also the Army felt that it would lose all influence if it did not do something for the good of the country." [15]

The Nation, an American liberal magazine, offered a remarkably able synthesis of Japanese-American conflicts and their historical evolution:

> Economic pressure has pushed our frontier ever westward; today our western frontier is in Asia itself. We have marked out China as an American market of immense potentialities. Under the Open Door policy, of course, we assume that we are giving all countries, and particularly Japan, an equal opportunity to do business in that market. But so vast are our natural resources and so highly developed is our system that the real advantages are all on our side . . . .

The Open Door, paradoxically enough, stands in the way of [Japan's] expansion. Washington and Tokio must come to a new understanding on the Asiatic problem.[16]

Secretary Stimson was willing to consider changing some of the terms of the Washington Treaties, perhaps, but he always insisted that Japan recognize first the Open Door's legitimate standing in international relations. Cordell Hull made much the same demand in 1941. This was the premise behind the nonrecognition doctrine of Japanese conquests in Manchuria. Exactly how far he would have gone to implement this doctrine would be hard to say, because he could get no backing either from the British or from President Hoover for anything more than a public letter to Senator Borah declaring that the United States would not recognize Manchukuo. Stimson had asked Hoover to keep the Japanese guessing about further steps the United States might take, such as an embargo or boycott, but the President had refused, noting that he could not see how China or Russia would allow their futures to be unsettled by a country the size of Japan.[17]

When the League of Nations's Lytton Commission finally investigated the Manchurian conflict, Tokyo stalked out of the League. Stimson sadly noted at the bottom of his copy of the Lytton Report that many of his worst fears had been confirmed: "Japan's ambition in . . . China could not be said to be limited to settlement of clash of interest in Manchuria—She (or a section of her bankers) has already put out definite claims for general exclusive hegemony [on] China's modernization." [18]

Like other American leaders, Stimson was anxious to settle the question before it got that far. He was disappointed that Hoover would not allow him to use stronger weapons; yet on the same day that the Stimson Doctrine was made public, he told the Chinese minister to the United States that Washington "had no quarrel with any of Japan's rights in Manchuria" and hoped to see the two countries settle their differences in ways which did not "impair our rights in China" and did not violate the Kellogg-Briand Pact. More pointedly, when Japan's military outburst at the Shanghai international settlement occurred in 1932, Stimson advised the Chinese sharply that other nations would follow Japan's example unless the Nationalist government changed the "picture of various Chinese factions cutting each other's throats and tearing each other to pieces . . . ." [19]

He remarked to Walter Lippmann that Washington did not insist upon a return to the *status quo ante:* "I gave him the analogy of a court of equity dealing with the abrogation of a contract." [20] "If Japan was willing to agree, conceivably it might have been arranged to arbitrate some of her claims, but . . . it depends wholly upon the consent of both sides whether any such arbitration shall be undertaken." Another time: "I explained confidentially to the press that the American note of January 7, 1932 was a statement of principles and not an attempt to describe a remedy, and that very many cases might come up where the situation had so changed that a restoration of the status quo ante would not be the best remedy . . . and often it would not do justice to restore the status quo ante and they do something else." [21]

That was the situation as Stimson left office. He advised those who followed that Asia's future depended upon China's future: "Our trade with the Far East," he wrote, in review of Far Eastern problems, "has stood the test of the depression more satisfactorily than has our trade with any other region abroad. The Far East in 1932 offered an outlet for 20 per cent of the United States' total exports, as compared with 17.4 per cent for 1931. It is thus apparent that our policy and action in the Far East are matters of great practical importance to the present and future welfare of the United States." [22]

In his book *The Far Eastern Crisis* (1936), Stimson reiterated the three basic points of his Manchurian diplomacy. First there was the direct damage to trade and the possibility of jeopardy to American nationals and territorial possessions. Next there was the threat to the peace treaties which were the hope of the western world. And finally there was the danger that American prestige in China would be destroyed if the United States, after taking the ideas of Christianity there, should abandon the country to Japan. But he went on again to emphasize economic factors: "We have recently been so absorbed in our own sufferings . . . that we forget the possibilities which should normally inhere in our commercial relations with China and the rapid strides which in normal times, particularly during the first decade after the Great War, have been made in the development of our commerce with that country. During that decade it increased at a much more rapid rate than our commerce with Europe." [23]

Both President Roosevelt and Secretary Hull readily agreed that *The Far Eastern Crisis* could not be ignored and that Stimson had outlined the salient points in it, but they too had great difficulty in finding "something else" that could be done. In his *Memoirs,* Hull wrote that he understood from the outset that Japan's way meant the absorption of

China, and he wanted to prevent it by reasserting the validity and the viability of the Washington Treaties. This was where Stimson left off in his January 9, 1933, conversation with Roosevelt, and the new President began by accepting the Stimson Doctrine: he kept the fleet at Hawaii, recognized the Soviet Union, and, as Admiral William Standley testified in 1936, maintained the "usual patrol of gunboats on the Yangtze River and in other troubled areas . . . . The employment of vessels on the Asiatic station," concluded the Admiral, "is dictated by special conditions and circumstances as they arise, making it impossible to predict exactly where their services will be required for the protection of American interests." [24]

The first decision, then, had been not to break with past policies towards Asia. But in the early months of the New Deal, Roosevelt kept probing for well-reasoned opinions on the disagreement with Tokyo. In one Cabinet meeting the possibility that Japan might force a war was considered. Less fatalistically, Roosevelt and Stimson discussed the "importance of maintaining the situation so that Japan could be controlled by joint naval action of Britain and America . . . ." [25]

THE END OF NAVAL DISARMAMENT

This premise set the foundation for American policy at preliminary naval talks in London in the fall of 1934 and through the London Naval Conference of 1936. Quite firmly the United States and England refused to grant a change in the 5:5:3 Washington Naval Conference ratio. Some wanted an even stronger policy towards Japan, on all fronts, but domestic considerations and the still prevalent belief that Tokyo could finally be brought into line discouraged such enthusiasts. In fact, in the months before the naval talks the State Department continued to take a firm stand with China on several issues of alleged discrimination against American interests. Though Stanley Hornbeck explained to the new Undersecretary of State, William Phillips, that the United States recognized that China was going through a trying period in its development and therefore wanted to pursue a liberal policy towards that government in the hope that it would survive and grow strong, only a few months later he admonished the Chinese ambassador that China's creditors in America had come to the Department with legitimate complaints and that no more aid could be given until those matters were settled. In addition, if China was planning to give new business contracts to any foreign nations, the United States "must ask that she offer the same or similar business to nationals of the United States." [26]

In 1934 the Department frowned upon parts of China's proposed "Industrial Encouragement Act." Nelson Johnson, Minister to China, wired the Secretary of State on June 26 that this Act would grant special advantages, such as tax rebates and monopoly privileges to domestic concerns. The most alarming provision, said Johnson, was the one which stipulated that industries with foreign capital investment "shall not receive encouragement under this act." William Phillips replied that the American Legation should present a brief note on the matter explaining that while the United States could understand China's desire to help its domestic industries, certain provisions of the proposed act "would appear to contravene various treaty commitments of the Chinese Government and that, in consequence, the Legation reserves such rights of American nationals as may be adversely affected by the operation of the Act under reference." [27]

But if American officials tried to perpetuate the Open Door Policy by scolding Chinese governments, they still assumed rightly that the major problem was Japan's forward movement. When Tokyo suggested a good-will tour by some prominent Japanese leaders of the United States as a way of relieving tensions and reinvigorating friendships, Ambassador Grew was instructed to reply that it would be but an empty gesture so long as discriminations against America were continued in Manchuria. Hull then personally warned the Japanese Ambassador, on May 16, not to go too far in China without American participation, for even if there had been no Washington Treaties, "my Government would . . . be interested in equality of trade rights." [28]

American oil companies most particularly wanted the State Department to back up such warnings, for they were the first large enterprise to suffer losses in Manchuria. "We feel that the strict maintenance of the 'Open Door' policy," declared the Standard Oil Company of New York, "is the only hope for the protection of American interests in Manchuria." Hull authorized informal representations to the Japanese Foreign Office, but to the disappointment of Ambassador Grew, who urged more forceful steps, he refused to "be drawn or pushed into a position of taking the initiative in actions or threats of action to coerce Japan . . . ." [29]

Although Hull recommended that the companies reach a settlement with a Japanese-sponsored oil monopoly, the Department was aware that the monopoly was one of the proofs of Japan's aspirations which helped determine Washington's policy in naval talks. Even the "internationalists" now saw for themselves what Japanese control would mean, said one Department official. "The lesson that Japanese superiority in the Far East would definitely mean the closing of the Open Door has been driven home in a way which I should not have anticipated." [30]

Treasury Secretary Morgenthau, perhaps seeing only the apparent backdown on the Manchurian oil question and like issues, became convinced that the State Department was too timid, and continued in this belief right down to 1941. He felt the United States should break out of the dilemma by extending direct financial aid to Chiang Kai-shek. Hull answered his criticisms by reasserting the collective and multilateral principle of the Washington Treaties. Disagreeing vehemently, Morgenthau belittled and scoffed at Hull's supposed "fears of British and Japanese predominance in China's trade," and then urged upon the President the opposite view, that America's trade could best be protected and furthered by helping China. In fact, the only way America could possibly lose out in Asia would be by refusing to aid China. Morgenthau enlisted economic experts Jacob Viner and John H. Williams to point out the qualitative importance of American exports to China. "Our trade with China is of considerable importance," began a Treasury memorandum to Roosevelt. "In the last nine months, the United States supplied 27 percent of China's total imports, double those supplied by Japan or Great Britain. During the last two years, we have absorbed 18 percent of total Chinese exports. Our trade with China comprises only about 3 percent of our total imports and exports; but this measure of the absolute importance of our trade with China is misleading because such trade is of very considerable importance to certain areas and industries in this country." Unmodified silver purchases from China and a refusal to grant financial aid would result in "the withdrawal of the United States as an active influence in Far Eastern affairs, leaving that field to Japan, Great Britain, and other countries.[31]

After hearing these arguments, Roosevelt surprised Morgenthau with a return memorandum in which he blasted past China policies, implying that the Treasury suggestion might even perpetuate them: "China has been the Mecca of the people whom I have called the 'money changers in the Temple.' They are still in absolute control. It will take many years and possibly several revolutions to eliminate them because the new China cannot be built up in a day." Perhaps it would be better to force China to stand on its own feet, independent of Japan and Europe, rather than aid in the "continuation of an unsound position for a generation to come." Roosevelt did, however, allow the Treasury to manipulate the silver purchase program so as to aid China's own stabilization efforts rather than to hinder them.[32]

As Morgenthau had asserted, Hull did fear the renewal of an informal Anglo-Japanese entente. Already the British ambassador in Japan, Sir Robert Clive, had argued with Grew over the Stimson Doctrine. Clive contended that all of Japan's actions in Manchuria and China were directed towards the one goal of achieving recognition for Manchukuo. If the western powers really wanted to keep the door open, some sort of recognition would seem to be necessary. Ambassador Grew had returned quickly that such a thesis courted disaster. Any retreat from the principles of the Washington Treaties would undermine the western powers' political and economic position. The State Department re-emphasized Grew's points with a cable to London backing him up.[33]

In the event, the only achievement of the London naval talks, as Norman Davis reported, was that the "British have come to realize that, if they are going to induce Japan to 'play ball' they must make her understand that she will have to play on the same team with both of us . . . ."[34]

The hope of a united stand against Japan seemed strengthened by the 1934 naval discussions, but the Administration was becoming more and more concerned that a rising philosophy of Japan's Manifest Destiny was replacing Tokyo's previous almost apologetic claim for self-protection in the Manchurian affair. J. Pierrepont Moffat noted that Roosevelt was "likewise concerned over their seizure of markets throughout the world by underselling, particularly in textiles, and their oil policy." "Japan is annexing parts of China," the President said, explaining these fears to Ambassador William Dodd, "and plans to annex more and control all of Asia including India. We shall spend a billion dollars building warships, and all of them will be antiquated in ten years." Still another time Roosevelt told Admiral Standley that the United States would build three ships for every new one that Japan constructed when Tokyo bolted the London Naval Conference and the

Washington Treaties. If the President did not share Morgenthau's ideas on how to aid China, he certainly had no intention of getting out of Asia and leaving the field to Japan.[35]

Admiral Standley had heard the Japanese point of view, and knew that Tokyo would denounce the treaties. Japanese naval officers had made it plain that they considered the heart of the matter their belief that America was unwilling to allow Japan's nationals to engage in enterprises within areas protected by the Monroe Doctrine, yet America insisted that the door remain open in Asia. Standley denied this. The American navy was not a threat to Japan, he had replied, but only a policy instrument "to protect certain of our interests, including our possessions and trade in the Far East." To the Japanese the use of this very instrument was precisely their objection to allowing their fleet to remain inferior to those of the United States and Great Britain. "We consider it only natural, logical, reasonable and fair," argued the Japanese naval officers, "that the Americans should refrain from building railways, working mines and doing things in general which would affect our vital interests in the countries immediately adjacent to our possessions in the Far East." The only kind of open door they expected in the Western Hemisphere was a commercial one, said a Japanese navy captain, and if the United States would accept the same for itself in Asia there would be no "trouble between the two nations on the score of the Open Door . . . ." [36]

American policy makers, like their Japanese opponents, also linked naval policy to economic and political situations. Nelson Johnson pointed out that the invasion of Manchuria and the subsequent discrimination which had occurred there would have to be considered seriously, "for we consented to a reduction of our navy and to an abandonment of our recognized right to build and maintain strong naval bases in the Philippines only after we had obtained agreement among the powers regarding the open door in China and the abandonment of the Anglo-Japanese Alliance." [37]

Led by Chief Delegate Norman Davis and Admiral Standley, the American delegation maintained that Japan's desire for naval equality was destructive of the "equality of security" which had prevailed since 1921. Japan withdrew and denounced the Treaties. "This is a tough situation," Davis wired Hull. "Ordinarily the logical thing would be, if we are not going to enforce our rights with Japan, to make peace with her. Unfortunately there are considerable obstacles in the way of doing the former and there seems to be no way to do the latter. At least not until in some way the Manchurian situation had been adjusted, and the Japanese are prepared to pursue a policy which is not in conflict with international law and fairness." [38]

Japan, decided one of the American delegates, "has clearly shown her hand at desiring only one thing, overlordship in the Far East, which means the expulsion of American rights and the closing of the Open Door . . . ." [39]

THE SEARCH FOR A NEW MODUS VIVENDI

So America rebuilt the Great White Fleet. Approving such Theodore Roosevelt-like policies, Ambassador Grew argued that this was the best way to support the "normal development" of American interests in the Far East. On March 16, 1935, Hull forwarded a long memorandum from the State Department's Far Eastern Division to the President. It advocated retention of the Philippine naval bases and pointed out that the United States could no more withdraw from the Far East than from Latin America. Though the Great China Market might never become as great as some had dreamed, "As our own population becomes more and more dense, as the struggle for existence in this country becomes more intense, as we feel increasingly the need of foreign markets, our definite concern for open markets will be more widely felt among our people and our desire for and insistence upon free opportunity to trade with and among the peoples of the Far East will be intensified. For in that region lie the great potential markets of the future." [40]

With the blessings of the Department, a former Ambassador to Japan, W. Cameron Forbes, led a twentieth-century-Marco Polo business expedition to the Far East in 1935 and returned with stories of new prospects of wealth and riches for the American trader in China. That country had constructed 50,000 miles of new roads, he exclaimed before the National Foreign Trade Council, and they awaited only Detroit's trucks and automobiles to turn them into vital arteries of commerce. K. C. Li, president of the Chinese Chamber of Commerce, further stimulated this meeting by describing the "extraordinary awakening" which had taken place in his country and predicting that it would soon become "the most important trade center in the world." [41]

A highly roseate view—but one that swayed sober minds. No doubt it was less appealing to those who more fully understood China's internal weaknesses and had learned from past experience about the illusion of the China Market. Yet the potential was there, and even if it were only an illusion, the United States wanted to see for itself. Japan's actions could not be allowed to prevent Americans from finding out. Trade with Japan might be of greater value in the 1930's, reasoned many, but then, as the State Department memorandum had said, what of the future? China's potential versus Japan's growing nationalism—*this* was the first consideration. Such a trend in American thought was reflected in Grew's cautioning of the State Department to avoid public "emphasis on the preponderant interest of trade with China over that of trade with Japan" during the American Economic Mission's Far Eastern tour.[42]

Nor could it be forgotten that Japan was threatening not only China but all of Asia. And as Secretary Hughes had said in 1922: "The Open Door policy is not limited to China." In the 1930's 33 per cent of America's iron and steel exports, 26 per cent of its copper exports, 15 per cent of its industrial machinery exports, and 40 per cent of its paper exports were destined for the Far East.[43]

But China was somehow bigger than life: It was the symbol as well as the reality of American interest in Asia. Henry Morgenthau's blunt comment that Asian affairs were an "international battle between Great Britain, Japan, and ourselves and China is the bone in the middle" was a crude caricature of the vision that held such fascination for Americans.

Having failed to keep Japan within the military and political fences of the Washington Treaties, some State Department officials wanted to resurrect the moribund Second China Consortium. Maybe cooperation could be resumed in economic matters.

In March, 1935, the State Department turned down another Chinese request for commercial aid with the comment that "financial assistance if given should be given by cooperative action among the powers." "We expressed doubt whether a settlement of the situation in the Far East should be made a condition precedent." Few besides Stanley Hornbeck and Thomas Lamont believed that much could come of this effort to use the Second China Consortium—and even they doubted the possibilities. Roosevelt and Hull were unenthusiastic, but agreed it was worth a try.[44]

Hornbeck's starting point was his conviction that China would never achieve peace and stability without outside help, nor would any plan which excluded Japan have a chance; therefore, some form of international cooperation was the only alternative. He had even discouraged some of Forbes's more grandiose plans for building Chinese railroads, because they would be too much of a challange to Japan.[45]

Lamont thought that the Japanese might still have an interest in the Consortium, and that the American participants could also be aroused. His past experience led him to assert that "the organization of the Consortium for the assistance of China and the cooperation of the American group in that consortium were beneficial to the whole situation and therefore to the American economy, so to speak." [46]

Because the New-Deal-sponsored Securities and Exchange Act prohibited the combination of savings and investment banking with bond flotation, very few of the American group could participate in international loans to China, but Lamont and the State Department counseled them not to dissolve the group until Washington had decided if any kind of economic and financial cooperation with Great Britain and Japan could be expected.[47]

At the very least, admitted Economic Adviser Feis, the Consortium might continue "to serve as a brake against action by any one power seeking special advantage." Hornbeck added that without the international banking group's restraining influence, "American nationals stand little chance" against the "emphatic methods used by foreign governments" in gaining participation in Chinese development loans.[48]

In making these plans, those involved could not cope with China's dislike for the international banking group, England's desire to take advantage of Chinese offers to place railroad loans with its bankers, nor Japan's independent course. A 1937 Anglo-Chinese contract broke the Consortium, and it was about this same time that Chiang Kai-shek told Nelson Johnson that the Nine Power Treaty had been a detriment to China from first to last. In short, no one except some United States policy makers saw any advantages in the Second China Consortium.[49]

THE BRUSSELS NINE POWER CONFERENCE

Hornbeck and Lamont did not have the answer, but neither did anyone else apparently. Everywhere the Japanese went, they restricted or eliminated American interests. Finally, in July, 1937, the China "incident" took on new proportions as the Japanese army moved out of Manchuria and North China following a clash at the Marco Polo Bridge in the area around Peiping. At once Cordell Hull appealed to the Japanese ambassador, asking him to persuade the Foreign Office to return to "a constructive program like the basic program proclaimed at Buenos Aires for . . . restoring and preserving stable conditions of business and peace . . . ." [50]

Morgenthau again charged that the Secretary of State was appeasing Japan, but he could not have been critical of Hull's sharp reply to Vice-President John Garner's worried suggestion that American marines be withdrawn from the international settlements. The marines were necessary to protect American interests, Hull had said bluntly. Finding a more positive policy or the "right course of action" was far less easy for Hull. The strain left him, observed an aide, "looking pretty drawn and haggard." [51]

Roosevelt was searching too. The Chinese had asked for, and the State Department had finally approved, a 25 million dollar credit from the Export-Import Bank. This supplemented a monetary arrangement which had been reached between the Treasury and Chinese finance officials. Since 1936, when China had gone off its silver standard (largely because of the disruptive impact of America's silver purchase program), Morgenthau had been making a series of temporary silver purchase agreements with China. Some believed that Morgenthau had saved China from Japan or an Anglo-Japanese sphere of influence. As the undeclared war against Japan continued to go badly, China asked for more and more of this tonic as well as for other aid. From 1934 through 1941 the United States purchased more than a half a billion ounces of silver from China, paying that Government $260,000,000. [52]

The President had promised Finance Minister H. H. Kung that his administration would continue to strengthen Chinese-American friend-ship "in every appropriate and practicable manner." The Shanghai Chamber of Commerce and the American Chamber of Commerce saw a great deal of self-interest in granting credits to China, recommending that it be stipulated that all purchases of materials and all employment of foreign technical services should be American. [53]

Roosevelt briefly considered a naval blockade of Japan, but dis-carded the idea, said Sumner Welles, because he knew Congress would not back him up. [54]

Somewhere between economic aid to China and the idea of block-ading Japan was Roosevelt's famous Quarantine Speech of early Octo-ber, 1937, in which the President suggested isolating those responsible for the "epidemic of world lawlessness." Receiving little public support for a strong stand against Germany and Japan, Roosevelt tried to channel the impact of the speech into a constructive program by initiating the Brussels Nine Power Conference shortly afterwards. Perhaps there was little to be expected from foreign opinion, for, as Roosevelt later wrote Stimson, the League of Nations powers had made it clear that no real pressure could be brought against Japan. Even so, the President overoptimistically entertained hopes that the Brussels Conference might in some way start the world back from the edge of conflict by providing a place for mediation between China and Japan.[55]

Once again it was Norman Davis who was chosen to make the attempt. The day before he left for the Conference, Davis met with Roosevelt to discuss American policy towards Japanese expansion. There were two main schools of thought about it, Davis contended: The first held that having defeated China, Japan would continue to reach out until war with the United States became inevitable. The other maintained that Japan could never defeat China, and even if this were somehow accomplished, Tokyo would still need American aid and trade.

Roosevelt, personally finding the first view the more plausible, felt that "our security and stability" were in danger; he therefore wanted to bring about a truce between China and Japan before it grew too late. But what if the Conference failed, asked Davis, and the war in China became worse? Roosevelt answered that if it came to that, American public opinion would demand that something be done.

Turning from these speculations, Davis produced a draft of a possible Far Eastern settlement. From even a brief examination Roosevelt could see that it began with a reassertion of the Nine Power Treaty and the Open Door Policy. After that, Japan was offered guarantees of fair treatment in and from China and the other Treaty signatories. The draft then suggested troop withdrawals and even the possible relinquishment of extraterritorial rights in China, and at the bottom of the paper the author noted: "All the economic provisions are in accord with our trade policy. If accepted by Japan and the other Powers, it would give valuable impetus to the universal acceptance of this policy." [56]

When Ambassador Grew discussed the purpose of the Conference with the Japanese foreign minister, he received the brusque reply that "if we wished to help the situation the best thing we could do would be to persuade Chiang Kai-shek to negotiate for peace." American delegates at Brussels talked to unofficial Japanese observers, who simply repeated their country's view that the Sino-Japanese dispute could be settled only by bilateral negotiations, anathema to the United States. Tokyo refused to send an official delegation to the Conference.[57]

The Brussels Conference was thus over before it began, but several secret conversations the American delegation had with representatives of other nations are of no little interest in demonstrating the dilemma involved in trying to reconcile Japan's ambitions and the Open Door Policy.

The Chinese were undoubtedly the most upset by the American attitude, since aid from the Treasury and from the Export-Import Bank seemed clear indication of United States support. They must have been startled, then, by United States expectations that their delegation would have to make some commitments to the Japanese, who could not, said the Americans, "simply stop and go away." "If they did that, there would still remain all of the issues out of which the present resort to force had arisen." Equally upsetting was Davis' remark that President Roosevelt hoped the Chinese delegation would make an opening statement and then retire from the deliberations, so that Japan would have no complaint that the Conference was one-sided. After all, concluded Davis, the Nine Power Treaty did not call for Chinese participation on such matters! [58]

Stunned by these developments, the Chinese went looking for aid from other delegations. Russia seemed interested in a strong policy, for example. Soviet Foreign Minister Litvinov had been invited to Brussels, not as a signatory of the Nine Power Treaty but because of Russia's obvious interest in Far Eastern questions and even more obvious usefulness as a counterbalance to Japan. Litvinov, however, declined to play a silent role, and much to the embarrassment of the American delegation insisted upon being a part of all the major deliberations. Point-blank he asked the American delegates how far their Government would go in using force against Japan. "I told him," Davis reported, "fortunately we had not reached a stage where we needed to consider this seriously and when we could even discuss it usefully." The Russian offered to provide pressure against Japan from the Asian mainland if the United States and Great Britain would guarantee the Soviet Union against a European attack. Davis replied even more coolly than before. "Any statement which went beyond the purpose of the conference," he said, trying to discourage further discussion, "would have a very adverse effect in the United States and might harm more than help the Chinese insofar as the United States was concerned." Davis had come to Brussels to bring Japan and China together under the shield of the Nine Power Treaty, not to talk of war.[59]

At the open sessions Litvinov jibed at those who were more interested in making the meetings a personal success than in solving the difficulties before them. After any conference like this had gone on for some time, he said, there was an almost irresistible urge to say to the aggressor, "If you will make peace and give us credit, you can have most of your terms," and to say to the victim, "Make peace with the aggressor, and God bless you." [60]

The British, on the other hand, refused to accept any sort of responsibility and were determined "to go just as far in the way of direct action in the Far East as the United States, but no further." Caught between the Russians and the English, Davis found himself trying to persuade Malcolm MacDonald that his delegation's attitude would give the Japanese a wrong impression. Slipping aside again, MacDonald replied that his government wanted to cooperate with the United States "not only in determining what we should do but standing together in what we refuse to do." [61]

The other nations at the Conference, taken up with their own problems in Europe, were anxious for the meetings to end with as little embarrassment as possible. Finally, the chairman of the American delegation had to report to his superiors that he could not carry out his instructions to keep the Conference going "for some time, even months if necessary" to make continued approaches to Japan.[62]

As the meetings ended, Davis was complaining about the bad press his efforts were receiving. Inside the State Department there was evident an atmosphere of futility and a general letdown feeling. Roosevelt lost his great interest in the project. For four years the Administration had tried to find a way of containing Japan. Yet the assumptions it worked from constantly hampered its ability to maneuver or to meet the specific challenge. Thus during the Brussels Conference, Secretary Hull had decided not to issue a neutrality proclamation during the Sino-Japanese War because it might mean that the United States would be obliged to recognize a Japanese blockade of China; but as the *Panay* incident demonstrated, the United States was not yet prepared to confront Japan in a final showdown.[63]

John Hay once stated that the United States must do everything it could for "the integrity and reform of China, and to hold on like grim death to the open door . . . ." Even before he left office the dilemmas had become apparent to Hay, who was the first to discover that other nations' ambitions always threatened the Open Door Policy and that China would remain a source of conflict so long as it continued to be an object of diplomacy rather than an equal or even any sort of sovereign entity. Although the United States had needed Japan's stabilizing influence in Asia, after 1937 it seemed impossible to work with Tokyo on the basis of the Open Door Policy and the Nine Power Treaty. But the tragedy was not played out for four more years.[64]

I have made it clear that the United States cannot take part in political arrangements in Europe, but that we stand ready to cooperate at any time in practicable measures on a world basis looking to immediate reduction of armaments and the lowering of the barriers against commerce.

President Franklin Roosevelt, *State of the Union Message,* 1934

5 · Political Isolation and Neutrality Unavailing

A few days after moving into his office in the State, War, Navy Department building across from the White House, Secretary Hull explained to a chief aide how he thought America should view European affairs. "As he saw it," his listener noted, "our role in foreign affairs was to be helpful whenever we could and to exercise our good offices towards a sane and reasonable solution of outstanding questions affecting the peace of the world, but not to go forward with any plan for leadership." [1]

Broadly speaking, this reluctance to exert leadership in European affairs was the isolationist attitude of the early 1930's, which has caused such puzzlement and embitterment when it was later debated by students of the era.

Nearly all Americans living in the 1930's shared in (or at least understood) the disillusionment that had followed the Peace of Versailles. They had little stomach for defending that settlement's political organization of Europe, and wanted nothing to do with future crusades. Like Ernest Hemingway's Frederick Henry, they had said their farewell to arms. Even Roosevelt, who certainly held few revisionist views about World War I or about munitions makers as merchants of death, and who was perhaps more willing than Hull to offer leadership to Europe, admitted to Oswald Garrison Villard that, "From the point of view of hindsight, we might have kept out, but at the time we were following the precedents of several centuries." [2]

People before World War I, the President continued, thoughtfully, "were thinking in terms of the old international law which is now completely disappeared." Another time he told one of his ambassadors in Europe that another war "would be disastrous to us as well as to Europe

85

and the rest of the world." Fear of another war tormented both liberals and conservatives and had a good deal to do with limiting American initiative in the mid-1930's.[3]

After 1937 American leaders realized that they were even more afraid of an Axis-dominated world. How to meet that challenge was what finally separated the isolationists from the interventionists. The first title was not very exact, for most in the former group really desired only nonintervention in the empire building of European or Asian powers, while the latter group insisted it would soon become impossible to live in the shadow cast over the world by these empires. That this was the key difference is illustrated by significant isolationist attention to, and support for, Roosevelt's Latin American policies. America Firsters such as Colonel Charles Lindbergh even suggested absorbing Canada into the United States.

Another reason some were giving for America's desire to remain aloof was the advantage gained by acting as a balancer, as England had supposedly done in the nineteenth century. Secretary Hull and many of his assistants would have liked that, especially since they believed that the United States had fallen heir to English economic power and could lead the world towards freer trade—through the most-favored-nation treaty system. Once the British "had got it started," Hull asserted, "it spread like the waves of the ocean . . . ." He saw no reason why similar waves should not now roll out in orderly and steady fashion from the United States.[4]

Other State Department officials pointed out that the seas had become churning maelstroms. If it were to enjoy economic advantages, America would have to try to calm the political storms of Europe. One Department officer told Hull "quite bluntly that no European power believed in words and that unless and until we were prepared to talk deeds they would not take anything from Washington too seriously." Sumner Welles later wrote that after 1936 no economic remedy could have healed the military and political sicknesses that confronted the world. "This Mr. Hull seemed unable to understand."[5]

As a matter of fact, neither point of view could count on Roosevelt's support. Hull constantly looked for more appreciation of his trade program from the White House; and the advocates of greater participation in political affairs were hurt several times between 1933 and 1937 by what Allan Nevins has called the "hot-and-cold Roosevelt policy toward Europe . . . ."[6]

The President's first act in European affairs was to attempt to influence the Geneva World Disarmament Conference, but his repudiation of the London Economic Conference and his refusal (or inability) to accept political responsibilities would have made the gesture futile even had the rest of the powers been willing to listen—a very doubtful proposition. Congress then tried to legislate neutrality, but found itself unable to do more than reassert neutral rights. As this period ended, Germany's aspirations to establish a hememony in Europe were revealed, and the United States, which had hoped to stay clear of political involvements, found itself seeking closer relations with England and France.

ROOSEVELT'S APPEAL TO THE GENEVA CONFERENCE

"The rest of the world—ah! there's the rub." This was the phrase President Roosevelt employed to begin his discussion of European affairs in his 1936 State of the Union Message. After describing the successes of the Good Neighbor Policy, he changed the tone of his remarks and admitted that the United States had not found similar ways to achieve its ends in Europe.

For a brief moment in 1933, Roosevelt had convinced himself that he might be able to cut through the tangled political issues of the 1932–35 Geneva World Disarmament Conference. If he could strike through to the basic problem, he was convinced that the reasonableness of arms reduction, in order to achieve world peace and to stimulate world economic recovery would then become apparent to all. The trouble had been, he told Henry Stimson, that President Hoover had never dramatized the issue in any way. Years afterward Roosevelt was still insisting that Europe's economic problems in the Great Depression had come from the burden of arms costs.[7]

But the American President's repudiation of the London Economic Conference was drama of another sort, at least to the Europeans who saw in it a rejection of cooperation with Europe. Of even greater impact than the Bombshell message to London, however, was Roosevelt's unwillingness or inability to make a political commitment to America's World War I Allies. The President avoided making this decision as long as possible.

After spending the day in consultations with Roosevelt and Hull, America's representative to the Geneva Conference, the omnipresent Norman Davis, took the midnight train to New York on March 17, 1933, with no plans having been decided upon and only "the prospect of using our influence to the best advantage that he can." A few days before, Washington had learned that the European powers were probably going to ask the United States to modify its traditional insistence upon neutral rights in order that effective measures could be taken against an "aggressor." [8]

A month later Davis confirmed this, and added that America would "have to pay for arms reduction in Europe." The price was limited political involvement: The United States would have to agree not to interfere with a blockade against a continental aggressor, after such a nation had actually been identified.[9]

At first, President Roosevelt seemed willing to meet the price. In talks with the German ambassador, as they were reported to Berlin, Roosevelt linked the Disarmament Conference to the London Economic Conference, saying that the "pulse of the world economy was growing constantly weaker and it had to be put on the path to convalescence" by a general approach by all countries. He took a direct and continuing interest in the Conference during May, 1933, and used strong words to German economics expert Hjalmar Schacht, in Washington on other business, to convince him that the United States was opposed to any change in the level of German armaments. The Germans had become, he said, the "only possible obstacle to a disarmament treaty." Schacht's government had raised demands at Geneva for arms equality, whereas the English MacDonald Plan proposed to solve the problem by measured reductions from each nation's existing level. Roosevelt concluded his remarks with the dour note that American opinion of Germany had not been so low since October, 1914.[10]

Besides Germany's attitude at Geneva, there were the Nazi anti-Jewish laws and acts, abhorrent to the United States and to most others. Direct American interests in Germany were suffering as Schacht manipulated his limited resources to increase Germany's economic power. Chagrined American diplomats were ready to remind Berlin how much Germany owed to the United States for its post World War I recovery. But all they could see was the German Chancellor, Adolf Hitler, threatening to create a nation and empire in central Europe that would once again menace American interests. "They have gone mad with a vengeance," the chief of the Western European division of the State Department wrote in his diary.[11]

Roosevelt's attempt to sever the deadlock at Geneva came on May 16, 1933, when, after talking with Hull, he decided to point out the "home truths" of economic and military disarmament. He addressed a message to the Geneva meetings calling for the repudiation of offensive arms and a world-wide nonaggression pact. Norman Davis followed with a tentative promise that America would not interfere with a blockade against an aggressor, and, of even greater importance, would not protect its citizens if they engaged in actions that might weaken the collective effort. This was a bold decision and a challenge to Congress in its later attempts to legislate neutrality.[12]

At this point everything fell through. France and Russia had second thoughts about the safety of the MacDonald Plan and wanted harsher demands made upon Germany. France also insisted upon firmer guaranties from the British; and in Washington, Congress refused to allow Roosevelt the discretion necessary to embargo goods against an aggressor—at least not without a lengthy struggle in which the President would not engage himself.[13]

Both domestic and international reasons were behind his decision not to fight Congress on this issue. He certainly did not want to jeopardize his antidepression attack, yet as he told an official of the League of Nations, "we are nearly through with our crusading and . . . if the nations did not soon get down to brass tacks" they should be willing to "let us go our own way." It was about this time that the United States began rebuilding its navy.[14]

Only weeks later, however, Norman Davis was on his way back to European capitals carrying letters from Roosevelt to each of the European leaders. To Ramsay MacDonald the President wrote soothingly that European armaments were "infinitely more dangerous" than disagreements over gold stabilization and tariffs. "Never before," Davis avowed to the French, had the United States been so concerned about the success of disarmament meetings. Washington was sure that further delays would only allow Germany time to rearm in secret. There were really only two alternatives for dealing with that country: The former allies could destroy Germany, "and I did not think it possible to get armies to go into Germany and murder the Germans after they had been defeated," or the three nations could bring Germany into a disarmament pact while there was yet time.[15]

America was closer to England's position on disarmament than to the harsher one of France, and Davis purposely strengthened London's hand by repeatedly mentioning to Sir John Simon his hope that fear of Germany would not drive Britain and France so close together that London would be unable to act independently. But when he finished stating the need for Anglo-American unity, the American was disappointed by Prime Minister MacDonald's response: If the United States was so interested in international cooperation, he asked, why had it destroyed the London Economic Conference? Davis answered obliquely that Roosevelt had been left no choice by English and French concentration on currency stabilization and their lack of interest in "how to raise the price level and to remove quotas." But all that was in the past, he pleaded, and the two nations must now look to these graver problems confronting them.[16]

French leaders raised embarrassing questions, too. If the Germans broke a disarmament agreement, what kind of sanctions would the United States approve—and act upon? Again Davis was indirect: "Anglo-Saxons were not disposed to define in detail what they would do in future contingencies whereas the French desire to attempt such a definition." [17]

Winding up this tour in Berlin, Davis tried to convince the resurgent Germans that their best interests would be served by a disarmament agreement. "Within a few months after such an agreement," he predicted to Foreign Minister Von Neurath, "economic and other conditions would greatly improve and we would begin to get the idle people back to work. Unless this is done conditions will go from bad to worse." It was a good argument to use with a nation of Germany's size which had six to eight million unemployed, and to a political leader who had come to power largely as a result of the depression, but Von Neurath countered that just as soon as Hitler could get people back to work, just that soon would the Nazi regime become less belligerent.[18]

When the Geneva Conference reassembled in the fall of 1933, there was very little chance that these leaders Davis had talked with would reach any agreement. Uneasily watching Hitler's fist waving, French diplomats insisted that there be a four-year trial period during which a permanent disarmament commission would carry on periodic inspections, and only in the second four-year period would there be any actual disarmament. United States delegates tried to ease certain harsh-sounding French phrases, particularly that of "trial period," but Secretary Hull directed his main effort to the German ambassador, advising him that Berlin would be assuming "a serious responsibility" if it demanded immediate rearmament instead of going along with the Anglo-French ideas and proposals. Davis was instructed to soothe

the Germans, but not at the cost of creating a breach between the three former Allies.[19]

Hitler defiantly denounced the Geneva Conference and took Germany out of the League of Nations as well. Roosevelt's early attitude towards political involvement now became clear. He had been willing to accept a limitation upon neutral rights, but when Hitler forced the issue he quickly made a transatlantic telephone call to Davis and told him that the United States had no place to go, for it could not be linked politically with France, England, and Italy: "We are not interested in the political element, or in the purely European aspect of peace." [20]

Roosevelt's 1934 State of the Union Message further emphasized United States disinterest in European political questions, but in April he mentioned the possibility to Norman Davis of United States support of an economic blockade of Germany if Hitler refused to allow an international commission to verify or negate reports of secret rearmament. In May he showed some interest in Davis' suggestion for doing away with private arms manufacturing, but these were momentary inspirations or flittings, having nothing to do with a plan of action.[21]

In Geneva diplomats were talking again, but with about as little real interest. Britain and France were at odds. Germany was no longer there. France berated both England and the United States for this situation, insisting it had resulted from refusals by these two nations to guarantee European security. Louis Barthou was now the French foreign minister, and he resumed France's earlier plan of constructing strong alliances in Eastern Europe, especially with the Little Entente and Poland. When Barthou kept returning to this subject at Geneva, Davis warned him that French attempts to turn disarmament discussions into political alliance talks would drive the United States away. Barthou retorted that in the past "sometimes the United States played a more active part when it was not present as a formal participant than when it was." [22]

Davis understood this allusion to the Reparations Commission and America's later sponsorship of German recovery through the Dawes and Young plans, but the French leader's thrust did not weaken the American representative's determination to reach his goal of bringing Germany into a negotiated agreement without taking sides in European questions. American diplomats were becoming impatient with what they assumed to be French illusions of grandeur. "If France will abandon her international role," Davis stated before the Council on Foreign Relations, "and live at home, she can have safety." [23]

Roosevelt was equally unresponsive to French political overtures, commenting that he could not understand how any foreigner could genuinely expect us "to tie ourselves up in contractual form." "None the less they come back, chiefly the French but also the others [with this] thought in a series of disguises, apparently unwilling to recognize its utter impossibility." [24]

Among the last to abandon this "thought" was Russian Foreign Minister Litvinov. In November, 1934, he approached an American diplomat at Geneva with an idea for a permanent peace organization designed to establish a united front "against the unruly ambitions of Germany and Japan." Ambassador Hugh Wilson shook his head at the idea of American participation and then went on to describe the bad situation which had resulted when Germany had walked out of the Geneva Conference "and accused us of trying to force her . . . . Public opinion in America indignantly repudiated the idea that we had mixed in an internal European squabble." [25]

Public opinion had been one factor all right, but so had Congressional attitudes, and Roosevelt's hot and cold attitude. The debate then beginning in America was not a simple case of an internationalist President and Secretary of State striving mightily to educate an isolationist or apathetic nation and Congress. From the way American policy developed in 1933 and 1934, it would be difficult to conclude that Roosevelt fitted either category. More useful in understanding this period than the later debate between court historians and revisionsts were the insights of the Council on Foreign Relations' Raymond Leslie Buell, whose comment went straight to the heart of the matter: "It was untenable for America to assert that it had no concern with the political disputes of Europe at the same time that it led a world-wide disarmament movement." [26]

Yet this was exactly what American policy had hoped to bring off during these two years. Of course Washington was unhappy to see Germany rearm, but it was unable and unwilling to make political commitments to that end. At the same time, the quarrels between England and France may have made this just an academic question. As the Executive branch thus struggled with its own mind and with European minds at

Geneva, Congress was seeking to shield America from war through the Neutrality acts—on the surface a much simpler task.

THE MEANING OF THE NEUTRALITY DEBATES

"I know I'm walking a tight rope," President Roosevelt confided to an adviser about the Italian-Ethiopian War, "and I'm thoroughly aware of the gravity of the situation." Roosevelt was talking about his use of the 1935 Neutrality Act to discourage aggression; Congress had passed it almost as an emergency measure to prevent United States involvement in the Italian forward movement in Africa. A committee headed by Senator Gerald Nye was investigating munitions profiteering and private loans to the Allies before American entrance into World War I and their influence upon the April, 1917, decision to go to war. The Nye Committee may not have proved this point, but it was influential enough to stimulate neutrality legislation in 1935 and again in 1936 and 1937. The operative clause of all these acts was the requirement that when the President found that a war existed between two or more countries, he must then declare an embargo on war goods to those engaged in the conflict. But it did not end there, for both Congress and the Administration were on the same tightrope: their balance, difficult to maintain under any conditions, was being overloaded by the weight of other factors. There was United States sympathy for the victims of aggression, and there was the more worldly desire to take part in world economic affairs. As Germany and Japan represented the usurping powers in the 1930's, it was very difficult to be neutral about the growing menace they represented. Besides the Reciprocal Trade Agreements Act, Congress passed and the President signed from 1933 to 1939 more legislation designed to open up and maintain trade outlets than in any previous period of American history. The Export-Import Bank Act, the Cellar Free Port Act, the Merchant Marine Act, the Civil Aeronautics Act, and many others added enough weights to the nation to pull it off the tightrope. "We are to a greater degree than ever before," said an Assistant Secretary of State in 1935, "meshing our domestic economy into the world economy." When the Reciprocal Trade Agreements Act came up for renewal in 1937, Hull's opponents picked the argument that his program led to political involvement, and many Congressmen voted against the bill, citing that reason.[27]

The State Department wanted to use the 1935 Neutrality Act to stop

Italian aggression. It appealed to Great Britain, unsuccessfully, to limit exports to Italy to "normal peace time proportions" and it encouraged semi-official discussions in a nonpartisan atmosphere among American businessmen, so that they would know why they were being asked to forego profits to support their Government's stand.[28]

Ironies and twists abounded in this confused atmosphere, where Congress had passed a neutrality law and the Executive Branch wanted to wield it as weapon against aggression. But neither branch wanted to initiate thereby a dramatic withdrawal from the world, and perhaps the greatest irony was that the President and the Secretary of State could not successfully employ the Neutrality Act against aggression because of the economic forces that had prompted the passage of the trade bills. American businessmen would not take the long-range point of view which the Administration had asked them to understand and appreciate. Exports to Italy averaged about $25,000 monthly in 1934, but in November, 1935, that figure had rocketed to $583,000.[29]

This irony worked itself out as the Administration and the business community gradually came to an agreement on the need to oppose fascism and Japanese militarism, but not before other "moral" embargoes failed to stop shipments of materials, such as the famous scrap-iron to Japan. In the meantime the Administration moved slightly closer to England and France. Secretary of the Treasury Morgenthau was given the go-ahead to negotiate a currency stabilization agreement with Britain and France, which he openly hoped would prevent further currency wars among the three and would protect each against German or Japanese currency manipulations. The struggle against fascism, thought Morgenthau, made necessary this reversal of American policy at the London Economic Conference.[30]

Whether or not Roosevelt intended the above to be a political move, he strongly complained that the 1937 Neutrality Act's cash and carry provision, under which belligerents could purchase war supplies provided they were bought with cash and carried away in the purchaser's ships, worked "all right in the Atlantic" but "all wrong in the Pacific." Hull and Roosevelt had concluded that any neutrality law which limited Executive freedom would have this or an equally dangerous flaw in it; therefore they would have preferred to have none. The Secretary remembered always in these years a comment Woodrow Wilson had made in 1916: "The business of neutrality is over." [31]

Congress did not see it that way. It hoped that, in a very literal sense, the business of neutrality could be enjoyed; or at least a majority of its members so hoped, and designed neutrality legislation accordingly. If the Secretary of State and the President distrusted the concept of neutrality legislation and tried to use it to defeat aggression, their acts did not mean until much later that they wanted political commitments to the Allies. Business and other economic leaders were not all agreed on a standard position on neutrality legislation; but one group, the Commerce Department's Business Advisory Council, warned that the 1936 law would "direct a large volume of normal peacetime trade in materials essential to the importing nations in time of war to other sources of supply." [32]

In this tangled state of affairs there began to emerge a few well-ordered lines of argument which could be followed through the maze to logical conclusions. Walter Lippmann began by raising a very cogent criticism about the 1935 Neutrality Act and the Administration's use of it during the Italian-Ethiopian War. The United States had turned its back on the League, he argued, but its actions through the Neutrality Law and its other maneuvers made it appear that the Administration had found a way of delegating to itself the "rights of a member without assuming any of the obligations." [33]

Lippmann was not so concerned with the morality or immorality of opposing Italy as with the inconsistency of avoiding political commitment while trying to influence European affairs. Isolationists who agreed with Lippmann's presentation called for complete disengagement. At the opposite pole stood those who wanted to end all pretense of neutrality and make any political commitments necessary to protect the United States and its interests abroad.

Charles Beard represented ably the first alternative; Lippmann pointed out weaknesses in both arguments; and Agriculture Secretary Wallace, though not a perfect representative of the other side, answered Beard's contentions.

Beard had argued forcefully in his *Open Door at Home* that America should seek prosperity and safety not through reciprocal trade agreements or collective security or neutrality acts, but through a reorganization of the American economy. By 1935 his early devotion to the New Deal had turned to distrust. His articles in the *Nation* and *New Republic* asserted that the United States was heading towards war as the result of its anti-Japanese policies and its rearmament program, which he feared were becoming attractive antidepression measures. On this latter point the *Nation's* editor, Oswald Garrison Villard, was also particularly alarmed, and he wrote Secretary Hull that "most liberals are appalled" by the billion dollar military and naval budget despite the "explicit warning of the founders of the country against large military forces of a permanent character." [34]

The equation implied between liberalism and Villard's point of view was not entirely accurate; another liberal, Henry Wallace, was an outstanding internationalist on both economic and political questions. He wrote in *America Must Choose* (1934) that a "clear-cut program of planned international trade or barter would be far less likely to get us into war" than wrong-headed attempts to isolate the American continent. "I have very deeply the feeling that nations should be naturally friendly to each other and express that friendship in international trade. At the same time we must recognize as realities that the world is ablaze with nationalistic feeling, and that with our own tariff impediments it is highly unlikely that we shall move in an international direction very fast in the next few years." [35]

Wallace said that he was surprised Beard had become an isolationist (though his own analysis could easily have led another to that same conclusion); but more revealing about the neutrality debate was Wallace's further comment that those in "the midst of business and political affairs" simply could not afford the time necessary to undertake Beard's program with its drastic changes in the American system. Before it could be accomplished the system would come crashing down.[36]

Walter Lippmann wondered in turn if Secretary Wallace really understood the implications of the "choice" he was outlining for the American people. Did America want neutrality or neutral rights? he asked. If the former, then American ports must be closed to all armed vessels, foreign enlistments must be forbidden on American soil, and no loans could be made to belligerents. "This is the problem we have to think about while Europe arms. It is another case, to use Secretary Wallace's phrase, where America may have to choose." Staying out of war might be possible, but not if the American people also wanted to exercise neutral rights. And they will "grow increasingly resentful if they cannot. This is the dilemma of neutrality." [37]

Roosevelt entered the debate at Chautauqua, New York, on August 14, 1936. Calling those who hoped to capture world markets during wartime seekers after fool's gold, he asserted: "If we face the choice of profits or peace, the nation will answer—must answer—'We choose peace.' " On the other hand, he continued, the United States rejected isolationism, except to isolate itself from war, and "We do not maintain that a more liberal international trade will stop war, but we fear that without a more liberal international trade war is a natural sequence." [38]

Here then was the full debate: the Roosevelt-Hull-Wallace thesis posited that peace could be maintained only as a result of a dynamic foreign policy. Hull stressed also (and Roosevelt was beginning to agree) that American recovery similarly depended upon a dynamic foreign policy; and even if domestic recovery did not depend upon freer trade, Roosevelt himself had said that without it war was a natural consequence.

Roosevelt tried to correct the faults of Congressional neutrality legislation himself and thus further his ideas on foreign policy; the Lippmann-Beard position was that the neutrality acts were a dangerous sham and America should clearly define its goals and understand the ramifications of each step as it went along in world affairs. Above all, it had to be realized that economic advantages could not be gained without eventually paying a political price. The Administration never satisfactorily faced up to that challenge.

The cash-and-carry provision of the 1937 Neutrality Act, for example, appeared deceitful not only to those who thought with Lippmann or Beard but also to writers for the Council on Foreign Relations, who noted sardonically: "The underlying principle was clearly isolation—but only so much insulation as the traffic would bear . . . . The law of 1937 was not designed to eliminate war by rendering it profitless. On the contrary, the 'cash and carry' plan was plainly a device for making money with a minimum of risk." Senator Key Pittman confirmed this analysis, explaining that the provision was necessary to the American economy, since "conditions with regard to industry and labor in this country today [are] so deplorable that further obstructions to our exports would bankrupt large sections of our country." As an experiment in methods of keeping out of war, the Neutrality acts could not succeed. As Robert Divine observed about the 1937 law: "Congress was determined to follow the Nye thesis only where it was politically feasible —it did not wish to antagonize farmers, laborers, and manufacturers who all were dependent to some degree upon foreign trade." [39]

Rounding out this discussion of the neutrality debate, one may find Assistant Secretary Sayre's remark about the world of the 1930's—"The economic world became a battlefield in which the issues were sometimes political as well as economic"—a very useful summation. There could be no better place to test Sayre's hypothesis than in the record of German-American conflicts from 1933 to 1937, and in the equally significant story of the Anglo-French-American rapprochement, which was well under way at the end of those years. Nor could there be a better person to observe than Sayre, since his role in these events was central.

THE GROWING GERMAN MENACE

"If this Government remains in power for another year and carries on in the same measure in this direction, it will go far towards making Germany a danger to world peace for years to come." This report by the Consul-General at Berlin, George Messersmith, was considered important enough in later years to be made a featured part of the State Department's White Paper on American entrance into World War II. Probably the most significant thing about this report was its date—June 26, 1933.

Further on, Messersmith contended: "It is impossible for us to talk about tariffs or monetary policy or any of these major matters with a Germany whose leaders do not think in any sense along the lines that we do." [40]

Obviously the inclusion in the White Paper of a prophetic dispatch such as this was accomplished largely through hindsight. The same can be said for Cordell Hull's affirmation in his *Memoirs:* "There was little doubt in my mind in March, 1933, that Germany would provide one of my biggest problems in the years to come." [41] Even so, both comments do reflect accurately the early concern the United States felt about Hitler's Germany: his was a *total* challenge certainly, but it was not the existence of Nazism *per se* that made World War II and America's entrance into that struggle inevitable; rather, it was the expansion of the system.*

* German-American differences by the mid 1930's were no longer primarily economic. Hitler defined the world in military terms very early; and perhaps only Cordell Hull among American policy makers continued to hope that Germany could be brought into line by economic pressures—and it is doubtful if his was more than a slight hope. On the other hand, Nazi Germany's autarchic economic policies were far more serious to American leaders than has been assumed. Germany's economic competition in South America constantly kept Washington on edge. Nor should it be passed over that Washington's views on Germany were consistent with its outlook on the rest of the world. In making this statement, I mean to call attention to the fact that American policy *was not* just a reaction to German or Japanese militarism. The disagreement with Japan came to a head with the signing of the Tripartite Pact in 1940, for example, but it was a much older struggle going back to 1900 and always, broadly speaking, about the Open Door Policy. So it was in Europe, where Germany's challenge was the same.

The spread of the Nazi system influenced the head of the Western European Division in the State Department, J. Pierrepont Moffat, never an avid interventionist, to deny that German domination of Central and Eastern Europe could ever be a good thing. It would mean, he told a questioner, "a still further extension of the area under a closed economy." Assistant Secretary Sayre was even more emphatic in pointing out to such persons as the director of the Reichsbank the bad influence German trade mechanisms and methods had on world recovery. "The only hope, we felt of producing such a condition, he told the German, "was through the most-favored-nation policy." [42]

With Roosevelt's active support, the Department brought pressure on Germany to accept that policy and to provide also for equality of treatment for American nationals who had loaned money to Germany or had interests there. To the State Department, George Peek's option—to seek short-run economic advantages—was an anathema. "To give in on this essential point," said Hull and his top aides, "would be inviting similar action which tends to drive our trade to a dollar for dollar exchange . . . against our ultimate interest." [43]

Russia also had a closed economy, yet the United States, albeit very reluctantly, made direct trade deals with that nation. Consequently, it was not a matter of principle only, but the very reasonable fear of German competition in all areas—and, only a few years later, of German military and political expansion in the Rhineland and then all of Europe —which most influenced American policy. Nazi anti-Jewish policies intensified these fears. Hull told the German ambassador in March, 1934, that the most outstanding cause of American ill-feeling toward Germany was the brutal treatment of the Jewish people. [44]

Quite possibly, then, American policy makers used economic weapons to punish (if they could) German offenses against humanity. American diplomats insisted that there were certain standards necessary to the conduct of international relations: Hitler's Germany violated all these—economic, political, moral—although, given the less moralistic attitude of the 1960's towards planned economies of all kinds, it is doubtful that today German autarchy would still be considered so evil in itself.

However that may be, on May 8, 1933, the German government announced that it had suspended interest payments on its private indebtedness to the American bankers who had helped float the Dawes and Young plans. Then the German government and its citizens took advantage of the market price decline of the bonds to buy them back at much lower cost. During June "orders to this effect from Germany through the National City Bank [were] greater than at any previous time." By the end of 1933 Germany was offering to pay 50 per cent of the interest indebtedness in cash and the other 50 per cent in scrip. This scrip could then be returned to a German Central bank for one-half its face value in Reichsmarks. German exporters purchased the depreciated bonds and resold them to their government at par, providing themselves thereby with a neat bounty that subsidized still more exports! "In devilish fashion," charged Cordell Hull, "the Germans tied in nonpayment of bond interest, depreciation of bond prices, redemption of bonds at these low prices, and subsidization of exports." [45]

At the London Economic Conference, Hull had a chance to see other German manipulations. Here Berlin's representatives tried to use the debt situation to angle for better trade terms with Britain and France, which would have adversely affected the United States, Hull reported to Washington. The Secretary glimpsed also other plans being laid between Germany and England, which E. H. Carr later identified more clearly as proposals for joint exploitation of the Russian market. It will be remembered that William Bullitt was also highly concerned at these doings and recommended diplomatic recognition of the Soviet Union for this and other related reasons.[46]

All through these months, irritation at German policies was spreading and deepening into conflict. In January, 1934, Schacht added another turn of the screw by announcing special favors to Swiss and Dutch creditors whose nations purchased more goods from Germany than they sold there. Consul Messersmith supplied Washington with a report by his commercial attaché, Douglas Miller, which tied these new strands onto what the United States saw was the main rope of Germany policy. The favors to Swiss and Dutch creditors would be an immediate aid to bringing pressure on Germany's other creditors, wrote Miller, but they also pointed to a German political and economic bloc in Europe: "This block is to be so constituted that it can defy wartime blockades and be large enough to give the peoples in it the benefits of free trade now enjoyed by the 48 American States." [47]

From this report and others like it, American leaders saw a rope being woven around them to force United States creditors to accept the expansion and strengthening of German autarchy—and rearmament.

Schacht then came to the United States asking for a credit to purchase many millions of dollars worth of cotton for resale in Europe, offering to use the profits to pay American creditors and stimulate American trade in Germany. President Roosevelt, suddenly becoming disturbed by these maneuvers, added his own comments to a protest, which made it "a disguised threat of retaliation." Hull was uncertain for a moment what to do about the proposed credit, recognizing that Germany did have economic difficulties to contend with, yet nearly convinced also that "Germany [was] deliberately trying to get the American creditor to finance her rearmament . . . ." [48]

George Peek wanted to trade with Germany, and he had no qualms about bilateral arrangements. He brought the export manager of General Motors to the State Department to convince Hull's advisers that there was broad support for dealing with Germany on such terms. Moreover, he claimed that President Roosevelt agreed with him. Assistant Secretary of State Sayre, taking up the challenge, answered that although Germany could afford to pay cash for airplanes, it refused to pay cash to its creditors. New credits would not change that situation; they would only be used for more munitions. Furthermore, public opinion was against Germany. And lastly, given current German commercial policy, it was difficult to see how any agreement could be made that would be advantageous to the United States. [49]

Department officers felt also that they had to justify their position to the President. They offered the above arguments as well as those of Consul Messersmith, whose reports carried great weight in the Department; he had sent in another long report which asserted that Hitler's regime was tottering. It would be indeed foolish to do anything to prop up a government which was "discriminating against American imports and American interests in Germany . . . . The only hope for Europe, and for us all, is that this regime does fall so that it may be replaced by a Government with which we can deal in the ordinary way . . . . As I see it, we have nothing to lose and everything to gain by a policy of waiting." [50]

Strongly anti-Nazi, even to the point of insulting the Berlin government upon occasion, William E. Dodd, the American Ambassador to Germany, was not sure this was the way to meet the "almost desperate" attempts by Schacht to "negotiate commercial reforms with us." When the State Department kept turning down all German overtures, Dodd appealed to Hull that "one cannot banish facts from one's mind no matter how patriotic one may be." And the German Foreign Office was intensifying its plea, instructing its ambassador to say that the German people would go in rags if necessary rather than be forced to accept an unbalanced trade situation. This met what had become the standard response in Washington to these German presentations: The United States could not accept a bilateral trade balance with Germany and yet champion a multilateral trade program with all other nations.[51]

American bondholders protested that Ambassador Dodd was not representing their interests forcefully enough. Reports also came in that Dodd was sympathetic with one of Schacht's schemes for settling Germany's indebtedness. On July 12, 1934, the Western European Division of the Department spent hours preparing a new instruction for the Embassy in Berlin. It was not the narrow interests of the bondholders that needed re-emphasizing, reasoned the Department officers, but Washington's determination to oppose "further discriminations that Germany might wish to make in favor of other countries." In writing this instruction, the drafters worked from the assumption that Berlin really intended to "blackmail us through one means or another into negotiating a trade agreement . . . on terms satisfactory to her, that is, that we should undertake to buy more German goods . . . . The drop in American exports to Germany from 15 million dollars to six million was in large measure due to deliberate activity against us on the part of the German Government." [52]

Still hanging on to the edge of American economic foreign policy George Peek tried to gain a stronger position by constantly sending business executives to the Department to question its handling of German questions. Not all came at Peek's prompting, and some bankers even "advocated our making an arrangement with Germany whereby we would take more of her goods in return for her paying the American holders of the Dawes-Young loans." [53]

These arguments could not be ignored, so the Department appointed its own "Special State Department Committee on Proposed American Policy with Respect to Germany." After studying the problem, the Committee came back with a full report on October 12, 1934. Its conclusions surprised no one: It would be unwise to negotiate a bilateral trade agreement with Germany. Taking its cue from the Messersmith reports, the special committee asserted that the "whole complexion of affairs may be quite different in a year or two. It is not likely that the current German commercial policy can last for any considerable period of time." [54]

The next day the German ambassador announced that his government was terminating the 1924 most-favored-nation treaty it had signed with the United States. The way was now open, he told newsmen in the halls of the State Department, for a "special trade agreement." In Germany, Ambassador Dodd was told that the United States would have to make some kind of arrangement like this or lose its market for raw materials there. Dodd, in no mood for such threats, replied sharply that even were there no other obstacles, Nazi acts against the Jews and German bellicosity would not permit the Department to negotiate in defiance of public opinion.[55]

Peek now tried a new approach. He quietly lined up President Roosevelt's support for a large barter exchange with Germany. He had already completed the preliminary negotiations before Hull came to the rescue of his trade program. At a special Cabinet meeting to discuss the matter, the Secretary admonished Administration leaders and the President that it would kill the reciprocal trade agreements idea—especially since the United States was pressuring Brazil into abandoning a similar agreement with Germany. Other nations simply would not follow the American lead if such hypocrisy characterized American dealings.[56]

Critical discussions with France and Italy were then under way, he continued. In each of these, Francis Sayre was avowing that "we rejected the bilateral theory of trade in favor of a triangular or polyangular trade." "I kept illustrating to the President," Hull wrote later, "the soundness of our plan, particularly the vital necessity of equality of treatment." Roosevelt withdrew his support for the Peek proposals.[57]

Completely rebuffed, the German ambassador came forward to ask the State Department what his country could do to meet American objections. Sayre replied that "the changes were so fundamental that . . . the next step would be for Germany to see if she could find a way of reconciling our commercial philosophy, but that he did not mean trying to find a halfway compromise." "He really meant a fundamental acceptance by Germany of our trade philosophy," recorded Moffat, "and a thorough-going partnership with us along the road of equality of treatment and the reduction of trade barriers." Did Germany have to adopt the most-favored-nation policy towards all nations or just the United States, asked the Ambassador. The United States had no wish to dictate to any country, answered Sayre, obliquely, but it was interested in the "effects of Germany policy upon American trade." The ambassador then replied that the two nations had to look at the situation between them realistically and not simply in terms of principle. Since World War I, he argued, Germany had purchased eight billion dollars more from the United States than it had sold here.[58]

During 1935 the Department continued to press Germany to change the fundamental characteristics of its trade policy; and the Germans just as persistently continued their efforts to force a change in American policy. Hull's patience wore thin at times. In October he threw up to the German ambassador American loans to the Weimar Republic and German lack of gratitude for such friendly acts since World War I. Besides the loans, the United States had allowed Germany to act as a "broker to buy vast quantities of raw materials which it redistributed in some form to Central and Western Europe at fine profits . . . ." [59]

Another time he reminded the German diplomat of America's crucial decision to forsake the chance to sell 800,000 bales of cotton to Berlin rather than jeopardize the trade agreements program. It would have been paying blackmail—and like "taking opium." [60]

Just at the moment when Hull thought he might be making some progress with German leaders, the Treasury imposed countervailing duties on German exports. Looking for a way to oppose Hitler, Morgenthau had hit upon a section of the Tariff Act of 1930 which called for retaliation against nations that subsidized exports. Hull objected. Morgenthau then took his case to the White House, but promised to present State Department rebuttals along with his own arguments. "If it is a borderline case," Roosevelt decided, "I feel so keenly about Germany that I would enforce the countervailing duties." [61]

Germany abandoned the offending practices, and the special duties were lifted. Yet these were only symptoms of a general malaise in German-American relations, which was growing steadily worse. On January 27, 1937, for example, Ambassador Dodd received a message from Secretary Hull describing the agitations fostered by unofficial German agents in order to disrupt the Buenos Aires Conference and to injure his commercial treaties with Latin American countries. On the same day, George Messersmith wrote Oswald Garrison Villard: "If the democracies maintain a firm attitude and are sufficiently generous, but wise and reserved, when the time comes a properly directed German Government should be established." [62]

Basing foreign policy upon the downfall of an opponent was highly speculative business. Roosevelt's Quarantine Speech that fall opened the way to many other speculations. Exactly what he intended by it remains uncertain even today. At the very least, said political columnist Dorothy Thompson, the speech was a recognition that "our chance of working out a solution for our internal problems [is] threatened by the convulsions which shake the rest of the world; and that a world war, or the continued spread of the present sort of international anarchy, will, whether we are drawn into it in a strictly military sense or not, disrupt our economy, and, in all probability bring down the whole social arch as it is now constituted." [63]

Miss Thompson's interpretation was fine, but the final interpretation of the Quarantine Speech was for Roosevelt to make. And he seemed unsure—both in Asia and in Europe—about what exactly the United States would do. Sumner Welles suggested holding an international conference in the White House on Armistice Day, 1937. If Berlin failed to send a representative, then those nations which did attend would be ready to accept the fact that the world had split apart into two systems. Both Roosevelt and Welles felt that they had to find out if it were at all possible to reach "a practical understanding with Germany both on colonies and security, as well as upon European adjustments." Welles hoped that the assembled representatives would then go ahead and define the rules of peace and, in the unhappy event of war, the rights and obligations of neutrals on land and sea.[64]

Engaged in an attempt to woo Mussolini from Hitler's arms, the British were cool. Secretary Hull called Welles's idea appeasment; he believed it would be represented as a "corrupt bargain" or a foolish "peace congress" called into being at a time when the democracies should be arming to meet the war threat from Germany.[65]

The conference was never held, although other proposals received a somewhat warmer reception in England during the next few months. Roosevelt became fatalistic: on December 8, 1937, he advised his new Ambassador to the Soviet Union that it was "perfectly clear that there was no possibility of doing anything to divert the forces in Germany which, under Hitler's concept of world domination and conquest, were driving inevitably to war." Probably there were times after this moment when Roosevelt's hopes rose that a conflict could be avoided, but just when the Administration finally decided there was no hope is really less important than understanding the German-American clash from 1933 to 1937 and its bearing upon the rapid sequence of events after those years.[66]

THE RAPPROCHEMENT WITH ENGLAND AND FRANCE

From a low at the time of the London Economic Conference and the Geneva Disarmament Conference, Anglo-French-American relations came up, like one end of a see-saw as German-American affairs went down. The situation might be temporary, since there was still no firm political alliance. Economic understanding between Great Britain and the United States, however, was strengthened by a 1938 trade agreement. Secretary Hull came to believe that if the English Treaty had been one of the first he negotiated instead of one of the last before the war, the catastrophe could have been avoided. Anyhow, he argued, "The political line-up followed the economic line-up." Besides being an example of Hull's near self-hypnosis resulting from concentration on foreign trade, this comment has merit as another indication that the conflict with Germany could not be divided into economic, political, and military fragments.[67]

It is also significant that the United States managed to dent the Ottawa Preference System as a direct result of the agreement. British willingness to make certain concessions was an indication that appeasement had failed and that London needed United States support to withstand Germany.

After practice had shown the first trade agreements to be sound, Secretary Hull turned to England and the Ottawa System. The progressive closing of the Empire "like an oyster shell," he told the British ambassador reprovingly on January 18, 1937, could not be happening at a worse time. Congress was considering legislation on wartime embargoes on goods and credits, the Reciprocal Trade Agreements Act was up for renewal, and favorable decisions on those matters were highly important to both nations.[68]

Assistant Secretary Sayre tried to make the president of the British Board of Trade see that there were two trade philosophies competing for the world, and that since the globe could not tolerate much longer the existence of both, Great Britain must stand with the United States. From London, Norman Davis, now a delegate to an international sugar conference, wrote Secretary Hull that he had been telling Foreign Minister Anthony Eden that so long as the world's nations continued to strangle trade, they would be committing international suicide. And he wrote to Prime Minister Neville Chamberlain that the President and he both viewed a trade agreement as a very important first step to "facilitate a solution of other questions which are of mutual interest and general benefit." [69]

These arguments did have their proper effect even before Munich. In the summer of 1937 the American Ambassador in London reported that he sensed a trend towards "attempting to retrieve some of their mistakes in dealing with us and attempting to bring about a fuller measure of co-operation . . . . " [70]

Chamberlain's cabinet officers never really thought there would be much economic gain in a trade agreement with the United States. As late as October, 1938, the Foreign Office maintained it could only reduce Britain's already "miserable" trade conditions. But Prime Minister Chamberlain had written Roosevelt a year before: "The conclusion of an Anglo-American commercial agreement when we have found ways of overcoming its obvious difficulties will undoubtedly be an important step in the right direction [in obtaining a] community of sentiment between our two countries as to the events in the Far East and the development in the European situation." [71]

Washington was determined not to join that community of sentiment without a genuine economic understanding and real advantages for the United States in British markets. "When war was threatening and Germany was pounding at our gates," Francis Sayre dramatically stated to the British in September, 1938, "it seemed to me tragic that we had not been able to reach and sign an agreement." But after many compromises a trade agreement was consumated in late 1938. [72]

This was the beginning of the United States's long ascendency to the leadership of the Grand Alliance after Pearl Harbor, and the way was marked by its growing assertiveness in other questions. In the fall of 1938, while the trade negotiations were going on, the British began varying the pound-dollar rate of exchange near the limitations set by the 1936 Tripartite Pact. Morgenthau had earlier established cooperation among the three as an antifascist measure, but Treasury officials now warned him: "[If] sterling drops substantially below $4.80, our foreign and domestic business will be adversely affected." [73] If sterling thus declined, so would other currencies, all upsetting American business prospects. To prevent this, Treasury aides suggested that a clause might be included in the pending trade agreement terminating its existence if Great Britain devalued the pound below $4.80. Harry Dexter White pointed out that England would have to accept these terms, since she "needs our good will much more than we need hers at the present time." The clause was so written and inserted in the formal agreement. [74]

White's comment, as will be seen, was a statement of the general understanding American policy makers were coming to as the war approached. For a few years the New Deal avoided political commitments in Europe. Most admitted readily that the policy was inadequate, yet no real alternative appeared possible either to the Administration or to the nation. The isolationist-interventionist split grew much sharper after 1937 as the nation completed its difficult transformation to a military outlook on the world. Isolationist criticisms of the Government's handling of foreign policy were sometimes cogent and penetrating, especially since the Administration had such difficulty in setting forth its objectives or in accepting the truth that economic advantages had political costs, but many isolationists then contradicted their own logic by desiring objectives once again obtainable only through world political leadership.

From 1938 to 1941, the Rome-Berlin-Tokyo Axis shaped American foreign policies more than in the previous four years. In Latin America the Axis threat supplied a reason for modifying the Good Neighbor Policy towards an economic alliance; in Asia, Japan's membership in the Tripartite Pact brought matters to a head. But Washington did not abandon past economic policies in the midst of a military threat, and it began thinking a good deal about the kind of world it wanted after the war.

I also hope that the policy of your Government will
be . . . a just attitude toward the American countries
which have felt themselves crushed under that same
pressure, almost always inspired by the improper aim
of impeding a solid economic constitution of the countries, even though it is obvious that the raising of the
standards of living of any people represents a greater
demand in favor of the industrialized countries . . . .

Lázaro Cárdenas to Franklin Roosevelt,
November 27, 1940

Suppose that Germany wins the war in the next two
months and does on the economic fronts what they
have done on the military fronts. What will they do
in South America presuming they win, and then, what
are we going to do about it?

Harry Hopkins, Press Conference, May, 1940

6 · Giving Latin America a Share

"That is a new approach that I am talking about to these South American things," President Roosevelt summed up his remarks to business
paper editors in 1940. "Give them a share. They think they are just as
good as we are and many of them are." Like many other American
leaders, especially political conservatives, these editors had come to
the President with their concern that the Good Neighbor Policy had
turned into an "out" for Latin American extremists, who were using
it to escape having to pay for confiscated foreign-owned properties.[1]

As Roosevelt had then informed them, he had a new approach to
this problem. Washington had been watching Latin American nationalism and Axis penetration coming closer together until, like two electri-
fied poles, a spark suddenly flashed between them. Its intensity startled
the observers, who realized that the Good Neighbor experiment would
have to be modified. Hence the President's remarks to the editors had
begun significantly with a reference to foreign-owned utilities in Brazil
and the dangerous frictions they produced.

The greatest shock came from the March, 1938, Mexican oil expropriation decree. At first the State Department refused to accept its
validity and tried to reverse it, but when Mexico turned to German and
Japanese buyers to sell its oil, it was admitted that the poles could not

109

be driven apart by force—only by shutting off the current could they be separated. Another oil crisis, agreed State Department officers, somewhere else in Latin America would jeopardize all United States interests; therefore they must "be prepared to give more positive advice as to the best method of handling problems as they arise." [2]

This shift to a more "positive" policy in Latin America was gradual and not without difficulties. Of course, in many instances nothing had to be changed. Having created the Guardia Nacional in Nicaragua, for example, it seemed wise at the end of the decade to grant Nicaragua's dictator money from the President's Emergency Fund to complete the Rama Road between the eastern and western sections of his country, for, as the Public Roads Administration affirmed, this highway would "have considerable value" for purposes of internal policy. [3]

Sometimes temporary expedients sufficed. Carleton Beals reported that a newly elected Colombian president who had shown unfriendly signs towards American property owners received an invitation to meet with Government officials and private businessmen on the Starlight Roof of the Waldorf-Astoria. Upon his return to Bogota, American airplanes saluted his inaugural and soon an FBI police mission appeared, to help him train a secret service organization. All in all, commented Beals, a new dawn of American interest had broken over Colombia. Another time a Latin American leader threatened to expropriate the United Fruit Company's lands in his country, but when he was informed that the trees would not be sprayed to protect them from destruction if he took such action, the official backed off from his threat. Military intervention was in the past, but other pressures, both official and private, still were in evidence. The problem yet unsolved was how to avoid force and how to give Latin America a share of the economic pie. [4]

At the 1938 Lima Foreign Ministers Conference, Hull had reasserted Washington's commitment to the Montevideo Program. "It was recognized," he reported, "that this liberal trade policy was the only one proper to a peaceful trading world, rather than one of competing and force-using alliances." But the Secretary of State could not add after the meeting that he had brought back an agreement on all out collective action to resist foreign intervention in the hemisphere. Latin Americans did not yet completely trust the United States; and besides, many of these nations enjoyed important advantages through trade connections with Axis countries. Despite Hull's contention that all Latin Americans

viewed his liberal trade policies as the only proper and profitable approach, another close observer of those countries said that they had
"greatly benefited by barter." That kind of trade did not hamstring
them with new debts, "and it is precisely a semi-colonial country that
cannot possibly do without trade restrictions." Beals's remark singled out
the changing temper of some Latin American economic thinkers, who
by 1945, at the Mexico City Conference, were ready to challenge
United States desires for low tariffs in Latin America.[5]

Privately, Secretary Hull was more pessimistic about American successes at Lima, telling Ambassador Josephus Daniels that the United
States had not curtailed German advances in the Western Hemisphere.
Clearly this *was* the case in Mexico, thought Daniels, but then he had
warned Secretary Hull against too firm a policy on the oil expropriations—and his advice had gone unheeded.[6]

Other Americans shared this concern about inter-American relations: The editor of the *Chicago Daily News* and soon to be Secretary
of the Navy, Frank Knox, wrote President Roosevelt: "Care must be
taken . . . to put the emphasis on participation by American firms
in South American enterprise as partners with South American interests
in the business rather than giving it the appearance of exploitation by
our people." Latin America remained the least developed area in the
world and should be a "promising new frontier for young Americans
who possess the pioneer spirit." Similarly, one of the business paper
publishers and editors Roosevelt had talked with explained that "in
the United States banks literally groan with idle surplus capital . . ."
but "this generation and the next have an opportunity for pioneering
far beyond that which existed a century ago. Then the Pacific
shores bounded our vision; today a hemisphere awaits our development . . . ."[7]

These statements were full of the rhetoric of an earlier vision of the
American on the frontier: Natty Bumppo and his Indian ally who
struggled with the elements, bad Indians, and Frenchmen. Only now
the opponents were "nationalist extremists" and Germans.

The American Pathfinders of the late 1930's had their allies in the
State Department. The International Telephone and Telegraph's Frank
Page was informed that the Department felt that his company's holdings
should be expanded, for IT&T supplied a "needed part of our export
trade and it was necessary to assure the predominance of American
interests in the communication field as against any European interest."

This example was typical of the political-economic link-up in the Good Neighbor Policy as World War II came closer.[8]

From 1938 to 1941 the United States was developing a way to give Latin America a meaningful share. This included aid for the establishment of basic industries, programs to absorb agricultural surpluses, and the "delousing" of South America to rid it of Axis pests. These alterations began as responses to Bolivian and Mexican expropriations, and were sustained, as a student of the Good Neighbor Policy put it, by "loans, grants, and technical assistance to Latin American governments . . . and from the beginning they had a political tinge. The exploration of the possibilities and limitations of the techinque became a continuous process when its potentialities were realized." [9]

Its potentialities were first realized in a negative sense when Bolivia nationalized Standard Oil Company properties. Washington refused to grant La Paz loans or technical assistance until that capital came to terms with the company. Pressure was put upon Paraguay and Argentina to discourage those countries from abetting the Bolivian action. On the other hand, there were pressures cramping the State Department also: German and Japanese representatives were watching just such frictions in inter-American affairs, hoping they would wear through openings for their interests. Secondly, this dispute hindered other Americans from gaining a share in the development of Bolivian resources. Hence when La Paz offered one million dollars, even though the companies claimed their holdings were worth seventeen million, the Department persuaded the companies to accept it. But it was in the Mexican oil dispute that the technique was first seriously tested.[10]

THE GOOD NEIGHBOR NEARLY DROWNS IN
MEXICAN OIL

Initially, the Mexican nationalization decree on March 18, 1938, left Secretary Hull puzzled as to how he could help restore the oil fields to the American companies when they had signed a pledge with the Mexican government promising not to invoke Washington's aid in just such disputes. But there was much more at stake, Hull soon realized, than the 600 million dollars the oil men demanded for the properties. The fundamental question, as the companies realized too, was what would happen to their ability to produce oil so much more cheaply not only in Mexico but all over Latin America? In 1932 it cost $1.90 to produce a barrel of oil in the United States; $1.41 in Mexico; $1.60 in Colombia, Ecuador, and Peru; and $.87 in Venezuela.[11]

"Should the government of Venezuela," Hull was warned, "follow the government of Mexico and expropriate the foreign owned oil properties . . . without adequate payment therefor, the proper interpretation of the Monroe Doctrine will become the gravest problem the State Department will have to face." [12]

The expropriations in Mexico were a threat to all other oil holdings in Latin America; moreover, in Mexico itself the expropriations were part of a larger revolution that began in 1911 and was reaching a climax in the 1930's. There was a possibility that all American interests in Mexico were in danger. Anticlericalism and attacks upon foreign landholdings, like the giant estate of American newspaper magnate William Randolph Hearst, highlighted Mexico's violent campaign against feudalism but other American investors and small landholders came under attack also. Washington had been trying to find some way to protect American landholders when the real storm thundered and broke over the oil fields. Ambassador Daniels doubted that a rigid approach could withstand these gusts and blasts and therefore urged his superiors to bend with them. James Harvey Rogers, returning from his currency study of Latin America, also advised Roosevelt that accommodation would be the safest course. President Lázaro Cárdenas was a Socialist, said Rogers, but the oil companies could drive "a fair bargain" if either "directly or indirectly through their bankers, they are willing to put up only a few million dollars." [13]

When Roosevelt looked over some diplomatic notes the State Department wanted to send to Mexico City about the agrarian expropriations, he, too, thought the Secretary's strenuous defense of property rights out of place in the middle of the twentieth century. Yet Hull finally convinced the President that any weaker approach would leave American nationals "to the mercy of debtor countries contrary to reason, the holdings of all international agencies and tribunals and the principles of long-established international law." [14]

But shortly after Hull thus triumphed in upholding Anglo-Saxon property principles, he was brought up short by the oil crisis. The dispute had begun in 1935, and in the following year Mexican labor unions advanced a series of demands which the companies claimed were preposterous. The latter also believed that Cárdenas was merely using the dispute as a reason for eventually taking over the oil fields. In the fall of 1937 the Mexican Labor Board had ordered the owners to pay substantial increases in the 3⅓ pesos per day that 13,000 of the 18,000 oil workers were then receiving. The total cost of such an increase might have reached 26,000,000 pesos annually. The wage increase would destroy them, cried the companies, and they threatened to close down the oil fields.[15]

This was the strongest card in their hand unless they could draw more from the State Department. And a calm and confident oil man told Daniels that the companies could not fail to win, since the Mexicans, even if they took over the fields, had too few tankers or tank cars to move the crude. A few days after this conversation, Secretary Hull did take up a stake in the game, sending Daniels a note expressing his doubts about the validity of the wage earners' demands. If the Administration of President Cárdenas supported them, then the issue ceased to be only Mexican internal affairs: "It is not always easy to draw a sharp line between matters purely of an internal and domestic character and those of an international character." The Good Neighbor Policy was a two-way street, he concluded, with a frown showing through every word. The State Department expressed its displeasure at the trend in Mexican-American affairs more demonstrably and asked the Treasury Department to delay completing a new special silver purchase arrangement with Mexico until these other questions were cleared up. Morgenthau, who was afraid already of German penetration in Mexico, refused.[16]

On March 9, 1938, the companies made a final offer to pay something over 22 million pesos, but their original defiance and arrogant manner had so goaded the Mexicans that the government demanded nothing short of full control of the fields. Or it may have been that the companies were right and Cárdenas had all along intended to take the fields. Since the time of the first concession-hunters, when corrupt presidents had sold their country's resources for clandestine bribes, the owners had been able to persuade, manipulate, cajole, or plain frighten Mexican officials; but now Cárdenas shouted, No more! On March 18 he nationalized the fields.[17]

The companies were reeling from this blow when they suffered an even greater one. The Mexican people rallied to Cárdenas and turned Expropriation Day into a national holiday. Recovering at length, the companies cried with one voice, Spoliation must be resisted. The New

York *Journal of Commerce* wailed that Latin American trade would be ruined if "other countries follow in the footsteps of Mexico"; and a former Ambassador to Germany, James Gerard, even wrote to give Roosevelt his estimate of the dollar value and the volume of trade that would be lost unless the oil wells were restored.[18]

"We thought they were awfully foolish," recalled one New Deal State Department officer. Another said that the Mexicans simply were incapable of running the fields. Hull and Welles were downright angry. Summoning the Mexican ambassador to his office, the Undersecretary peppered him with objections. The United States had just gone out of its way to help stabilize Mexican finances through the silver purchase agreement, he began. Mexico could not pay cash for the properties, so the act bordered on confiscation. Nor could Mexico possibly run the fields at a profit. "Furthermore . . . as the ambassador knew, in view of the way in which oil was sold in the world market and of the control by the companies of the oil tankers," it was out of the question for Mexico to sell the oil "except at ruinous prices. As a result, Mexico would have to dump it into the hands of Japan, Germany, and Italy." Unhappily for the Administration, Welles's prophecy proved to be only too accurate.[19]

From the beginning the Department tried to create a favorable climate for a pro-company settlement as best it could, without acting directly as the oil companies' international lawyer or policeman. As the crisis lengthened and deepened, into it sank the Good Neighbor Policy until it was nearly drowning in the oil, and it took Roosevelt himself to pull his Latin American policy out to safety.

All along, the President was urged by his former chief in the Navy Department, Ambassador Josephus Daniels, not to smear the Good Neighbor policy with oil. It could never be worth it "in a mad world where Pan American solidarity may save democracy." In the State Department, however, Daniels suffered the reputation of being more Mexican than the Mexicans, and his admonishments went unheeded. How ironic this, for Josephus Daniels was the very man who in support of Woodrow Wilson's moral imperialism had ordered American ships to shell Vera Cruz. His transition into the most responsible and mature of Washington's Good Neighbor diplomats stood in obvious contrast to the inability of several Department liberals to come up with anything more than the barest advance on past policies.[20]

Only a week after the nationalization—March 25, 1938—several

State Department officers and Senator Key Pittman went to see Secretary of the Treasury Morgenthau. They wanted to "re-examine certain . . . financial and commercial relationships with Mexico." They especially wanted to go over the special silver purchase agreement with Mexico under which the Treasury bought stated amounts of the metal each month at prices above those in the world market. A Department policy memorandum on this subject was already circulating describing the probable psychological results of cutting off American silver purchases. In addition, directly cutting off Mexican silver and buying the metal only at the world price could cause a decline in Mexican government revenue, a lowering of Mexican purchasing power, and a fall in the dollar value of the peso. The memorandum closed with a warning against undertaking such a step unless "friendly countries" were protected from suffering losses on silver.[21]

At the meeting with Morgenthau, Senator Pittman spoke out firmly: A decision to end the silver purchase agreement with Mexico was "in the interest of our foreign policy." Most of the others thought so too, with only Morgenthau unconvinced. Consequently, two days later the Treasury announced its suspension of the monthly silver purchase arrangement. At once the world price fell from 20½ cents per ounce to 18½ cents per ounce. The United States soon resumed open market purchases of Mexican silver, in large part because this was not a very good lever to use against Mexico City, as the mines were often owned by Americans also, and because Secretary Morgenthau had never agreed with the idea. But the special high price Mexico had enjoyed was not restored.[22]

Laurence Duggan said that the Department had acted principally to forestall even more stringent Congressional action against Mexico, but this hardly explains Hull's and Welles's later efforts to use the silver price as a diplomatic Big Stick, nor does it explain other Department-initiated pressures. Combined with a business-organized and State-Department-supported boycott of Mexican oil (and even other goods), the decision soon resulted in a 28 per cent fall in the peso's value. To withdraw the silver market so suddenly, Daniels said, was "like taking anesthetics from a patient too soon . . . ." Throughout 1938 and 1939 the United States officially blocked Mexican oil sales to the navy, encouraged other Latin American and European nations to boycott it also, and cast benevolent rewards to Venezuela in the form of large oil quotas.[23]

President Roosevelt never fully subscribed to the companies' position or to that of the State Department. He thought the companies very unrealistic in expecting compensation not only for current value plus depreciation but also for oil still under the ground. "These companies ought not to have prospective profits given to them," he told newsmen on April 1, 1938. "If I have a piece of land at Warm Springs that is worth $5,000, and the Government, or the State of Georgia wants to take it over, I ought to get $5,000 out of it. I ought not to be able to say, 'In a few years this is going to be worth $20,000, so you have got to pay me $20,000.' " [24]

But the President did not as yet interfere with Hull's firm approach, exemplified by the boycotts and Hull's remarks to the Mexican ambassador that nations which confiscated foreign property became decadent and sank steadily backward and downward. The Secretary of State assured the oil companies that his Department would uphold the principles of an orderly society, but he had to confess that there seemed little chance of recovering the properties short of military intervention. [25]

While these and other discussions were going on, State Department aides were preparing a note to Mexico City that was little shy of being an outright demand for payment. Daniels shortstopped it, and in the ensuing confusion Cárdenas denied having received a note from Washington. Angered by this lack of cooperation, the Secretary of State sent another strong note on agrarian expropriations—but he did not force Ambassador Daniels to deliver the original note or one like it. This second thought helped save the Good Neighbor Policy, but Hull turned to the Treasury Department almost at the same instant and urged Morgenthau to drop the price of silver still another cent, so that he could deal with the "Communists" down in Mexico. [26]

Morgenthau refused: on his desk were memos describing the inherent dangers of this State Department policy. Always carrying great weight with him was the information, shared by Daniels and his superiors as well, that German and Japanese interests were making steady gains in Mexico and Latin America. One he no doubt had seen began: "Our international trade is being forced into ever-narrowing channels. More and more areas of trade are being dominated by clearing agreements, barter practices, blocked balances, multiple currencies, and others which run counter to the trade policy the United States has been pursuing." [27]

"Yes, but . . ." was Hull's theoretical answer. "What if Mexican nationalism spilled over into Venezuela?" Either alternative—Axis penetration or Latin American nationalism—threatened the Montevideo Trade Program. Hence the State Department was not yet ready to accept Morgenthau's counterproposal to put money into Mexico to help that country through the oil crisis rather than continuing to take it out by lowering the price of silver. No settlement, said one Department policy maker, which left Mexico in control of the fields could be tolerated, for it would set a bad precedent.[28]

Morgenthau recorded in his diary that the President approved his approach, but once again the White House did not interfere with State Department handling of Mexican proposals on the oil question and related issues. In June, 1938, Cárdenas suggested that the Mexican government put aside 120,000 pesos monthly to pay for some of the smaller agrarian claims. Welles replied that a better idea would be for Mexico to put in escrow $337,646.27 each month to pay for all properties expropriated since 1927. This was doubly offensive to Mexico City, for it not only made an impossible financial condition the *sine qua non* for a Mexican-American settlement but contained an impossible psychological condition. The Cárdenas administration could never agree to give the giant landholders with their feudalistic estates an equal chance at compensation without destroying the spirit of the revolution. President Roosevelt had recognized this and had commented that the small landholders should receive first consideration.[29]

The Department's ideas on an oil settlement were equally objectionable to the Mexican government. Washington decided it wanted the question settled by arbitration, but the Mexican president considered this a challenge to Mexican sovereignty. Moreover, the Department insisted that any amount found owing to the companies by a negotiating committee should be paid in three years. In answer, Cárdenas advised Daniels that Mexico could pay no more than one million dollars a year without giving up the revolution, and Mexico would be "scraping the bottom of the barrel" to do that.[30]

"It looks like the oil companies are dominating to such an extent," Daniels wrote in his diary, "that the manufacturers will sell to everybody in the world except Mexico." The Ambassador had written gravely after hearing from other Mexican officials that American manufacturers had returned orders and money from the Mexican nationalized oil company.[31]

With private pressures mounting and with the State Department and Mexico at odds over even the means for reaching a settlement, Daniels returned to Washington in January, 1939, for a series of conferences on the oil question. Roosevelt's attitude pleased the Ambassador. The President insisted that the companies would have to take the initiative in negotiations "and he would take no part in them until all others had done everything." But he found Cordell Hull in a dark mood, staring out the window of his office as they talked, and bitter at Mexican ungratefulness. Disturbed, Daniels wrote in a special diary: "He had no sympathy with them and wishes to be as hard as nails to them, but says no force can be employed. In heart he would like to use a Big Stick, but hopes strong language, very strong (almost threats) will enable him to dictate to them." [32]

This impasse continued for two years. The State Department remained firm in its approach, but it got no closer to any kind of solution to the specific problem. Elsewhere in Latin America, however, the Administration was moving to correct deficiencies in the Good Neighbor Policy and to prevent a repetition of the Mexican situation.

Part of the difficulty in the latter was that Expropriation Day had become at once symbolic and prophetic in both Washington and Mexico City. Boxed in by this assumption and fear, the State Department was inflexible. It backed a company-sponsored plan for a management contract with the Mexican government, for example, which was no compromise at all and which would have given the former owners practical control of the fields for forty or fifty years. At the end of that time Mexico would have received full title to a string of holes in the ground. The Mexican president said he was willing for the companies to have a voice in the management of the fields, but he wanted to pay for the expropriations out of Mexico's receipts from oil exports. Cárdenas's plan was equally unacceptable to the oil companies, for they saw it would require them to drink up their life's blood in oil in order to quench their thirst for compensation. [33]

In 1940 Sinclair Oil settled with the Mexican government, but Hull was not ready to encourage the other companies to make a settlement on a similar basis, and he made public a note in which he criticized the Mexican government for not accepting his arbitration proposal. The Mexican foreign minister replied, also publicly, that there was "no rule in international law universally accepted in theory or practice" to uphold the American Secretary of State. He added that boycotts, tariffs, and quotas had made it impossible for Mexico to obtain sufficient funds to pay for the properties.[34]

Exactly as Welles had predicted, Cárdenas turned to Germany and Japan for markets. He was aided by a maverick American shipper, William Rhodes Davis, who ignored Washington's finger-wagging and in the best entrepreneurial tradition provided Mexico with the means to sell its oil. Bryce Wood in *The Making of the Good Neighbor Policy,* comments significantly that Mexico's economic health would have been much worse in the years 1938–40 if Davis had not seen and taken advantage of this opportunity.[35]

One of the company negotiators, Standard Oil's T. R. Armstrong, pretty well pinpointed State Department assumptions and, perhaps unconsciously, the difficulties these assumptions created in the face of German and Japanese competition, especially since W. R. Davis was helping Mexico out of a bind. Speaking to the National Foreign Trade Convention of 1938, Armstrong informed the assembled businessmen that the goods they sold to Mexico were being driven out by barter agreements the Mexicans were making with Germany and Japan and Italy. This was a result of the oil expropriations, he contended, since Mexico now had no other market for its oil. "Bilateralism thus gradually shuts out certain lines of American trade." If these trends continued, the Hull reciprocal trade program could not be extended to any nation which expropriated property.[36]

There were probably many in Armstrong's audience who thought to themselves either then or later, if indeed they did not discuss it openly, that perhaps the oil companies had better re-examine their position, for it was becoming more difficult to convince those who had lost Mexican markets that the integrity of the oil properties was more important than the expansion of Mexican-American trade. Daniels came away from meetings with the American Chamber of Commerce in Mexico thoroughly upset at the evidence of a "practical boycott against Mexico." German agents had indeed moved swiftly to take over American markets, lamented Chamber of Commerce members, and these intruders charged lower prices for typewriters and electrical appliances. And there would be other losses, for, as Daniels learned, German agents had taken up Cárdenas' offer to buy as much oil as Mexico could supply.[37]

Daniels soon drew a particularly significant distinction between the old order of Americans who held on to outdated concessions in Mexico and the new generation who had "come here representing American houses and wish trade and are getting it . . . ." The Ambassador was determined to help this group in opposition to the reactionary old one. German diplomatic reports confirmed that Daniels was hard at work: "There is no lack of reliable indications that the American Embassy and the trade commissioner of the United States are working against us with all means at their command." [38]

Gradually this commonsense attitude penetrated the minds of even the most stubborn defenders of the oil companies. Daniels still complained, though, that while Secretary Hull supposedly agreed with Roosevelt that the oil men should initiate negotiations with the Mexican government, the Secretary had attacked the Cárdenas administration for not taking more initiative. Daniels agreed with Adolf Berle, who had said only a few months after the nationalization decree that he knew of no historical case where outside diplomatic intervention had canceled or even delayed any agrarian reform.[39]

Cárdenas was replaced by a more moderate Mexican president in 1940 elections, one who, a former Cabinet official wrote to Roosevelt, was committed to the fullest cooperation in defending the hemisphere. Roosevelt was now ready to take a stronger hand in the matter and sent Vice-President Henry Wallace to Mexico to attend the inauguration of Ávila Camacho with instructions to raise the question of closer relations. The United States then promised Mexico a continuing market for other minerals if it would agree to embargo such goods to keep them from going to the Axis. From Mexico City came indications that Sumner Welles's new suggestion for a "global" settlement might be acceptable.[40]

The gentleman's agreement on minerals gave Hull room to maneuver with the oil men. He had not suddenly reversed himself and, as he told them, he still upheld the "principle of property rights"; but with war coming nearer, Roosevelt dissatisfied with the State Department's approach, the reasonableness of Ambassador Daniels' arguments, and the general frustration of the last three years, there was no real alternative. Even so, as late as October, 1941, at least two high officials still wanted to delay final negotiations until more pressure could be brought into play: Sumner Welles, for example, asked the Treasury once more to use its silver policy as a lever. "If the Treasury does not cooperate, the other pieces . . . will not be put together." But Ambassador Daniels had the last word. Further delay, he told the President, would be "akin to intervention" to the Mexicans. "You are right," said Roosevelt. "See Hull. I am sure he feels as deeply as we do that the time has come for action." [41]

There followed an exchange of notes which set in motion the mechanics of a settlement which left the oil fields in Mexican hands. Moreover, a Mexican-American committee was established to investigate ways that economic and political relations between the two countries could be improved, and the Export-Import Bank granted Mexico a $30,000,000 loan ostensibly to complete the Mexico City–Guatemala section of the Pan-American Highway; but of course it would help in any monetary settlement on the oil fields. Relieved, Secretary Hull said that the settlement would be "further concrete proof of the fact that problems existing between nations are capable of mutually satisfactory settlement when approached in a reciprocal spirit of good will, tolerance, and a desire to understand each other's point of view." [42]

This was said shortly before Pearl Harbor; within two years the Secretary and his aides would be seeking to use wartime cooperation plans to restore American oil men to Mexican fields.

But looking back a few months to an exchange between the President and the Senate Military Affairs Committee, the influences at work upon American policy and President Roosevelt in 1941 show up quite clearly. The exchange began when one senator wanted to know why the United States did not punish Mexico.

"All right," came the President's reply. "All right, suppose we did not buy any Mexican silver. We are buying today, in small amounts, much less than we did. If we stopped buying Mexican silver, they would sell it to somebody else, possibly for a smaller sum." And what if the United States curtailed its tourists? "The President of Mexico would, I am inclined to think, sell more oil to Italy and Germany to make up for that amount. There isn't very much more you could do."

Roosevelt then broadened his commentary to give the senators a lesson from European history and its application to the current predicament. England had put a blockade around Napoleon in 1807, he stated, and now the Germans wanted to put a fence around the United States—in fact their "whole threat" was wrapped up in this attempt to dominate world trade! [43]

"By no stretch of the imagination," wrote two historians on the coming of World War II, "could the Administration be accused of

having exerted pressure on Mexico in behalf of American interests."
For those whose imaginations can be stretched more than these authors
suppose, this is not quite all the story. The settlement owed a good bit
to Axis competition and, as Roosevelt had put it, there wasn't very
much more anyone could do—unless, as some suggested, William
Rhoades Davis could have been prosecuted under the old Trading
with the Enemy Act.[44]

"DELOUSING" LATIN AMERICA

Like the Cuban Revolution of 1933, the Mexican oil crisis was big
enough and serious enough to contain most of the problems of the Good
Neighbor Policy. Axis competition had been a major consideration in
Mexico—and it was so all over Latin America. Roosevelt's sometime
conservative adviser, Bernard Baruch, returned from a European trip
at the end of the 1930's anxious to tell Administration leaders about
the need for "establishing better cultural and economic relations with
Latin America, where German economic penetration could bring that
[region] under her control without firing a shot." Undoubtedly the State
Department reassured him that it understood the problem and was
taking measures to correct the situation. "For some 3 years prior to the
outbreak of war between the United States and Japan," said Assistant
Secretary Berle, describing one important move to a Senate committee,
"the Department of State had been cognizant of the existence of Italian
or German-controlled lines in South America. We had initiated a
campaign to clear these lines out." [45]

A more general campaign had also been under way at least since
the time of the Buenos Aires Conference. In the months after that
meeting the State Department had secured the cooperation of the War
Department for closer military coordination with Latin America. There
should be more Latin Americans in West Point and Annapolis, thought
the diplomats, more good-will overflights and naval visits, and more
invitations to Latin American officers to visit the United States. The
Italian and German colonies in South America, concluded a supporting
policy memorandum, were controlled by their national governments—
and these nations practiced an "aggressive commercial policy founded
on bilateral balancing, subsidization, and currency depreciation." [46]

The War Department agreed. It asked the State Department in turn
to back American-owned commercial aviation companies and to promote American munitions sales there. In 1938 this Administration

team underbid German competitors for the right to send military missions to South American countries to replace those Germany had earlier sent to some countries to train their armies. And the United States also offered to train Latin American officers in the United States schools.[47]

In the Treasury Department, Morgenthau was still advocating his form of dollar diplomacy to counter German advances. In January, 1939, Morgenthau called Commerce Secretary Hopkins' attention to a German locomotive sale to Chile. *"I am particularly interested in learning whether the conditions which led to the business being given to Germany are such as will gravely handicap our manufacturers from obtaining a reasonable share of Chile's additional purchases of equipment and machinery"* (emphasis in original). Since the question of commercial credits for Chile was about to come up, would Hopkins give him a report on the matter?

These sales took place in 1937, Hopkins responded. And when a new call for additional bids went out in 1938 and American firms were not even asked to present an offer, the commercial attaché at Santiago told his Chilean counterpart over an informal luncheon that this action would create a "very bad impression in Washington." The bids were reopened, and the Baldwin Locomotive Company received the contract even though its price was 17.5 per cent higher than a German bid. As Hopkins went on to explain, his attaché had successfully forced this issue, but the real problem "facing us with our Chilean trade" was that Germany was "forcing Chile to trade on a bi-lateral basis." [48]

These were the tactics Roosevelt was talking about when he suggested to newsmen that Germany could gain control of Latin America without sending troops over. "And that applies, of course, to exports and imports, and it would be a perfectly logical conclusion of the domination of Europe by those powers." [49]

Later the President's Republican Secretaries, Frank Knox and Henry L. Stimson, shared his concern and made it a bipartisan one. Speaking before the Canadian Society of New York, Knox predicted that a victorious Axis would command the South Atlantic, "establish hostile bases in the Americas, and drive this country's essential foreign trade from the seas." Testifying on the Lend-Lease Bill, Stimson asserted that Latin American allegiance would follow trade routes. If Germany controlled Spain, the threat would be intensifed because of the cultural links between South America and that country.[50]

Of more immediate concern were the German and Italian air links with Latin America. For a time they seemed to be the most dangerous threat to American interests in the Western Hemisphere. Each day Brazil's *Condor* and Colombia's *Scadta* lines flew Axis commercial representatives into South America. After the German victory over France, there arose the possibility that Hitler would use them if he could to jump from North Africa to Brazil.[51]

The most obvious weapon against the Axis lines was the chosen instrument of the 1920's, Pan American Airways, which the Administration decided should be called upon to help clear them out. Until that was accomplished, it was decided not to do anything that might lessen Pan American's ability to perform this task. Ironically, Pan American was somewhat reluctant to reorganize the Axis-controlled airlines as it already owned shares in them. All government agencies were directed to help in this campaign of "replacing them by United States controlled airlines," and the State Department choked off their American oil supplies, even threatening to blacklist any company selling them gasoline. Finally, with the aid of Colombian troops, *Scadta* pilots were forced to retire, leaving the line in "neutral" hands.[52]

President Roosevelt set aside eight million dollars to help any South American country which wanted to eliminate German airlines but had not yet accomplished that goal because of a lack of funds to establish new ones. Under this plan *Condor* was reorganized, and two subsidiaries of Pan American took over nearly all the connecting trade routes in South America.[53]

Using Pan American to "delouse" South America had other positive results. The Administration soon decided to grant Pan American an additional 12 million dollars for the construction of landing fields to be made available to the Air Corps, but Roosevelt insisted that along with the money, the Government should hold first lien on these bases in case Pan American should become bankrupt. Along with other innovations in American air policy, this attitude revealed a changing temper and a desire to rationalize American foreign economic policy. It seemed that Pan American was being nationalized into something like the British Overseas Airways Corporation. At least the desire to work air policy into over-all planning was there, as evidenced in a statement of the Commerce Department's *Foreign Commerce Weekly:* "The future in inter-American trade will show a direct relation to the improvement . . . of air services in this hemisphere." [54]

From the office of Nelson Rockefeller, the newly appointed Coordinator of Inter-American Affairs, the Administration combated other German and Italian business firms through public relations media and, failing to drive them out that way, through pressuring American businessmen who had not taken the hint.

Josephus Daniels applauded Rockefeller's efforts, pleased that the real enemy was under fire instead of the Mexicans. He also approved the Coordinator's campaign to remove German employees from American businesses in Latin America, reasoning that such men might, after the war, use their contacts to promote German goods at prices below America's ability to compete.[55]

And while the main thrust of this campaign was against Axis interests, the Administration's approach was a comprehensive one. Roosevelt's musings upon the future (or the lack of a future) of British holdings in Latin America was not atypical. "As you know, the British need money in this war," he had told the business magazine publishers and editors. "They own lots of things all over the world . . . such as tramways and electric light companies. Well, in carrying on this war, the British may have to part with that control and we, perhaps, can step in or arrange—make the financial arrangements for eventual local ownership. It is a terribly interesting thing and one of the most important things for our future trade is to study it in that light." If Axis competition had forced modifications in specific and general policies, it had also opened up, Roosevelt more than implied, new fields for exploration and thus started new trains of thought rumbling along the tracks of the Good Neighbor Policy.[56]

OUTLINING A NEW SHARE FOR LATIN AMERICA

Finding a way to meet the other half of the challenge—Latin American revolutionary nationalism—was not nearly so direct and easily done. It still is not in 1963.

Washington's very success in eliminating Axis interests made the problem more acute, since normal trade patterns with the European Continent were disrupted by the war. Besides trying to rearrange its own economy for war, the United States had to prevent, if possible, a collapse of South American economies under the weight of surpluses or the pinch of shortages occurring in different places at the same time. Some policy had to be evolved out of these tensions which would meet the economic and psychological needs of the present and allow for the kind of planning and development Roosevelt had described in his conference with the publishers and editors.

Not all at once and not without some stragglers, Administration leaders decided that more should be done to help basic industrialization in Latin American countries. Like those who questioned Stimson's plan to bring the Marines out of Central America and the Caribbean, there were many who now disagreed with this conception. Nevertheless, the decision to extend aid through the Export-Import Bank, first began in the late 1930's, was later developed into such generalized foreign aid plans as Point Four, and still later into the Alliance for Progress. In 1940, though, it was only an embryo.

During the Recession of 1937–38, the year of the Mexican oil crisis and also the year that the State Department started clearing out the German and Italian airlines, there was more than a little uneasiness about the future of inter-American trade. In that regard the times were not unlike those of the early 1960's. Like the attention of businessmen to the Alliance for Progress, the Commerce Department's Business Advisory Council gave special attention to Latin America in its own meetings and in sessions with Harry Hopkins and President Roosevelt. The situation prompted John L. Lewis to tell the 1939 CIO convention that the Good Neighbor Policy needed to "be bulwarked with definite arrangements and facilities and provisions and stipulations which will mean that the extension of credits to the southern countries will place men to work in the idle factories of American industries. . . . It is time for our own government and our own Department of Commerce, and our own State Department to look at this problem with eyes that see realistically and tear themselves away from the ancient traditions and the ancient practices which have ruled these Departments, to undertake to see that America has an equal break in the foreign markets of the world . . . ." [57]

Congress had refused Roosevelt's request for 500 million dollars for just such credits, but the sight of Hitler's armies marching through Poland and France changed the legislators' minds, and the Administration sponsored on its own a special conference at Panama City to set up an Inter-American Development Commission to promote "further development of national resources." Sumner Welles addressed this conference, stressing the responsibilities of Latin American nations in making sure that American investors could have confidence in the just treatment and protection their properties would have when they came south to help with industrialization.[58]

On the other side, Roosevelt and Hopkins made sure that powerful leaders of American industry like Curtis Calder of American and Foreign Power and Graeme Howard of General Motors and Clarence Dillon of Dillon, Read and Company, knew of their earnest desire that United States firms hold onto the Latin American trade which had been diverted into their hands because of the war.[59]

"This is no time for a timorous or traditional approach to the task," began a Treasury Department memorandum. "Now is the time to harmonize our economic program with our new political program of a Good Neighbor Policy. Here is the opportunity for the exercise of great economic statesmanship at a point in history which may well prove decisive." Another Treasury official added a practical amendment to these sentiments: "It would be politically unwise to allow American capital to be used to the detriment of American exporters. And in the case of repeat merchandise, where the first order determines largely where the re-orders will go, American exporters cannot afford to allow the initial business to go abroad." [60]

Latin American countries, as a representative of the United Fruit Company asserted at a symposium at the University of Michigan, "have been left inaccessible and underdeveloped largely because of the lack of capital. We have a large reservoir of unemployed capital, and every dictate of self interest, national policy, and good neighborliness indicates this sphere in which to put idle dollars to work." [61]

And finally another old South American hand Juan Trippe, writing in *Survey Graphic,* summed it all up: "Our commercial intercourse with Latin America [has] become a vital part of our national economy. Banking transactions incident to the movement of goods from the United States to Latin America mounted to an $80,000,000 peak only last year, and are certain to increase still further in the current year." [62]

Nelson Rockefeller's congratulatory letter to Roosevelt on his 1940 re-election set forth the anxiousness and anticipation United States policy makers felt about Latin America: "Today as never before the opportunity exists to make permanent the cultural and commercial ties between the American Republics which you have done so much to strengthen during the past few years." At the 1940 Havana Foreign Minister's Conference, United States delegates had made a start towards making "permanent the cultural and commercial ties" and accepting the challenge of finding markets for raw materials and providing capital for industrialization projects. "The Havana Conference," Adolf Berle solemnly advised Roosevelt, "is built upon the theory that a message will be sent to Congress on Monday, July 22nd, recommending that an additional half-billion dollars be given to the Export-Import Bank." [63]

The Bank, then, had been chosen to stimulate Latin American industrialization, or at least to make a beginning, with the expectation that increased American capital investment would carry on the work. This idea of developmental loans through the Bank was almost accidental in origin: a public works loan to Haiti in 1938. By mid-1940 Administration leaders had moved from that small example to the much larger concept suggested by Assistant Secretary of State Berle that the Bank's funds be used to finance the purchase of Latin American surpluses. Sumner Welles picked up this idea, and similar ones, and wove them into a dramatic presentation at a confidential meeting of the Inter-American Financial and Economic Advisory Committee on July 11, 1940. The United States planned to extend both the volume and the character of the Export-Import Bank; it planned to make better arrangements in monetary and exchange matters; and it planned to finance and store certain surplus commodities.

Almost at once, under this program the American Ambassador in Havana seconded Cuba's request for a $25,000,000 loan to help in "maintaining stability in Cuba." [64]

But it was in Brazil—where, as we have already seen, German-American rivalries had been the sharpest in the 1930's—that the new parts in the Good Neighbor Policy were given a full test. Brazil had to have steel, especially after the war cut off supplies from Germany and Belgium. Private American capital had looked into the feasibility of building a steel complex there but like British companies had rejected the notion as impracticable in the immediate future. It was known, however, that the German Krupp interests as well as a Japanese company were still interested in the project. In the first part of 1940 the Brazilian government went to the State Department with its disappointment and displeasure about the decision of the American companies. Picking the most sensitive spot, Brazil hinted that it might look favorably upon a German proposal. Roosevelt immediately took a direct hand in the matter, instructing Jesse Jones to ask United States Steel to reconsider its decision and also to get in touch with other companies and suggest the idea to them. Jones's aide, Warren Lee Pierson, president of the Export-Import Bank, had traveled in Latin America in the late 1930's and had his own ideas concerning the need to "decolonize" the economies of that region so as to sustain inter-American harmony and prosperity.[65]

Thus when Brazilian President Getulio Vargas reacted against further efforts to bring the steel companies into the project on the old basis and himself suggested an Export-Import Bank loan, the agency was quite ready to make such a multi-million-dollar loan, even though the Administration said it would rather it had been handled entirely by the steel companies. One good reason for making the loan, thought Jones, was that Great Britain was going to give up iron ore holdings as part of the deal. One of Pierson's assistants could think of four more: the project would stimulate the sale of American goods and services; it would produce strategic goods for the war effort; and the loan would foster industrial progress and make Brazil an even better customer in the future. The State Department *Bulletin* noted approvingly that besides easing the burden of Brazil's rearmament, the twenty-million-dollar loan would be spent among 250–300 American manufacturers.[66] But even if all these stated reasons were just a public relations campaign to sell the project to American skeptics—and this is so unlikely that it hardly needs to be mentioned—the competition with Germany was real enough and motive enough to bring about the loan. By 1943 this investment by the United States Government in Brazil had climbed to over 176 million dollars, which included loans for a variety of other projects as well. Foreign aid had grown out of its infancy.[67]

So the Volta Redonda steel complex was built. This was only one example of where the United States and Brazil could cooperate, declared the Business Advisory Council after surveying the new situation, but the Council did not want the Commerce Department to forget that a firm policy was still needed in order to "establish the proper psychology necessary to encourage the investment of American capital in Latin America." Even before the steel loan, the BAC had advocated joint enterprises to provide what Frank Knox had called a sense of partnership rather than of exploitation. In fact the group went him one better: This partnership would give the enterprises a nationalistic character. "It may even be the means whereby certain industries now restricted to Brazilians can have the benefit of American capital and American technological skill in their development." [68]

"Brazil has in the past represented our chief market in South America," noted a writer in *Foreign Commerce Weekly,* "and, in view of the large construction program now under way, it would appear that the Republic is in a fair way of maintaining that position." "A number of American concerns," another representative of the Commerce Department confirmed, "are planning to expand their existing branch factories or establish new ones. The products involved are fertilizers, toilet preparations, ladies dresses, safety razors and electrical goods." [69]

American trade and investment increased by over 390 million dollars in the single year between September, 1939, and September, 1940. As the war came to the United States, this increase seemed small compared with the next four years, and it should be noted that the war was far and away the most important influence on inter-American economic affairs in those years; but let it also be remembered that new foundations had been laid in Brazil and elsewhere. Such foundations supported and facilitated expanded investments. Along with other new currents stimulated by the war, the net effect of the modifications in the Good Neighbour Policy, was to make the power and influence of the United States and its nationals even more important, and the reason, as set forth by James Fred Rippy, is simple enough: Americans already controlled large segments of the Latin American economy. By 1941 the United States—or, rather, its nationals—owned railroads in eight or nine countries and light and power companies in six. "All the cable, radio-telegraph, and radio telephone systems providing connection with foreign countries belonged to capitalists of the United States or of the British Empire . . . . Nearly all of the transoceanic steamship lines were likewise owned by foreign companies . . . . All of the trunk-line airways and some of the branch systems were controlled by the companies of the United States. Most of the mineral areas in active production belonged to the Anglo-Saxons, with citizens of the United States owning the major part except in the case of petroleum." Foreign ownership of fruit and sugar lands was equally dominant.[70]

Thus the share Latin America was to get depended much more upon how this investment pie was cut than upon other factors. Postwar planning for inter-American relations began with these modifications and was completed with the generalization of them into a full-blown revision of Adam Smith's division-of-labor thesis. On the night of the Pearl Harbor attack, Roosevelt instructed Secretary Hull to keep Latin America informed and "in line with us." The State Department had some trouble fulfilling that order, and the tensions which arose between the

United States and a few Latin American countries over their reluctance to break completely with the Axis were not solely political but a continuation of the rising nationalism of the previous decade. And in 1945 this nationalism was present at the Mexico City Foreign Minister's Conference ready to challenge United States proposals once again.

In the case of China our chief object should be, not a favorable balance of trade, but a strong China. A strong China, able and willing to defend the principle of the open market in the Far East, would be worth billions of dollars to the U.S., not alone in terms of exports, but in terms of the security of the system under which we want to live.

Fortune, May, 1941

When I said that the matter depended entirely on the President's statesmanship, he replied that the United States was not in favor of the "closed door" and that it was Japan's turn to figure out ways and means of opening it.

Ambassador Nomura to Tokyo, 1941

7 · Japan Tries to Close the Door in Asia

Prior to World War II and Japan's decision to join the Tripartite Pact a year later in September, 1940, some American diplomats still hoped that the Far Eastern problem would remain manageable within traditional limits. Events since 1933 had dented badly, but not yet demolished, that hope. Economic pressure probably would have to be brought into play, maybe even military displays, but few—at least before 1939 —really expected anything like an attack on Pearl Harbor.

The war in Europe changed Washington's attitude: Japan's somewhat reluctant (but complete) turn to Berlin and Rome enlarged the dimensions of the problem, making it part of the European struggle. Perhaps the Tripartite Pact made a Japanese-American war inevitable; a strong case can be made for that point of view, but it is probably a nearsighted one. This Pact might better be understood as a sudden-recognition scene, where tensions which have been rising in the early acts of a tragedy are finally resolved.

Japan's membership in the Axis Pact did encourage Tokyo to strike southward in 1940 and 1941, not only endangering British imperial lifelines but also cutting American security lines. And in explaining his reasons for aiding Great Britain in its war with Germany, President Roosevelt, in a letter to Ambassador Grew, linked Europe and the Far

East: "We must . . . recognize that our interests are menaced both in Europe and in the Far East. We are engaged in the task of defending our way of life and our vital national interests wherever they are seriously endangered." [1]

The President did not mean simply the preservation of the British Empire in the Far East. "Something bigger is at stake," wrote Admiral Harold Stark to a colleague. "So far as China is concerned, we have 'our foot in the door—the door that once was "open," ' and if I had the say so, it would remain there until I was ready to withdraw it—or until the door opened to such a point that I could withdraw if and when I saw fit." [2]

Though not so pugnacious, Secretary Hull was equally determined. A few days after the European war started, the Japanese Foreign Office presented a note to the American Embassy suggesting the prompt removal of all the belligerent's troops from China. America was not directly concerned, since it was not at war, but like Roosevelt in his letter to Grew, Hull feared that a challenge to Britain or France was only a way to get rid of all Occidental influence in China: "Not since the middle of the nineteenth century has any one power claimed a right of preponderance or predominance of influence there. The United States has its rights and interests there just as Japan." [3]

A few months later, the State Department rejected out of hand a British suggestion that London and Washington work to achieve a compromise peace between Japan and China. Washington felt that the British wanted to surrender too much to Japan, and the State Department was unwilling, possibly even for the sake of easing Britain's situation in the war with Germany, to agree to any scheme by which Japan might solidify its forward position in China.[4]

From 1933 to 1937 the United States had sought a way out of the dilemma in attempting to convince Japan that its best interests would be served by subscribing to the Open Door Policy. That effort continued, but after the failure at Brussels it became more legalistic, more moralistic, and more persistent. Put another way, Stimson had first labeled Japan a defendant in a civil suit; after 1937, the Administration came to see Japan as a criminal offender and therefore subject to restraint.

Some recorders of these events have rightly stressed Japanese militarism and duplicity, especially in connection with the negotiations leading to the Tripartite Pact and in general right up to the day of the attack at Pearl Harbor. Others have pointed out that American insistence that Japan conform to its way of thinking and give up the path of empire was of equal importance—if not more so.[5]

However that may be, these two things are certain: Japan wanted an Asian Empire, and the United States would not yield it. The United States firmly insisted that all nations would prosper through the Open Door Policy; Japan just as firmly denied it.

Nor were the Japanese army warrior-politicians the only ones, as some have contended, who denied the universal value of the Open Door Policy and set out to destroy it. Japanese naval officers made this fact plain to Norman Davis and Admiral Standley at the time of the London Naval talks, when they protested that Japan desired a navy equal to that of the United States primarily because of America's defense of the Open Door Policy by using its navy. Japanese statesmen such as Prince Fuminaro Konoye, Hachiro Arita, and Yosuke Matsuoka had held similar views for a long time. Japanese liberals, on the other hand, were unable to convince these fellow countrymen that Tokyo should stay away from an alliance with Berlin and Rome and stay with London and Washington.

Herbert Feis unintentionally, but precisely, gave the best reason for the defeat of the Japanese liberals. American policy, he wrote in *The Road to Pearl Harbor,* offered Japan no rewards, no advantages for returning to the "company of peaceful and orderly states and accepting a place below the salt." Certainly a Japanese chauvinist could point to Hull's March, 1938, speech to the National Press Club on American overseas interests and rights as contradictory of the principles Washington was pressing upon Tokyo, if not in letter then in spirit. The Secretary had avowed that the United States could not adopt isolationism without "incalculable injury to the standard of living" or exposing its nationals and "legitimate interests abroad" to injustice and outrage.[6]

But America's advance into Asia had been a peaceful one through the Open Door (with the somewhat embarrassing exception of the pacification of the Philippines after the Spanish-American War), and Japan employed ruthless military conquest. A sympathetic account of the last talks between Secretary Hull and the Japanese touched upon these differences, and the mental barrier between them: Secretary Hull's mind was that of the "orderly nineteenth century when imperial ambitions could be satisfied without provoking war . . . and the powers professed regard for the law of nations." "Nomura's world stretched back to the Emperor Jimmu, traversing centuries of samurai militarism, unmodified by Christian idealism and scarcely touched by democratic individualism." [7]

A significant contrast in method—yet in each instance, the dynamic force was expansion. And Japan *did* imitate Western imperialism from the 1890's on into the next century. Hull strove mightily to convince the Japanese to accept an orderly framework for its expansionism, but buried within scattered State Department reports on Japanese-American relations were precise refutations of the arguments he was using. "The evidence advanced in this report," said an American vice-consul in Osaka, "demonstrates that Japan has not derived any material benefits from the trade agreements program of the United States, either in its trade with the agreement countries or with the United States. It is believed that the trade agreements have been largely responsible for Japan's inability to secure advantages from the so-called 'free gift of reduced duties.'" Perhaps this should not be surprising. After all, Sayre and Hull had promised Roosevelt that third nations would not benefit greatly from the reduced duties that the United States granted to trade agreement countries. [8]

The Vice-Consul's report was supported by the director of the Trade Agreements Division of the State Department, Harry Hawkins, in a memorandum to the Far Eastern Division as late as November 10, 1941. It was clear, asserted Hawkins, that most nations which had recently negotiated trade agreements with the United States discriminated against Japan in one way or another. Even the United States itself did not really give Japan an open door into the Philippines or into Cuba. Hawkins recommended that Washington consider the situation and then open these markets, for the small losses it would suffer there would be far outweighed by the advantages the United States might then expect in China if a *quid pro quo* could be arranged. [9]

Japan's union with Germany and Italy had raised additional political questions that precluded such an understanding. But Japan's choice had been influenced by an increasingly militant economic policy the United States had pursued since the summer of 1938, in response to Japan's forward movement in China. The "moral embargo" of that year was followed in 1939 by the failure to renew the Japanese-American Commercial Treaty. In the summer of 1940 Japan's quest for raw materials and economic self-sufficiency motivated a drive into Indo-China; from then on, there was really no turning back for either side. A year more of conflict followed. On July 2, 1941, Japanese leaders declared in secret: "We will not be deterred by the possibility of being involved in a war with England and America." [10]

Japanese militarism was a brutal and ugly thing; it cannot be justified, for the same reason that American excesses against the Indians and questionable motives in the Mexican War and the Spanish-American War cannot be. But in each instance some factors behind the expansionist drive can be identified. The starting point is obvious: Japan opposed American presence in China, and perhaps in all of the Far East.

REASSERTING THE TRADITIONAL AMERICAN POLICY

Critics of American Far Eastern policy prompted Secretary Hull to reassert its fundamentals in an open letter to Vice-President Garner on January 8, 1938. The failure of the Brussels Conference frustrated and rankled American diplomats in these months, probably because of the bad press Davis had received near the end, but also because of the inability to find any kind of answer to the Far Eastern dilemma. Like Secretary Stimson's letter to Senator Borah announcing the nonrecognition doctrine, Hull emphasized United States support "by peaceful means [of] influences contributing to preservation and encouragement of orderly processes." [11]

Having cast this moral cloak over his policy, Hull continued to play down direct material interests in the Far East which had brought American gunboats to Chinese rivers, a successful demand for extra-territorial rights, or marines to various treaty ports since the Allied defeat of the Boxers.

The following excerpts from Ambassador Grew's diplomatic records provide much more evidence that the cloak Hull had thrown over American policy had a very materialistic lining. On March 4, 1937, he called on the vice-minister for foreign affairs: "I spoke of the fundamental basis of the commercial policy of the United States as favoring the maintenance and extension of the open door . . . ." On November 28, 1937 : "I . . . went into an extensive explanation of the American Government's interest in the preservation of the integrity of the Chinese Maritime Customs presenting every possible argument to the effect that the Japanese military in Shanghai must not tamper therewith." On December 28, 1937: "I said to the Vice Minister that in my opinion the integrity of the Chinese customs certainly represented one of the

American interests envisaged in the final paragraph of our PANAY note of December 14 . . . ." On May 17, 1938: "I said that American missionaries and businessmen are becoming increasingly restive at this arbitrary interference with their legitimate interests which cannot be explained by pleading the dangers of the war zone . . . ." And finally, on July 4, 1938, Grew presented the Japanese Foreign Office a twenty-two page list of depredations against American businessmen, churches, schools, and individual nationals.[12]

"It is inconceivable to me," Admiral Leahy wrote to the President two days before Hull's letter to Garner, "that we as a nation are going to give up our rights of trading or living in China and confine our activities to our own continental limits." The similarity to Hull's speech to the National Press Club of this letter from Leahy is striking, and the Admiral gained a chance to support his contentions publicly when Roosevelt sent an Administration bill to Congress calling for an enlarged navy. "At the present time," Leahy testified before a Congressional committee, "it is the national policy to protect our commerce. The naval policy is designed to support the known national policies, such as the Monroe Doctrine, the protection of nationals abroad, the protection of American shipping, and the protection of American territory, including island possessions, against invasion." [13]

A key moment in the ensuing debate on the President's decision to enlarge the navy came when New Deal supporter Senator David I. Walsh answered an opponent's remark that the navy had no business on Chinese rivers at all. "The navy never enters a foreign port or goes near a foreign country," retorted Walsh, "without directions from the State Department." [14]

And when the proposed naval strategy for the Far East, PLAN DOG, later was submitted to President Roosevelt during November, 1940, Admiral Stark's transmittal letter might well have been written by Admiral Mahan: "I believe that we should recognize as the foundation of adequate armed strength the possession of a profitable foreign trade, both in raw materials and finished goods. Without such a trade, our economy can scarcely support heavy armaments. The restoration of foreign trade, particularly with Europe, may depend upon the continued integrity of Europe." [15]

Even those State Department planners who had urged caution and the consortium principle began recommending direct aid to Chiang Kai-shek by the time of Grew's presentation of the twenty-two page list, and for all of the above reasons. Admittedly, they were still shy of the advanced position of Henry Morgenthau, who was now predicting in the darkest terms that if China fell, the President would have to go, hat in hand, to the Mikado and beg him not to take the Philippines. Morgenthau had definite ideas on the need to aid Latin American countries, and his views on the Far East fit easily into that overview: in each instance he argued that credits were necessary if "foreign domination" of these areas was to be prevented. For Morgenthau, a revised dollar diplomacy thus had world-wide opportunities to take up and challenges to overcome.[16]

Hull also wanted to keep these opportunities open. "American opinion believes it to be incompatible with the establishment and maintenance of American and world prosperity," he instructed Grew on November 20, 1938, "that any country should endeavor to establish a preferred position for itself in another country." [17]

Influential segments of American private leadership were also concerned about stopping Japanese plans to establish a Far Eastern hegemony. Such leaders formed the "American Committee for Non-Participation in Japanese Aggression." The Committee undertook to persuade those who still enjoyed profitable trade with Japan in metals and other strategic goods that they were cutting their own throats. Pamphlets were issued covering every group which the Committee felt was endangered by Japanese expansion—for example, *American Business and the Far Eastern Conflict, The American Church and the Far Eastern Conflict,* and *American Labor and the Far Eastern Conflict.* Publisher Henry Luce formed his own group, with the intention of offering Chiang Kai-shek direct aid "to supplement any more large-scale efforts which may ultimately be made by the United States Government." [18]

Another leader, former Ambassador W. Cameron Forbes, the leader of the 1935 Economic Mission to the Far East, berated Japanese officials for choosing a path of conquest. "I have advised the State Department of some vigorous language I recently used in telling the New York Japanese Consul General how quickly and completely Japan would serve her own interest by getting out of China and staying out," he wrote Henry Stimson—himself a key figure in these groups.[19]

Far Eastern expert Nathaniel Peffer brought together in one place many of these opinions in the October, 1938, issue of *Foreign Affairs.* Those who naïvely hoped that the Great China Market would finally become a reality under Japanese management had better take another look at the results in Manchuria. Tokyo had made that whole area into a source of raw materials for Japanese military needs. The rest of China, he concluded, would have industrialized at a much faster rate had it not been for the debilitating struggle with Japan. And if Japan did win, what then? Tokyo lacked the ability to complete China's industrialization, and so it was illusory to believe in a new prosperous China under Japan's guidance and development.[20]

Cordell Hull had made this same argument to Japanese diplomats several times over in the 1930's; Peffer's article hit close to the center of America's dilemma of desiring a stable prosperous Japan to lead in Asia, but increasingly fearful that Japan intended to take it all for itself. The Japanese, on the other hand, deduced from such statements and attitudes of the Secretary of the Treasury, the Secretary of State, Ambassador Forbes, and Mr. Peffer that the "have" nations would never allow them what they considered was rightfully theirs in the Far East. Ten days after Hull had instructed Grew that the United States considered that its own and world prosperity suffered every time "any country" secured a "preferred position for itself in another country," Grew sent to Washington an article by Hachiro Arita, soon to be foreign minister, who wrote that the League of Nations was an instrument of the nearly self-sufficient powers who protected themselves against rising powers and employed sanctions to hold back such challengers. "It is with this thought in mind that Japan is preoccupied in realizing an economic Japan-China-Manchukuo bloc." [21]

As it had been for the past several years, the Administration was debating how to help China without provoking war with Japan. Morgenthau wanted to loan money to the Universal Trading Corporation, a Chinese government agency, for the purchase of American trucks. Undoubtedly the statements and opinions of the anti-Japanese organizations made their weight felt in this discussion. Hull was still afraid of going too far and admonished Roosevelt that if such a loan were made, with all its implications, the President must act responsibly and inform Congress and the nation of the possibility of war and then be prepared to send the fleet into the far Pacific.[22]

Morgenthau contended that in addition to propping up China, this loan would mean markets for forty-three million dollars worth of goods. "And to this extent business in this country will be stimulated and employment created." The Export-Import Bank could handle the arrangements. Speaking for the Bank, Jesse Jones added: "The Bank is prepared to make the loan under suitable provisions to assure the disbursement of the funds in this country for the purchase of American products." [23]

Regardless of the influence such narrow and direct economic arguments may or may not have had (and coming in the midst of the 1937–38 recession they could hardly have been overlooked, especially if the President did not share Hull's view that the loan might lead to war), the general conclusion that could be drawn from them was central to Hull's entire outlook on foreign affairs. Two years before, the Secretary had sent Roosevelt a memorandum of a conversation he had with the famous John A. Hobson. This student of economic imbalance had impressed Hull with his comment that the "last large possibility of maintaining capitalism lies in the Orient. . . . Whether the Americans will care to play second fiddle to the Japanese, whose character and behavior are so baffling to the Occidental mind, is very doubtful." [24]

Even as he spoke against the Morgenthau loan to China, Hull expressed agreement with its general goal: "Naturally, all American Government officials are *equally desirous* of getting rid of surplus production and they are also *equally anxious* to see Japan defeated in her purpose by the exercise of force to dominate the Far East and repudiate and render inoperative the Nine Power Treaty" (emphasis added).[25]

ECONOMIC WARFARE AGAINST JAPAN

In January, 1939, Secretary Hull was still trying to dissuade Japan. Referring to the recently concluded Lima Foreign Ministers Conference, he described its trade resolutions to the Japanese Ambassador as the "only basis for real commercial progress." The Ambassador replied simply that he hoped that the question of discrimination against American rights would be solved soon, so that the two nations could go ahead with the development of China. That was an interesting thought, said Hull, but of course the United States stood, as it always had both in Europe and Asia, for broad equality of opportunity.[26]

The year just passed had indeed been a disturbing one. However one interpreted it, Japan's surpassing for the first time the volume of American trade with China could not be ignored. Nelson Johnson informed Hull on March 30, 1938, that his talks with some businessmen had left him with the feeling that they still failed to understand what

Japanese dominance would mean. He knew well enough that the "respect extended to foreign interests will be the respect which is given to exhibits in a museum retained because of their historic value." [27]

As worried, yet as reluctant to face a final break as Hull, Stanley Hornbeck could not avoid the thought in February, 1939, that "military opposition" might have to be mounted against Japan. Economic Adviser Herbert Feis suggested a less militant course, proposing that the 1911 Commercial Treaty with Japan should be allowed to lapse. This would give Washington direct control on a day-to-day basis over Japanese-American trade and serve to put Japan on notice. Adolf Berle turned over this idea and mused: "It is a curious fact that the United States, which bolts like a frightened rabbit from every remote contact with Europe, will enthusiastically take a step which might well be a material day's march on the road to a Far Eastern War." [28]

Hull hesitated, considered for a time allowing only part of the treaty to lapse, became concerned with Roosevelt that Congress was going to force their hands, and finally gave notice in July that the Commercial Treaty would be allowed to lapse, though he carefully explained that the action meant no immediate change. The United States had decided to conduct its relations with Japan on an *ad hoc* basis. During that month the Japanese Ambassador had proposed to a skeptical Hull another reason for his country's continuing military actions in Asia: Japan was preventing the spread of Bolshevism. The Secretary turned the point beautifully by replying that although the United States also "fights Bolshevism," Japan by "steadily lowering the standards of life of their own and other peoples by a course of militarism and military conquest," had become the greatest supporter of Bolshevism.[29]

A few months later, Roosevelt had a related point to make to Ambassador Grew. The President denied that a point of no return had been reached in Japanese-American relations; the United States was more incensed for the moment by Russia's attack upon Finland, "but things might develop into such a feeling if the Japanese Government were to fail to speak as civilized twentieth century human beings." [30]

To Tokyo the European War seemed a perfect opportunity to advance Japan's cause, and at the outset of 1940 its foreign policy became much more militant. For example, the Japanese began demanding of the Dutch government in the East Indies unlimited access to that colony's oil resources. To the United States this was a clear indication of what even indirect cooperation between Germany and Japan would mean.

In a letter to the *New York Times,* Henry Stimson called for an end to scrap-iron sales to Japan. "We think Mr. Stimson is right," editorialized the New York *Daily News,* "and we hope Congress takes his advice. This country has a golden opportunity to put the squeeze on the Japanese military caste now, the proper object being to squeeze the Japanese out of China with economic pincers. If we let the chance slide for the sake of a few dollars for a few people, we'll be inviting a Japanese onslaught on us after Japan has conquered and reorganized huge, rich and industrious China." [31]

Japan's leaders did not intend to be caught in an economic pincers, nor did they think of getting out of China. Grew reported that new trade negotiations had begun with France, Argentina, and Paraguay. Mexico and Spain had also been invited to send trade missions to Tokyo. There remained a few among Japan's leaders, continued the American Ambassador, who realized that only the large volume of Japanese-American trade prevented a complete break, but they were losing out to the extremists. [32]

On the Fourth of July, 1940, Hull sent one of his longest appeals to the Japanese Foreign Office. He stressed the similarities between the two nations instead of the known differences. Each attached great importance to foreign trade, for instance; and both had a large stake in maintaining that trade through the Open Door Policy. In both countries respect for private property rights constituted the "foundation of the social and economic system." [33]

This message arrived as Japan was getting ready to make demands upon French Indo-China. When it went ahead and asked for the placement of military observers in the colony to counter Anglo-American "encirclement," Hull urged the Vichy French government to resist. If Japan ruled supreme over the Pacific area, he warned the French, "all foreigners would be driven out and could return only by paying skyscraping preferences." The Vichy French set a high price on their cooperation, the kind of economic and political guarantees that Washington could not make or even bargain about. [34]

In September, 1940, Japan adhered to the Tripartite Pact. There had been a long debate in Tokyo; and even those who were strongest for the Axis Alliance wanted to limit Japan's commitment to as vague a one as possible. In theory, at least, Tokyo did reserve the right to determine when the pact should come into play militarily if the United States should enter the European war. This did nothing to calm Washington's anger—and fear.[35]

Sumner Welles responded in a speech at Cleveland, Ohio, which summarized the Administration's feelings. He had already stated in policy memoranda that the Tripartite Pact elevated China to a position of equal importance to Great Britain in American security planning. At Cleveland he began by reviewing the events of the past few months in the Far East and American objectives in the light of those events. Nothing had changed; the United States still demanded complete "respect by all powers for the legitimate rights of the United States" and "equality of opportunity for the trade of all nations" and Japan's "new order in Asia" had violated all international treaties and law. Welles concluded with references to Japanese pressures on the East Indies and Indo-China, where the events of even the last few weeks had "culminated in measures undertaken by Japanese military forces which threaten the integrity of the French Colony." [36]

In Administration discussions, Roosevelt raised the question whether Russia might be wooed a little. Hull jumped all over the idea, exclaiming that the Soviet Union could never be trusted. But newly appointed War Secretary Stimson defended the suggestion against Hull's battering, remarking that the Russians and the Americans had parallel interests in Asia. Then Stimson began recalling past plans for dealing with the Japanese. In 1918, he told the meeting, Woodrow Wilson became infuriated at Japanese actions in Siberia and imposed an economic boycott against that country, "with the result that she crawled down within two months and brought all her troops out again from Siberia like whipped puppies." [37]

Left unsatisfied and still searching, the President mulled over his next move. A day or two after this Cabinet meeting, he casually remarked to Admiral James Richardson that he had considered stringing light ships across the Pacific to enforce a boycott of Japan. But as he went on talking to the Admiral, he grew less and less positive and admitted that he did not know if America would fight if Japan attacked other European colonial possessions or even the Philippines.[38]

On September 27 Roosevelt had advised Stimson and Knox that he did not intend to pick quarrels with Japan, but he would not back down on any key issue. Economic pressure was still the best weapon, and the door should remain open for "discussion and accommodation within the framework of our historic position in the Far East." [39]

Acting upon this premise and his hunch that something had better be done about direct aid to China, Roosevelt asked Sumner Welles to clear the way for a large loan to Chiang Kai-shek. Years later, staff writers for the *Reporter* magazine called this loan the first victory of the China lobby, and so it may have been; but America's "historic position" in Asia was of long standing. Moreover, Chiang always assumed that he should give a prominent place to economic arguments when appealing to the United States for funds. In asking for this loan, he cited the dangers of trade disturbances and discriminations "against American economic interests" which would follow a collapse of the Chinese economy. The American Information Committee at Shanghai, added the Chinese leader, was undoubtedly supporting the loan because of the realization that "Japan's renewed attack on Chinese currency is seriously detrimental to American trade." [40]

Besides the loan, Washington also cleared the way for volunteer pilots to join the famous Flying Tigers squadron and cut off shipments of scrap iron.[41]

A State Department memorandum of December 10, 1940, set forth the reasons why the United States had stepped up its economic warfare to stop Japan: Tokyo has made its choice for Germany. If the Japanese should succeed in driving out the British from the Far East, "our general diplomatic and strategic position would be considerably weakened —by our loss of Chinese, Indian and South Seas markets (and by our loss of much of the Japanese market for our goods, as Japan would become more and more self-sufficient) as well as by insurmountable restrictions upon our access to the rubber, tin, jute, and other vital materials of the Asian and Oceanic regions." [42]

PROLONGING THE AGONY—THE HULL-NOMURA TALKS

Out of contacts some American clergymen had with Japanese leaders came an opportunity (the last one, as it turned out) to resolve the dispute short of war. These men carried to the State Department certain ideas for a *modus vivendi* which they had received in Tokyo. Hull and Roosevelt accepted the gambit and so informed the new Japanese Ambassador, Kichisaburo Nomura, who had been selected for just such work because of his acquaintance with America, its naval officers, and President Roosevelt. Perhaps with a wave of the hand, the American

Commander-in-Chief had been reassuring and confident at their first interview, saying: "there is plenty of room in the Pacific for everybody." Hull, who was making these notes on the conversation, said that here the President "elaborated a little in order to emphasize this suggestion." [43]

In his *Memoirs* the Secretary revealed his own state of mind at the outset of these prolonged discussions with the Japanese Ambassador. Japan wanted a direct bilateral negotiated settlement in Asia, but he would accept nothing short of a broad agreement on the rights of all nations there and the Open Door Policy.[44]

Hull then asked Nomura to meet him at the Wardman Park Hotel in his apartment on April 14, 1941, for the first of a continuing series of meetings which lasted almost to the very day Japan bombed Pearl Harbor. The Secretary posited four principles as the only satisfactory basis for negotiations; in fact, as Nomura learned, Hull would not even begin serious talks until Tokyo had accepted them. These were:

1. Respect for the territorial integrity and the sovereignty of each and all nations.
2. Support of the principle of non-interference in the internal affairs of other countries.
3. Support of the principle of equality, including equality of commercial opportunity.
4. Non-disturbance of the *status quo* in the Pacific except as the status quo may be altered by peaceful means.[45]

Later on, the question of Japan's membership in the Tripartite Pact became a fifth principle. Nomura apparently failed to report these American prerequisites in full until some months later, out of fear that they were so objectionable to Tokyo that his superiors would call off the discussions immediately.[46]

Four days after this first meeting, recalled Ambassador Grew, a Strictly Confidential memorandum on Japanese-American relations was circulated within the State Department. Its main point was that Japanese expansion would be curtailed only when Tokyo had been made to understand that its militant policy and leaders could not take and keep an area against the wishes of the United States and other powers.[47]

Not all advisers in the State Department agreed that Japan could be forced to retreat. "Japan is making a bid to establish itself as a major power," Maxwell Hamilton observed. "To do that, supplies of certain commodities are essential. A conclusion that Japan is likely, in the present world situation, to acquiesce in measures which would deny Japan essentials would not seem to be well-founded." [48]

Hamilton's dissent was swallowed up in the emotional and ever more rigid atmosphere of the State Department, just as dissenters in Tokyo lost out to the war-planners. When Nomura, for example, asked that the principle of equality of opportunity be made part of the negotiations proper, the Secretary retorted that the United States would not even consider entering into discussions if Japan "should even hesitate in agreeing" to this principle. [49]

Through its "Magic" formula the United States had broken the Japanese code and therefore knew Nomura's instructions at the same time he did. The State Department learned thereby of a new move into Indo-China scheduled for mid-July. When it came, the United States nearly broke off the talks completely. A State Department press release spoke gravely of "the vital problems of our national security" raised by the Japanese action and of the danger of the loss of such "essential materials . . . as tin and rubber which are necessary for the normal economy of this country and the consummation of our defense program." [50]

Then the last economic shot was fired: Washington froze Japanese assets on July 26, 1941. Sumner Welles accused the Japanese of supporting Nazi Germany and he and Hull agreed privately that "nothing will stop them except force." "The point is how long we can maneuver the situation until the military matter in Europe is brought to a conclusion . . . ." [51]

Playing for time was the primary tactic from now on, but Roosevelt did suggest to Ambassador Nomura that his country should accept a neutralized Indo-China from which foodstuffs and raw materials would be guaranteed to all nations by international agreement. In response to this suggestion, Tokyo instructed Nomura to ask for a meeting between the President and Prime Minister Konoye. The ambassador raised this question at an interview after Roosevelt's return from the Atlantic Conference with Prime Minister Winston Churchill in August, 1941. Roosevelt seemed taken with the idea at first, but Hull and other Cabinet officers opposed it unless the Japanese first agreed to the four principles. The President's reply, therefore, was restricted to stressing Japan's responsibility for peace in Asia, and to warning that if Tokyo continued its movement into Thailand, the United States would have to take steps to "preserve its security and safety." This was the carefully phrased statement that Churchill and Roosevelt had worked out at the Atlantic Conference. They hoped it would forestall Japanese action for at least a few months.[52]

Some later interpretations of this document insist that it was an ultimatum, or nearly so, but a more critical historical question centers in how much Secretary Hull expected from the Japanese before agreeing to a Konoye-Roosevelt conference. Stimson noted, for example, that the Secretary of State was firmly set on achieving a Japanese evacuation of China up to Manchuria as a prior condition. The evacuation of the latter area would be discussed afterwards. Moreover, Japan would also have to promise not to attack Russia.[53]

Konoye's shaky government could not end the China Incident that way; and Ambassador Grew also felt this was too much to expect before even beginning negotiations, and he had been one who felt that Hull was not tough enough back in the mid-1930's. If the idea had been to bring the Japanese leaders to a willingness to compromise with the United States, then that end had been accomplished by August, 1941. Sending reports to the State Department during these months seemed to him "like throwing pebbles into a lake at night; we were not permitted to see even the ripples." [54]

Tokyo's response to the freezing order reaffirmed its position, with an added twist of fatalism: "In an atmosphere of world crisis and international confusion, it is sometimes difficult to ascertain when an event is a cause and when it is a consequence." As Grew could attest, the remark suited the occasion. But when he had presented a copy of the freezing order, such bothersome questions were put aside, and he made the point plainly: "The American freezing order in effect works along lines similar to the restrictions and handicaps which American business and trade and commerce have encountered in Japan and Japan occupied areas during the last several years." [55]

During October and November, Washington continued to stall, as Secretary Stimson put it, "so as to be sure that Japan was put in the wrong and made the first bad move—overt move," and so as to "get that big stick in readiness." [56]

Hull, fatalistically, like the Japanese Foreign Office, played out the tragedy of the Open Door Policy. "It cannot be doubted for a moment," he said, going over past ground with Nomura on October 17, that if Japan "adopts this basic policy" of peaceful change, "she will have the advantage over all countries in her area because of her geographical position, her race, and because of her business acumen." [57] Japanese leaders had by this time decided, however, that United States policy would soon strangle Japan unless a sharp blow could force the United States to let go its economic grip. It is unlikely that the more realistic leaders in Japan expected to gain more than an extended breathing space during which they could build up their defenses in depth and discourage the United States from fighting a long and difficult war.

A few Administration policy makers thought about proposing a short truce to the Japanese. At worst it would give Stimson and Knox more time; at best it might even cool off things enough so that negotiations might begin again. Stimson was adamantly against the idea; and when Roosevelt mentioned it to him, he retorted that "it has always been our historic policy since the Washington Conference not to leave the Chinese and Japanese together, because the Japanese were always able to over-shadow the Chinese and the Chinese knew it." [58]

Even so, Hull came close to making such an offer for a three month's truce on November 25, 1941. In exchange for United States resumption of limited economic relations with Japan, Tokyo was to have promised to send no more troops into areas it then occupied and not to invoke the Tripartite Pact if the United States entered the European War. Finally, the United States would "introduce" Chinese and Japanese representatives to one another, so that they could begin talks anew. The Chinese opposed the truce scheme; there was confusion in the British cabinet, and at least one negative response was received from London; and various cabinet members were against it; so that Hull and Roosevelt decided against making the offer. It may be that Hull never fully believed in the idea anyway.[59]

Hence the Secretary of State informed his two colleagues of the War and Navy Departments that "we were likely to be attacked perhaps next Monday." On November 26, the Secretary of War prepared his now famous message to the Western Defense Command: "Negotiations with Japan have been terminated without an agreement on disputed points. Japanese future action unpredictable but action possible any moment. If hostilities cannot, repeat cannot, be avoided the United States desires that Japan commit the first overt act." [60]

In the Pearl Harbor investigations, this message became an important piece of evidence. Senator Homer Ferguson pressed Sumner Welles about this decision:

> Well, do you agree that we did turn it over to the Army and the Navy on the 27th as indicated by Colonel Stimson's note or language?
> MR. WELLES: I think that is a question only Mr. Hull himself could answer.[61]

Around the possible answers to this question has spun a whirlpool of argument over American entry into World War II. This question and others like it have been debated and argued without any satisfaction and have only resulted in limiting American political thought and attitudes even today. The debate picks up the issues too late; it assumes that American policy was either narrowly moral or unmoral; it concerns itself too much with the irrelevant idea of a huge conspiracy to lead America into war; and it obscures many other issues entirely. Harry Hopkins probed to the nexus of the Japanese-American dialogue: [62]

> Apropos of the Roberts report, which indicates that the State Department had given up all hope of coming to an agreement with Japan, it seems to me that hardly squares with the facts. It is true that Hull told the Secretaries of War and Navy that he believed Japan might attack at any moment. On the other hand, up to the very last day, he undoubtedly had hopes that something could be worked out at the last moment. Hull had always been willing to work out a deal with Japan. To be sure, it was the kind of deal that Japan probably would not have accepted but, on the other hand, it was also the type of a deal which would have made us very unpopular in the Far East.

Hopkins missed the point only by failing to stress more plainly that Hull always insisted upon prior acceptance of American principles. In the ten years before Pearl Harbor, and not just from November 25, 1941, the United States feared that Japan would attack the Washington treaties, and then American interests. Tokyo's 1931 assault on the Washington treaties met an uncertain response. Stimson and Hull both hoped (along with many others) that something could be worked out. Secretary Hull was hardly as alone as Hopkins' statement would indicate in trying to achieve a settlement.

From 1931 to 1937, Washington tried logic and persuasion. The Brussels Conference demonstrated how unsatisfactory this approach had become. After that the United States firmly reasserted its position, began a series of economic measures, and kept hoping this would be enough. Japan responded with increased belligerency, and climaxed its opposition by joining the Axis Tripartite Pact. When President Roosevelt told the Japanese it was their turn to figure out ways and means of keeping the door open in Asia, the attack on Pearl Harbor was Tokyo's answer.

The year and a half between Sedan and Pearl Harbor
was an immensely creative period in foreign policy,
as creative as that earlier period at the beginning of
this century when the Atlantic and Open Door policies
were made articulate.

Forrest Davis and Ernest K. Lindley,
How War Came, 1942

Over eighty years ago Abraham Lincoln pointed out
that a nation could not endure permanently half slave
and half free. It would have to become either all
one thing or the other. Today we are forced to
recognize this truth in respect to the world at large.
That world cannot endure permanently half slave and
half free . . . .

Henry L. Stimson, June, 1940

8 · From New Deal to New Frontiers

Unwilling to see Germany and Italy establish a joint hegemony in
Europe, the United States finally plunged into the very fields of political
involvement it had hoped to avoid through neutrality.

Hitler's military challenge forced the issue. The strain of finding a
way to meet it cracked and shattered domestic political alliances, especially after the Administration called for serious rearmament in 1938.
The Progressive-Northern Democrat front fell into many fragments.
Although not all Progressives refused to follow the Administration,
many did, including some of Roosevelt's strongest allies on social legislation.

Undoubtedly many former opponents of the New Deal found the
growing emphasis on foreign affairs to their liking. The militancy of
Southern conservative Democrats has long been a feature of American
politics. The isolationist wing of Progressivism in the Republican party,
on the other hand, was much less happy at sharing a bed with the
Chicago Tribune and the Hearst Press.

Thoughtful interventionists had concluded, perhaps reluctantly, that
America could not work out its destiny in the same world with the
Axis—the world could not endure, Stimson had said in a radio address,
half-slave and half-free. Some isolationists admitted the force of this

argument, but replied that even if the country could lead a crusade against the Axis, it would surely lose its soul in the process. A few conservative isolationists, however, did not hesitate to advocate a Fortress America that would have imitated fascist economic—and perhaps later on political—methods in the Western Hemisphere. Socialists had a vision of the Western Hemisphere, too. But whatever their disagreements on the future, both believed the interventionists exaggerated the threat and that a strong America need not fear for its existence as a free nation.

This brings one to the question of New Deal shortcomings and specific failures in the recession of 1937–38. The recurrent specter of unemployment and low prices did hover over the New Dealers well into the period when the Administration was aiding the Allies with "everything short of war," but to blame this spirit's influence, at least in the narrow sense, or to call it the demon which drove Roosevelt into the war, simply is not warranted.

One of Roosevelt's ablest defenders, Basil Rauch, quite rightly pointed out that although domestic economic problems sharpened many issues, they did not make the Axis challenge "either more or less minatory." Rauch goes on, however: "Besides Roosevelt had made it clear from the beginning of his administration that the danger was real to him." Now whether one agrees with Rauch that this was the role Roosevelt essayed or not, he has raised an important question: When and for what reasons did the New Deal undertake political involvement in Europe? To answer simply in order to stop Hitler's military thrust is right but only the first cut in a probe that should go much deeper. The Anglo-American conservative poet-intellectual T. S. Eliot had some scathing words for contemporaries which represented a thoughtful corrective to the growing emotionalism of the times, but far more importantly, to the idealization of the Anglo-American Alliance after the war. He said in his *Idea of a Christian Society* (1940): "Sometimes we are almost persuaded that we are getting along very nicely, with a reform here and a reform there, and would have been getting along still better, if only foreign governments did not insist upon breaking all the rules and playing what is really a different game." [1] *

---

* The hostile reception given to A. J. P. Taylor's *Origins of the Second World War,* despite his disclaimers, which are borne out in the book, of pro-Hitlerism are evidence not only of a desire to point out his specific errors of fact and judgment, but perhaps a dangerous desire to see only the villainy of one man behind the war and to seek no more.

Whether one agrees even partially with Eliot, there is another point to be made: the years before and after World War II demonstrated that the United States regarded the defense of its liberal trade system as central to the conduct of its foreign policy and the stem of that policy's ideology. This is not to say that Americans did not regard Germany as primarily a military threat, especially after the violation of the Munich promise, but when the United States looked to the postwar world, it planned for one that was liberal economically and politically.

And of course Cordell Hull always led the Administration in linking foreign and domestic matters under the umbrella of his reciprocal trade agreements program. He remarked to Henry Stimson in 1938 that he had truly hoped to force Germany back into line through the creation of a trading bloc of twenty or thirty nations, but national economic difficulties stemming from the recession were choking both the domestic economy and his foreign economic policy.[2]

But the Secretary's troubles in pre-war years more generally resulted from an inability to sustain neutrality, matched with a reluctance to involve the United States, and though Sumner Welles and William Bullitt criticized Hull for wanting his cake and eating it too, the Secretary's attitude better typified the country as a whole.

The gold problem and the question of the Spanish Civil War were good examples of the American predicament. These were two issues among many which led American leaders to the conclusion that intervention was the only way out of the world of the 1930's, for it was impossible to accept the possibility of an Axis victory. Committed to defeating the Axis, the United States at once began postwar planning for a better world. The State Department was determined that the economic reorganization of the peace should follow the broad outlines of the Reciprocal Trade Agreements Act, and there should be no political deals between other members of the Grand Alliance to mar the vision of an open world.

NEUTRALITY BECOMES A DEAD-END STREET

Opened to their cores, the relatively peripheral gold problem and the Spanish Civil War question both display the failure of American neutrality, and therefore are representative of the kind of developments and situations that led the United States towards intervention. The former directed attention to shortcomings in the Hull program; in fact, some thought that if the gold situation was any real indication of the direction of future events, the trade program was heading nowhere. The Spanish Civil War and the key question that rose out of it, recognition of Francisco Franco's regime, created both an economic and a political issue. The Administration wanted to protect American interests in Spain and it wanted to keep Madrid separated as much as possible from Berlin and Rome, but it found it could do neither very successfully.

In an encouraging letter to the President at the end of 1937, the State Department pointed out its gains for the country as a result of significant increases in trade with Agreement countries. About the time he read this report, Roosevelt was asking Treasury Secretary Morgenthau what would become of American foreign trade if other nations followed Germany's example and left the gold standard entirely. The Secretary had no satisfactory reply.[3]

Fortune magazine had an unhappy one: "The Hull trade agreements have been a useful step in the right direction. But to open up real frontiers, under a general policy of raising the standard of living of other countries, we shall have to go much further." [4]

Treasury purchases of gold, like the Export-Import Bank, had become an adjunct to the trade agreements program. It was international pump-priming of the most obvious kind. First used in 1933 to reinflate the dollar, the Treasury's continued buying of gold put dollars into the world economy, and as Treasury expert Alvin Hansen explained, it was "a form of intensified protectionism, and, on the other hand, tend[ed] to force exports through what is known as 'exchange dumping.' " [5]

But as *Fortune* suggested, the water supply from such wells was not unlimited. Gold purchases were at best only a temporary palliative, albeit a most effective one in the 1937 recession when American exports fell only 7 per cent despite a drop in imports of over 36 per cent. The preservation of this "favorable balance of trade" owed much to the billion and a half dollars the Treasury sent into the world economy in exchange for gold.[6]

But the more gold that the United States drew off in this way, loaded into truck caravans, and carted off to Federal Reserve banks or Fort Knox, the less other nations had to sell. South African mines were pressed to keep up with the demand. By the end of the 1930's America owned more than 60 per cent of the world's gold. "Here we are," quipped Tom Lamont, "sitting on top of this heap of gold with nowhere to go with it, unless we can encourage foreign trade." But, and almost as an afterthought, he added, "There are no frontiers to the mind and genius of the American people." Yet the practical question of how to increase world trade in an Axis-dominated situation, which was at the base of Roosevelt's question to Morgenthau, remained to be answered. Nor could it be until American political involvement opened new frontiers.[7]

Perched on top of this less and less valuable and more and more exposed heap of gold, the Administration was also an open target for critics of its Spanish policy. Liberal malcontents scornfully referred to it as intervention by nonintervention. And Herbert Feis later agreed: "The governments of the Allies came, in the midst of war, to rue their consent to Franco's victory." [8]

Before the Spanish dictator's victory, the United States had followed England and France in their efforts to keep the Spanish Civil War just that and not the beginning of a final showdown with Germany and Italy. After the Republic was crushed, the State Department was chagrined at its inability to restore satisfactory relations with Madrid. Once again German and Italian influence seemed to stand in the way politically and to encourage Franco to imitate fascist autarchy. This was especially galling because the Department had allowed commercial agents from Franco's forces to come to American ports "for the purpose of validating shipping documents and hence helping our trade . . . ." [9]

A number of businessmen had very badly wanted renewed trade relations with Spain even before Franco's victory had become assured. Representatives of the National Foreign Trade Council called at the Department to make a final plea that the Administration get in "on the ground floor after Franco wins." [10]

A special conference considered such pleas on March 24, 1939. Department officials decided that the right thing to do would be to recognize Franco in "two or three days, partly because our business interests demand it, partly because it is vital to all to maintain American control over all communications between Europe and Latin America which center in Spain; [and] partly because we and Soviet Russia alone have not recognized the inevitable—an embarrassing partnership." [11]

As soon as recognition had been granted, the National Foreign Trade Council's spokesmen were right back with suggestions for an Export-Import Bank loan to Spain—based, significantly, upon the example of new loans to Brazil. These businessmen thought that such a loan would not only stimulate a resurrection of Spanish-American trade but also release blocked American credits. State Department officers were somewhat piqued at learning that they had already contacted the Commerce Department and the Export-Import Bank. Moreover, the Agriculture Department also seemed to be out in front of the State Department (despite its leadership by the "liberal" Henry Wallace) because it wished to dispose of surplus cotton and keep in touch with Spanish markets for the future. The State Department wanted to achieve political results before making any such loan.[12]

Sumner Welles was able to use the potential Export-Import Bank credit as a lever to pry out of the Spanish ambassador promises concerning the release of Americans who had been imprisoned during the Civil War for serving in the Republican army, the return of International Telephone and Telegraph officials to Spain, and a "firm guarantee," which the ambassador personally initialed, that "American business would be treated in Spain on the basis of equality and in accordance with the principles of international law." [13]

But once again, without American participation in a more direct fashion, relations between a European nation and Washington never became satisfactory. The attempt to bribe Franco away from Hitler and Mussolini only partially succeeded, though he did stay out of the war. International Telephone and Telegraph quarreled with the Franco government over the terms of its future participation in that country, and it took a good deal of State Department pressure to solve that question. Indeed, a retiring Spanish Ambassador thanked the Department for making it plain that return of American properties "was the central and vital issue." [14]

THE ADMINISTRATION ACCEPTS THE CHALLENGE

The central and vital domestic issue, said a group of experts for the Brookings Institution, was the evidence they found to demonstrate that the New Deal had actually destroyed the confidence necessary to promote expansion. America's economic malaise could not be overcome so long as the "combined savings made by insurance companies and savings institutions . . . were more than three times the value of corporate bond and note issues" as had happened in the 1937–38 recession.[15]

Practically all conservatives shared or sympathized with the Brookings Institution findings. It was plain enough to them that the New Deal had undermined the venturesome spirit of American capitalism.

Roosevelt admitted the difficulties, but he and the New Dealers considered that the monopolists and malefactors of great wealth were pursuing deliberately restrictive policies in an attempt to regain control of the Government. On March 4, 1938, the President described the situation in straight and simple language: "We have fifteen or twenty million Americans in this country who today have no purchasing power. There are fifteen or twenty million Americans falling into that category." [16]

A month later the President formally launched the Second New Deal (some call it the Third) as his counterattack against the recession and his enemies of the Left and the Right. Led by Solicitor Robert Jackson and Harry Hopkins, it was designed to be a two-pronged maneuver. Jackson was to join the Temporary National Economic Committee's fight against monopolists, while Hopkins officially introduced Keynesian deficit spending as Administration policy.[17]

Even as they initiated this attack on the country's domestic economic problems, Roosevelt's advisers were becoming more and more disturbed by the external threat and both consciously and unconsciously comparing and sometimes linking the two in ways that Cordell Hull had done in his discussion with Henry Stimson. One can speculate forever on this matter and never reach solid ground, but the methods a few of these advisers used to bring the problem into focus can be set forth in some detail.

We begin with Harry Hopkins. Hopkins was given a new job in the fall of 1938. As a possible successor, Roosevelt wanted him to dispel notions of his radicalism by accepting and serving well in the position of Secretary of Commerce. Secretary Hopkins did make a good impression, though illness kept his actual participation in Department matters at a below-normal level. Later, as a trusted lieutenant in the fight against the Axis, Hopkins further succeeded in obtaining the backing and confidence of the Dollar-a-year Men as well as many others in the business community.

In the Congressional hearing on his nomination to the Commerce Department post, the former relief administrator defended the PWA and the WPA appropriations by pointing out that during the 1937 recession the nation had suffered the sharpest drop in employment in any "period of time that has ever occurred in our history." But as befitted his new assignment, Hopkins declared that "business must succeed and must be able to work with Government, if our economic system is to be preserved." The New Deal was already on the statute books, he told newsmen on March 8, 1939, and if the low 62 billion dollar gross national product were to grow into a prosperous 80 or 90 billion, the Government was going to have to aid business on "101 fronts." "With 12 million unemployed, we are socially bankrupt and politically unstable." [18]

Speaking in his home state of Iowa, the Commerce Secretary pledged himself to business recovery: "This country cannot continue as a democracy with 10,000,000 or 12,000,000 unemployed. It just can't be done. We have got to find a way of living in America in which every person in it shares in the national income, in such a way, that poverty in America is abolished." [19]

From the Commerce Department's Business Advisory Council, Hopkins received reports and recommendations on domestic affairs which served also to focus attention on new trade outlets in Latin America and other world markets. He attended White House Conferences where he and these men, as he told newsmen, had "some very considerable discussion of foreign trade . . . ." [20]

When fused with his own ideas on the Nazi menace, these influences found their way into speech drafts and remarks such as the following:

> We must also recognize that today foreign trade is being used by some countries as a vehicle to support political and cultural penetration. Unless we acquiesce in such penetration, we must be prepared through the adoption and use of national powers to meet quality, quantity and price on such a basis as to get the business.[21]

For Hopkins, the Axis challenge was a very real threat no matter what sort of ideology spawned it.

Adolf Berle had rebelled against resurgent trust-busting, yet his opposition to this "hole in the program" came at a time when domestic differences in the Administration were being subordinated to the international question. One should not neglect Berle's criticisms of the Second New Deal and their revelation about his worried state of mind because they contrasted so sharply with his views once the United States had chosen to oppose the Axis. Testifying before the TNEC, the former Brain Truster said that if the country had truly come to the point where creation of wealth was demanded as "a function of the government . . . the choice should be the considered choice of the country and not the result of a policy of drift." Even more pointedly he wrote Roosevelt: "The paramount necessity now is to do some thinking at least one lap ahead of the obvious financial and industrial crisis, which is plainly indicated within the next few years." [22]

Like Hopkins, Berle had great fears for the future in these months, and also like Hopkins he was familiar with the external threat. When he prepared a speech for the President after the Munich Conference in September, 1938, the adviser described darkly the dangers of a world dominated by fear and the sword; then he justified "the need for re-armament unless there were honest disarmament." Roosevelt looked at this draft and put in a strengthening paragraph to dramatize Berle's points "in a way which left little doubt that the line of demarcation between democracy and Nazism was one which could not be bridged or marked by a high wall with each side keeping his ideas to himself without interference from the other." [23]

In sober discussions with the President and Sumner Welles during these months, as it became more and more obvious that appeasement had failed, Berle prophesied gloomily that an Axis victory would isolate America in "the unfortunate position of an old-fashioned general store in a town full of hard-bitten chains." The only alternative would soon be all-out aid to the democracies to prevent a total Axis victory.[24]

When the war did come, Berle wondered if there were another choice, wondered if it would be possible to prepare a Fortress America against a Russo-German Europe. Such plans ran against the "process of men's minds," but eventually, in years, this domination would break up. "But they will be ghastly years." [25]

So Berle concluded that a Fortress America was not really a possibility to be preferred to a dramatic showdown with the Axis. "I could wish," he then impatiently wrote Stimson, "that the country were a little more interested in preparedness than it appears to be." An associate in the State Department recorded Berle's "lurid picture" of the British fleet being driven out of Gibraltar even back as far as Canada, and behind it Hitler menacing the whole Western Hemisphere. Against this dark vision, Berle tried to build up a crusading spirit, said the observer.[26]

J. P. Moffat feared that this spirit had too great a hold on another colleague, Assistant Secretary of State George Messersmith. He had allowed his anti-Hitlerism to fill his thinking about American foreign trade. Messersmith had first tied these two up, it will be recalled, back in 1933. Now he pointed to Hitlerism as a time-bomb not only in Europe, but also in America. "How futile it is to believe and to argue, as some still do," he declared before the National Foreign Trade Convention in 1938, "that a value of trade such as this [six billion dollars] does not have a vital bearing upon our internal life and upon the standard of living of our population." The year before, he had advised this export-minded group: "There is practically no phase of the relationship between states in this day in which economic factors do not enter . . . ." Every day, the Department worked on problems intimately concerned "with our whole economic structure . . . ." [27]

Messersmith opposed any sort of deal with Germany which might compromise American trade principles and/or allow Berlin to obtain money for armaments. He, Francis Sayre, and Cordell Hull thought alike on this problem. On February 18, 1938, Hull forwarded one of his memorandums to Roosevelt. After outlining the difficulties the United States would come up against if England and France fell before Germany, he continued: "our troubles" will "come a little later" and that thought "does not give me any comfort." Already Germany's advancing forces had left little "prospect for our progress in Southeastern Europe." And to give the aggressor a free hand there would be to give him one everywhere. [28]

Secretary Hull had also spoken to the 1938 Foreign Trade Convention, and his words complemented Messersmith's message. When nations like Germany and Japan reject orderly trade practices and patterns, first comes regimentation, then preparations for war. The Secretary brought a new aide into the Department at this time, the well-known author and publicist George Fort Milton, to help older aides in the public campaign for the reciprocal trade agreements program as the best protection against domestic regimentation and foreign trade aggression. "We are confronted with a choice," read one of Milton's letters to a former president of the United States Chamber of Commerce, "between a healthy competitive economy linked to a freely functioning international market, and a regimented economy operating on the basis of federal subsidies and quotas, in accordance with the principles of self-containment." [29]

Other advisers were convinced, along with *Fortune,* that the trade agreements program could never do the job without American leadership in the Grand Alliance. Always among the first to make the leap from thought to action, Henry Wallace spoke for stronger action in his new book, *The American Choice* (1940): If the nation were to prevent intolerable increases in unemployment, it had to invest monies and export goods totaling at least four billion dollars each year. "I think we ought to face the fact that with a Hitler controlling the exports, imports and exchanges, it is impossible to get an adequate outflow of exports from the United States, and that an increase of governmental intervention is inevitable." [30]

To Roosevelt's quickening interest in the task of stopping Hitler's advances, Hull's methodical presentations and cautious maneuvers appeared inadequate (even though the Secretary seemed to have a pretty free hand in Asia); yet the Secretary sensed a more sympathetic interest in his work and goals emanating from the White House at this very time. He was confirmed in this belief when the President ordered Cabinet officers to become familiar with a speech Hull had delivered before the Farm Bureau Federation on December 5, 1939. Looking ahead for a moment, the spirit and even the letter of the President's declaration of a national emergency on May 27, 1941, were in perfect accord with Hull's general view. There were always alternatives to a showdown with the Axis, Roosevelt said, but:

> Tariff walls—Chinese walls of isolation—would be futile. Freedom to trade is essential to our economic life. We do not eat all the food we can produce; and we do not burn all the oil we can pump; we do not use all the goods we can manufacture. It would not be an American wall to keep Nazi goods out; it would be a Nazi wall to keep us in. [31]

Although this quotation is typical of his speech, it should be pointed out that Roosevelt obviously tried to pick out arguments that would demonstrate American self-interest in the fight against Hitlerism. They were not necessarily his own views, though other evidence would indicate they were. Even if they were not, it is significant to see what kinds of arguments he used to make his point.

GROWING SUPPORT FOR INTERVENTION
OUTSIDE THE ADMINISTRATION

American public opinion on foreign affairs had separated into an antipodal structure by the time of this speech. The extremes were defined in the Committee to Defend America by Aiding the Allies, and by its opposite, the America First Committee.

Among the leading interventionist voices was that of the *New York Times,* which editorialized on the Hull trade agreements in even better style than the Secretary himself. The RTA program had become the best protection against "some form of totalitarianism" erupting in America. It had been Germany's loss of foreign markets which had forced that unhappy country to Nazism—and (significantly enough) had been the key factor in forcing the United States to try the NRA and AAA experiments, concluded the editor.[32] The lesson was obvious.

During the war, *Times* publisher Arthur H. Sulzberger looked back on the immediate prewar years and stated his belief that the United States had consciously chosen war "because we knew that our future could not be as we had mapped it unless we halted the aggressor as quickly as we could." [33]

Sulzberger was reviewing a complex and emotional era but *Fortune's* 1940 poll of executive opinion revealed at that time how divided and uncertain American business leaders were over the advisability of trading with the German economic bloc, and also how sure over 60 per cent of them were that America had to maintain and expand its foreign trade. Nearly half predicted a totalitarian reorganization of business if Hitler were to win the war. This magazine had recently reported a sudden shift in business opinion after the outbreak of war in Europe and the November, 1939, repeal of the arms embargo of the Neutrality Act. "For a time the easychair conversations in the Union League Club sounded like a conference of Administration whips. Indeed, the broad shift in business's attitude toward Roosevelt was almost as phenomenal as the get-together of Nazis and Soviets." Itself an able molder of public opinion, this magazine had several times gone on record in favor of "Mr. Hull's trade policy" both in editorials and in letters by the editor to President Roosevelt. Thirty-two of fifty newspapers polled in one survey and eighty-eight out of 120 in another favored a repeal of the arms embargo.[34]

Another Hull booster and sometime participant in New Deal diplomacy was Tom Lamont, who observed that the editors of the more cautious *Collier's* had the greatest respect for the trade program; and Lamont early offered his services to help repeal the arms embargo, as did other like-minded economic leaders. They felt as Bernard Baruch did, who later recalled that his differences with the New Deal were "submerged in my growing awareness of an imminent danger as the troubled thirties drew to a close"; or as W. Averell Harriman did, who wrote Roosevelt of his personal admiration and that of "my friends in industry and finance upon your masterful handling of our foreign policy"; or, finally, as did Wendell Willkie, who warned the Indiana Bankers Association that a German victory in Europe would endanger the American "system of free enterprise." [35]

Congress reflected this growing desire for an interventionist foreign policy, concluded an observer from the State Department who watched President Roosevelt issue a call for an end to the arms embargo. The applause at every place where the President declared his intention to keep out of war was equaled every time he mentioned the "cash and carry" amendment, which, said this officer of the Department sardonically, was "immensely popular with the Congressmen who had just returned from their districts." Senator Key Pittman could not have given a more direct explanation of this feeling: "The condition with regard to industry and labor in this country today is so deplorable that further obstructions to our exports would bankrupt large sections of our country." [36]

And Secretary Stimson could affirm from his new position in the War Department that "cash and carry" was successful in the period before Lend-Lease. Between 1938 and 1940, he noted in his War Diary, $1,400,000,000 were spent in the United States for war materials. "The vast majority of people and of Congress saw the need for these orders, financed by foreign capital and developing American industry, and believed the United States safeguarded from war by the Neutrality Act." [37]

This was what had become of the neutrality debate of the 1930's: Americans deceived themselves into thinking that they were protected from war and were able to gather up the profits from the belligerents. Other Americans were so convinced that their country had to enter the war either for self-protection or for self-interest, or for a combination of both and morality, that they went along with or even encouraged the deception. The Business Advisory Council was sure of one thing: "An enlargement of our opportunities for trade and investment in foreign countries *is now essential* to maximum national prosperity" (emphasis in original). Self-containment with its regulations and controls would destroy "free enterprise and . . . the democratic processes which we prize so highly." [38]

Another semi-official business group, the newly formed Committee for Economic Development, pointed out to Undersecretary of Commerce Jesse Jones that the "importance of foreign trade" had to be considered of fundamental interest to the nation. On the other hand, many businessmen, while desiring foreign trade, thought Roosevelt's foreign policies were as bad as his domestic ones. But the isolationist Senator Burton K. Wheeler was dismayed to find in his travels around the country that so "many of the Chambers of Commerce, and Lions Clubs, and other organizations are for doing everything short of war." [39]

An Administration complaint in late 1940—that the "business people of the country," though enjoying the benefits of cash and carry, were still slumbering and unaware of their responsibilities for the Defense Program and the sacrifices they would be called upon to make—was probably only too accurate. Ironically, the defense effort had temporarily reversed the basic economic problem of the 1930's. Instead of overproduction, the Administration found itself trying to pull more out of the American economy. Alarmed by the slow reaction of American productive machinery to this crisis, Roosevelt concerned himself as late as August, 1941, with the task of getting the meaning of the defense program "down to the little man of America." [40]

Rousing American economic leaders to meet this production problem was difficult in part because of the President's own soothing assurances that America was not going into any foreign wars unless attacked. As Stimson had explained, cash and carry was supposed to free the country instead of involving it. Then, too, there was a well-justified fear abroad in the nation that the surpluses would come back as soon as the war was over. Roosevelt was thinking "about this matter" and informed an adviser that he was determined that "there shall be no depression of prices after the war." But this kind of assurance did not dispel the doubts about the defense boom. "The defense effort," wrote Bruce Catton in *War Lords of Washington,* "was rather like a brand new baby, which—for all anybody could predict—might grow up to be either a horse thief or a clergyman." [41]

Isolationists argued that it would be worse than a horse thief. They contended that the United States did not have to participate in a foreign war to preserve political democracy and free enterprise. Sears Roebuck's forceful leader, General Robert Woods, spoke for the America First Committee before the Council on Foreign Relations and offered their views:

> Americans like myself feel that our true mission is in North and South America. We stand today in an unrivaled position. With our resources and organizing ability we can develop, with our Canadian friends, an only partially developed continent like South America. . . . I think we

should also make it clearly understood that no government in Mexico, Central America and the Caribbean South American countries will be tolerated unless it is friendly to the United States and that if necessary we are prepared to use force to attain that object.[42]

The first real test between these two points of view came when the Administration called upon Congress in January, 1938, for a two-ocean navy. Thus began the debate which lasted until the passage of Lend-Lease.

THE LAST GREAT DEBATE BEGINS—
AMERICAN NAVAL POLICY

Three days before the end of 1937, President Roosevelt sent an open letter to the chairman of the Senate Subcommittee on Naval Appropriations. He began with a reference to the European arms buildup. "I have used every conceivable effort to stop this trend, and to work toward a decrease of armaments. Facts, nevertheless, are facts, and the United States must recognize them." It was likely, therefore, that he would soon request new ship construction.[43]

Within the month came the expected request for authorizing the construction of six new battleships and stand-by authorization of an additional twelve. When completed, this program would provide a two-ocean navy. Admiral Leahy's testimony has already been cited in another place, but to present the framework once more, Leahy had said that United States naval policy was designed to support the Monroe Doctrine, to protect American nationals abroad, to protect American shipping, and to protect American territory, including island possessions, against invasion. He had also said: "At the present time it is the national policy to protect our commerce." [44]

When the floor debate began, several unhappy congressmen demanded to know just how far the Administration would go to support these national policies, and to what extent was America's rearmament tied to Great Britain's foreign policy.[45]

Senator Robert Reynolds had joined the issue on January 6, 1938, insisting that "the time has come when the American people should interest themselves in America first, last, and all the time." The nation should seek foreign markets in Latin America and stop fooling around in the Orient and in Europe. Senator Harry S. Truman rose to give the answer: China's troubles with Japan came from the "very policy which the Senator is now advocating for America, that is, to live within them-

selves, and not have communications with the rest of the world . . . ."
Truman's rejoinder seems all the more significant if it be kept in mind
that Reynolds had not called for total isolation.[46]

Two western senators returned to the attack with a different maneuver;
they cited Roosevelt and Hull for the prosecution of the noninterventionist
case. Colorado's Edwin Johnson quoted a 1928 speech by Roosevelt
which had raised the "pertinent question" why Congress was being
called upon to authorize ships to be built "next year and the year after,
and the year after that." "This brings the naval question," Johnson
continued, quoting from Roosevelt, "out of the realm of our immediate
naval needs and into the realm of diplomatic juggling." [47]

Homer T. Bone of Washington scored Hull's notion of "our interests"
in the Far East as the Secretary had enumerated them in an address to
the National Press Club. "When there are ten or twelve million idle people
in this country," charged the Senator, "to prate about 'our interests'
in China is both dangerous and useless." [48]

Administration spokesman Senator David Walsh of Massachusetts
replied simply that America no less than Great Britain had interests in
all parts of the world. "It is estimated by our experts that unless we are
able to keep open certain trade routes the United States of America
could not maintain itself for more than 2 years without being defeated by
a powerful enemy."

Walsh went on: "The Federal Government may give up everything
else, but it cannot give up the lives of its people and its property. It
must have a navy! And it is only a question of what kind of a navy and
what size navy we must have. The navy is our police force. It is our
fire department. It is our protection. It is our life." [49]

Though the Administration won this point easily enough, the isolationists
rose up again in the 1941 Lend-Lease debate. Before moving to
that, however, the concomitant reconstruction of the merchant marine
should be described, since it has gone pretty much unnoticed—a circumstance
that is particularly unfortunate, for the basic arguments and
logic were the same as for military or naval rearmament: the necessity
to maintain trade routes against any Axis attempts to dominate the
seas.

As far back as the fall of 1936, Roosevelt had informed Michigan
Senator James Couzens of the plight of the American merchant marine;
it had suffered a series of ups and downs since the 1840's: "What I need
and what the country needs is a fearless Chairman of the Maritime Com-

mission, who will take the responsibility in setting up and putting through a new and permanent Mercantile Marine policy." [50]

He soon found his man in Admiral Emory S. Land. Reviewing his first years as Chairman of the Commission since 1937, Land said that the United States had by 1941 come a long way in building merchant shipping so that "the productivity of American farms and factories" would not again "lapse into the inactivity which followed the last World War and plunged our nation into economic distress." To that end the government had by 1941 committed $1,750,000,000 to the Maritime Commission, and it expected to receive still another $1,250,000,000 for the construction of "two ships a day for each of the next two years." In 1944 a Congressional Committee on Post-War Policies asked Land why the merchant marine had once been so weak. Land's reply said much about the intellectual development of American foreign policy: "Primarily Horace Greeley's maxim, 'Go West, young man.' We cannot go West anymore." [51]

Senator Royal Copeland defended a Maritime Commission appropriation in 1938 by arguing that even if the merchant marine was not self-supporting and even if the Treasury had to keep pouring funds into it, ". . . who can question that it is part of wisdom for the United States of America, having a surplus of American products and a surplus of manufactured products to create services in South America which would eventually lead to increased exports?" [52]

Land and Copeland had developed a theme which was taken over with only a minor variation by an interventionist speaker at a rally in May, 1941: "It is a corner stone of American destiny that the seas be free . . . ; they will not be free under Hitler's domination. The lifeline of our country is the sea routes leading variously throughout the world. They must be preserved so that the productivity of American genius may further enrich the world and inspire all friendly nations to the greater effort in the ways of better living." And for a coda there was Admiral Land's exuberant declaration: "Does Hitler really think he can stop us?" [53]

THE LAST GREAT DEBATE ENDS—LEND-LEASE

The State Department first greeted the Munich Pact with a "sigh of relief and pleasure," though only a few in that department thought that a chance would now arise for "real appeasement on sound economic foundations." [54]

But, *pro forma,* the Department kept up its pressure to bring Germany back into line, and goods from the Sudeten area were separated from those coming from the rest of Czechoslovakia. A few months later, countervailing duties were reimposed on all German goods. The German chargé told Sumner Welles that the duties would upset his government. "To this I made no reply," Welles recorded coldly. The German diplomat then reported to Berlin that Secretary Hull believed that all political problems were capable of an economic solution. "The preponderance of the economic over the political is the result of the involvement of American commerce with the whole world," cabled the German. "Hence the national interest of America is in the greatest possible encouragement of international trade and in the maintenance of peace. She feels that both are threatened by the totalitarian powers." [55]

As 1939 began, the Administration was indeed responding to this dual threat. Rearmament continued, of course, and the President launched a campaign, not successful until November, to repeal the arms embargo; he also took personal responsibility for selling military airplanes to the French government. When a public storm arose over this issue, Roosevelt called the Senate Foreign Relations Committee to a White House conference, where he tried to satisfy his critics among them and in the nation. He discussed the world in geopolitical terms: If "one nation dominates Europe, that nation will be able to turn the world sphere." The current struggle was one "between different kinds of economies"— between the have nations and the have-nots.[56]

"Why dammit," exclaimed Secretary Hull about this time, "these nations have told us again and again what they mean to do . . . . If they succeed, we will have to transact our business with the rest of the world through Tokyo and Berlin." [57]

In March, Hitler moved his legions all the way into Czechoslovakia. The American President asked Hitler and Mussolini to guarantee the rest of Europe that there would be no more territorial rearrangements. If Berlin and Rome would do that, then "the United States would be prepared to take part in discussions looking towards the most practical manner of opening up avenues of international trade to the end that every nation of the earth may be enabled to buy and sell on equal terms in the world market as well as to possess assurance of obtaining the materials and products of peaceful economic life." Hitler laughed; Mussolini sarcastically called it "a result of progressive paralysis." [58]

On September 1, German armies rolled into Poland and the war began.

Within three months, Congress had repealed the arms embargo and the United States was selling war goods and munitions to the Allies. If only to keep the record straight, the President sent Sumner Welles to Europe the following spring to see if there was any basis at all for a negotiated peace. Welles found none.

Traveling to the capitals of each belligerent, Welles repeated the President's long-standing economic offers. In Berlin the German Foreign Minister reasserted his country's claim to close economic and political ties with Central Europe, but more ominous was the dark declaration which stayed in Welles's mind that the United States should not "forget that one thousand years ago German Emperors had been crowned in Prague." [59]

Without doubt the Lend-Lease discussion and debate climaxed the Great Debate over foreign policy in the 1930's. It was Welles's answer to the German foreign minister, and it was the nation's decision to oppose the Axis—and to make a commitment to that goal. At the end of 1940 Great Britain declared that its dollar supplies had fallen too low to permit further purchases on the cash and carry plan. Even if there were some differences of opinion about this claim, and some downright skepticism, everyone in the Administration accepted the broad conclusion that if aid to Britain was essential to victory over the Axis, then it had to be given. On December 18, 1940, the British government was told to go ahead and place orders totaling over three billion dollars; a way would be found to pay for them. [60]

House Resolution 1776 was introduced in January, 1941, to provide that way. Administration spokesmen explained that this Lend-Lease idea and its fulfillment was fully as vital to American security as the creation of the army and navy at the time of independence. Navy Secretary Knox referred also to another historic time and act—the Monroe Doctrine of 1823—and he said that for 118 years that Doctrine had prevented non-American military and political intervention in the Western Hemisphere. It had been "enunciated for preserving the territorial, economic, and social integrity of the United States." Germany threatened that integrity and had to be stopped. [61]

Secretary of War Stimson described Lend-Lease as a "skillful Yankee bargain." To begin with, Great Britain had already spent over 605 million dollars in cash and had thereby provided "our manufacturers working capital with which to build factories and take care of her orders." Consequently, England had contributed "vitally" to our productive capacity. And finally, since management of the new aid program would always be in American hands, it would make for a coordinated and effective war effort.[62]

Before workers in the offices of the War Department, the Secretary called it unprecedented and magnificent realism. Furthermore, if anyone asked them if Congress' war-making power had been bypassed, his personal reply would be, "Congress has declared war to this extent at least." And the President reportedly told the Polish Ambassador on March 6, 1941: "We Americans will have to buy this war as such. Let us hope at the price of Lend-Lease only. But who can say what price we may ultimately have to pay?" [63]

Acting partly upon the momentum supplied by the passage of Lend-Lease, President Roosevelt now began that last series of "complicated maneuvers" which revisionist-minded historians have so belabored. And it is noteworthy that even Secretary Stimson considered the April, 1941, decision to order the navy to report German ship movements to the world a "disingenuous" means of supporting British convoys: "I wanted him to be honest with himself. To me it seems a clearly hostile act to the Germans and I am prepared to take the responsibility of it." Roosevelt may have assumed that Hitler still did not want to risk a shooting war with the United States even after this "clearly hostile act." Nonetheless, Stimson was justly worried about the President's haphazard approach to such an important matter of peace and war. This sterile debate on Roosevelt's personal morality, though barely relevant, has thus taken precedence over the political economy of American foreign policy.[64]

Incidents did occur on the Atlantic between German and American ships, but war came from the other direction. On September 11 the President told the American people in a "fireside chat" about the decision to convoy Lend-Lease ships to England. For if the Axis won, he said, the "Atlantic Ocean which has been, and which should always be, a free and friendly highway for us would then become a deadly menace to the commerce of the United States, to the coasts of the United States and even to the inland cities of the United States." [65]

TURNING THE CHALLENGE INTO OPPORTUNITY

Planning for the postwar period had already begun; the Atlantic Conference between Roosevelt and Churchill, for example, was divided into strategy sessions on how to deal with Germany and forestall Japan and sessions devoted to more long-range matters, such as the disarmament of the aggressors and prospects for continuing the Anglo-American alliance.

A letter from former President Herbert Hoover to Secretary Hull in March, 1941, typified the American mood in approaching these problems. Though discredited by the New Dealers and turned down by the voters, Hoover's summary of the alternatives before the United States, like his earlier one in 1933, ably outlined the situation: "The passage of the Lend-Lease Act obviously involves us deeply in the consequences of the war. But it also gives our government a measure of responsibility to see that the policies pursued by the British are in the interest of both winning the war and winning a peace, and in the interests of the United States." Hoover was particularly worried that the British food blockade "negatived" all the principles England had advanced in war propaganda against fascism. These were exactly the same arguments Mr. Hoover had advanced to Woodrow Wilson just after World War I when he described how Central Europe was "rumbling with social explosion" and on the verge of "total collapse." Then, as in 1941, Hoover sought to "use food control to aid in winning the war and the peace and in the special interest of the United States." [66]

Great Britain would have to follow policies not incompatible with American plans, it was contended: "No help to Germany," one State Department official said in September, 1939, "but no dominion status for ourselves." Most of the officers in the Department suspected that London wanted to organize a huge trading orbit after the war, to the exclusion of American interests.[67]

Compared to the protests and sanctions against Germany before the United States entered the war, those sent to Great Britain were mild and they could have been simply for the record, but past experience with British trade policies made them more important than that. Indeed, they were like Woodrow Wilson's protests against British naval policies before American entrance into World War I, which he tried to eliminate in the Fourteen Points. "This Government has made it clear," read a typical protest against restrictions on American exports to British Africa, "that it attaches the highest importance to the sanctity of treaties and that violations of treaty rights wherever they occur tend to spread still further the forces of disorder." [68]

In plainer language still, Secretary of Commerce Hopkins reported to the Cabinet on April 4, 1940: "There is no doubt that relative to our pre-September position we stand to increase our net exports because of the war." Since the British were being forced to buy more from the United States, "We are, of course, in a position to exercise considerable influence upon [them] in decisions of policy which affect us." [69]

Lend-Lease was the best lever to use to achieve this goal, and from the beginning the State Department wanted to use it to pry open the Ottawa Agreements. These developments will be considered in a later chapter; suffice it here to indicate that President Roosevelt thought a framework agreement on Lend-Lease repayment should be made first, while the details could be left to continuing negotiations.[70]

Sumner Welles tried to establish such a framework at the Atlantic Conference, and he and Roosevelt spent much time on their way to meet Churchill discussing the problem of opening trade so that underdeveloped countries could help themselves and increase their standards of living. The more prosperous nations would then enjoy the reciprocal benefit of larger foreign markets for their goods. Without the cooperation of the British Empire this was useless talk, and Welles realized it clearly. Lord Halifax, the British Ambassador to the United States, confirmed that Roosevelt had spoken "earnestly" to Churchill about economic matters and noted that the President and Welles seemed worried already about a possible rebirth of isolationism in America. Halifax gave it as his opinion that the two American leaders were determined to have a share in "moulding and running the world" after the war.[71]

A key example of this determination was Washington's flat opposition to Anglo-Russian preliminary attempts to define possible spheres of influence in Europe. This question was touched on at the Atlantic Conference, but the very urge to join with the British in making a generalized postwar statement like the Atlantic Charter had come partly from Roosevelt's concern about Churchill's unilateral pronouncements on the postwar world. On July 14, for instance, the President had sent a message to the Prime Minister disclosing his interest in "rumors regarding trades or deals" in Anglo-Russian talks. He asked for a public statement from London, which he would then back up, reassuring the world that "no post-war peace commitments as to territories, populations or economics have been given." The Atlantic Charter was just such a statement.[72]

American leaders decided from 1938 to 1941 that the country could not achieve its destiny in a closed world dominated by the Axis. Having gone that far with its assumptions, the Administration had to accept political commitments, not only for the war period but also in order to restore an open world society. The doubts and uncertainties since 1933 in European policy were gone; World War II provided a new chance to reshuffle for another "deal" both in domestic and in foreign policy.

In this changed world and in a changed mood, Adolf Berle felt exhilarated about the future: "There is no need to fear. Rather, we shall have an opportunity to create the most brillant economic epoch the U.S. has yet seen. It is entirely feasible to make the country at once more prosperous and more free than it has ever been. And . . . without sacrificing any of the essential freedoms." [73]

Berle's new optimism presupposed (perhaps unconsciously) the extension of American commitments far beyond anything in American diplomacy before 1941. Were Americans up to that challenge as well as to the lesser, immediate one?

We could not alienate them in the Orient and expect
to work with them in Europe.

Cordell Hull, *Memoirs,* 1948

The fourth objective of the trusteeship system—
"equal treatment in social, economic and commercial
matters for all members of the United Nations and
their nationals"—seeks to establish in all trusteeship
areas sound economic foundations for world peace.
Here, again, another distinctively American ideal, expressed at various times as the Open Door policy, is
made a binding obligation in all trust territories.

Francis Sayre, 1947

9 · America and the
Colonial Empires

Political leadership in the anti-Axis Alliance suddenly brought the
United States into new and sometimes uncomfortably close relations
with the colonial empires of its allies. The British, French, and Dutch
empires were rocked by Japanese successes, starved because of German
victories, and inhabited by peoples who had just discovered that the
white man was not invincible.

America's historic dissociation from European rulers, and its own
revolutionary heritage, had created reservoirs of good will in Asia and
Africa. Native leaders, and potential revolutionaries, from these places
had studied with admiration the thoughts and deeds of the first American revolutionaries, Tom Paine and George Washington, along with
those of the next century, Henry Thoreau and Abraham Lincoln.

The image of America which they carried back to their fellows was
generally happy, one on which Americans liked to pride themselves.
How crushing, then, that so many Asians and Africans held up to
America after World War II a new image in which Uncle Sam had
become corroded and evil. Communist propaganda! This was the easiest
answer, and of course a valid one, as far as it went; but it, too, brought
up the sticky matter of how communist influence had replaced America's revolutionary image.

One group of sophisticated neo-orthodox liberals has held that this was part of the Irony of American History: there never was an America (or any nation of mortals) so pure or so innocent. Liberals at home who had believed this and expected perfection and those abroad who wished for perfect understanding from the United States had both misread the Nature and Destiny of Man.

This explanation and similar ones from later State Department and academic realists offered a general view of man but often begged the specific question. Even if one believes that any American response to the colonial question could not have won over Asian nations, as I am inclined to believe, this does not change the fact that American leaders never met the issue squarely. Moreover, during the war and after, even those sophisticates who had adopted neo-orthodox views often did exactly what they cautioned others not to do—they saw things in absolutes of black and white. The Devil's imprint appeared most plainly, for example, upon European colonial rulers. This taint was particularly evident in monopolistic privileges or imperial preference systems. Americans considered such relationships both unholy and unhealthy: unholy for the colonies and unhealthy for American interests. Their own Open Door Policy, by promoting equality of treatment for all nations, was obviously much superior—the American record in the Philippines proved it beyond doubt.

When it came time to advance proposals for a United Nations trusteeship system, Washington tried to include this policy as its fundamental approach despite the obvious limitations imposed by the need to work with the European rulers during the war and afterwards. *Fortune* had its own version of this new proposal, clearly and satirically expressed as a plea for a new imperialism. "American imperialism can afford to complete the work the British started; instead of salesmen and planters, its representatives can be brains and bulldozers, technicians and machine tools. American imperialism does not need extraterritoriality; it can get along better in Asia if the tuans and sahibs stay home. . . . So long as Asia does not try to foist an economic feudalism of the Jap type on its neighbors, the U.S. can believe in Asia-for-the-Asiatics too." In almost one long breath, the magazine had got it out: American optimism, American superiority to European colonialism, and American opposition to economic feudalism or extreme nationalism.[1]

Harry Hopkins wrote up, in notes he planned to use for his memoirs, a similar evaluation of British colonialism which both liberals and conservatives might accept: "There is constant friction between our business interests and we think—and I have no doubt with good reason —that Great Britain would take an unfair advantage of us in trade around the world. It is footless to ignore the fact that the American people simply do not like the British colonial policy . . . ." [2]

When the leader of that policy, Prime Minister Churchill, tried to restrict the Atlantic Charter to European matters, President Roosevelt suitably countered on Washington's Birthday, 1942, "The Atlantic Charter applies not only to the parts of the world that border the Atlantic but to the whole world." Obviously these remarks were a counterattack on Axis claims, especially in the Far East, but they were part of the President's belief: "We are going to have to take some positive steps [to change colonial relationships] or find ourselves pushed out completely." And later when a disturbed adviser questioned the direction American policies seemed to be taking, a direction that favored the imperialists, Roosevelt replied—turning over his palm— "Why, Pat, I can change all that at the proper time, as easily as this . . . ." [3]

Pat Hurley had his doubts then, and they grew into bitterness. As Roosevelt's trouble-shooter in the Middle East and China, he became increasingly irked at Britain and Russia, who, he charged, "gave eloquent lip service to the principles of democracy" but were clandestinely reconstructing old empires. Even worse, they were doing it with United States aid and comfort. "We finished the war in the Far East," Hurley bitterly wrote President Truman, "furnishing lend-lease supplies and using all our reputation to undermine democracy and bolster imperialism and communism." [4]

Though Hurley exaggerated American support to Allied reconquests and oversimplified the political issues involved, his criticism was offered by other conservatives as well as a large number of liberals who voiced complaints about American policy. Roosevelt had not been able to "change all that" as he might have wished. For one thing, American leaders soon realized they could not have it both ways: They could not build a postwar world in cooperation with their allies and still take away their empires. United States military planners had assumed at the start that America's goal would be to re-establish its position "and that of the European powers in the western Pacific." As the war continued, this original assumption was modified and enlarged to include postwar security problems. The French colonial empire, for example, already weakened before the war even began, was a bothersome question to both military and political strategists. These thinkers considered possible amputations in order to save the body, but Great Britain wanted to save it intact.[5]

When confronted by colonial nationalists with the letter of the promises in the Atlantic Charter—the "right of all peoples to choose the form of government under which they will live"—the United States fell back to its record in the Philippines. Washington held it up to European capitals as a worthy goal, and assured African and Asian leaders that their freedom would come just as surely and just as completely.

THE AMERICAN RECORD IN THE PHILIPPINES

Only a few years after taking the Philippine Islands, the United States started talking about their independence. It was a moral issue to some; others recognized that the Islands had been difficult to pacify, their products competed with domestic agricultural interests, and, finally, they represented a political commitment which many Americans did not want to see continued. Besides, American expansion in the Pacific was commercial and ideological rather than territorial. The Philippines were an expanded base or, more traditionally, an entrepôt; hence absolute political domination would not be necessary.

With an eye on these objections, when they found expression in the 1932 Democratic national platform, Candidate Roosevelt supported Philippine independence. Inside the White House, Herbert Hoover was deciding what to do about a bill providing for that very thing. The Hawes-Cutting Bill would have made the Islands independent at the end of a ten-year transitional period. Much to the relief of his secretaries of State and War, however, Hoover finally vetoed this bill. Stimson opposed independence, he told the President, because the Philippines had "become a physical and spiritual base for American influence—political, economic, and social—in the Far East. There we demonstrate before the eyes of all Far Eastern peoples and all governments which exercise authority or influence in the Far East, American ideas and methods." [6]

The Hawes-Cutting Bill would give the Filipino people independence, said Secretary of War Pat Hurley, but it would also give them too much say in "the future international position and basic trade and other policies of the United States in the Orient." Hurley's anti-imperialism during World War II was based upon the same sort of considerations. Speaking about Britain's future role in the Middle East and elsewhere, Roosevelt's special representative said that the United States was willing to maintain England as a first-class power but only if it "discarded the principles of imperialism *and monopoly*." [7]

One of the authors of this bill felt it had been misinterpreted. The "efforts of Mr. Huey Long and others" had got it all turned around. It was not intended to hinder American economic interests in the Far East at all. "You will remember," he added to Stimson some years later, "that our trade with China was considered of such great importance that we passed a special law relating to Americans doing business in China, exempting them from income tax assessments on their exclusive Chinese business." [8]

Whatever Congress as a whole intended by the Hawes-Cutting Bill, President Roosevelt signed another independence bill in 1934, the Tydings-McDuffie Act. And he suggested giving up American military bases there, though he reserved the question of naval bases for negotiations after independence. [9]

The President was irritated when Congress then placed what amounted to a tariff on Philippine cocoanut oil, a processing tax which, he believed, repudiated promises given to Filipino leaders when the independence bill was still being considered. These leaders complained to Roosevelt and asked for a full Congressional study of Philippine-American economic relations. If it had been carried out then, such a study would have revealed that American capital owned 30 per cent of the sugar *centrales,* 70 per cent of the electric power sources, and nearly 40 per cent of the mining industry; furthermore, over 70 per cent of the Islands' trade was done with the United States. [10]

"The Philippines," wrote one student of American relations with the Islands, "have developed economically in a typically colonial fashion. Money crops for which there was a duty-free market with protected price levels in the United States have been stimulated by the use of American capital; foodstuffs for domestic consumption have been crowded out; domestic industries have not been much encouraged." [11]

Agriculture Secretary Wallace gave life to these statistics and forwarded to Roosevelt a first-hand account of economic conditions among the sugar workers, who were "permanently in debt with an income so low it beggars description." There was wealth aplenty being created in the sugar industry there if the worker "got what he produced. . . . But they get damn little if any help from any Americans in connection with their economic wrongs—most Americans out here only know of the New Deal as something awful. It means taxes and disrespect of the courts." [12]

The Independence Act did not reverse this trend. In 1938 Manuel Quezon, president of the Commonwealth, wrote to the American High Commissioner, Paul McNutt, "You seem to favor the present economic policy that imposes no limitations as to the amount of articles and goods coming into the Philippines from the United States and under full tariff protection, whereas Philippine articles and goods will be subject to quotas and excise taxes and without any safeguard as against tariff changes in America." Quezon's "ideas of government often differed profoundly from my own," recalled another High Commissioner, Francis Sayre, "nor was I willing in those cases falling within the scope of my official duties to yield to proposals and desires that ran counter to American interests and ideas." [13]

When he became Secretary of War, Henry Stimson was pleased to learn that Roosevelt, though he had signed the Tydings-McDuffie Act, was firmly opposed to "any irresponsible and faithless abandonment of the Islands." But when the Japanese successfully invaded the Philippines, native leaders began repudiating that protection. "This war is not of our making," charged Quezon. The United States had known the Islands were weak but had failed to build up its defenses properly. Reinforcements were not on the way, nor were any planned. The United States had abandoned the Philippine front. A few days later Quezon asked for immediate independence so that he could approach the Japanese with neutrality proposals. Military commander Douglas MacArthur appended his own estimate of the situation to this message: "The temper of the Filipinos is one of almost violent resentment against the United States." Far from recovered from the Pearl Harbor attack, Roosevelt resisted this idea and repeated the pledges of independence in the Tydings-McDuffie Act.[14]

Quezon's resentment abated after his government was evacuated to Australia and then to the United States. American strategic planners were taking another look at the Philippine situation at this time and also planning ahead to the postwar years. Their conclusion was that the United States would have to have bases in the Islands. Secretary of War Stimson, always concerned about the Philippines, told Senator Millard Tydings in September, 1943, that there would be "a great many dangers to still be guarded against, and that's just one reason" for such bases. Tydings responded that the President had agreed that the Philippines should receive "help and understanding" in the adjustment period after independence. Also speaking for the President was Harry Hopkins, who told Allied representatives at Teheran that the United States would in all likelihood maintain naval and air bases in the Islands, "as part of the Pacific security system." [15]

Representative James Wadsworth suggested to Stimson that "acquiring or the eventual acquiring, of posts in the Philippines will be part of a great pattern," which Congress would oversee. "Yes, we'll have mandates," replied the Secretary of War.[16]

In 1945, when Congress enacted a Philippine Rehabilitation and Trade Act, Representative Jasper Bell declared: "We are the great source of capital investment and this bill was designed so that American capital could and would flow into the Philippines." Section 341 of the Trade Act assured equal treatment for American citizens in the "disposition, exploitation, development, and utilization of all agricultural, timber, and mineral lands of the public domain, waters, minerals, coal, petroleum and other mineral oils . . . ." [17]

Relations between the United States and the Philippines remained close after the war, but Philippine President Carlos J. Garcia restated the Philippine criticism of the American record in the Islands. Foreign interests still dominated the nation's economy, he complained. "Reduced to stark realities, such a condition makes a mockery of our independence and robs it of substance and meaning. As long as this condition persists, we shall remain in many ways a colonial country." Having subdued an insurgent movement, and fiercely anticommunist, Philippine leaders had to face up to such "stark realities" as well. Perhaps if President William McKinley had started the American record in the Philippines with a Rehabilitation and Trade Act like that of 1945, he would not have had to seek God's sanction in taking the Islands, but could have controlled them through economic means.[18]

INDIA AND THE BRITISH EMPIRE

Stimson's remark, "Yes, we'll have mandates," and Harry Hopkins' attitude at Teheran on Philippine bases indicated an acknowledgment of some American political responsibilities in the postwar world. In 1942, when the Japanese threatened to sweep away British power in India, President Roosevelt was suddenly brought face to face with his own prophecy: ". . . we are going to have to tell our friends the Allies that they must have faith in the Orientals and their ability to govern themselves." This was precisely the role the President himself essayed in the Anglo-Indian crisis of that year.[19]

Led by Mohandas Gandhi and Pandit Nehru, the Congress party of India had demanded full and immediate independence, rejecting all offers of dominion status after the war as merely devious schemes to perpetuate the British *divide et impera* policy.[20]

At the first wartime strategy conference between Churchill and Roosevelt (December 22, 1941, to January 14, 1942), American policy towards the Indian problem was simply, as Hull phrased it, that the President believed "that if she were granted the promise of independence after the war, she would co-operate more with the British and their war effort." [21]

Churchill accepted Roosevelt's idea that India be allowed to sign the United Nations Declaration on war aims—so long as the Indian delegate signed merely "India" and not the "Government of India"— but when Roosevelt kept pushing him on the subject, the prime minister "reacted so strongly and at such length" that the President never raised the question directly again. But Roosevelt was far from through reminding his Ally about it. Washington suspended trade negotiations with India in order not to encourage the Congress party to expect interference, but when Singapore fell, and with it much British prestige, the President asked Special Ambassador Averell Harriman to make sure that Churchill knew that Washington was concerned about the difficulties with India. Harriman reported that the Prime Minister was insisting that the other great faction in India, the Moslem League, absolutely rejected the Congress party's program for independence, and as the great fighting strength of India came from that former group, he could not "take any political step which would alienate the Moslems." [22]

The prime minister did, however, send Sir Stafford Cripps to negotiate with the Congress party and the Moslem League; Roosevelt designated Colonel Louis Johnson, already a member of the American mission to organize Indian war industries, as his special representative to keep him informed on the Cripps mission. At the same time he urged the prime minister to try a temporary solution similar to the American experience with the Articles of Confederation. That kind of government could take over the public services but devote most of its attention to the preparation of a permanent constitution for the formation of a new government after the war.[23]

The Congress party rejected the Cripps mission, citing as a specific complaint British retention of the Defence Ministry, but intimating that Cripps's plan for a constituent assembly was no more than a sophisticated way of postponing or even denying India its freedom. Louis Johnson, who had tried to mediate by a suggestion that an Indian be named Defence Minister at least "on paper," reported to Washington that he shared such suspicions.[24]

Gandhi and Nehru turned away from these negotiations and talked about a campaign of civil disobedience to force the British to grant India independence.[25]

Roosevelt asked Churchill once more to try his idea patterned on the Articles of Confederation and to make a promise of postwar independence, but the Prime Minister believed that such ideas bordered on madness. "Anything like a serious difference between you and me," he managed to reply calmly, "would break my heart and surely deeply injure both our countries at the height of this terrible struggle." [26]

Meanwhile, Johnson was trying to save American prestige in India by dissociating Washington from the policies of the government of India. It was imperative that he do so, at least to the extent of rebutting Gandhi, who was telling newsmen that the United States could have stayed out of World War II: "Even now she can do so if she divests herself of the intoxication her immense wealth has produced." [27]

"There is no damned thing in all this fine country that we in America covet at all," Johnson countered to Indian newsmen. "You can look at our record in the Philippines and see how we handled Cuba. America is the greatest self-contained nation in the world. Happiness in India and prosperity in India means happiness for America and prosperity in America." [28]

Colonel Johnson's assurances were not enough; like Quezon's bitter messages during the invasion of the Philippines, Indian protests were the beginning of what we now call Asian neutralism. Even though he had such different ideas about what kind of war it was, Gandhi hoped that his threat of disobedience would bring American intervention. "Tell your President," he confided to the journalist Louis Fischer in the summer of 1942, "that I wish to be dissuaded." So Fischer carried his message orally and in a letter to the President, a letter that openly asked for American "sympathy" in effecting a British withdrawal. "I venture to think that the Allied declaration that the Allies are fighting to make the world safe for freedom of the individual and for democracy," Gandhi wrote the American President, "sounds hollow, so long as India and, for that matter, Africa are exploited by Great Britain, and America has the Negro problem in her own home." Roosevelt answered that India should make common cause against an enemy which would "deny forever all hope of freedom throughout the world." [29]

But privately, Roosevelt continued to criticize the way Britain was handling what had by now become a crisis. "You are right about India," he wrote Harold Ickes, who had expressed his irritation at British policy, "but it would be playing with fire if the British Empire were to tell me to mind my own business." [30]

When the Civil Disobedience campaign began, Gandhi and Nehru were arrested, and in Washington there were fears that Japan would be the only victor out of the chaotic state of affairs Hull feared would surely come. Increasingly uneasy about this possibility, Roosevelt ordered former Undersecretary of State William Phillips to go to India as his personal representative. His instructions ruled out direct intervention, but he understood that he was to speak to British officials "in a friendly spirit"—though quite bluntly—about American concern for a happy solution. Soon thereafter Gandhi began to fast in his prison quarters.

Phillips sent back several less than encouraging letters in the next few weeks. They all carried one main point: India was disillusioned at America's unwillingness to intervene. The diplomat hoped that Washington would take the initiative and call a conference of Allied leaders to establish a provisional government for India with a promise of self-government at some fixed date in the future. Without this kind of action, warned Phillips, the United States could never retain either its moral position or its influence in postwar Asia.[31]

Since Gandhi ended his fast a few days after Phillips posted his final letter to Washington, Roosevelt did not have to worry so much about his decision not to act upon Phillips' recommendation. The Indian crisis eased, and Phillips was recalled to the United States, where, before the Senate Foreign Relations Committee, he pled for intervention. "India is dynamite," he said, and several senators responded by urging Roosevelt to put pressure on Churchill. But Roosevelt, now wanting to do almost anything but that, tried to sidestep further trouble by explaining

that American troops were being stationed in India for military purposes only and had no political connections with the government of
India.[32]

The Anglo-Indian problem was a severe but temporary headache for
Churchill; he left it to his successors to grapple with Indian nationalism
after the war. What worried the Prime Minister much more was that it
indicated a growing interest in the political affairs of the Empire by the
United States. Though he had "contained" international New Dealism
once, he feared it was a powerful force having at its disposal many
weapons. American technical missions in India, for example, were
criticizing London for not allowing India to keep its dollar earnings
in New Delhi. If this practice were not stopped, concluded one group,
England would be able to deny American exporters entrance into an
important postwar market.[33]

In another part of the world, the 1940 Anglo-American destroyer-
bases deal brought into being the Anglo-American Caribbean Commission, charged with the area's security and with promoting increased
standards of living. The Prime Minister defensively reacted to the Commission by asking the American President to announce that its establishment had brought no transfers of sovereignty.[34]

The American Ambassador to England, James G. Winant, told the
Royal Empire Society, in the sort of speech that Churchill could not
have been overly pleased about, that a great opportunity now presented
itself to the two nations because of the creation of the Commission to
"give greater security to the peoples who live in the Atlantic islands
off the coasts of the Americas, under our separate jurisdictions, but
now in several instances with a degree of joint responsibility because of
our base-lease agreements, and yet without interference with sovereign
rights." [35]

No doubt the Foreign Office was also aware that some Americans
were even suggesting that title deed to some of the British West Indies
might be a start towards settling the Lend-Lease debt at war's end.
But Roosevelt had turned this idea down, disclaiming any desire to
take on the myriad political problems of the Caribbean.[36]

He and Harry Hopkins were interested, however, in nonterritorial
expansion there, and in 1944 Hopkins wrote about American desires
in the British West Indies. In the *American Magazine,* the presidential
adviser informed his readers that there was no intention of giving up

the West Indian bases after the war. They were needed for both military and commercial purposes. After the war, he declared, the United States would be trading across the seas by air and by maritime carriers—both needed the bases.[37]

This concern paralleled Hopkins' interest in the Philippines, and it also might be compared to Washington's desire to secure Pacific stations for United States air commerce in the late 1930's. Here, too, the Administration invaded places the British had previously claimed for their own. At the turn of the century the United States had been interested in coaling stations for its merchant fleet; in the 1930's Pan American Airways' clipper ships sped across the Pacific, and they too needed refueling stations, especially in the Canton and Enderberry Islands. The British had a shadowy claim also to these islands, but, more important, they had a similar desire to expand their air commerce in the Pacific.

For a time the ensuing contest between the two countries—complete with dramatic races to occupy the islands and land colonists—seemed almost like a comic opera, but Roosevelt was very serious indeed about protecting American rights. On February 16, 1938, he informed the State Department that unless the British agreed to settle the dispute, he would place all the islands "not permanently occupied in the area generally situated between Samoa and Hawaii" under the Interior Department's jurisdiction by means of an executive order. That executive order would have been a dramatic footnote on the American frontier thesis.[38]

Two years later, and back to the Atlantic and the destroyer-bases deal, Roosevelt rejected the original British offer for airfield and port facilities in the West Indies until the terms were changed to allow the United States 99-year leases "with the right to fortify and defend regular military bases not only in Newfoundland, Bermuda, Jamaica, St. Lucia, Trinidad, and British Guiana, but also in the Bahamas and on Antigua." In the 1960's many of these bases have come under the control of Pan American Airways, which runs them for the Government as part of the Atlantic Missile Range.[39]

Roosevelt often chided Prime Minister Churchill on conditions within various parts of the Empire, especially in the Caribbean and Africa. "You can right a lot of wrongs with 'pitiless publicity,' " he told a group of Negro publishers. He also expected that a United Nations victory would result in the creation of a new trusteeship system to improve colonial situations.[40]

In the case of the French colonial empire, he had doubts about whether parts of it should be restored, but these ideas never left the planning stage.

TO RESTORE OR NOT TO RESTORE—
THE FRENCH EMPIRE

The American government had been very much upset at French weakness in allowing Japan into Indo-China in 1940 and 1941. It was also concerned about a German occupation of French North Africa, for Saigon and Dakar had become Axis springboards.[41]

To forestall, if possible, a complete Axis take-over, Roosevelt sent a watchdog ambassador to Vichy France, Admiral William D. Leahy. Leahy was instructed to use any one of a wide range of diplomatic and economic promises (or even clubs) to keep French North Africa out of German hands. The Admiral used all his weapons, including promises of aid and threats that France would never see its influence restored in North Africa if Germany were allowed to occupy the area. He was even more definite about Indo-China; on July 19, 1941, Leahy bluntly told the French that if Japan won in Asia, Tokyo would take Indo-China, and "if the Allies won *we* would take it." [42]

All through the war, Leahy's threat hung over both Vichy officials and then Free French leaders, who searched for some way to dissipate it and reassert France's voice among the colonial powers. At times Roosevelt spoke softly, promising Marshal Henri Petain that France would be reconstituted in all its past glory, including the French Colonial Empire. Such assurances pointed up United States ability to determine these questions and therefore accentuated France's current inability to influence the decisions of its Allies.[43]

Moreover, the French knew that the American President often had less friendly thoughts about the future of their empire. In the fall of 1943 the De Gaulle Committee of National Liberation pressed their case for representation on the Pacific War Council, but they were re-buffed wherever they went in Washington. Roosevelt had thought out the Indo-China problem to the point where he now considered installing an international commission or trusteeship there. Actually, this idea followed from his prewar proposal to the Japanese that the country be neutralized.

On his way to the Cairo and Teheran conferences, the President mentioned the idea to the Joint Chiefs of Staff. The British thought that

France could resume its former big-power status after the war, he began, but for his part he could not believe it, and therefore he did not want to return French rule to Indo-China, New Caledonia, the Marquesas Islands, or Dakar. This last place was now a continental outpost of the Americas, he added significantly.[44]

Realizing that the British would represent the main obstacle to his plan, Roosevelt lined up the support of the other Allies. First he approached Chiang Kai-shek at the Cairo meetings, asking him if China wanted to assume suzerainty over Indo-China after the war. The Chinese leader returned the compliment neatly by suggesting what Roosevelt wanted anyway—an international trusteeship. At Teheran the President then conferred with Stalin briefly on Indo-China. The Russian ruler seemed interested, and Roosevelt later informed his new Secretary of State, Edward R. Stettinius, that he had talked with these two, so that when the Prime Minister objected he could say, "Now, look here, Winston, you are outvoted three to one." [45]

In January, 1944, Roosevelt sent a note to Secretary Hull pointing out that British opposition stemmed from their fears about the probable impact such a move would make on their own possessions, especially Burma. They suspected it would mean independence, and in the case of Indo-China, said Roosevelt, that was exactly what he did mean.[46]

Throughout that year the President kept the idea in the back of his mind, while deferring French requests for more participation in Far Eastern strategy and economic matters. At Yalta in February, 1945, he repeated his proposals, but the British so strenuously opposed all American trusteeship planning that Roosevelt advised reporters on the trip home on board the U.S.S. *Quincy* that he had decided it was better to "keep quiet just now." In March, Roosevelt warned Ambassador Hurley and China Theater commander Albert Wedemyer to maintain a close watch over British and French political maneuvers in the Far East. At the conclusion of this discussion the President added that at the coming San Francisco United Nations Organization Conference, a trusteeship system would be organized "that would make effective the right of colonial people to choose the form of government under which they will live as soon as in the opinion of the United Nations they are qualified for independence." [47]

Whatever Roosevelt intended or desired, nothing like that happened at the San Francisco Conference: the trusteeship system (following agreements at Yalta) was very narrowly defined, at least so far as actually placing any territories under its jurisdiction. And with President

Harry S. Truman's tacit consent at Potsdam and after, French forces re-entered Indo-China. Within ten years, filled with almost constant war against nationalists and communists, they were driven out. Much the greater irony was that the United States, which had backed out of political responsibility for Indo-China at the end of World War II, found itself locked in the country from 1954 to 1963—with no way out in sight.[48]

That Roosevelt's strength was nearly gone at the Yalta Conference is no answer. The tragic attempts by the French and the Dutch to reclaim Asian empires would have taken place anyway. Nor was the American attitude entirely clear, for as Admiral Leahy noted late in 1945 (and he was hardly a friend of French imperialism), the Dutch East Indies had always been considered in the "British zone of control." And prior to that, Roosevelt had smiled upon Queen Wilhelmina's plans for reform and reconstruction in Indonesia. Secretary Hull had a narrow concern about the Dutch colonies; he wanted assurances that American oil companies would regain their properties there.[49]

Much of the answer to American policy problems at the close of the war against Japan has to be found elsewhere than in Roosevelt's personality or weariness. Sumner Welles regretted that the United States had missed an opportunity to establish a positive trusteeship program, proving to have been "altogether timid and vacillating in its approach." The timidity came from a concern not to cripple the British Commonwealth at a time when it was increasingly needed as a postwar Ally; the vacillation originated in United States ambiguity about the extent of political responsibility that it wanted to exercise in the colonial world. Roosevelt never had a burning desire to pick up the shattered pieces of ruined empires. American policy makers did propose a trusteeship system, but the timidity, the vacillation, and the desire for an Open Door Policy in the territories in question undercut their political proposals.[50]

The State Department's trusteeship system was designed to meet the aspirations of colonial peoples, promote United States security and economic well-being, and yet be acceptable somehow to European metropolitan rulers. It was expected that these contradictions could be worked out.

THE TRUSTEESHIP PROPOSALS

Roosevelt had early rejected a renewed quasi-League-of-Nations mandate system as unsatisfactory for the solution of the colonial problem. The United Nations had to come up with something better. In the past, he wrote to South African leader Jan Christian Smuts, League members had taken the mandate system as an excuse to exercise sovereignty over areas assigned them. There were many unstable places in the world which should be taken away from weak rulers, he then informed Russian Foreign Minister V. M. Molotov in June, 1942. Many colonies, too, would achieve self-government some day soon. In the dangerous transition period ahead, international trusteeships over such areas might be the best idea.[51]

These random thoughts became the foundation of Washington's planning for the colonial question; and, as before, American spokesmen likened their ideas on European empires to America's performance in the Philippines.

Secretary Hull presented Roosevelt with a policy memorandum on March 17, 1943, which outlined the Department's thinking on a United Nations declaration on dependent peoples. If a trusteeship system were to succeed, Hull wrote, colonial administrators must do at least five things: provide protection and opportunity for the colony to advance its general welfare; allow colonials a large share in local government; grant progressively increasing self-government; establish dates when the colonies would become independent; and, lastly, pursue development of the colonies and their resources to the interest of the peoples and to the world at large. Hull pressed each of these points upon British Foreign Minister Anthony Eden several times, and especially at the Moscow Foreign Ministers Conference in the fall of 1943.[52]

Economic Adviser Herbert Feis, in an article in the April, 1943, number of *Foreign Affairs,* discussed what the United States hoped to achieve. England and the United States "are pledged to avoid imperialistic adventures. Both are also pledged by the temper of the times to grant a reasonable share of opportunity to the capital and enterprise of other peaceful nations in the development of resources over which they may have decisive influence." [53]

Francis Sayre later put it differently: "Here, again, another distinctively American ideal, expressed at various times as the Open Door policy, is made a binding international obligation in all trust territories . . . . There can be no economic peace in the world except upon the basis of equality of treatment." [54]

Securing agreement to such a "binding obligation" became more important, it seemed, than securing the placement of specific territories under its jurisdiction—with the exception of the former Japanese mandated islands, and the way in which administration of them was settled weakened United States ability (and desire?) to persuade its Allies to turn over their possessions to international control. It might almost be said that the American trusteeship proposal was Hull's corollary to the Open Door Policy.

When Stettinius became Secretary of State after Hull, this policy of securing generalized promises or obligations was continued. At a planning session for the United Nations in 1944, Stettinius stressed that then—and later at meetings of the United Nations—the trusteeship discussion would be limited to general principles and the subject of specific territories would be left for future determination.[55]

Stettinius' chief aide, Joseph Grew, prepared a paper for the President's use at the Yalta Conference summarizing Anglo-American differences on the trusteeship question. There were three main ones: The British wanted a single power to exercise the trust authority in any given area, while the United States favored international control over some areas. The British thought in terms of self-government, but the United States believed a free choice should be offered between self-government and total independence. Both nations felt the need for international accountability but differed sharply on the details of such accountability.

In view of these differences, the State Department was working on three draft proposals: first, a general declaration on minimum political, economic, and social standards, for *all* non-self-governing territories; second, a specific trusteeship plan for Japanese and Italian possessions, former League of Nations mandates, and possibly other kinds of territories voluntarily put under trust; and, third, a draft plan for regional advisory commissions like the Anglo-American Caribbean Commission.[56]

As Grew expected, the British countered at Yalta with proposals that would have made the European colonial rulers the primary guarantors of the trusteeship system. Stettinius had already decided to place his greatest emphasis on the point that, beyond captured Axis territories and former League mandates, only areas voluntarily put under trusteeship would be administered by the United Nations.[57]

He was taken aback, then, when the Prime Minister violently turned on him at the Sixth Plenary meeting at Yalta as soon as he finished reading the proposals. "Never, never, never," growled Churchill. "Under no circumstances would [I] ever consent to forty or fifty nations thrusting interfering fingers into the life's existence of the British Empire." Stettinius tried to convince the Prime Minister that the machinery was "not intended to refer to the British Empire" but did not succeed until Roosevelt took Churchill aside during a recess in the formal meetings and assured him that what Stettinius had said was true. No one wanted to destroy the British Empire, nor would any specific territories be put under trust at San Francisco.[58]

Unknown to him at Yalta, Churchill had allies, within the President's circle of advisers, in the Secretaries of War and Navy, who were both dubious about the President's interest in making the former Japanese mandated islands into trust territories. Their interpretation of American security needs included military bases on these islands, which they were afraid could not be managed if the islands were under the United Nations. Actually, all the State Department wanted was a *pro forma* trusteeship in order to strengthen the trusteeship proposals in the United Nations.

And in the summer of 1944, the President had expressed this same opinion in a note to the Joint Chiefs of Staff. "I am working on the idea," he said, "that the United Nations will ask the United States to act as Trustee for the Japanese mandated islands." On another occasion he told State Department advisers lightly that he did not want to take over the former mandates, because that would contradict the Atlantic Charter; besides, he did not "think it was necessary." The islands would only supply jobs for "inefficient Army and Navy officers or members of the civilian career service." [59]

Finally, as he later explained to Navy Secretary James Forrestal, an Australian suggestion that the United States actually take all the islands north of the equator and that they, the Australians, take all those below that line, was in reality too limiting, for there were many islands south of the equator which figured in American security planning. If further assurances were needed, there was the President's remark to newsmen that while the United Nations would be the responsible agency for the former Japanese mandates, "It seems obvious that we will be more or less responsible for security in all the Pacific waters." [60]

But the Army and Navy kept on pressing for absolute control, and Admiral Ernest King argued that the retention of the bases was necessary for another reason: "Throughout the ages centers of civilization and power have gravitated toward the water. Access to the seas has made nations prosperous in times of peace. Control of the seas has made them powerful in times of war." Secretary Stimson approached the new President, Harry Truman, and obtained yet another promise that no specific territories would be discussed at San Francisco.[61]

"Our security interests were zealously guarded in San Francisco where high officers of the Army and Navy acted as advisers to the American delegation," declared Charles Taussig of the Anglo-American Caribbean Commission. As a result, the United States obtained administrative responsibility for the islands, and when the American delegate explained Washington's plans for promoting their self-government, the Russian delegate insisted upon adding the words "or independence" to the draft plans. The United States representative accepted this amendment but recorded his opposition to "the thought that it could possibly be achieved within any foreseeable future . . . ."[62]

During the debates on a general trusteeship system at San Francisco, the United States aligned itself on several crucial issues with the metropolitan powers and against semidependent nations, such as Egypt, who wanted to alter the plan in favor of the countries that would be administered under the proposal.

The Egyptian delegate found the United States opposed to him on two resolutions he had offered as amendments. He suggested first that the dependent peoples be given a voice in the selection of the administering power. Losing this vote, the Egyptian then unsuccessfully pressed for an amendment that would allow the General Assembly to declare a territory ready for self-government—and then make it so.[63]

As these votes indicated, the United States was not willing to challenge the metropolitan rulers in a showdown on the trusteeship system. During the war the United States had obviously been restricted because of its relationship to European nations; and its hope that general statements of United Nations principles would solve the problem were entirely too optimistic: Roosevelt was simply not able to "change all of that." Would a truly strong approach and stick-to-it attitudes have made any difference? "Positive neutralism" in Asia and Africa would have arisen with the Cold War as it did anyway, even after the United States had stepped in to help certain areas (such as Indonesia) to find their freedom. More than that, the United States could not escape other political problems of South East Asia and Africa, problems appearing in ever-increasing numbers after 1945: Hull's corollary to the Open Door Policy was just not enough.

But after the war, the major burden of cooperative action in the development of the hemisphere will rest upon the initiative, the imagination and drive of individuals and private groups throughout the Americas.

Nelson Rockefeller, 1943

10 · Adam Smith, Latin America, and the New Deal

One conspicuous result of World War II in the Western Hemisphere was Washington's new burden of almost total responsibility for political and economic leadership in the Americas. Rationalized into a full-blown theory of inter-American affairs, Roosevelt's phrase "giving them a share" became the working thesis. In Latin America there were no European rulers to challenge United States policy, as in the case of the colonial problem, and this gave Washington a freer hand. But there were other factors, particularly the war-created inflation there, which militated against American policy makers.

Making the Good Neighbor Policy a success from 1933 to 1938, as *New York Times* writer and editor Herbert L. Matthews observed, was fairly easy and uncomplicated: "To desist from doing things we had been doing was relatively easy. There was an element of risk, and specific American interests sometimes suffered, but on balance the policy paid off handsomely." [1]

As early as 1935, though, Cordell Hull added that Good Neighborliness had to be something much more positive: "If the Platt Amendment was symbolical of an early epoch in our inter-American relations, its recent abandonment is an emphatic symbol of a new era in which it becomes our manifest destiny to enter into ever closer relations of free and voluntary collaboration for the furtherance of the prosperity of each and the peace of all." This statement was prophetic of the development of inter-American relations after 1938, probably more so than even Hull imagined at the time for he was one of the last in the Administration to give up older ideas about how the oil crisis in Mexico should be handled. But when he did, he too became a staunch supporter of the "new" Good Neighbor Policy. His associates in the State Department, as well as many of the political and economic leaders in the

194

Administration from the "dollar a year" men, were building a new theory (or modifying a very old one) on top of the realities of South American nationalism, the memory of Axis penetration, and their own new conception of economic interests in inter-American affairs.[2] Important private leaders and high officials of the United States had not failed to notice that trade developed more rapidly and more completely with nations like Canada, where the production of semifinished goods and finished manufactures was encouraged, both internally and by the patterns of Canadian foreign trade. If this were so, argued such thinkers, then outlets for direct and portfolio investment would also increase in more prosperous areas than in places where the standard of living stayed mired around the subsistence level. From these two postulates followed yet a third: The creation of a strong middle class would promote stability and security.

The more one looked at this set of postulates and assumptions, the more one became aware that they were in reality a modification of Adam Smith's division-of-labor thesis. The United States would produce manufactures and heavy items; Latin American countries would turn out semifinished goods and branch off into light industry while still producing raw materials.

Using not-so-hidden hands to straighten out contradictions and reconcile short-term and long-range objectives in South America, policy makers set out to implement this theory. They encountered difficulties from the first wartime conference of importance at Rio de Janeiro in 1942 to the last at Mexico City in 1945, including the almost insurmountable one of inflation. These difficulties lessened the chances that the theory would ever get a full trial, and this in turn prevented an answer to the real question of how workable it would have been under ideal conditions. But almost all American policy since World War II has been based upon a variation of that theory.

BRINGING ADAM SMITH'S THEORIES UP TO DATE

"The ancient mercantilist fallacy that an industrial exporting nation should strive to impede the industrialization of its overseas markets was ridiculed and exploded nearly 200 years ago by Adam Smith," declared the American Ambassador to Argentina, Spruille Braden, "but, like so many mistaken theories, this one dies hard." [3]

Sumner Welles and Laurence Duggan had already reached similar conclusions by 1940 and were propagating the new faith in speeches to various segments of the American community. Welles told the Advertising Club of Baltimore that the inter-American economy after the war would have a "much higher degree" of diversification "both of raw materials and manufactured goods." Duggan told another group that the resulting diversification would relieve Latin America of any dependence upon European markets.

But even these State Department officers who were so much up on what to expect after the war were surprised by what did happen. Not only did old South American-European trade channels dry up, but a sudden flood in North-South trade channels nearly washed away their plans to direct the development of inter-American relations. In the five years between 1939 and 1944 the dollar value of American exports to Latin American doubled to $1,034,000,000 annually. Inflation accounted for part of this rise, but it still denoted a tremendous new current in inter-American trade.[4]

But some did not give up trying to find a way to direct it. Adolf Berle, for example, explained at a 1944 meeting of the Inter-American Development Commission that the United States had moved away from the notion that it should fear competition from Latin American industrialization, for "what we lose in competitive industry we more than make up in markets occasioned by the increase in wages and the growing prosperity of the countries which improve their economic life." Since the Americas were a hemisphere of private enterprise, he continued, the burden would naturally fall upon private investment, principally upon that kind of investment and upon those investors who accepted their responsibility to society. Unfortunately, the good market in Latin America, created by wartime conditions, clouded memories of events even in the very recent past, and so many found it much easier just to float along and enjoy it.[5]

Like Berle, the sober-minded Eric Johnston, Chairman of the United States section of the IADC, tried to explain to the members of the National Foreign Trade Council what the government and business had to do in cooperation: "We know, of course, that the laissez-faire of earlier days would be ridiculous and impossible in complex modern times. But what business must have, nationally and internationally, is an alliance with government."[6]

An Assistant to the Secretary of Commerce more directly referred to Adam Smith's ideas in a discussion of the need for a balanced hemisphere development to "provide maximum productivity and levels of living by making use of those resources in which a country has a comparative advantage." A Congressman probed into this Commerce Department thinking during hearings on the postwar economy and asked one of the key questions: Had the United States set out to raise the standard of living in Latin American countries "in order to find a market for our output"? And the reply was: "I think it is to our advantage to assist them in every way possible." [7]

Presented in this way, this series of remarks shows the outlines of the neo-Adam Smith discussion then going on among United States policy makers. Admittedly, the analogy is not perfect, but more important than that, these men believed that like Adam Smith, they were providing "theories which met the political wants of the new age [and] . . . the productive energies of the age." As Johnston had said, American policy makers did not want a return to nineteenth-century laissez-faire. Quite the opposite—what they were interested in was a way of adapting Smith's international division-of-labor thesis to fit the new age.[8]

In a radio discussion, "Is the Good Neighbor Policy Here to Stay?" Eric Johnston remarked that many Latin Americans wanted to work with North American businessmen and were willing to put up 20 to 40 per cent of the capital for such projects. Johnston avoided the sticky question of how long this arrangement would remain satisfactory and what would happen when the Latin Americans decided they wanted the majority share.[9]

For the moment, most Americans were willing to leave that question in abeyance and approve the concept of such a partnership. It was especially appealing to many New Deal Keynesians, who were looking ahead to the postwar era. If the continuing expansion of exports to Latin America could be thus sustained, an expanding economy at home could be assured. Keynesians repudiated Adam Smith all right, especially the popularizations of his theories by reactionary and conservative businessmen, but, as Gunnar Myrdal suggests, they often sought ways to bring up to date his ideas on international trade. Lord Keynes himself was doing it within the British imperial system.[10]

With a growing awareness that their goal was the same—the successful development of Latin America—private leaders exchanged positions with public leaders. Nelson Rockefeller, Will Clayton, and Spruille Braden, coming into the State Department, provided managerial know-how, while Henry Grady and Warren Lee Pierson, among others, returned to the business world with a deeper understanding of governmental relations with business and with a storehouse of contacts to promote private investment and foreign trade.[11] *

JOINING THEORY AND PRACTICE

The Export-Import Bank's developmental loan policy (which began almost accidentally in 1938 and became so purposeful in Brazil), together with the Inter-American Development Commission and the Inter-American Economic and Financial Advisory Commission, supplied the mechanics of the Good Neighbor Policy during World War II.

The Bank's expanded loaning practices made it, as one of its students noted, an equivalent of the British Colonial Development Corporation. Besides offering insight of some value into United States relations with Latin America, this suggestion also provides a clue to some of Washington's later difficulties in Latin America. The British Colonial Development Corporation and the Export-Import Bank simply could not satisfy the aspirations or the basic needs of underdeveloped countries.[12]

Having said that, however, it is necessary to add that, as far as it went, the Bank was a very useful aid to United States policy makers. It was important in implementing the Good Neighbor Policy by financing such projects as Brazil's Volta Redonda steel complex. To complete it and related projects, the Bank by 1943 had loaned Brazil just short of 200 million dollars. Eric Johnston, already known to be vitally interested in Latin America, spoke happily about the project at a 1944 meeting of the IADC: "The increase in Brazil's productive capacity in steel will result in increased earning power which the steel plants in the United States can enjoy by selling steel to Brazil in fabricated form. We will be selling automobiles, refrigerators, railroad equipment and those other products based on steel and at which we excel." [13]

Elsewhere in Latin America the Bank made loans for the production of strategic materials, the Inter-American Highway in Central America, and various public works. Reviewing these achievements, a director of the Bank testified before a congressional committee: "In addition

---

* Anyone who has traveled even a few miles south of the Rio Grande cannot but be impressed by the tremendous impact made by Coca-Cola upon even the smallest villages. It was another business executive who had trained in politics and government, James A. Farley, who headed the export branch of the Coca-Cola Corporation after World War II and, with the aid of the State Department, promoted its expansion with the same efficiency he had displayed in securing the nomination of Franklin Roosevelt in 1932.

to its contribution to the foreign trade of the United States, the Export-Import Bank has served often as an instrument of foreign policy." And President Roosevelt noted in a letter to Warren Lee Pierson as Pierson returned to business: "The Export-Import Bank has played a vital part in the conduct of our good neighbor policy with the South American countries." [14]

Nelson Rockefeller's Inter-American Development Commission supported the efforts of the Bank and initiated cooperative food production schemes, health and education programs, and other projects of its own. Rockefeller, in his pronouncements on the postwar period, always emphasized the role of "individual and private groups throughout the Americas"; and after the 1942 Rio de Janeiro Foreign Ministers Conference, one of his agencies published a handbook which outlined the ways in which the Rio resolutions on hemispheric cooperation would be realized. An industrial revolution in Latin America would require: "(a) Participation of United States capital, either alone or in combination with national capital; (b) The services of technicians or specialists from the United States; and (c) The acquisition of machinery, equipment and other products of United States industry." Both North and South America would thus profit and prosper.[15]

Although the economic foundations for inter-American relations were seemingly well set, they were faulty in various ways. World War II inflation, with its supercharged demand for raw materials, negated much of the too little industrial progress that was being made with the aid of the United States. Postwar Latin American economies were being shaped by their northern neighbor's demand for raw materials, while the cost of living in many of these countries was rising by 200 or even 300 per cent.[16]

A second weakness was an indirect result of the first. The tremendous increases in inter-American trade made postwar planners feel less pressed to find a solution to the dilemmas of earlier years, and businessmen saw fewer reasons to cooperate with long-range planning. At a Foreign Ministers Conference in 1945, South American delegates complained that the United States now seemed only casually interested in measures necessary to Latin American industrialization—if not actually opposed to them. Immediately after World War II, Washington shifted most of its attention and aid to Europe to combat the communist threat, while Latin Americans received an occasional nod or fatherly advice to make their countries safe for investment.

A third weakness was that the plan originated in Washington and was directed from there, and therefore the projects undertaken were not necessarily those which Latin American countries most needed to balance their economies. Nor was aid automatically granted; the unspoken prerequisite was generally full cooperation with the United States, which again meant cooperation with its investors.

In the 1950's and thereafter, Latin American leaders raised the possibility of regional economic planning as the path to industrial progress. This seemed to be too far advanced for many Central American countries which had hardly left the feudal age. Even so the United States encouraged some of this planning, but Washington was worried at times about the direction it might take. Brazil's Operation Pan America was received skeptically by the International Monetary Fund and other lending agencies, which wanted to know much more about the type of economic thinking behind the Brazilian plan.[17]

If anything, the "new" Good Neighbor Policy gave the United States an ever-increasing dominance in inter-American relations on economic issues because of this power of the purse. The United States called for hemispheric planning, initiated some itself, and thereby extended its control over ideas coming from Latin America. Though this is a harsh analysis, it is essentially accurate. Washington still demands reforms in Latin America and then sets the boundaries upon reformist leaders, trying to keep them from becoming revolutionaries; it still gives aid and then demands the creation of a favorable climate for foreign investment, often without pausing to see if the two aims are in conflict either generally or specifically.

Going back to 1941, the American Minister to Canada heard a comment from a Canadian official which went to the center of this problem. The Canadian said that if Great Britain lost the war against Germany, he personally hoped that Canada would join the United States rather than remaining independent. "You'd be damned good friends politically to an independent and weak Canada," he stated, "but you'd be ruthless in putting the screws on us economically." [18]

Latin American leaders would probably have agreed with the Canadian if they could have heard Joseph C. Rovensky, a former member of Rockefeller's staff, an important shareholder in Bolivian mining enterprises, and vice-president of the Grace National Bank, address a meeting of businessmen in October, 1944. The problem was to sustain and advance the tremendous advantages the United States now enjoyed in Latin American markets, he told his Boston audience.

to De Gaulle which insisted upon "a peaceful and orderly solution . . . which will not prejudice the legitimate rights of the nations concerned." [27]

Faced with the inevitable, De Gaulle backed off. Grew advised the President that this policy had greatly increased America's prestige in the Arab states, but he was still concerned that the Levant was a keg of dynamite ready to set off the entire Middle East. Hence the Department's Briefing Paper for the Potsdam Conference rejected the idea of allowing the British and the French to settle the issue between them. In fact an approach towards reaching a solution could only begin with a simultaneous Anglo-French military withdrawal.[28]

The Russians first spoke up about the Levant at Potsdam. Just as firm on this question as he was to be on many others, President Truman shut off the discussions with the declaration: "We are in favor of equal treatment for everybody in the area, with no one having a privileged position." [29]

Premier Stalin, satisfied, withdrew a Russian paper on the subject. But he was to be much less happy about Truman's equally determined stand on the Dardanelles issue and that of the former Italian colonies. Russian leaders had opened discussions with the British back in 1944 on possible revisions of the 1936 Montreux Convention governing the use of the Turkish Straits. Prime Minister Churchill had indicated that he was willing to grant some Soviet desires, but he opposed bilateral control by Russia and Turkey of the Dardanelles—as did the Turks. For a time the United States, much to the annoyance of the Turkish government, had remained on the sidelines, with the State Department only advising the White House that America desired "(a) freedom of commerce (b) a regime of the Straits which would appear most effectively to promote the cause of world peace . . . ." [30]

When the Straits question came before the Allies at Potsdam, Truman delayed a specific discussion of that area and suggested that the Russian request for a military base on the Black Sea and a review of the Montreux Convention should be postponed to later sessions. But on the following day, July 23, 1945, he linked the Straits issue with his own "paper on the free and unrestricted navigation of inland waterways." Now it was Stalin's turn to ask for a delay; he wanted time to consider Truman's neat counterplay.[31]

Stalin replied the next day. The Dardanelles should be considered separately, since the President's proposals really pertained only to the

Danube and the Rhine. Truman then became insistent that they should be considered together, and he declared himself in agreement with the British position that freedom in the Black Sea straits should be guaranteed by all the Big Three.[32]

By the end of the Conference, neither side had changed its position, and Stalin was pressing another request—to administer one of the former Italian colonies in Africa when it was placed under trusteeship. As Herbert Feis noted, England and America feared the strategic advantages Moscow would gain thereby—for the first time Russia would be able to extend its power far below Turkey and the Persian Gulf. Anglo-American leaders thus visualized the situation on the map and, shuddering at the thought of it, put off discussing the question at Potsdam. The Russians held a strong hand in this game, however, for former Secretary of State Stettinius had already agreed in principle that the Soviet Union was eligible to administer a trusteeship. At the September, 1945, London Foreign Ministers Conference, Molotov duly suggested that each of the Big Three be given one of the former colonies to administer, noting that Russia wanted Libya. Amidst the clash on major issues, Secretary of State James Byrnes denied that Stettinius had actually promised Russia one of the colonies—it had been said only that she would be eligible. Then he joined his British colleagues in proposing that the Italian colonies be placed under the United Nations Trusteeship Council.[33]

RIVALRIES IN IRAN

Russia would have preferred spheres of influence among the Big Three in Iran as well as in the Dardanelles and Italian colonies. But here, too, the United States had different ideas. Since Great Britain had also followed spheres-of-influence diplomacy here, American diplomats had to overcome each rival, though of course they were much closer to British ideas than Russian. Still, Washington was unsure how far its own influence and penetration should go in Iran. Some advisers wanted to follow a hands-off policy so far as the Iranian government was concerned; others desired a more positive approach; but, like President Roosevelt, they wavered on the question of extending the New Deal to Iran.

One disappointed advocate of the New Deal approach complained that the United States had mistakenly chosen to back up the "racketeers, and the profiteers, against the welfare of the masses and contrary to majority opinion." And it must be conceded that by the war's end American policy in Iran had narrowed almost to the single line of opposing Russian penetration.[34]

When Great Britain and Russia occupied Iran to secure their supply lines in August, 1941, the State Department, concerned, appealed to American missionary schools to add to their good works by staying in Iran and countering bad influences at work there. Wallace Murray, Chief of the Near Eastern Division, suggested to the Presbyterian Board of Foreign Missions that its school at Tabriz would restrain "Soviet separatist and ideological activities in that area, of which much has already been heard." Murray advocated also the resumption of trade negotiations with Iran "for reasons of political expediency and in order to safe-guard American trade interests in Iran during the post-war period." [35]

Conferring with representatives of American oil companies interested in Iran, Murray assured them that he did not want to see a repetition of the era following World War I when the United States had been obliged to force its way into the Middle East.[36]

Before State Department officials was a British request for Lend-Lease funds to build several pipelines across Iran. Washington held back its approval, asking for assurances that these lines would be made available to American companies after the war. The Department had already protested against Article IV of the Anglo-Soviet-Iranian Treaty, for under its provisions these two occupying powers might settle the future of just such joint transport improvements without consulting the United States.[37]

With these doubts prodding them, Administration leaders responded favorably and quickly when Iran requested a financial mission to help it order its fiscal affairs. Arthur C. Millspaugh, who headed this mission, was given to understand that he was supposed to pave the way for other American interests: "Our control of revenues and expenditures not only served as a stabilizing influence but also was indispensable to the full effectiveness of Americans in other fields." [38]

The State Department had also sent to President Roosevelt's desk a series of memoranda on Soviet-Iranian relations in anticipation of talks he was to have with Foreign Minister Molotov at the end of May, 1942; Hull hoped that Roosevelt would put the Russians on notice that the United States expected "trustful cooperation" between Russia and Iran and, more than this, that Russia would be made aware of America's interest in helping Iran. Hull also spoke to the War Department about Iran, requesting Secretary Stimson to bolster the military mission there which was engaged in facilitating the shipment of Lend-Lease supplies to Russia. Stimson said he was unable to increase the mission as such, but he was ready to send additional experts and advisers to the Iranian government.[39]

Still, Hull remained unsatisfied, and so did special Ambassador Patrick Hurley, who returned to Washington from a tour of the Middle East and Asia, anxious to tell Roosevelt that he believed that the United States had to put forth a much greater effort and exert much more leadership if Iran were to remain independent.[40]

Because of his recent acquaintance with the problems of the Near East and relations with Russia there and elsewhere, Hurley accompanied the American delegation to Cairo and Teheran, where he succeeded in securing signatures from each of the Big Three on the Teheran Declaration that pledged them to respect Iran's independence after the war. Sometime during the Teheran meetings Roosevelt asked both Hurley and Millspaugh to submit their thoughts to him on strengthening Iran so that the Declaration would not be a meaningless one.[41]

Hurley suggested changing the control of Lend-Lease distribution from British to American management, and he offered plans for building a democratic government in Teheran based upon a "system of free enterprise." This could be accomplished, said the adviser, by the aid of American experts "fully indoctrinated in the policy of our government toward Iran . . . ." Millspaugh was much more expansive: he projected a full-scale twenty-year aid program which he believed would also serve as a general plan for "develop[ing] and stabilizing backward areas." [42]

"I was rather thrilled with the idea of using Iran as an example of what we could do by an unselfish American policy," Roosevelt exclaimed to Hull after looking over these reports, but his enthusiasm was never so great that he failed to see the difficulty of finding experts idealistic enough and honest enough to make the plans work. Then, in a letter to a personal friend, Roosevelt outlined some of Iran's agricultural and social problems, only to conclude that if he were thirty or forty years younger he himself would take on the task.[43]

Whatever hopes and doubts these two reports had stirred in Roosevelt, he definitely shared Stettinius' conviction that America's position in Iran should not "lapse again in any way to that of relative unimportance . . . ." America was going to be there, and in February, 1944, Hurley's recommendation that the American legation be stepped up to an Embassy was carried out. In March another Hurley suggestion was adopted when Lend-Lease distribution was taken over by American agencies. Later that year the American military mission was also strengthened, as Stimson noted, "for the protection and advancement of our interests . . . ." And Admiral Leahy was pleased at this time to see the President taking a "very strong attitude toward Britain" on future oil concessions in Iraq, Iran and Saudi Arabia.[44]

Leahy's observation was only one comment on what was becoming the key issue in Iran. Apparently without informing either Russia or Great Britain, the United States had moved to obtain an oil concession in Iran. Never before had American interests had a clear shot in this country, but now prospects were especially good, since two Americans had been employed by Teheran in 1944 to advise on applications for petroleum concessions and on petroleum legislation and administration.[45]

The British found out soon enough, however, and scrambled in to seek a similar grant; the Russians followed shortly thereafter, but asked for the right to seek oil in all of Azerbaijan, the northernmost province of Iran. Suddenly alarmed, Teheran called off (possibly at Anglo-American urging) all talk of concessions until the end of the war. The State Department's Economic Adviser later explained: "Any gesture intended to assist the USSR to secure control over the oil resources of Northern Iran would have been resented in Britain and regarded as betrayal by the ruling element of Iran. Besides who knew with certainty what use the USSR would make of the concession?"[46]

Interestingly enough, *Fortune* magazine was not at all pleased with this treatment of the Soviet Union: "Did we in this case try to outsmart the Soviets? The situation is not an argument for the U.S. to 'get out of the Middle East.' It may well be an argument for closer collaboration with our allies."[47]

The State Department felt otherwise and started working to terminate the joint occupation as soon as possible. Narrowly concentrating upon removing this menace threatening Northern Iran, the Administration sidetracked positive attempts to cure that country's other ills. Perhaps it was feared that Russia would also ask to share in "New Dealizing" Iran and then use this opening to expand its influence; but quite probably it also had much to do with the wish not to offend the "ruling element" in Iran.[48]

However that may be, the State Department wanted Roosevelt to obtain Stalin's acquiescence at the Yalta Conference in Iran's decision not to continue concession negotiations until after the war. No joint or even unilateral rehabilitation plan was discussed except the President's vague references to the United Nations.[49]

Always suspicious of the Russians, Iranian diplomats told Acting Secretary Grew how Teheran had maneuvered thus far to avoid meeting the Russian request; then they expressed the hope that American companies would play a prominent role in developing Iranian oil resources. Aware of this encouragement, Anglo-American diplomats mulled over what they called their "grievance against the Russians" during pre-Yalta talks at Malta. The negotiations had gone ever so smoothly until they had been "arrested by the hamhanded procedure of the Russians in demanding a concession in the north which raised political issues." [50]

At the Fourth Plenary meeting on February 7, 1945, Roosevelt undertook to placate both sides. Repeating some of the things he had no doubt learned from Millspaugh and Hurley, he urged upon his colleagues the necessity of cooperation in Iran. The country was a prime example of the kind of economic problem that would confront the postwar world and the United Nations, he concluded hopefully.

On the next day, when the Foreign Ministers met, there was less hope and much more argument. Molotov pressed the other two to recommend to Teheran that it reconsider and reverse itself on the proposed Russian concession. Eden and Stettinius said that they thought Russia should have an oil concession in Iran—but not before foreign troops were withdrawn. Finally Molotov decided to let the question ride with the remark: "The situation [is] not acute at the present time." [51]

But it rapidly degenerated and became acute in the months following, when Iranian officials asked the United States to help extricate their country from the Anglo-Soviet vice. At Potsdam the British offered a step-by-step withdrawal, first in Teheran and then all through the country, but Stalin rejected that proposal, insisting upon the letter of the Anglo-Soviet-Iranian Treaty, which provided for a withdrawal six months after the end of hostilities.[52]

In September, 1945, the Administration pulled out its financial mission to placate the Iranian government and as a gesture to that country's sovereignty in answer to possible Russian contentions of undue American influence. Although the United Nations was finally brought into the controversy, American-led Iranian soldiers replaced Soviet occupation forces in Northern Iran, and American influence probably was the determining force in blocking the granting of a Soviet oil concession in 1947.[53]

Gone were the impressive dreams of rebuilding Iran. Great Britain and Russia had withdrawn their troops, but the country's basic ills remained. Foreign ownership of oil resources led to the nationalization crises of 1951 and 1952, at the conclusion of which the United States finally got a share of Iranian oil as part of an international consortium set up to run the fields. The continuing burden of absentee land ownership plagued the country, and the rising tide of Middle Eastern nationalism made the area unstable. The Shah was attempting a program of reform from above; perhaps it would be enough.

But Iran's situation was much like that of Iraq. There, too, the United States sought access to oil resources, communications facilities, and entrance rights for American commercial aviation. In 1959 Abdul Karim Kassim, a revolutionary leader, repudiated the spirit of past dealings with the European-American concessionaires: "These concessions were given at a time when Iraq was fettered, but we are now free and deal with the companies on a basis of mutual profit." Although Kassim was himself overthrown a few years later, his words were the words of Middle Eastern nationalism, and not that of radicals but of middle-class reformers.[54]

MR. ICKES' ARABIAN NIGHTS

"Manifestly, this project of Mr. Ickes was no global boon-doggle cut to the measure of *The Arabian Nights*. Here was no petroleum equivalent of milk for the Hottentots. The Secretary of the Interior, far removed from his usual imperialist-baiting, trust-baiting, reformer role, was playing for stakes that Cecil Rhodes at his most extravagant never contemplated." [55]

International rivalries there were in Saudi Arabia, though the unsettled relationship between the Administration and the oil companies participating in the ARAMCO concession was equally important. The above colorful quotation from *Fortune* touches upon it, but is far from explicit in describing what the "stakes" were. Relations with Saudi Arabia were a four-handed poker game. Washington had to bluff, raise, and call each of the other three players—King Ibn Saud, the oil companies, and Great Britain.

The game had begun when after several years of negotiations the Texas Oil Company and the Standard Oil Company of California secured from King Saud the right to explore and develop the oil resources in nearly all of his realm. This occurred in 1939. There arose a myth that King Saud believed that the Americans were the only bidders who did not want to subvert his rule in Arabia. Recent students of the Middle East and the oil companies have pooh-poohed that notion and insisted instead that he granted the concession to the Americans because they were the only ones who would pay what he demanded.[56]

Secretary Hull smiled upon this achievement and defined the government's role mildly enough as protection and support for the over 300 citizens connected with American interests in Arabia; therefore he asked President Roosevelt to approve the sending of the American Minister resident at Cairo to establish relations at Jedda. Roosevelt noted briefly on the Secretary's memo: "Excellent idea." [57]

Until 1941 the companies felt secure in this benevolent, noninterfering attitude at Washington and in their own ability to satisfy King Saud. But German successes at the outset of World War II weakened ARAMCO's favored position at court. Saud saw his revenues from Mecca pilgrims dwindling; oil shipments fell off. What could he do? Then the answer came to him: Demand from ARAMCO an out-and-out subsidy of six million dollars a year.[58]

The King's demand shook the oilmen. Though they could probably raise the money, they were alarmed by Saud's dickerings with Japanese and British concession hunters. Moreover, they could see that Saud's regime was in fact in danger of coming unhinged. In short, there was nothing for the oilmen to do but admit that Saudi Arabia was a "political problem" beyond their capacity to act alone.

Fortunately, there appeared a facile way out of their troubles: If the Administration could be persuaded to grant Arabia a loan under the recently passed Lend-Lease Act, then Saud's financial difficulties would be at an end and the American government's protective shield would shelter the ARAMCO concession. There was another advantage to this proposal which the oil companies did not talk about out loud. The plan would still leave them much freer than their European counterparts, whose governments were often major stockholders (and policy makers) in return for their protection.[59]

ARAMCO's representative went to see Roosevelt with this plan on April 9, 1941. The President was sympathetic, but unable to see how Lend-Lease could be applied to Arabia. A few days later oil executive James S. Moffett suggested an alternate plan—direct purchases by the United States Navy of six million dollars worth of Saudi Arabian oil each year. Moffett closed his appeal dramatically, "We believe that unless this is done, and soon, this independent kingdom, and perhaps with it the entire Arab world, will be thrown into chaos." Once again Roosevelt was sympathetic, even anxious to help, but stymied as to how to do it legally.[60]

Harry Hopkins had an idea: "It occurred to me that some of it might be done in the shipment of food direct under the Lend-Lease Bill, although just how we could call that outfit a 'democracy' I don't know. Perhaps instead of using his royalties on oil as collateral we could use his royalties on the tips he will get in the future on the pilgrims to Mecca." The President said no again; he still thought he could go no further than to stipulate that the British use part of a 450 million dollar RFC loan to "to take care of the King's financial requirements." The companies might even help make the arrangements between the English and the King, wrote Jesse Jones of the RFC to Moffett.[61]

This was the wrong kind of response, thought the oil men. They fretted that Britain's prestige would go up and up and Arabia "might be drawn into the so-called sterling area and we might not be able to maintain the American character of our enterprise." [62]

They tried to convince the Administration of the reality of this threat for the next two years, concentrating on the Petroleum Administrator for War, Harold Ickes. The companies brought him evidence that the British were undercutting the American holdings. Loans, banking establishments, and even concession hunters disguised as locust-hunters were all alleged to be part of this plot. And they succeeded in creating a state of alarm in Ickes' office, although once again the results were not quite as they had planned. Ickes said later that his "mind at once moved to the conclusion, on the analogy not only of Great Britain, but of other European governments, that our economy and our own ability to fend for ourselves in time of war would be greatly increased if we had an interest in this big oil pool, and so we moved in right away to try to acquire some interest." [63]

When a letter came from an ARAMCO executive which even suggested that this might be a possibility as a sort of *quid pro quo* for

Lend-Lease aid to Arabia, Ickes went at once to the President, and on February 18, 1943, Saudi Arabia was declared eligible for Lend-Lease aid. A month later Secretary Hull increased American diplomatic representation at Saud's court because he wanted the United States to have a full minister there if negotiations for government participation in the oil reserves were to begin.[64]

In June the Petroleum Reserves Corporation was set up to carry out multiple negotiations with the companies, Saudi Arabia, and perhaps even the British on a more general oil agreement. The drive for government participation was gaining momentum—too much, thought the oil companies, for they thought very little of Ickes' idea that the government purchase 51 per cent of the stock in the Arabian oil reserves. Conditions in the Middle East were improving now, what with Saud's subsidy from Lend-Lease and the changing course of the war. Most of all, ARAMCO disliked the Petroleum Reserves Corporation's intention of negotiating directly with King Saud through the Minister and an oil expert "who was not associated with any commercial oil company." [65]

Ickes was no more popular in the State Department either. Though the Navy and War Departments generally approved of the Petroleum Reserves Corporation's plan, the State Department had suddenly found it had many objections to it. Secretary Hull and Economic Adviser Feis were not backward "about the need of getting the reserves of oil," but they felt Ickes had adopted strong-arm methods and was trying to use too much power diplomacy. If he upset the small nations in the Middle East which still had untapped oil resources, or if the repercussions of his blunt approach reached Latin America, then the United States might never be able to regularize the whole Middle Eastern oil situation and thus "prevent a race or a scramble which would perhaps prevent us from getting what we ought to have." [66]

Ickes had many projects under way at this time, and one of them, he believed, would regularize the Middle Eastern oil situation and thereby ease Hull's worries. His idea was to announce the intention of the United States government to build a pipeline across Arabia into the rest of the Middle East: "The primary purpose in that suggestion was to alert the British to the idea that we really meant business in the Middle East on oil." But again Herbert Feis had reservations. Admittedly the idea would achieve one of the State Department's goals, but would it not also be the start of a general forward movement with all the as yet unconsidered—and unexplored, even—ramifications that such a movement would mean? One thing for sure, it would make the oil companies wards of the government, force the United States to maintain military bases there, and involve America in all the ancient problems of the Near East.[67]

Amidst these conflicts came a clear reaffirmation of the Open Door Policy upon which all the agencies and departments of the Administration could agree. On November 5, 1943, the Foreign Operations Committee of the Petroleum Administration for War submitted a general declaration to Ickes entitled "A Foreign Oil Policy for the United States." This policy memorandum asserted that the government should "aim at securing for American nationals access to the world's oil resources on equal terms with the nationals of all other countries." Discrimination and state oil monopolies were "harmful not only to our nationals but to the nationals of all countries." Royalties and taxes paid to the producing country should be directed at preserving "incentives adequate to attract capital and insure continuity of expansion." Even if equal access were theoretically achieved, "it [would] be illusory unless the government undertakes to see that acquired rights are respected." In conclusion, all the above was "in line with the traditional Open Door Policy of the United States now incorporated in the Atlantic Charter"! [68]

Although the pipeline project never got off the ground, it did serve, as Ickes had expected, to "bring a favorable response from 10 Downing Street." And from this response the United States hoped to begin discussions to achieve the aims of the Foreign Operations Committee. But the State Department did not want Ickes to lead or even to take a lesser role in the diplomacy which would have to follow. Herbert Feis went to London in October, 1943, to start talks on an Anglo-American oil pact. Russia was not invited to take part in these preliminary discussions or even in later ones in Washington, recalled Feis, because the Soviets had not been closely associated in pooling Middle Eastern oil during the war, but also because it was "impossible to guess what types of proposals the USSR might make; they might bring the whole pattern of ownership in the region into question. It seemed foolish to take this risk before our own policies were defined." [69]

In early August, 1944, a tentative agreement was reached. Surrounded by the usual optimistic and idealistic pronouncements and promises, the key sentence was: "With respect to the acquisition of exploration and development rights in areas not now under concession, the principle of equal opportunity shall be respected by both Governments." [70]

"While the oil business was settled," Harry Hopkins reported to the President, "it indicated to me how difficult it is to hold a formal economic conference with Great Britain on any single subject at this particular time." From London's point of view, Hopkins should have realized, the Open Door Policy may not have been so advantageous. As the power balance tipped so far in favor of the United States at the end of the war, the oil companies once again saw the terror of creeping socialism in any government proposals—even though they had been perfectly willing to solicit intervention in their affairs in less secure times. In 1946 it appeared that some companies had actually gone beyond the stage of the Open Door Policy and wanted to determine for themselves when the door should be open and when it should be closed. The Sinclair Oil Company, for example, sought an exclusive concession in Ethiopia. And their influence had much to do with Congress' refusal to ratify the Anglo-American oil agreement in 1945 and again in 1947.[71]

Nonetheless, the old Red Line Agreement had been wiped away and the Open Door Policy was triumphant throughout the Middle East. How long it would be so was another question. A decade after the war found the United States fighting to maintain its influence there. In Iran it was the 1951 nationalization crisis; in Iraq, revolution and military intervention; in Egypt, Nasser's "neutralism" and the seizure of the Suez Canal. At the time of an American intervention in Lebanon, the *Wall Street Journal* took a look at American policies in the Middle East and stated: "We are on the wrong side of a social revolution and it is an uphill battle."

A strong, friendly China would do much to lighten
our task and to promote mutually beneficial cultural
and commercial intercourse.

State Department Policy Paper, 1945

Our Committee instructed me to express to you their
appreciation of the unequivocal assurance that the
Open Door and the Territorial Integrity of China are
still America's policy in the Far East and that there
is no intention of relinquishing the same.

Alfred Kohlberg, American China Policy
Association, to President Harry Truman,
1946

12 · The Ambiguous China Policy

"Following the outbreak of war between the United States and Japan,"
read the introduction to the 1949 State Department's China White
Paper, "the United States Government took a number of important
steps which demonstrated the desire and intention of the United States
to treat China as an equal among the Major Powers and to contribute
to the strengthening of the Chinese nation." Four years of civil war
in China had culminated in victory for Mao Tse-tung and the Chinese
Communists. The Kuomintang was chased off the mainland to Taiwan.
And the Truman Administration was suddenly put under attack by
domestic critics who blamed it and the preceding Administration for
the loss of China. The Truman Administration replied by publishing
selected documents in the White Paper to demonstrate that the desire
and intention of making China into a great power had been thwarted
by internal dissension, internal and external communist intervention,
and, above all, Chiang Kai-shek's inability to rule efficiently and meet
these challenges.[1]

For some Department officers the White Paper was a sigh, perhaps,
and a sophisticated shrug of the shoulders. And among these a few
boldly asserted that America's China policy had always been a dangerous delusion, ever since the turn of the century and the Open Door
Policy of John Hay. "In this highly subjective picture of the Chinese,"
wrote the most famous of the China policy debunkers, George F.
Kennan, "there was no room for a whole series of historical and psy-

237

chological realities." Kennan aimed this and other arrows at those who had foolishly put on blinders and insisted that China should have grown strong and secure behind the aegis of the American Open Door Policy. Those who failed to follow Kennan's argument or who disagreed with it could still use the White Paper to justify American policy. According to it, the Chinese had just simply been unable to find themselves in time to save their country from communism. This group was willing to concede that possibly the Yalta Agreements had been unwise, but they would go no closer to Roosevelt's critics than that. In the aftermath one of the President's closest advisers did comment that the Yalta Agreement made it impossible for a newly unified China to exercise complete sovereignty over Manchuria, but that did not cause China's downfall.[2]

Such criticisms of the Yalta accord were pertinent, even if they are strengthened a very great deal by hindsight. Roosevelt did abandon the Open Door Policy, on the surface at least, in favor of a spheres-of-influence approach to Manchuria, and we have already seen (and will see again in later chapters) that this was almost the only exception and the only place where this happened.

Japan's strike at Pearl Harbor had cut through the earlier dilemma of the China policy and the Open Door Policy. After Japan's thrust had been blunted and then turned back on itself, American leaders perceived that they would have to bear arms permanently in Asia to protect their interests unless some country, probably China, could be called upon to replace Japan and play the role of stabilizer in the Far East. How to make China strong enough to do that within the framework of the Open Door Policy was the new dilemma of that policy. Walter Lippmann wrote cautiously in early 1942: The "controlling American purpose in the Far East is trade and cultural intercourse," but to achieve those things after the war, America would have to deal with Asians "as allies and not as protectors." Lippmann had put his finger on the problem, and a business journal looked on the optimistic side of things and rejoiced at the opportunity to help China's economy, for it "would open up new outlets for the energies of man, new cultural and commercial areas; and these would give to freedom an economic meaning that it has lacked for more than a decade." How easily did dreams of the Great China Market come back again and again![3]

The President's son James was perhaps the most enthusiastic of all, writing to his father's confidant, Harry Hopkins, that after the war

China could become America's greatest export market—ever. Our other allies might throw us out, but never China. His father, however, remained among the more skeptical. The same doubts he had harbored in 1934 had stayed with him; yet during the war these very feelings seemed to pull him towards China and the idea that the United States could influence, perhaps decisively, the final outcome of the Chinese Revolution that had begun around 1910. Certain it is that he saw himself as China's protector and principal spokesman at his wartime conferences with Churchill and Stalin.[4]

Those close to the Chinese government, such as Joseph Stilwell and Ambassador Clarence Gauss, had scarcely any hopes at all that the Kuomintang would survive. General Stilwell was blunter than most in setting forth his opinions. Chiang "rules by fear and favor," Stilwell wrote Secretary Stimson as early as June, 1942. "Despite his apparent despotic power, he does not dare disturb the structure by tearing out any of its members, for fear of amalgamating the opposition to where it may threaten his hold." [5]

By late 1944 attempts to keep the props under the Kuomintang seemed to be failing everywhere, and the State Department and the President turned over the idea of working with Mao Tse-tung's communist forces in North China. But there were too many obstacles to such an entente; so in lieu of it Roosevelt tried to convince the Chinese leader to absorb the communists into a broadened and more democratic nationalist government.

Whatever happened to that idea, it was imperative that the United States reach an understanding with the Soviet Union on Chinese affairs, preferably before Moscow declared war on Japan. The Yalta accord was reached largely to satisfy that requirement. As mentioned above briefly, this bargain was a repudiation of the literal meaning of the Open Door Policy, but was also an attempt to secure and even perfect its spirit.

First, the Soviet Union was supposed to support the Nationalist government of China as part of the Yalta Agreement—thus dividing two possible enemies of the Open Door Policy, the Russians and the Chinese Reds. Second, Roosevelt had other plans, such as a proposed trusteeship over Korea, which would block Russian expansion in the Far East. Third, the United States always expected to take an active part in protecting its policies, not only through the occupation and democratization of Japan and former Japanese mandated islands, but also through its continued military presence in the Philippines and Formosa. So the Open Door Policy was not abandoned, except superficially, at Yalta. It was Mao Tse-tung's victory which forced the writing of the White Paper; but in a larger sense the Chinese Communists' victory came about because of their repudiation of the kind of diplomacy which made them an object, almost a thing, rather than an equal. America might have been able at one time to influence the Communists, but never to control them. The China policy from 1941 to 1945 was ambiguous in that it wanted a strong China, but always within the bounds of the Open Door Policy. (It was the same sort of dilemma that Japanese policy had presented a decade before.) [6]

THE CHINA THEATER

The China Theater, wrote War Department historians, was "a device by which the President sought to accord Chiang a position due the head of a major Allied state, and still limit his participation in discussions on Allied strategy to those matters involving war in the Far East." No better description of the China Theater and its inherent political difficulties has been offered anywhere else.[7]

In creating the China Theater and assigning parts to its main actors, Washington faced political problems with its Allies right at the outset. At the first wartime strategy conference between the Prime Minister and the President, the two leaders decided to defeat Germany first and fight a holding war against Japan. Naturally the Chinese, who had not been consulted, were disappointed, and in the months and years that followed, Chiang sometimes tried to use his disappointment, as a weaker partner will, both as a lever under Anglo-American consciences and as a threat to quit the struggle. This contributed no little bit to the trials of all concerned.

Roosevelt was never tempted thereby to change his strategic decisions, but he did want to soothe the Chinese. And he felt that the British had greatly compounded the injury by refusing to accept Chiang's offer of troops for the defense of Burma. He pressed Churchill hard on this point at their first wartime meeting in Washington, and he kept it up through his military representatives. Trying hard to heal the irritations, Roosevelt then suggested in his covering letter to President Chiang creating the Stilwell Mission "the possibility of [a] Chinese command under you and General Stilwell in North Burma and British defense further south. This will give the British the chance to cover the approaches to India." [8]

The Stilwell Mission was thus thrust into the midst of political complexities and confusions. General Stilwell's dual role as Chiang Kai-shek's Chief of Staff and as the representative of American policy and interests tangled even the simplest military problems. Stilwell wanted to make China an effective ally in the fight against Japan, even if it meant stepping on Chiang's toes or enlisting the legions of Mao-tse Tung. Since Washington had made Chiang the center of its postwar plans for China in Asia, the dour General was at last placed in an untenable position and withdrawn from China.

Roosevelt had even warned Stilwell not to talk too tough to the Nationalist leader about his country's shortcomings in the war against Japan: "He is the Chief Executive as well as the Commander-in-Chief, and one cannot speak sternly to a man like that or exact commitments from him the way we might do from the Sultan of Morocco." [9]

Brooding in his capital, Chiang chafed at his assigned role. In April, 1942, he wrote to Roosevelt expressing his distrust of the Soviet Union and Great Britain, and suggested that he had doubts about the United States as well. India's Ghandhi had warned him, he said, that the Western powers thought of China as a pawn during the war, and would still do so at the peace table. Two months later he had a more concrete grievance; only 10 per cent of what President Roosevelt had promised to give China had actually been delivered. He did not accuse Roosevelt, he concluded; it must have been done without his knowledge.[10]

Just as Roosevelt tried to soften and tone down Stilwell's language, sometimes the Chinese foreign minister would soften Roosevelt's messages before they were sent on to Chiang. The Generalissimo once saw an original message from the President before it had been expurgated by T. V. Soong and declared that if Roosevelt had sent such a message, he would not continue as the Allied Commander in the China Theater. China's major complaint, however, was that too often "when Far Eastern matters were discussed, China was not consulted as there were no representatives present, only after decisions were made, were they communicated to the Chinese Government." [11]

Soong spoke thus shortly after the Casablanca Conference, and he repeated the charge over and over again. Through Roosevelt, China undoubtedly received a stronger voice in international affairs than it could have received any other way. But this made little difference; for it was still just a dependent's role, this business of receiving favors and bearing disappointments. It became a particularly loathsome one for Chiang when the President unilaterally reversed a Cairo Conference decision to invade Burma, in order to meet British objections that the invasion of Europe would have to be called off if men and supplies were to be diverted to the Burma campaign.

Chiang's resentment at General Stilwell's arrogance and bluntness reached its peak in September, 1944, when the American General succeeded in obtaining Roosevelt's strong backing in his private campaign to make Chiang fight in Burma: "It appears plainly evident to all of us here," the President wrote from the Second Quebec Conference, "that all your and our efforts to save China are to be lost by further delays." Hence Chiang was to put Stilwell in full command.

"I understand," Chiang said calmly when Stilwell brought him the message, and put the top on his teacup to signal an end to the meeting. "I handed this bundle of paprika to the Peanut and then sank back with a sigh. The harpoon hit the little bugger right in the solar plexus, and went right through him. It was a clean hit, but beyond turning green and losing the power of speech, he did not bat an eye." [12]

Chiang demanded and received Stilwell's recall, but Roosevelt did not intend to listen to Chinese requests for more representation at Big Three meetings, and he announced at the Yalta Conference that the Big Three alone would write the final peace terms.[13]

This statement failed to calm the British, who constantly sought to find out how far the United States intended to go to boost China to big-power status. As Foreign Minister Anthony Eden once put it to Roosevelt and Hopkins, his government disliked thinking about China "running up and down" the Far East. The President had once implied that China should become one of the Big Four policemen to keep world peace. The British variously interpreted American policy as naïve (Churchill called the China policy the great American illusion) or as a devilish clever attempt to undermine British Far Eastern interests. The truth was, of course, that it was something of both—and more.[14]

POSITIVE STEPS TO HELP CHINA

Though Chiang Kai-shek was not to be in on Big Three strategy decisions, the United States wanted very badly to increase his stature, and especially to strengthen the Nationalist government at home. Stil- well's mission was to have been part of that effort, but it backfired, and by the time General Albert Wedemeyer took his place in China it was almost too late for any military adviser to save the situation.

More successful was America's initiative in breaking with the past to the extent of negotiating away extraterritorial rights; in achieving the Cairo Declaration, which promised China that its lost territories would be returned; and in insisting that China be one of the signatories of the Moscow Declaration on the postwar world.

China had narrowly escaped Africa's fate in the late nineteenth century, but nevertheless had been reduced to a semicolonial status after the Boxer Rebellion and the subsequent imposition of unequal treaties. The once proud Celestial Kingdom was obliged to grant the foreign devils special navigation rights on Chinese rivers, permission to station troops in treaty cities, and the privilege of allowing their nation- als to be tried only in special consular courts for civil or criminal of- fenses. These treaties were not only humiliating to the spirit but often hurtful to the pocketbook, since the foreign devils used their advantages to overcome native competition.[15]

Half-hearted negotiation pointing towards the elimination of extra- territorial rights had begun before the war, but even if they admitted the Nationalists had stabilized China, neither the United States nor Great Britain was in any great hurry to surrender them. When the subject came up again in 1942 in the context of the war, some advisers still flatly opposed relinquishment—including the American Ambassa- dor to China and Political Adviser Stanley Hornbeck, both of whom wanted to save this card to play "at some later date." [16]

Hull felt compelled to act even so, and enumerated his reasons to the Ambassador in London, cabling him that short-run psychological and long-lasting political and economic considerations were at stake. Not for publication was the Secretary's aside that an Anglo-American renunciation might also ease the British out of their special advantages at Shanghai and Hong Kong.[17]

Thus spurred by Secretary Hull, the negotiations came to a successful close in early 1943. Article IV of the proposed treaty specifically pro- tected American property owners and their heirs, and Commerce Sec- retary Jesse Jones assured the President that his Department was at work seeking ways to adjust to the new state of things and to expand commerce: "In the foreign field problems of primary significance to

American businessmen include difficulties arising from the termination of extra-territorial rights in China. Existing Chinese commercial codes will quite certainly require revision with a view for facilitating the postwar participation of foreign firms in the industrial development of China." [18]

Foreign traders heard the Department's principal China adviser address their convention and affirm that the Kuomintang was already undertaking the needed legislative revisions. One old China Hand, William P. Hunt, praised the Department for despatching an economic adviser as well as a legal adviser to help in the clarification of Chinese laws.[19]

At the end of the negotiations Hull had turned to the Chinese foreign minister and explained that the United States had set forth all its foreign policy principles at the 1933 Montevideo meetings; relinquishing these special rights was "part and parcel of the good neighbor policy." [20]

Hull had more than a little hoped that the British could be persuaded to be good neighbors about Shanghai and Hong Kong. Roosevelt had spoken eloquently several times in trying to convince the British to give up the crown colony of Hong Kong. Both Anthony Eden and Ambassador Halifax heard him say that such a *beau geste* would eliminate one more vestige of the bad old imperialism. Sumner Welles and General Stilwell listened while he told them what a good thing it would be if Hong Kong were made into a free port, "free to the commerce of all nations—of the whole world!" [21]

English leaders reacted negatively, and strongly so, yet the President pressed the question right up to the Yalta Conference, when he finally decided that he could not drive Britain out of Hong Kong and at the same time grant Russian claims to special rights at Port Arthur and Dairen, though he did insist that Russia keep these Manchurian ports open to foreign traders.[22]

Hull had even brought the crown colony into the conversations at the Moscow Foreign Ministers Conference in October, 1943, remarking that the British possession typified dependent peoples who must be satisfied after the war. The Secretary's main desire, though, was to see that China was included among the signatories of the final declaration of the Conference. But he found both Britain and Russia suspicious. Hull persevered, thinking to himself that inside such a declaration China could be influenced, but if it was left outside, this might prove difficult. Moreover, if China and Russia were both part of the same pact, Moscow's cooperation in Asia, including American plans for China's rehabilitation, could be more easily obtained.[23]

On his way to Cairo and Teheran while Hull was thus engaged, the President sent special congratulations to him for securing China's right to sign the document. The President also expected to discuss China's postwar aspirations not only with Chiang but with his other Allies as well, and he was especially anxious to probe into Premier Stalin's intentions in the Far East. In these circumstances the Moscow Declaration might be useful at any moment, for in talks with the Joint Chiefs he predicted there would be clashes between Russia and China over Manchuria. These might be avoided, he hoped, by establishing a number of free zones in the area. Somewhat modified, this idea was the basis for the Yalta Agreement on the Far East.[24]

So Roosevelt, when he faced Stalin, wanted the Moscow Declaration, and he in fact did allude to it at Teheran. The United States had insisted upon Chinese equality, he told Stalin, because it was better to have this nation of 400 million as a friend "than as a potential source of trouble." At Cairo a few days earlier, Chiang had listed his wants and expectations in Manchuria, Formosa, and other areas. Chinese notes of these discussions record that Roosevelt had even offered China a place in the Japanese occupation, and that the President had then "proposed that China and the United States should consult with each other before any decision was to be reached on matters concerning Asia." [25]

Russian aspirations for warm-water ports in Manchuria were discussed at Teheran, the President listened to them in a friendly but noncommittal manner. Each time the topic arose, Roosevelt slid over it or expanded the discussion to cover the Dardanelles and the Baltic area, suggesting similar treatment be given to all. Truman used this general approach at the Potsdam Conference. Roosevelt initiated a topic of his own, a plan for a trusteeship over Korea, and this idea appeared in the background of the Cairo Declaration.[26]

American China policy in 1943 had thus attempted to boost China's internal and international standing within the context and by the method of buttressing the Open Door Policy. Sometimes American diplomats appeared to be carried away with these really very limited and momentary successes. Cordell Hull, for example, was overly sanguine in a discussion with the Chinese Ambassador in 1943, predicting that the

"Generalissimo would live to see a general renaissance take place in China on all important lines of human endeavor, such as swept over Europe like a sunburst during the fourteenth and fifteenth centuries." But anyone who bothered to go outside the State Department building found that the atmosphere over China was really very heavy, and any sunburst was hidden behind storm clouds. "The existing situation cannot endure very much longer," reported an American diplomat from China's capital. "A number of intelligent Chinese of affairs with sober, conservative and balanced minds have variously estimated . . . that under present conditions China 'can last' only from six months to a year." [27]

Excited by Chinese possibilities but fearful of the darker realities, American diplomats had taken the steps recounted above, but they heard Chiang's pleas for direct financial aid with uncertain reserve.

Chiang Kai-shek had asked for a 500-million-dollar loan to stabilize his economy as early as January of 1942. Now undoubtedly part of the reason for Washington's reserve was that this request came at a time when the later largesse of American foreign aid was undreamed of, but the American Ambassador, Clarence Gauss, had warned that certainly no more than that amount should be given, for he was skeptical if even that money would be spent properly. He was not alone. Others in the Administration were also worried lest the funds be spent "mainly for the benefit of persons or groups close to Chiang Kai-shek rather than in ways which would help the Chinese people and encourage their resistance." [28]

The State Department first approved a lowered figure, 300 million dollars, but upon re-examination of the political factors boosted it back up to 500 million.[29]

Chiang made another big request at the Cairo Conference. This time he wanted a billion dollar gold loan to reverse inflationary tides sweeping over his country. After the Teheran Conference scotched the Burma campaign, Chiang wrote the President dolefully that the decision would allow the Japanese to win in China unless his country received the billion dollar grant, redoubled airlift operations, and was guaranteed 20,000 tons of supplies per month.[30]

Treasury Secretary Morgenthau was one of the first asked to comment on the Chinese loan. He doubted it would do much good in Chiang's effort to defeat inflation, and, more important, it was still too soon to tell how such large sums could be best employed for

China's reconstruction. In brief, there were too many good reasons why the loan should not be made.

Ambassador Gauss was just as adamant: China was already exploiting the United States financially, he said. For example, American forces in that country had to pay an exorbitant exchange rate for the yuan. The Chinese currency was only worth ½¢, but Chiang refused to consider adjusting the official rate of 5¢ per yuan, so his treasury made 4½¢ on every yuan exchanged. Millions spent in China on airfields, charged Gauss, wound up in Chiang's treasury.[31]

Gauss ended his remarks on the loan, and turned to rumors that China planned to close its economy after the war. The United States should not allow this to go beyond the rumor stage. Serious negotiations for a commercial treaty should be initiated at once, so that Washington could make clear its desires.[32]

But the Ambassador's superiors cautioned against sending the Chinese a flat refusal. For one thing the Chinese leaders at Cairo had been given the impression that such a request would be acted upon favorably, but far more important to the Department of State were politicosocial arguments. True enough, China might not be very effective in the struggle against Japan, but that country's attitude and standing in the postwar world would be of great importance in the alignment of major powers in the future.[33]

In this instance Roosevelt listened to Morgenthau, and the loan was not granted; he sent Chiang a copy of the Morgenthau recommendations, commenting along with them that they actually expressed great confidence in Chinese abilities to meet their problems. The Chinese leader's reactions were harsh, including a threat to compel American forces in his country to pay all of their expenses, and he absolutely refused to modify the outlandish exchange rate, but the loan question dropped out of sight for the time being.[34]

GREAT EXPECTATIONS AND GREAT FEARS

As suggested by the State Department policy memorandum on the 1943 loan request, big-power rivalries in Asia played an ever-increasing part in America's China policy. In dread that the internal and external threat to China would overwhelm the Chinese government, policy makers clung ever more tightly to past assumptions, constantly repeating to themselves that China was this or was that without ever looking up to see if it were at all true.

Sumner Welles, for example, seemed only to be repeating the story of the 1930's dilemma when he wrote: "For reasons of strategy as well as for reasons of legitimate economic interest, the United States could not agree passively to acquiesce in the establishment of a Soviet dominated China." This was not so bad, except that Welles and the others who thought this way had substituted Russia for Japan without recognizing more important changes on the other side of this equation: unfortunately for American planners, the future power struggle in Asia did not follow any recognizable pattern of the past.[35]

For one thing, as Harry Hopkins noted realistically, China would truly require vast amounts of aid if the Open Door Policy were to be sustained. He estimated as much as 250 million dollars per annum for several years, and he was too low. For accepting this burden, however, the United States could expect to receive several benefits, he wrote in *American Magazine:* A strong China would be an Asian peacemaker: "Our compelling interests in the Pacific make essential a friendly and close relationship with China, economically and in every respect." [36]

Several other policy makers recognized with Hopkins the need to aid China, but their emphasis was on the advantages Hopkins had listed and how to obtain them. Francis Sayre emphasized military bases: "China needs American goods. The United States in the post-war world will need Chinese markets if we are to keep our men at work. The same is true of Australia, of New Zealand, of Malaya, of the Philippines . . . . If we accept that view, what follows? Should the United States establish naval or air bases in the Philippines?" [37]

To Assistant Secretaries of State Will Clayton and Dean Acheson, rebuilding the Chinese economy was a challenge and an opportunity. "I think if we put China on a sounder economic footing," stated the former cotton exporter before the Senate Foreign Relations Committee, "she will become a better customer for our goods and that the trade between the two nations could increase greatly." Acheson reminded a nation-wide radio audience that one person in ten in the United States depended upon foreign trade for a living. "The U.S.S.R. may be one of our best customers after the war. And China—a nation of 450 million about to have a great industrial development"—might well be another.[38]

From China, journalist Theodore White reported a renewed business interest in that country, one which might actually accomplish what Clayton and Acheson were talking about. "China may afford the greatest single outlet for American surplus producing capacity, machine tools, and heavy goods after the war. American business firms with long standing interest in the Far East are well aware of this." Standard Oil, William P. Hunt and Company, C. V. Starr and Company, and the National City Bank of New York were all "reaching written and unwritten understandings with the Chinese Government . . . ." [39]

In the United States, the China-America Council of Commerce and Industry held a banquet for 1,700 persons to welcome the Vice-President of China to the United States. The American Vice-President, Henry Wallace, was asked to be the principal speaker. "In view of the great importance of our relations with China we feel that this meeting will have a significance of the greatest importance," read Wallace's invitation, "especially as it will include representatives of the foremost business firms of the United States." [40]

Because he had just returned from China after talking with Chiang Kai-shek about the dissident communists in North China and the whole country's economic problems, Wallace was on the inside of Chinese-American relations. At this time the Administration fully understood the need "for broadening the base of support of the Chinese Government," the Department of State told Ambassador Gauss. "Anything . . . we can do to hasten such a reform will be all to the good." [41]

As early as 1943 disappointment and continuing dissatisfaction with the Kuomintang, plus the notion that somehow the United States might squeeze in between the Chinese Reds and Moscow, led a few State Department officers to suggest opening up direct contacts with Mao Tse-tung at Yenan. They argued that such contacts could be an important means of preventing a renewed Kuomintang-Communist civil war after Japan surrendered. In the summer of 1944 Wallace hoped to learn from Chiang if he would agree to bringing the Communists into the government. As tactfully as possible he tried to give things a little shove by conveying President Roosevelt's suggestion that inasmuch as the "Communists and the members of the Kuomintang were all Chinese, they were basically friends . . . . If the parties could not get together they might 'call in a friend' and [President Roosevelt] had intimated that he might be that friend." [42]

Chiang refused to commit himself and kept going back to the sore subject of the reversal of the decision to invade Burma. Other missions would also come to the Chinese leader in hopes of finding a basis for national unity by bringing the two factions together, but neither General Hurley nor General Marshall were to be any more successful.

Yet Wallace had taken War Production head Donald M. Nelson to China with him to organize a counterpart there to the American agency. "I consider the whole question of our economic relations with China," Roosevelt had written Nelson, "to be one of utmost importance to this country." He went on to explain that Chiang should be given to understand that Americans would not be coming to his country as exploiters. "Yet I feel sure that we have a proper function to perform to help to put China on its feet economically." And Chiang was more pleased by far with Nelson's part in the mission than with Wallace's call for unity. The production expert returned to Washington full of the exciting industrial potentialities in the Yangtze Valley: "For the United States, the Yangtze development would mean large exports, the stimulation of key industries and many jobs for workers. Several agencies of our government, and members of the House and Senate, are actively interested, as are a number of private industrial and engineering concerns." [43]

Representatives from 1,700 of them had met to welcome the Vice-President of China. Roosevelt and Grew were impressed by the Nelson report, but it "got progressively more dessicated in its dreary shuttle around government offices." Nelson's vision of postwar China as the "workshop and supply house of the Far East" may have seemed farfetched to many at a time when that country could not even sustain an offensive against the Japanese. On the other hand, it was charged by Bruce Catton that the report was put aside because it clearly implied a "profound change in the Oriental world." Whatever the reasons, the Nelson plan probably was the only way in which the Open Door Policy could have succeeded after the war. Chiang's inability to make good use of American military aid after the war would indicate, however, that even if the Nelson program had been adopted, the civil war still would not have been won.[44]

"There is still hope that everything will work out all right," Roosevelt wrote Henry Grady at the end of 1944. And that was about the best that any realistic policy maker could say about the China situation.[45] The Foreign Service officers now located with the Communists at Yenan were pushing their candidate for American aid. John Stewart Service reported that the Communists seemed favorably inclined towards foreign investment and the principles of private property even for Chinese citizens. Such paradoxical attitudes from the Communists gave some the idea that the Open Door Policy could be preserved by working with Mao rather than Chiang. Though he reversed himself later, Ambassador Hurley was one of those responsible for the idea that the United States might be able to work with the Chinese Communists. This momentary uncertainty led General Albert Wedemeyer to ask for very specific instructions about the purpose of his mission in replacing Stilwell: Was he to fight only the Japanese, or was he also charged with the task of strengthening Chiang Kai-shek's regime? [46]

THE YALTA FAR EASTERN AGREEMENT

Wedemeyer's problem was that if he were to fight the Japanese effectively, he might have to arm and use the Chinese Communists. This might result, of course, in the arms being used against the Kuomintang. Also if he were to work to unify China as well, American forces might become involved in a Chinese civil war. Roosevelt did his best to forestall and preclude this and other Far Eastern crises at Yalta through his dialogue with Premier Stalin.

The State Department had prepared for him detailed briefing books on the Far Eastern situation, but Roosevelt had little need of them. He had already gone beyond the goal-setting stage and was now thinking about how he could achieve his desired ends. But to keep the matter clearly in focus, one or two points in these papers need repeating. "Our policy toward China," began one, "is not based on sentiment. It is based on enlightened self-interest motivated by considerations of international security and well-being." Sino-Soviet agreement was the *"sine qua non* of peace and security in the Far East." Only then, concluded this paper, could equal opportunity be assured and permanence be accorded to any treaty of commerce and navigation the United States signed later with the Nationalist government.[47]

There was also the plain and simple desire to buy Russian military participation in the Far East, but this did not crowd out of Roosevelt's weary mind and body other political considerations. The Yalta Agreement was a logical conclusion to Roosevelt's China policy. After all, he had first raised the matter of Russian political desires at Teheran, and he had already done a good deal to try and bring the Nationalists and Communists into accord before the war ended, leaving Asia in turmoil once again.

Not until Stalin promised that the Soviet Union would support Chiang Kai-shek after the war did Roosevelt agree to Soviet desires in Manchuria. Moreover, none of these concessions could be claimed until the successful completion of a new treaty between the Soviet Union and China. It will never be known how this treaty would have been honored if Chiang had been able to stabilize China after the war.

Still, the Yalta Agreement was naïve, said many, for expecting even a modicum of Soviet good faith. Perhaps, but it is equally necessary to point out that even the American Chamber of Commerce in China felt that it had to recommend cutting off aid to Nationalist China in 1947, unless Chiang genuinely reformed and broadened his government.

Russia further agreed to approach the Chinese Communists on the question of support for the war against Japan in cooperation with the Kuomintang. Only then did the President accept Stalin's bid for lease rights to Dairen and Port Arthur. Even under Russian management, these Manchurian ports were supposed to remain free to international commerce. Roosevelt also agreed that Russia should share control of Manchurian railroads with China, and finally, that the Soviets should have the Kurile Islands north of Japan, lost to Moscow since the Russo-Japanese War.[48]

Russia played it tough on the Yalta bargain, extracting the full letter of its due (and perhaps then some). One observer has commented that the best that could be said for the Russian promise to aid Chiang was that Moscow did not openly intervene on the side of the Communists in 1945–46. As Allied relations rapidly deteriorated, some called the Far Eastern agreement a Russian variation on the shell game. And the pea was gone. But even General Hurley, who was among the first revisionists on the Yalta exchange and who undertook to reconcile Chiang and Mao, maintained that the more crucial problem still was how "to hold up the Chiang Kai-shek regime." Likewise did Ambassador Harriman warn from his post in Moscow that if the Kuomintang-Communist fissure were not pushed together by the time the Soviets marched, Stalin would happily employ the Chinese Reds to set up a "puppet government in Manchuria and possibly in North China . . . ."[49]

Of the two threats to Nationalist China, then, the internal one looked to be the greater. Besides, being realistic about it, there was not much that could be done about the Russians. Therefore, when the War Department was asked by the State Department whether the Yalta Agreement should be reconsidered in part or completely, it replied that Russia could take what it wanted in the Far East anyway. Nonetheless, by late April, 1945, the Administration had decided to do some rethinking about the bargain. Roosevelt's death, quarrels among the

Allies in Europe, long-range political considerations, and the growing conviction that the United States could defeat Japan alone were the major factors which led to such discussions.[50]

The Joint Chiefs of Staff recommended "introducing at least token U.S. forces into China" to counter Russian presence in Manchuria. As if it were privy to intra-government debates, *Fortune* printed an article entitled, "U.S. Meets U.S.S.R. in Manchuria": "What the U.S. needs basically in Asia is peace and and commerce, but if these advantages are to be secured basic policy commitments must be honored."[51]

Acting Secretary of State Grew wanted to find out if Moscow was going to honor its obligations. After a discussion at the White House, it was determined to hold up Ambassador Harriman's return to Moscow until some sort of decision was reached. This was on May 12, 1945. That same day Grew sent a list of questions to his colleagues in the War and Navy Departments:

> Was Russian entry into the Far Eastern War of such vital concern to the United States as to preclude an attempt to obtain "certain desirable political objectives in the Far East prior to such entry"?
> "Should the Yalta decision be reconsidered in whole or in part"? Should a Soviet demand for participation in the Japanese occupation be granted or "would such occupation adversely affect our long term policy for the future treatment of Japan"?

In addition to these questions, Grew included a list of political objectives the State Department had in mind. At the top was the express desire to obtain a firm commitment from Moscow that Russia would aid the United States to bring about Chinese unification under Chiang Kai-shek. Another objective was to obtain "unequivocal adherence" to the Cairo Declaration on Manchuria and Korea. A third concerned the acquisition of emergency landing rights in the Kuriles for commercial airplanes.[52]

Secretary Stimson pondered these vital questions from his colleague and could not keep from noting in his diary that they were inevitably connected to S-1—the atomic bomb project. "Over any such tangled wave of problems," he wrote down, "the S-1 secret would be dominant and yet we will not know until after that time [the Potsdam Conference] probably . . . whether this is a weapon in our hands or not. We think it will be shortly afterwards, but it seems a terrible thing to gamble with such big stakes in diplomacy without having your master card in your hand." [53]

As the Secretary was looking over his hand and worrying about not yet having the master card, he received a letter from former President Hoover. Hoover had been thinking about Russian-American rivalry in the Far East, too. And he believed that total victory over Japan would be costly in the event and would open the way to Russian expansion over the "balance of China and over all of Japan by ideological penetration"; he suggested that the United States should urge Chiang to approach the Japanese on the basis of their evacuation of China and Manchuria, after which the United States and Britain would offer peace terms based on Japan's total disarmament. If accepted, these terms embodied all that America had been fighting for, including the prevention of Russian expansion, the maintenance of "free enterprise" in Asia, and the return of Japan "to cooperation with Western Civilization." All these could be accomplished without more suffering and the expected loss of 500,000 to 1,000,000 lives in another eighteen months of war.[54]

A week after receiving the Grew memorandum and questionnaire, the War Department gave its answers, concurring in the need to reach an understanding with Russia before advising the Chinese to negotiate a Sino-Soviet Russian treaty under the terms of the Yalta Agreement. But then Stimson went on to say that Russia probably could take what she wanted just by entering the war. The crux of the matter, as everyone else was saying, was the "present schism in China." The Administration should intensify its efforts to bring the rival factions into one government.[55]

"Yes," Grew in effect replied, sending Stimson another memorandum elaborating on the State Department's current China policy—yes, the United States *was* trying to get Chiang to open his government to include all legal parties, even the Communists if they were prepared to observe the laws and decrees of the Nationalist government. It was hoped that an interim conference of Nationalist, Communist, and nonparty political leaders would be convened prior to the meeting of the proposed people's assembly in November, 1945. This would ensure the assembly's legitimacy and ability to promulgate a democratic constitution.

In addition, the United States desired to set up a supreme war council of Communists and Nationalists operating under an American com-

mander with staff assistance from British, Russian, and Chinese officers. Economic reforms, including coordination of postwar plans with
American, British, and Russian advisers should be initiated. "Enactment of new commercial laws and regulations embodying liberal commercial and economic policies and principles and insuring the 'open
door' and equal commercial opportunity to all countries" should be
encouraged.

If any of these steps were to be taken, Russian cooperation on three
main points was required: respect for Chinese territorial integrity (significantly though, and in relation to the contention that Roosevelt abandoned the Open Door Policy, the State Department was not opposed
to settling Chinese boundary disputes by negotiations); the return to
China of Formosa and the Pescadores; and the maintenance of Nationalist China's prestige and influence in international affairs.[56]

To seek an agreement on those terms, the now ailing Harry Hopkins
went to Moscow with Ambassador Harriman to talk with Premier
Stalin. By this time, however, enough disagreements had sprung up
among the Allies to make his visit remembered as the first Cold War
exchange.

After discussing European questions at two meetings, Hopkins and
the Russian leader took up Far Eastern matters on May 28, 1945. The
presidential adviser began: When would Russia enter the war in Asia?
In two or three months if T. V. Soong agreed to the Yalta decisions,
the Russian Premier answered. Hopkins went deeper: What about
Chinese unity? Stalin came back neatly, remarking that the United
States would have to assume the political lead in China. Moreover, he
thought there was no communist leader there strong enough to command national support. Ambassador Harriman interjected a question
about the Open Door Policy. The Premier quickly assured the Americans that it would be honored, "and went out of his way to indicate that
the United States was the only power with the resources to aid China
economically after the war." Hopkins demurred slightly, noting that
the United States did not have an "exclusive interest in China or the
Far East and that we did not wish to see any other nation kept out."
The discussion concluded satisfactorily with additional Russian assurances that Soviet military authorities would allow the Chinese Nationalists "in any areas where the Red Army were."[57]

President Truman was pleased. He took these conversations for positive replies to the State Department's list of political objectives and

wired Hopkins his personal congratulations. Secretary Stimson, though, had not stopped thinking about the tangled wave of problems, and when Truman brought up the reports from Hopkins in one of their conversations, the War Secretary came back to the ticklish question of sharing atomic secrets with Moscow and the "quid pro quo which should be established in consideration for our taking them into partnership." Truman said that he had been thinking of those questions, too, and "mentioned the same things that I was thinking of, namely, the settlement of the Polish, Rumanian, Yugoslavian, and Manchurian problems." [58]

The Hopkins-Stalin talks encouraged the President enough so that he called T. V. Soong to the White House to tell him about the Yalta decisions on the Far East. The Chinese diplomat reacted by asking for United States presence and intervention, if necessary, in the negotiations which would have to follow in Moscow. Truman declined at first, but he softened this a few days later, telling the Chinese government he realized that Dr. Soong could not discuss such critical matters with Marshal Stalin without the presence of others. [59]

Almost at once, Soong invoked American aid through Ambassador Harriman. The American diplomat then asked Washington for a further clarification of its understanding of the Yalta arrangements. The new Secretary of State, James Byrnes, answered that the United States declined to act as an interpreter, but it understood that the Manchurian railways should be jointly owned and operated, "and that while the American government did not wish to share in the control of the administration of the port of Dairen, it would expect to have free and equal access to the port as well as to the railways." This was still not detailed enough for those in Moscow who were facing the Russian negotiators every day. Harriman asked for more study of the Outer Mongolian and Korean situations, especially since the Potsdam Conference would occur before Soong and Stalin could possibly agree anyway. [60]

THE DOWNHILL RUN AFTER POTSDAM

By the time Truman left Washington for Germany on July 6, 1945, many of his advisers had come out against pulling or pushing Russia into the war against Japan. Truman disagreed. He accepted Roosevelt's military reasoning that many lives would be saved by Russia's entry, and he also accepted Roosevelt's political reasoning that Anglo-American-Russian cooperation would be the key to Chinese unity and stability. Moreover, as the War Department had said in answer to Grew's original inquiries, Russia could take what it wanted if it entered Manchuria with or without the Yalta agreement. There was still good reason to think a political arrangement with Moscow was far better than none at all.[61]

The American delegation had the Open Door Policy very much on its mind at the outset of the meetings. Soong had received Stalin's demands on the Manchurian railways and ports, and they went much further than was ever envisioned by United States representatives at the Crimean Conference. "The proposals relating to Dairen, as they now stand," Grew advised Truman, "are open to legitimate objection on the part of the United States and other of the United Nations." [62]

Long familiar with problems of the Open Door Policy, Secretary Stimson took it upon himself to keep the new President on the straight and narrow of American diplomatic principles. "I had talks with him," reads his diary for July 15, 1945, "and I gave him a memorandum on the conflict between the supposed plans of Russia as to Dairen in Manchuria and our Open Door policy, and went over them with him carefully, again and again warning him to be absolutely sure that the Russians did not block off our trade by their control over the Chinese Eastern railway. I pointed out that an open port would be useless if our trade could be smothered by railroad control behind that, and that was what it looked as if the Russians were planning to do." [63]

At the first meeting between Stalin and Truman on July 17, the Russian Premier facilely explained the difficulties which had held up the Sino-Soviet negotiations, and Truman came away, according to one version of what took place, thinking he had clinched the Open Door Policy once and for all. Admiral Leahy's record of the day's conversation was somewhat different. He contended that Byrnes and Truman had come to believe that Moscow would demand radical concessions from China. Whatever happened, the next day Truman was very "greatly reinforced" by Stimson's news that a successful atomic bomb had been tested in New Mexico, and its power exceeded all expectations. Truman "again repeated that he was confident of sustaining the Open Door policy, and I took the occasion to emphasize to him the importance of going over the matter detail by detail so as to be sure there would be no misunderstanding over the meaning of the general expressions." Can it be, as some have claimed, that such matters were really unconnected? [64]

The President now decided that it was time to review both the military and the political situation in this new light. He sent off a message to the Chinese government urging it not to go beyond the letter of the Yalta agreements in making concessions to the Russians. The State Department even prepared a draft protocol designed to secure written pledges from both Russia and China to honor "the principle of equality of opportunity which underlies the historic 'open door' policy." The President called together his military advisers to ask them if Russian entrance into the war in Asia was still required. Once again the War Department spokesman, General Marshall, pointed out that Russia would come in anyway and get "virtually what they wanted in the surrender terms." [65]

But Secretary Byrnes came away from this discussion shaking his head and hoping only that the Sino-Russian negotiations might stall and thereby "delay Soviet entrance and the Japanese might surrender." "The President was in accord with that view," revealed Byrnes to Navy Secretary Forrestal, and the Secretary of State "was most anxious to get the Japanese affair over before the Russians got in, with particular reference to Dairen and Port Arthur. Once in there, he felt, it would not be easy to get them out . . . ." [66]

Despite the encouragement not to yield, the treaty between Russia and China, signed on August 14, 1945, did go beyond what the United States wanted to see China concede. Ironically, the atomic bombs exploded at Hiroshima and Nagasaki came too late to keep Russia out and in fact probably speeded up its entrance into the conflict. Stimson had told Truman on July 24 that he was opposed to bombing Kyoto because it would be a "wanton act" against a non-military target and would make it impossible to reconcile the Japanese to American policy after the war. "It might thus, I pointed out, be the means of preventing what our policy demanded, namely a sympathetic Japan to the United States in case there should be any aggression by Russia in Manchuria." [67]

Byrnes issued strong representations against a clause in the Sino-Russian pact allowing the Soviet Union to put Dairen in a Russian military zone, and even considered landing American troops to back up his policy, but decided to allow developments to run their course. There was a feeling that the rest of the treaty was not too bad. After all, Russia had pledged itself therein to support the Nationalists. Moreover, it was difficult to send troops into Manchuria in August, 1945, when at the same time the United States finally refused to support

Chiang's claim to Hong Kong. Truman had bluntly asserted that "without aid from us" China could no more get troops to Hong Kong than to Manchuria.[68]

As the months went by, however, the United States did airlift half a million of Chiang's soldiers into North China and Manchuria, and American soldiers, ostensibly in the same areas to accept Japanese surrenders, stayed and became loosely involved in the reborn civil war. Admiral Leahy heard President Truman tell the Chinese Ambassador that he wished he could do more, such as arming and shipping thirty-nine divisions of Chinese troops to Manchuria. The Russians were making things difficult by restricting Chinese ships from disembarking in Manchuria and arming Chinese Communists with Japanese weapons. Nor were these isolated developments: In Japan, the United States avoided giving Russia a share in high policy decisions of the Allied Control Commission; Admiral Leahy commented gravely that the establishment of a Soviet influenced or dominated Japan would mean that the United States had lost the war in the Pacific.[69]

Why not, then, an all-out policy to preserve Manchuria? There are many answers, each of them providing part of the over-all picture. The atom bomb, for one thing, though it brought the war to an end quickly telescoped Asian problems. The Russian advance had been surprisingly easy and rapid against what had been assumed to be strong Japanese opposition. European problems diverted American interests and, as Joseph Grew put it in November, 1945, "We are surrounded by a sea of international troubles. If we start cleaning up China by force we might just as well make up our minds to police the world." The next factor followed from Grew's comment: Chiang Kai-shek was simply not going to be able to rule China. Even Stilwell's successor was reported by a British general as having said that American aid to China might actually be a hindrance and that the only solution might be found in making China into a United Nations trusteeship! [70]

In December, 1945, General Marshall set out to find some way of bringing the Communists and the Kuomintang into a unified government. Marshall was unable to bring it about, and the two billion dollars of aid the United States poured into China in the next two years (far more than the Russians ever gave Mao) was equally unrewarding as an attempt to save the American China policy. Finally, even the American Chamber of Commerce in China wrote requesting that no more aid be given Chiang until he eliminated the extremist elements in his government: "The cry has continually been for more, more, and again more aid, but it is an established fact that little or no effective use was made of the huge surpluses and postwar shipments of supplies, and that a considerable part of aid went to favored groups and individuals." [71]

Unfortunately such awakenings came too late; probably they would have been too late even before World War II. The emphasis on the maintenance of the Open Door Policy, while of course it did not lose China, still made that country the object of diplomacy, and support of Chiang Kai-shek forced American policy makers into ambiguous postures: They asserted that China should be a member of big-power decision-making teams, but sharply limited its presence and participation in such meetings. They looked for the Great China Market but were unwilling to force Chiang to carry out genuine reforms until it was a case of too little and too late. As late as September, 1946, an official of the State Department wrote the American-China Policy Association: "We have no intention of relinquishing the 'open door' policy in China." So very typical of Washington's attitude since the turn of the century, it revealed a state of mind which was no longer adequate to the changed situation. Roosevelt had tried hard during the war to improve China's internal and external situation, but his first inclinations about China back in 1934 were more realistic. The failures of the Open Door Policy were ideological ones as much as anything else, for they cramped American thinking from 1931 to 1949. [72]

As a nation we have built to the limit of our geographical frontiers. Certainly, we must concern ourselves more and more, if we are to be a prosperous people, with building a realistic basis of sharing in the development of the frontiers abroad—in making foreign trade something more than our own one-way street.

Henry Wallace, *Sixty Million Jobs*, 1945

The capitalistic system is essentially an international system. If it cannot function internationally, it will break down completely.

Assistant Secretary of State Henry Grady, 1942

It seems to me by this bill that your bank [the International Bank for Reconstruction and Development] is going to have the power to decide whether this country is developed or that country is developed, whether this country can successfully trade or that country can successfully trade.

Senator Robert A. Taft, 1945

13 · Restoring an Open World

When Americans set out to restore and rebuild an open world and to erect in it a more lasting superstructure than had been destroyed ideologically in the 1930's, and militarily in the war, they started with the belief that international security had to exist on two levels simultaneously —political and economic—and all major nations had to participate in the construction of the foundations of this new world. "To put it another way," an American Defense Department official explained at a later time and in a different context, but one which was related to the outcome of World War II, "we believe that while defense provides the essential security of the alliance [NATO], trade provides the substance." "We regard these trade measures as a forward step designed to provide the cement of the free world alliance in which defense has already erected the framework of steel." [1]

Going back to 1938, Roosevelt's adviser and later Ambassador to France William C. Bullitt had similar thoughts on the choice between Nazi Germany's autarchy and the American system: "Perhaps the absolute importance of the international market [has] been exaggerated.

261

Whether that be so or not, its relative importance appears today to be as great as ever; its marginal influence is real and powerful; whatever may be the role of the home market, the fostering of international trade must remain an element of capital importance for economic prosperity within the national frontiers." Bullitt was one of many who were coming to see the Axis threat in that way. He was also one of many who later perceived the same threat from Russian expansionism. "Every time the Soviet Union extends its power over another area or state, the United States and Great Britain lose another normal market." [2]

In reviewing much of what has been written about World War II diplomacy thus far, one is taken by the absence of any real concern about these economic factors. It almost seems that in striving to purge themselves of economic determinism, diplomatic historians have returned to an earlier point of view and re-emphasized political interpretations. More than that, the impression is left that only Churchill and Stalin indulged in political maneuvers, while the United States wanted merely to win the war and let the postwar world develop from there. This legend swells and swells (and with it the notion that America therefore always gets taken at the peace table by shrewder bargainers), and no matter how many needles are thrust into this balloon, it refuses to explode.

A partial reason for thinking this way could well be that since the United States was the strongest of the Big Three, American maneuvers were not devious and were comparatively uncomplicated. In Anglo-American economic discussions, for example, the United States, when all else failed, simply reminded Britain that it was the stronger partner.[3]

One founder of bipartisan foreign policy making was Senator Arthur H. Vandenberg, who certainly had few doubts that "Americans [would] mix their idealism with large and ample doses of enlightened self-interest." [4]

Vandenberg's hypothesis, which he had arrived at after abandoning isolationism, offers a more logical point of departure than a useless repetition of supposed American innocence or naïvete—a theme Henry James was the last author to use successfully. American leaders *did* follow through on their ideas and premises. From their first assumption that security was indivisible, it followed that international political organization had to supersede tight regional groupings. Economic planning closely paralleled this political concept, for policy makers reaffirmed multilateralism as against regional or closed systems, represented in the state trading monopolies of the Soviet Union (which had so upset Bullitt in the mid-1930's) or even the British Ottawa Preference System. In this the postwar planners simply picked up the story at the point of the U.S.–U.K. 1938 trade agreement. And the State Department's *Postwar Foreign Policy Planning* quite correctly made this the general theme and pointed out that economic planning was much farther advanced than political planning, since the former was primarily an amplification and refinement of the basic tenets of the 1930's. Herbert Feis said it all very simply during the war: "The extension of the Open Door remains a sound American aim." [5]

Also of great consequence was the discovery by many conservatives and liberals that economic planning for the peace afforded a meeting ground similar to the anti-Axis struggle. On that ground former Liberty Leaguer Will Clayton and New Dealer Harry Hopkins could easily reach a bipartisan understanding on foreign economic policy. In November, 1944, a disturbed Clayton wrote Hopkins that he was alarmed by a prominent economist's remark that strong measures by the National government could maintain domestic employment without the need for expanded foreign trade.

"Does he face with equanimity," marveled Clayton, "the possibility of a reconversion in our export industries from the present level of 15 billion dollars annually to the prewar level of 3 billion dollars?" True enough, some countries had achieved full employment without enlarged trade, but then, "Do we want to adopt the Russian system?" America's goal was a 150 billion dollar gross national product, with employment of 56 million persons; with that would come surpluses, and the only markets for these were foreign markets. Perhaps the United States would even have to assume Great Britain's role after the Napoleonic Wars and become the world's source of credit in order to finance its own foreign trade and investment. In any event, concluded Clayton, the alternatives were clear: either business and industry would provide the employment or the government would have to.

To each of these arguments Hopkins readily assented. "I just cannot understand what is going through the minds of those fellows who wash up foreign trade in such cavalier manner," he wrote back. "It seems to me they are quite unrealistic about what makes the wheels go round." [6]

No conservative outdid Hopkins in championing foreign investment, and its protection: "Whoever borrows must see to it that expropriation will be impossible," he wrote in 1944. "The people of this country have a right to expect that kind of protection from their Government. It must be further agreed that money lent by this Government to other nations must be spent for purchases in this country . . . . And it is highly important that business and government have an early meeting of minds as to general policy governing private investments abroad." The Hopkins-Clayton exchange was part of a very broad and very deep concern among American leaders that the Depression would fall upon the United States with even greater weight as soon as war-stimulated production could not be absorbed by the economy.[7]

There were harsh critics of this coalition: Rexford Tugwell mulled over its beginnings in his mind and concluded that it may have started a long time before, when businessmen were asked to aid recovery in 1933. Regardless of where it began, he said, by 1945 the enemies of progress were seated "in all the strategic places of power." Bruce Catton was upset at the postwar world and sat down to write, in the *War Lords of Washington,* an explanation of what he thought had happened. This book was based upon the contention that the dollar-a-year-men had perverted the New Deal to their own ends. Perhaps Archibald MacLeish was the most outspoken: "As things are now going, the peace we will make, the peace we seem to be making, will be a peace of oil, a peace of gold, a peace of shipping, a peace, in brief, of factual situations, a peace without moral purpose or human interest, a peace of dicker and trade, about the facts of commerce, the facts of banking, the facts of transportation, which will lead us where the treaties made by dicker and trade have always led." [8]

These criticisms did hit at a soft spot in American postwar planning, for all too often specific plans for Latin America, the Middle East, and the Far East got swallowed up as victory came closer and the drive for expansion and still more expansion of foreign trade grew intense. Planning for the United Nations escaped this early end because it was recognized that without such a political structure the future world could not stand.

THE BIG FOUR AND THE UNITED NATIONS

Sumner Welles and Harry Hopkins listened to the discussions between President Roosevelt and Prime Minister Churchill at the Atlantic Conference in August, 1941, and advised the President to commit himself more fully to a world political organization. Roosevelt's mind, however, was full of the memory of Woodrow Wilson's failures after World War I, and besides, he was fairly sure that an "international police force composed of the United States and Great Britain" would be the best kind of a security organization.

With the addition of Russia and China to the Grand Alliance, Roosevelt changed it to the Big Four, at least in theory, and divided the regions of the world among them for security purposes. They would be the "guarantors of eventual peace." In reality this was not an "either . . . or" sort of question, since Roosevelt knew that a world organization would be needed eventually if not right away; and for their part, his advisers well understood the realities of the balance of power among the Big Four, and that they would dominate any world body.

In the spring of 1942, though, the President had used the phrase "guarantors of peace" almost exclusively in discussions with Russian Ambassador Litvinov, who was somewhat surprised by Roosevelt's concluding question: Was Moscow "ready to abandon the League of Nations" in favor of the Big Four? "Anything for the common cause," came the reply.[9]

The President saw multiple possibilities as both a peace-making and a peace-maintaining mechanism for the Big Four balance of power. The two European members would balance each other, and together the United States and China could balance Russia and England on non-European matters.[10]

In Roosevelt's kaleidoscopic interpretation of the Big Four, China would "undoubtedly line up on our side" in any policy conflict with Russia. Foreign Minister Eden and Prime Minister Churchill saw other patterns, and felt that a more realistic interpretation would be that the United States would use China's "faggot" vote to further its own policies —probably to the detriment of British imperial interests.[11]

Hull and his aides, including various postwar planners from such semi-official groups as the Council on Foreign Relations, which were then meeting in State Department offices, wanted to turn the kaleidoscope a different way so that the President could see that there were less satisfactory patterns in Big Four regionalism, and that with a slight turn more, these would collapse into those terrifying ones which had characterized the closed blocs that had dominated the world between the wars.

The Secretary asked Norman Davis and Myron Taylor to point out these things to President Roosevelt. His own thinking ran along these lines: American isolationists would never allow themselves to be persuaded that the United States should sit on regional Big Four European or Pacific Councils, therefore they would negate postwar planning under that system. Moreover, regionalism inevitably led to special relationships arising between dominant powers and all the small nations within a given area. The final step in this domination was always "closed trade areas or discriminatory systems." [12]

By the fall of 1943 the Secretary believed that the President had come to see for himself the dangerous designs in the Big Four power balance. At any rate he had approved a draft for a Moscow Declaration calling for a security organization "based on the principle of the sovereign equality of all peace loving states, and open to membership by all such states, large and small . . . ." [13]

Admittedly the "sovereign equality" of all states was a fiction, but it was a protective one, thought Hull and his associates—protective against the kind of calamity that befell the globe after World War I. The United Nations would restore and help maintain an open world.

When Roosevelt himself outlined this future organization to Premier Stalin at Teheran, the latter fell back on arguments Roosevelt had spoken from in 1942 conversations with Litvinov and Molotov. Their positions had crossed in a figurative "X" and Admiral Leahy noted that "Stalin did not seem to be favorably impressed by the President's proposal to give the smaller nations of the world an equal position in the preservation of world peace." [14]

Leahy did not express the President's position completely in this summary, but it reflected how Roosevelt's outlook had changed since 1941. If Stalin was suspicious, Churchill, too, was uneasy. He had seen unhappy possibilities in the Big Four concept, but this new policy bore looking into also. They were further put off balance when in 1944 they met to discuss political influence in the Balkans and Roosevelt cabled them: "It is important that I retain complete freedom of action after this conference is over." To draw out these developments and see their interrelationship, it is evident that the State Department hoped that the creation of the United Nations would give the United States the greatest possible measure of freedom of action to protect its own interests while helping to maintain the peace. [15]

The following year, shortly before the Potsdam Conference, the State Department recommended establishing a Council of Foreign Ministers to prevent the rise of regionalism in the transition period: "Such a Council would tend to reduce the possibilities of unilateral action by either the

Russians or the British and would serve as a useful interim means through which the United States could work for the liquidation of spheres of influence." There is very little more to add to this general policy paper concerning the need American leaders saw for a general peace organization, but the following specific statement by Lauchlin Currie before a Congressional committee concerned with the postwar world, and America's place in it, perhaps epitomized Secretary Hull's economic reasoning. Currie was a deputy administrator of the Foreign Economic Administration and was one of Roosevelt's advisers on many questions; he told the Colmer Committee that the first prerequisite to expanding American exports was an "adequate peace organization. The first requirement for healthy international trade is, of course, military security. Efforts to achieve national self-sufficiency are hardly conducive to the expansion of international trade." [16]

Germany had violated Currie's pronouncements against self-sufficiency in the 1930's and had also violated the peace of the world. It was natural, then, for policy makers to assume that the first task of any security arrangement would be to see that Germany did not repeat its crimes. In this instance, too, Roosevelt began with different ideas from those of many of his advisers, and, once again, he altered his views to meet objections from those who favored restoring the "international system" as opposed to those who wanted Germany dismembered and deindustrialized.

At the time of the Teheran meetings, Roosevelt had tentatively decided upon partitioning Germany into five or more small states. But he was far from settled in this position, for, as he told Stimson, Germany probably could not feed its population by agriculture alone. Then he added that care must be taken "not to create by the result of this war another helpless Austria such as was created by the Versailles Treaty." Treasury Secretary Morgenthau wanted Roosevelt to pursue a tough German policy, and he gained a temporary victory at the Second Quebec Conference in September, 1944, when Roosevelt and Churchill initialed a paper he submitted to them calling for breaking off the Saar and the Ruhr from Germany and "pastoralizing" the whole area. [17]

The President had asked Morgenthau to devise a plan for dealing with Germany after he had rejected an army memorandum as too soft. He did not, he explained to the whole Cabinet, want Germany to have a subsistence level above that of the lowest level in those nations Hitler had conquered. [18]

Secretary Morgenthau had another source for his plan; conversations he had held with Foreign Minister Eden in August, 1944, had left him with the impression that the British government felt as he did that the Grand Alliance's real test would come over the postwar treatment of Germany. If the Allies failed to adopt a tough policy, Morgenthau insisted, then Russia would undoubtedly return to its prewar isolation from the West and seek its own means and methods of security. Eden indicated that this was indeed his view, adding that "restoring Germany" would "inevitably lead to war." Well satisfied with this response, the Secretary then pressed Eden to define Churchill's position. The Prime Minister stood somewhere in the middle, said Eden.[19]

Acting upon what he no doubt believed was an Anglo-American consensus, Morgenthau started campaigning for his program. Treasury experts attacked the post World War I fallacy that recovery in Europe depended upon revitalizing German industries and exports, circulating a long memorandum to other executive departments and the White House asserting that Germany could easily survive without restoration of its heavy industries and any supposed "disadvantages will be more than offset by real gains to the political objectives and the economic interests of the United Nations as a whole."

Indeed, the United States and Great Britain would greatly benefit from supplying former German markets. What was supposed to catch Churchill's eye, as in fact it did at Quebec, was Morgenthau's contention: "Not only will England be in a position to recapture many of the foreign markets she lost to Germany after 1918, but she will participate in supplying the devastated countries of Europe with all types of consumer and industrial goods for their reconstruction needs in the immediate post-war years." [20]

This memorandum fell like a stunning blow on Stimson, who suffered again when he discovered that Hull at least partially agreed with it. "Sound thinking," he hurried to write the President on September 15, 1944, "teaches that prosperity in one part of the world helps to create prosperity in other parts of the world . . . . The benefit to England by the suppression of German competition is greatly stressed in the Treasury memorandum. But this is an argument addressed to a shortsighted cupidity of the victors and the negation of all that Secretary Hull has been trying to accomplish since 1933." So Stimson remained faithful to his prewar insistence that the world could not be divided politically and economically.[21]

Even so, Morgenthau held the edge at the Quebec Conference, despite a reversal in Eden's attitude, for Eden now sharply disagreed with the Morgenthau Plan. Churchill, though, was "greatly intrigued" by the prospects laid out for English trade, reported Morgenthau, and exclaimed, "This is a matter of the good fortune of my people against the good fortune of the German people, and I am for my people." Morgenthau also held out a large credit (6.5 billion dollars) as an added inducement to the British leader. And as Roosevelt later explained to Hull and Stimson, the President had thought that "the real nub of the situation" was the problem of preventing future English bankruptcy and had hoped "that by something like the Morgenthau plan Britain might inherit Germany's Ruhr business." From that point of view the Morgenthau Plan was perfectly consistent with Lend-Lease and American support for Britain.[22]

Absent from the Quebec meetings, Hull exploded at this usurpation of his prerogatives—and at the deeper significance of what had happened. He recalled later that he was as angry over this as anything that ever happened "during my career as Secretary of State." By then he had come to agree with Stimson that in striking at Germany, the Treasury program "was striking at all of Europe." Equally disturbing, the Lend-Lease credit Morgenthau had apparently given away had been granted without a firm commitment from Churchill concerning his willingness to cooperate with America's postwar economic plans, and Hull considered the removal of British trade restrictions the key to all his economic planning. If a harsh German policy meant the destruction of European integration, as Roosevelt had indicated it might, and could be achieved only at the cost of giving away huge credits without any promise of cooperation, then Hull was dead set against it.[23]

Confronted by Hull's and Stimson's strong opposition, as well as by an untimely leak to the press, Roosevelt retreated from his commitment to the Morgenthau Plan and adopted a wait-and-see attitude, which he sustained throughout the Yalta Conference in February, 1945. The question still was not settled at his death. As Morgenthau had predicted, the German question severely tested Big Three unity and was one of the principal issues which broke it. At Potsdam the United States and Britain opposed Russia's claim to 10 billion dollars in reparations, as well as to the ways the Russians were already using to collect what they wanted. Anglo-American planners argued that Germany could not be left prostrate because of reparations, for then England and the United States would have to subsidize the nation to keep it afloat. On the other hand, Stalin's actions stemmed partly from his interpretation of his Allies' political plans for Germany. An American briefing paper on Germany might have confirmed the suspicious Premier's fears that the United States wanted a strong Germany: "Any break up of the effective unity of Germany at the present time would mean either a poorhouse standard of living in the West with Communism the probable end-result or an elaborate relief program at American and British expense." [24]

An exchange at Potsdam between Truman and Stalin, if viewed through the latter's eyes, suggests that there would be much trouble in the future over Germany. Adamantly against Stalin's assigning sections of Eastern Germany to Poland on a unilateral basis before the Conference had met, Truman commented that a reparations settlement in such circumstances would be difficult to accomplish. Stalin snapped back that the Soviet Union "was not afraid of the reparations question and would if necessary renounce them." [25]

Though a quadripartite zonal arrangement was reached at Potsdam, it broke down within a few years, and Russia did indeed find ways to protect its own security in Central Europe. Germany's dismemberment was accomplished, but not by agreement.

AIR POWER BRIDGES POLITICAL AND
ECONOMIC PLANNING

Among the lesser known issues of World War II diplomacy, the future of international air routes and air power in general was an excellent example of New Deal postwar planning. Conflicts of interest with Great Britain and Russia occurred here as in other questions; efforts to negotiate an open sky policy extended the Open Door Principle; and finally, the Administration's desire to regulate the international doings of private American companies exemplified Washington's desire to prepare the national economy for the new world to come.

As mentioned before, the United States had subsidized Pan American Airways' expansion into Latin America and then its development of a trans-Pacific route to the Orient. No wonder Juan Trippe considered that his airline was the "instrument of national policy." One of the last great entrepreneurial empires to come under government control, this segment of the American corporate structure was brought under close regulation not by the depression but rather by the coming of the war and the sudden expansion of both military and commercial air power. Many

New Dealers wisely came to look upon aviation as a valuable public utility, or at least as an industry heavily involved in public welfare responsibilities. Vice-President Wallace once described air power as the "key that will unlock the resources of the world." And one good reason for postwar cooperation with Russia, he contended, was the need to keep air routes open across the entire Pacific area to speed its development. In consequence, Wallace desired "perhaps a dozen airports in Soviet Asia." [26]

Herbert Feis warned that such international cooperation could never be an easy matter, and he, too, discussed air power questions very seriously: "The quarrels over opportunity for the privilege, for example, of flying to Timbuctoo could become as lively as an old-time frontier dispute; for the air is the new frontier." [27]

As it awakened to such potentials, the Administration quickly saw the need for supplying direction to its own air power representatives. By 1941 over 70 per cent of the world's commercial airplanes were owned in the United States, and several experiences with Pan American Airways had emphasized the need for regulation. This airline had been reluctant to cooperate at first in the Administration's drive against Axis-dominated airlines in South America, and in 1939 it had ventured into international diplomacy by trying to negotiate reciprocal landing rights with the British Overseas Airways Corporation. This effort failed both abroad and at home, where the State Department noted the attempt in its growing list of grievances against Pan American. And in 1941 the President even suggested government purchases of stock in Pan American and spoke sharply of Juan Trippe as a man who would pursue his own way despite the public interest.[28]

It was not surprising, then, that the Administration openly opposed Pan American's attempts to monopolize air traffic to Europe—and to secure for itself still another Congressional subsidy to pay the way. When the American Export Lines also appealed to Congress for money in the form of a Post Office subsidy, its request gave Assistant Secretary of State Adolf Berle a chance to define the Administration's air policy. One Senator had questioned the Administration's spokesman by declaring that he did not like "exclusive monopoly in transportation," but Pan American's argument that the monopoly was necessary to the survival and the prosperity of American air interests had impressed him. Berle countered that the Administration no longer supported Pan American's famous monopoly-producing "Form-B" contracts. Government negotiations with other countries were now aimed at securing landing rights on a general basis and not for the exclusive use of one line. "For instance," continued Berle, "air landing rights were recently negotiated by Pan American in Liberia, on an exclusive basis. They did not consult us about it. We do not like that feature." [29]

Berle went on to say that increased business between Europe and the United States made necessary at least two routes. The State, War, and Navy Departments had all agreed that the United States should establish another airline to Europe.[30]

Disturbed about what he believed was a campaign against his airline, Juan Trippe went to Chief of Staff Admiral Leahy with a plea that more be done to protect private rights, remarking that he had heard the army wanted to absorb all private lines. In 1943 Trippe's opponents pointedly announced that henceforth negotiations for landing rights would be on the broadest possible basis, "so that they might be assigned or allocated among American carriers by the competent Government authorities, and also to obtain rights in a manner which would make them subject to the authority of the C[ivil] A[eronautics] B[oard]." Berle then blocked Pan American's attempts to secure exclusive rights to or on government airports and facilities built in foreign countries because of the war.[31]

"You cannot deal with air routes and air lines in a piecemeal way and therefore the discussions must be much broader," explained Assistant Secretary of State Dean Acheson to Congressional critics. "But I can assure you there has been no subject which the Government thinks is more important." [32]

Much more purposeful than a New Deal take-over, these moves aimed at building a negotiating position to confront other big powers. Since the beginnings of air commerce and travel, most nations had reserved the air space over their territory for their own commercial aircraft. Like the centuries-old debates to establish "freedom of the seas," "freedom of the skies" brought forth basic arguments. A well-satisfied nation such as the United States wanted open access to more markets, whereas an aspiring nation such as Great Britain still needed special arrangements. Russia stood aside and criticized both. "Recent speeches in the British Parliament and Congress," reported the *New York Times,* "notably those on the future of international air lines, have revealed apprehensions in each country that the commercial interests of the other country were already plotting to seize strategic positions for the Anglo-American economic war they expected." [33]

"I haven't the least doubt," Harry Hopkins reassured American leaders, "that we will come to an understanding with Great Britain about our respective air bases throughout the world. And that understanding will be beneficial to both of us. We're going to trade through the air, as well as by sea, in this world to be. And the American people are quite right in emphasizing the importance of air bases." [34]

Still suspicious, Trippe thought that the settlement Hopkins was talking about would be internationalization of air routes, which, he told Leahy, would surely destroy American commercial aviation. His friend, Congresswoman Clare Boothe Luce, made a name for herself in her maiden speech to Congress by labeling American air policy "Globaloney." [35]

President Roosevelt carefully told reporters that he understood the free air policy to mean simply the reciprocal use of air bases, and he believed that Mr. Churchill shared that opinion. But he opened up much more to his advisers in private discussions. Axis postwar aviation industries must be controlled, he began. "He did not wish Americans to own or control" internal aviation companies in such places as Brazil. "The scope of international aviation," Roosevelt went on, "was too great to be trusted to any one company or pool." Increased subsidies might be needed to stimulate expansion, but the President hoped that the same policy "he had worked out for shipping lines after the last war" would be applicable to this situation. The government should use its planes and men to run federal lines, "but always on the understanding that if ever a private line was prepared to bid for the route, the Government would promptly retire from the business." [36]

Berle, then, went before Congress again to re-explain American policy. The army was not plotting to take over private lines; in fact, the military had contracted with these companies in such a way as to preserve their basic organizations unharmed. Thus they would be "equipped to take up the business of postwar aviation." As far as international policy was concerned, Navy Secretary Knox joined in by pointing out that America had a number of "chips on our side of the table" to bargain with Great Britain. Berle cited one in his presentation: since the United States had started sending Lend-Lease cargo planes to England, that country's factories had nearly ceased producing that kind of aircraft and concentrated instead on making fighter planes for the Royal Air Force.[37]

Unhappily aware that protracted Anglo-American competition would catch them in the middle, Canada and New Zealand initiated a series of diplomatic moves which led to the calling of an International Civil Aviation Conference in Chicago in the late fall of 1944. There the two Dominions proposed internationalizing all air routes involving more than one country—or, failing that, of all main routes across the Pacific and the Atlantic. Both the United States and Great Britain turned down that idea at once.

Chief Delegate Adolf Berle explained to the Conference that it was meeting at a time and in a situation not unlike that which had confronted the great international lawmaker Grotius. Unfortunately, the world had not yet progressed to the point where such bold plans as those of the Dominions could be accepted. But the United States sought no monopoly of air commerce; rather his government was prepared even to give airplanes to those countries "which recognize, as do we, the right of friendly intercourse, and grant permission for friendly intercourse to others." [38]

Having talked privately with Berle before the Conference opened, Admiral Leahy was well informed about the American position. "The United States represented by Assistant Secretary Berle," he wrote in his diary, "was determined to support American interests." England "was endeavoring to break the more or less monopolistic control of overseas commercial aviation heretofore held by American companies." [39]

When the English delegates addressed the Conference, they insisted upon the right to regulate the number of trips non-British airplanes could make into the United Kingdom and to limit the number of passenger stops on each flight. Sumner Welles put his finger on the issue raised by the British delegates. If the United States ever accepted this sort of limitation, it would destroy the "incentive to excel in competition, for which American aviation interests are superbly qualified . . . ." Of course this was exactly what the British feared! [40]

The United States then presented a series of resolutions collectively labeled the "Five Freedoms." In essence these would have committed the Conference to Washington's open sky policy; and this would have paralleled neatly the most-favored-nation policy and the Open Door Policy. Particularly noteworthy was the resolution which would have forbidden the establishment of "closed air" blocs between any group of nations or against any one nation. British representatives at Chicago sought to modify these proposals, but without notable success. In Washington, Knox's successor, James Forrestal, suggested to Harry Hopkins that they might be brought into line by pulling the strings on Lend-Lease. The Conference closed with seventeen nations pledging themselves to the

Five Freedoms, but future aviation questions were far from settled. Great Britain continued to offer opposition to American "prospective air carriers in the Near and Middle East" and to "prevent the use of dollar exchange in the sterling bloc countries for the purchase of American aircraft." [41]

Russia had stayed away from the Conference: this situation, noted Berle some time later, had been one reason why the United States would not accept New Zealand's internationalization plan. And within a few months, Russia became more obstinate about air matters when the United States tried to obtain military and commercial air bases in the Kurile Islands. Moscow bluntly refused to grant the request, which it said amounted to an unfriendly demand, unless the United States granted reciprocal privileges in Alaska. President Truman decided not to press the matter, but from such disappointments United States policy makers concluded that they could not rely upon any single instrument, such as the Five Freedoms, to settle postwar international civil aviation problems.[42]

ARTICLE VII OF THE LEND-LEASE AGREEMENT

The World War II air power debate took place on the outer edges of the main problems of Anglo-American economic planning; so, too, did a discussion between Roosevelt and Churchill on the distribution of former Axis merchant ships. Roosevelt suggested that after giving many of them to nations which had suffered merchant marine losses, the rest should be divided equally between the United States and Britain. "Whereat 'Winston' had jumped up and said 'How so? How so? Don't you remember that at the beginning of the war Britain owned twice the size merchant marine that the United States did?'" The President retorted, "Well how about the fact that at the end of the war the U.S. will own twice as large a merchant marine as Britain has then?" [43]

As in this instance, and that of air power, United States policy makers in economic discussions with their British counterparts spoke (and acted) from this irony-tinged confidence in America's new world position, though they tempered its harsher implications with the expectation, as Thomas Lamont expounded on it, that "we will all look forward to a post-war world in which Great Britain will be our prosperous friend, not another depressed area. She must be kept a going concern." Lamont grew serious, "America must have a partner." [44]

The Lend-Lease Act proved that the United States was, as Lamont further contended, "against stripping England of her liquid assets." Yet Washington never intended thereby to write London a blank check, nor did the State Department want another war debts tangle on its hands after the war, clogging international trade. Churchill called Lend-Lease the most unsordid act in history, but even he was aware that the United States was going to demand repayment—perhaps sooner than he thought, however.

State Department aides feared that the Treasury Department was developing a bookkeeper approach to Lend-Lease that threatened to bring on a "new war debt and war debt psychology." Hoping to reverse that tendency, and to reopen international trade channels, these aides wanted most of all to secure a promise from the British that they would open up the Ottawa Preference System. This would be payment enough, even if England never gave back a cent of Lend-Lease. If such a promise could not be obtained, even more tangled trade barriers could be expected when the British Empire closed around itself as it did in the previous decade. So the story picks up just at the point where it had unfolded at the end of the 1930's.[45]

The chance to impress these views upon British statesmen came shortly, when John Maynard Keynes arrived in Washington in the summer of 1941 to work out the details of the Lend-Lease master agreement. The acknowledged godfather of much of the Second New Deal, Lord Keynes was busy at work in his own country with economic warfare against Germany and postwar planning. He had sent on ahead a draft statement of Allied war aims designed primarily to counter German propaganda. This British memorandum emphasized sharply different points from those being developed in the State Department. Keynes stressed national measures such as social security (in the broadest sense) to prevent a recurrence of the depression. It even looked as if Keynes was determined to perpetuate a closed empire, albeit the rest of the draft promised a wide restoration of European trade. Germany could not provide a program, Keynes avowed: "But we and the other free democracies of America and the Dominions alone possess a command of the material means." American leaders were not quite sure how to take these ideas; to most of them Keynes's memorandum meant socialism if not something worse.[46]

The President asked the British economist to lunch with him so that they could discuss Allied postwar aims. During this informal meeting, Keynes could not get beyond the President's affable but noncommittal front. He reported of their talk only that the President had mentioned a possible joint defense establishment, suggesting that the American people would not be so insistent upon withdrawing from world political affairs as they had done after World War I. The President, speaking to Adolf Berle about this conversation, told him that he had informed Keynes that although the two countries shared pretty much the same hopes and objectives, he was not at all ready to have Foreign Minister Anthony Eden and Secretary Hull sit down and define the peace machinery.[47]

Across the street in the State Department, Keynes found a much more decisive attitude. There he was immediately presented a copy of the draft of the economic sections for the Lend-Lease Agreement. Keynes's memo had given first place to national measures, but the proposed Article VII emphasized international trade as the main road to postwar prosperity. Furthermore, the Department had worded Article VII so that Keynes rightly assumed that the United States meant thereby to commit England to specific terms upon which Lend-Lease aid was to be given. The two nations, Keynes read warily, "shall provide against discrimination in either the United States of America or the United Kingdom against the importation of any product originating in either country; and they shall provide for the formulation of measures for the achievement of these ends." [48]

Reaching this sentence, Keynes paused and asked Assistant Secretary Acheson if the draft was referring to Imperial Preferences. Acheson replied that it was, but he added quickly that there was no wish here to force unilateral obligations upon the British Empire. Article VII would only require the two countries to review all questions of discrimination "and would lead instead to cooperative action in preventing such practices."

The British thinker had already leapt by that kind of generalization to the unhappy conclusion that the United States was trying to force an opening into the Ottawa System by Lend-Lease, and, as Acheson remarked in his notes of the meeting, objected "wildly," insisting that the American plan would fasten a nineteenth-century formula on England when the only hope for the future existed in exactly the kind of controls which Article VII forbade. This was the same kind of reasoning Keynes had used back in 1933 in praising New Deal nationalism. Acheson declared that Great Britain could not expect to take aid from the United States and then cut off American trade; the American people simply would not stand for it.[49]

On the day following, Keynes gave Acheson a written version of his views on the American program; he began by stating dramatically that Article VII called up "all the old lumber, most-favored-nation clause and the rest which was a notorious failure and made such a hash of the old world . . . . It is the clutch of the dead, or at least moribund, hand." Reactionaries would seize it to regain power. The United States and Great Britain, he finished, must remain free to work out new and better arrangements.

Upon seeing this statement, one State Department officer retorted that the most-favored-nation principle had not made a hash of the old world, but British bilateralism had made a hash of the most-favored-nation idea. "And above all, he fails totally to see that after the sacrifices the American people are being called upon to make to help Great Britain in the present emergency (even though we are thereby helping ourselves), American public opinion simply would not tolerate discrimination against our products in Great Britain and, at Great Britain's instance, in other countries." [50]

Keynes returned to his country without capitulating to Washington's views on Article VII, but he knew that he was going to be up against a determined nation, and his later modifications were largely a result of these experiences with American planners. Secretary Hull punctuated his declarations on the subject of Anglo-American economic planning by making known his intention to negotiate liberal trade agreements with all the Commonwealth Dominions before stringent nationalism returned after the war.[51]

Sumner Welles offered an even more direct challenge to English planners by raising the Imperial Preference issue at the Atlantic Conference. On the first day of these meetings he told Sir Alexander Cadogan that he "had unfortunately received the impression that Professor Keynes represented at least some segment of British public opinion which was directing its energies towards the resumption or continuation by Great Britain after the war of exactly that kind of system which had proved so fatal during the past generation." [52]

Such discussions were muted undercurrents, however, for Roosevelt and Churchill were met to declare themselves Allies in the struggle against the Axis, to counter Axis propaganda with a statement of their principles (Roosevelt was also worried, it will be recalled, about the Anglo-Russian negotiations then going on), and to consider the kind of aid which the United States should give England and Russia. Yet Welles still tried to substitute the essence of the proposed Article VII for the Prime Minister's vague fourth paragraph dealing with economic matters in the Atlantic Charter. But the English leader protested that Welles's pet phrase "without discrimination" would force him to consult the Dominions. Moreover, the Prime Minister would have to add to this a clause "with due respect for their existing obligations," so that the paragraph would then read: "They will endeavor, with due respect for their existing obligations, to further the enjoyment by all States, great or small, victor or vanquished, of access, on equal terms, to the trade and to the raw materials of the world which are needed for their economic prosperity." [53]

Welles was keenly disappointed by Roosevelt's instructions to accept the British changes for the sake of completing the joint declaration of Anglo-American war aims. But less than a month afterwards the President assured a State Department officer that the United States would receive "certain advantages or privileges" in return for Lend-Lease and he was already thinking of "much closer currency cooperation"—a subject about which the Treasury would negotiate with London for the next four years. [54]

As Churchill complained at the Atlantic Conference meetings, it looked to English leaders as though the United States wanted to destroy all Imperial Preferences without touching its own high tariffs. In addition, some English economists at home were asserting that the United States was headed straight for a postwar depression, and they saw nothing in announced American proposals which would indicate an understanding of the need for the kind of planning Keynes had stressed. If Britain agreed to American multilateralism, she would surely go under in the critical period after the war even if America only faltered. [55]

To meet these objections, the Department revised its draft and included a promise of "domestic measures" to complement its international proposals, assure the expansion of production and employment, and ease British fears. On the other count, "the reduction of tariffs and other trade barriers" was appended to the clause calling for the elimination of discrimination. [56]

With these revisions, Hull was ready to confront the Prime Minister with a new Article VII when he came to Washington in December, 1941, for the Arcadia Conference. Churchill tried to sidestep, pleading more pressing considerations, like the Declaration of the United Nations or military strategy problems, which he said were taking all his time. This other matter should not be decided upon until he returned to London. Hull, adamant, warned the British ambassador that Congress was about to debate Lend-Lease renewal and it would be indeed embarrassing if the State Department could not explain why the Master Agreement had not yet been signed.[57]

Ambassador Winant reported from London that the British cabinet opposed Article VII mostly because of domestic political reasons, fearing that a split in the Conservative party would occur if the government accepted guns, tanks, and planes only after bartering away empire preferences. Some cabinet members apparently believed that President Roosevelt was not really interested in Article VII, only the State Department. Hull acted at once to correct such misapprehensions. First, his aides tried once again to explain to British officials that there was no attempt under way to force a unilateral obligation out of them, but, as Undersecretary Welles advised Ambassador Halifax, "this issue was fast becoming a very serious issue and . . . I feared the British did not realize how serious an issue it really was." [58]

Then the Secretary secured Roosevelt's signature on two letters to the Prime Minister which were intended to disabuse him and his colleagues of any mistaken notions that the President was disinterested or indifferent. On February 23, 1942, these letters brought the desired response, and the Master Lend-Lease Agreement was signed. Secretary Hull's intense campaign had been a success: "The foundation was now laid for all our later postwar policy in the economic field." [59]

DRIVING HOME THE WEDGE

Naturally enough, the British refused to admit that any such thing had happened, and they contended that they had received definite assurances that abolition of Imperial Preferences and lowering of American tariffs would be taken up during the peace settlement proceedings. But American leaders, having placed their wedge, went about the task of driving it home.

This general attitude was readily apparent in Herbert Feis's article "Restoring Trade after the War." "Most countries live in chronic fear of unemployment," began the Economic Adviser strongly. "Thus each believes it is important to have foreign markets for its chief export products on reasonably satisfactory terms and each is apt to bear resentment against the other when these markets fail." Dean Acheson picked up where Feis left off as he explained the significance of Article VII to Congress, placing great stress on the argument that it would alleviate just such international tensions by discouraging closed economic blocs. With Article VII, said the Assistant Secretary, the President had in effect told other nations: "You must agree to sit down with us and work out an arrangement which will have the effect of increasing the whole volume of production in the world, of consumption and employment and reducing the barriers of trade and doing away with discriminations." [60]

American Chamber of Commerce President Eric Johnston told a London audience in the fall of 1943 what great things were in store for the two nations if they could get up in full agreement from the table Acheson had described. Great Britain and the United States faced a fundamental choice: the two countries could easily become bitter rivals or they could become the "world's mightiest force" in "lifting all the world's regions toward a higher and higher level." The United States opposed cartels and spheres of influence, said Johnston, but no one in America had ever wanted to destroy the British Empire. "I am not talking about gratuitous expenditures either by you or by us for parting the hair and brushing the teeth of so-called backward peoples. Better and better customers all over the world; that is the objective of the cooperation I would like to see between the business of Britain and the business of the United States." [61]

As Johnston was delivering this challenge, official representatives from the two governments were meeting at a Washington "seminar on commercial collaboration," but they soon tied up over the original question of social security versus freer trade. Both sides were afraid not of the men across the table from them but of those they called "extremists," and the influence they might have on policy. The English, for example, shuddered at the kind of pamphlet the Council on Foreign Relations was distributing confidentially to its members, called *Postwar Agreements on Commercial Policy.* Its author declared that the United States could settle for nothing less than the fullest possible access to foreign markets. Past economic foreign policy had been too slow and cumbersome to be of any value in breaking down barriers after the war; there must be an agreement on tariffs, capital investment, and commodity trade. American planners, on the other hand, looked balefully at socialist economists like Thomas Balogh, who were attacking the whole rationale behind the United States' position: "How is one to reconcile the Most Favored Nation clause and similar paraphernalia with the professed aims of liberalism when, in the last few years before the war, they were almost exclusively used to prevent a sane organisation of the international exchange of goods." [62]

Washington suspected its Ally was searching for some way to reduce American leverage or, worse yet, to force the United States to assume specific economic responsibilities in the reconstruction period. Actually it would have been surprising only if this were not occurring.

In November, 1943, Treasury Secretary Morgenthau called Ambassador Halifax's attention to growing British dollar holdings. These were morally, if not legally, contrary to the original Lend-Lease Act. Halifax admitted the fact, but justified his country's action on the grounds that no provision had been made for the immediate postwar period when England's dollar shortage would be acute but its needs great. [63]

The following spring Lord Keynes used this argument to explain British reluctance to adopt United States commercial proposals. Particularly worrisome to English economic planners was Washington's strong desire to eliminate quantitative controls on imports. They argued that this would weaken English manufactures and badly damage their export trade. The British could foresee their nation falling more and more under American dominance, but United States officials replied that without increased trade, especially between America and the British Empire, these dire prophecies might come true—a new depression would surely come. [64]

This fear permeated American planning. One observer, to show how far this kind of thinking went, singled out the Lend-Lease agreement with Ethiopia with its clause forbidding the British from gaining an exclusive right to air bases in that country, as a model of the most-favored-nation principle that might well be repeated in all colonies and underdeveloped countries. In this way the United States would not have to depend upon the outcome of talks with Britain at all. And this is what Washington hoped for in the trusteeship system it advocated from 1943 on. [65]

Fear of a renewed depression was the other side of the coin to Adolf Berle's statement before American entrance into the war—"We shall have an opportunity to create the most brilliant economic epoch the U.S. has yet seen"—and it oppressed American policy makers. Witnesses before the Colmer Committee filled volumes of printed testimony with their hopes and fears about the world after the war ended. The organizer of American war production, Donald M. Nelson, warned on the day after the invasion of Europe, June 7, 1944: "Unless we can develop a broad export market, for capital goods, I do not see the chance in the reconversion period for the capital goods industries to be prosperous." [66]

How can the country, asked Nelson, find a market for 8,900 airplanes a month? One of the Committee's members related the half-serious answer he had heard from an airplane manufacturer on that very problem. He had suggested destroying all their current production and then "start building them over again." No one, testified Dean Acheson, believed that the United States could absorb its entire production under its present economic system. The country must export goods worth ten billion dollars a year. "We cannot go through another 10 years like the 10 years at the end of the twenties and the beginning of the thirties, without having the most far-reaching consequences upon our economic and social system." [67]

Roosevelt's letter to Foreign Economic Administrator Leo Crowley summed it all up: "In varying degrees every workman, every farmer and every industry in the United States has a stake in the production and flow of manufactured goods, agricultural products and other supplies to all other countries of the world." [68]

Writing in the *Atlantic Monthly,* the perceptive Swedish Economist Gunnar Myrdal insisted that this intense concern with foreign markets revealed that Americans were panicky about the future. Much of their "brave new world" talk was actually designed to prevent the spread of radical ideas. Myrdal may well have exaggerated these tremors or have projected his own fears onto American planners, but there was no denying that Cordell Hull had consistently maintained since 1933 that the alternative to radicalism was freer trade to restore employment and production, nor could it be doubted that many joined with him during the war in asserting that the country might be facing its last chance to save the system.[69]

"I have a feeling that the Prime Minister thinks that this is a pet hobby of Secretary Hull's and that you may not think it of great importance," Hopkins told Roosevelt just before the Second Quebec Conference. "I think it essential to our future bargaining that you disabuse the Prime Minister's mind of this."

As noted above, the President's actions at this meeting upset Secretary Hull, who felt that the Morgenthau Plan and the proposed 6.5 billion dollar credit would undercut the foundations he had laid in Article VII. Hull believed Roosevelt had "given away the bait." Morgenthau's rejoinder that Roosevelt had actually persuaded Churchill to accept joint committee discussions on the matter of Lend-Lease settlement did little to calm Hull.[70]

But Hull was able to repair his foundation with little difficulty. Following the Quebec Conference, the State Department and the Joint Chiefs made it clear that Lend-Lease would be restricted to military needs in the war against Japan. London had not, therefore, gained a promise of aid in the immediate post-victory period. With this pressure on London, Washington resumed informal commercial discussions in the first half of 1945. The British were ready with a new twist on Keynes's theme; they suggested that simultaneous and parallel conferences on full employment and international trade would be the best way to approach transition problems. Acting Secretary Grew threw four buckets of cold water on the idea:

1. Separate conferences could not be productive, since the two questions were inextricably linked.
2. Appropriate international cooperation on full employment could not be obtained in the absence of reasonably firm commitments on trade, commodity, and cartel policy.
3. Requirements necessary to full employment were likely to lead to mountainous barriers against international commerce, unless prior agreements had already been reached. (Perhaps Grew was remembering America's own experience with the NRA and the AAA!)
4. Attention could best be given to employment problems in a general conference on trade and employment.[71]

These commercial talks got nowhere and became merged first into the financial talks which were leading to the Bretton Woods agreement, and later into the discussions centered about the Anglo-American Loan Agreement at the end of 1945.[72]

Once again to the irritation of the State Department, the Treasury had taken the lead in trying to develop complementary financial instruments for the commercial plans of the State Department. This led to the Bretton Woods proposals for an International Monetary Fund and an International Bank for Reconstruction and Development. In effect, Bretton Woods offered to the world a modernized international gold standard complete with a replacement for the old international banking system.

"I wonder whether the Senators fully appreciate what this means," asked Senator Robert Wagner. "It means that at long last we have the prospect of getting the other countries of the world to subscribe to the same principles of stable and orderly exchange relationships for which we have always stood." [73]

Wagner's admonition was also a good one for historians of this period; they, too, must "fully appreciate what this means."

THE NEW GOLD STANDARD

The Treasury proposals which Wagner so warmly applauded had been devised in early 1942 by Harry Dexter White and his aides. They were described to President Roosevelt, fittingly enough, as "a New Deal in international economics." In creating the outline of this new New Deal, Treasury experts had worked from their unhappy memories of German, Japanese, and even British currency manipulations in the 1930's. Morgenthau had originally put forward the 1936 Tripartite Currency Agreement as an antifascist weapon, and the idea of an International Monetary Fund constituted a greatly expanded version of that plan. This Fund would be the keystone to an expanding foreign economic policy after the war by establishing a clearing union for international payments. Member nations could thus join in an effort to prevent crises of the sort which had led to the currency wars of the previous ten years. The International Bank would complement the Monetary Fund and make available capital resources for investment in war-ravaged areas. Both were designed to speed world recovery; some said that without them there would be no international recovery.

In England, Lord Keynes had worked out similar proposals for an "International Clearing Union." He and his colleagues in the British Treasury, shrinking from the horrors of a possible economic war with the United States and hoping that they might find some form of multilateralism in currency exchange not incompatible with their own national plans, came up with a fund which would enable Britain to participate in international commerce yet preserve its own domestic freedom for social experimentation.

The principal contrasts between the White Plan and its coeval Keynes Plan are worth going into in some detail, for they define the basic agreements and disagreements between London and Washington on this subject—and many other related ones.

The White Plan was originally limited to five billion dollars. Member nations could purchase one another's currency to meet an adverse payments situation; Keynes's Plan (designed to aid the debtor) centered around an overdraft principle which would have inflated the fund up to 26 billion dollars. The British desired to discourage creditor nations from maintaining a permanent "favorable balance of trade" (more exports than imports), but if creditors insisted upon doing so anyway, they would have to allow their liability to the fund to increase correspondingly. "The object is that the creditor should not be allowed to remain entirely passive. For if he is, an intolerably heavy task may be laid on the debtor country, which is already for that very reason in the weaker position."

The White Plan gave the Fund's officers the right to express opinions and to make recommendations on its members' national policies and even to hold back currency from debtor countries who continually avoided making internal adjustments to correct their balance of payments or if they "failed to carry out measures recommended by the Fund designed to correct the disequilibrium in the country's balance of payments"; the Keynes Plan put "virtually the whole responsibility for adjustment" upon the creditor country.

The White Plan originally contained very strict provisions for the elimination of exchange controls, though they did not appear in the published form. The Keynes Plan reserved such questions for each member's own determination.[74]

Adolf Berle explained to an English diplomat the outstanding question in American minds about the Keynes Plan: "What it really came to was a method by which American, and possibly other goods, could be made available to certain countries, notably Britain, on what was in fact though not in form a credit arrangement . . . . I said that this raised squarely a problem which the American Government would have to face, and in facing it would have to take account of Congressional opinion and public sentiment." [75]

Some sharp edges on these contrasts were rounded off by direct negotiations between Keynes and White in 1943. Often when they reached an impasse, White would finally remind Keynes that the United States was the stronger nation, and therefore more able to support its plan. Since both shared the conviction that some form of Anglo-American collaboration was essential, many of their conflicts were simply passed over by one side or the other. Critics in each country were not so understanding. In England, a left-wing–Conservative alliance attacked the Keynes proposals and asserted that Britain's salvation depended upon socialist planning or Imperial Preferences (or even both). Keynes had been through all this himself, and he had not stopped pressing for social security measures, but he thought his critics shortsighted and unrealistic: "Those who talk in this way, in the expectation that the rest of the Commonwealth will throw in their lot on these lines and cut free their commercial relations with the rest of the world, can have very little idea of how this Empire has grown or by what means it can be sustained." [76]

White had his detractors, too. They contended that the stabilization fund would fail to secure open markets for American goods. Debtor countries would dominate it, reasoned Senator Robert A. Taft, and force the United States to put up an unending supply of dollars without themselves eliminating "one exchange restriction, one trade restriction, or one sterling area . . . ." White replied to this by citing a Treasury policy memorandum in which such a possibility was considered and answered: it "will be the duty of the Fund to make a report not only to the country whose currency is scarce but also to the member countries who are exhausting or are using the resources of the Fund in a manner which is not consistent with the purposes of the Fund." [77]

Adolf Berle was not the only State Department official who had reservations about the Anglo-American financial plans. Another aide disliked the anonymous nature of the proposed Fund and International Bank. As the largest single contributor, the United States would hardly be willing, for example, to grant a loan to another power to establish rival airlines in this hemisphere. Obviously there needed to be political agreement among the big powers if economic planning were to bear fruit. The State Department wanted to amend the plans in order to make them less anonymous, but in the end United States dominance in the IMF and the IBRD made such amendments unnecessary. [78]

Delegates from forty-four nations met at Bretton Woods, New Hampshire, in the summer of 1944 to consider the Anglo-American joint proposal which had been arrived at after negotiation and compromise. Roosevelt welcomed them with a stirring message: "Commerce is the life blood of a free society. We must see to it that the arteries which carry that blood stream are not clogged again, as they have been in the past, by artificial barriers created through senseless economic rivalries." [79]

A long Treasury report to Roosevelt re-emphasized what the United States wanted out of these negotiations: "We in the United States believe that the greatest possible freedom should be given to our own businessmen engaged in international trade. But we know that this freedom will be meaningless unless other countries accord an equal measure of freedom to their businessmen." The Bretton Woods proposals will assure that they are able to do so. "After the war, our economic policy will be aimed at full employment and full utilization of a greatly enlarged industrial plant. These objectives, however, cannot be realized unless we find new outlets for products of farm and factory —outlets that will be steady and profitable after war demands have dropped off." [80]

The Administration employed these arguments to sell all those who still did not fully appreciate what Bretton Woods meant. Both congressmen and businessmen were told that the proposals would secure economic well-being for the nation. Morgenthau, for instance, really went out on a limb to the automobile industry, promising a steady export market of one million cars annually to the managers, and promising the CIO five million additional jobs if Congress passed the necessary legislation! [81]

If Congress did not act favorably, Dean Acheson darkly predicted, then "I should think that we might look with some apprehension upon the whole state of the world." [82]

Undoubtedly Administration spokesmen stretched things a bit on both sides to make the issue more dramatic, but even so, the support these promises and pleas engendered among the business elite came primarily from dread at a renewed depression in America and fright at rising radicalism in England and Europe.[83]

THE MEETING GROUND

As Congress was making up its mind to affirm the Administration's financial plans, Executive representatives came before it appealing for something more—a bigger appropriation for the Export-Import Bank. Leo Crowley said that the apparent duplication with the proposed International Bank was not really so. The latter would not be ready to function for at least a year and a half; in the meantime the United States wanted to "sell to Russia and other countries certain equipment and certain things that will help them to expand and rehabilitate their economy . . . then over a period of years repair business and other related new business are going to flow to us. There is a great advantage to us getting our machinery into some of these countries of the world and doing it while they are in the process of rehabilitation."

SENATOR TAFT. You would . . . require that [funds] be used only for a particular plant . . . and that the plant be built in a certain way?

MR. CROWLEY. We do that now.

SENATOR TAFT. You require . . . that perhaps the money be spent in this country?

MR. CROWLEY. Insofar as we possibly can. It is to finance, Senator, equipment and materials that they buy just in our own country.

SENATOR TAFT. Whereas the International Bank expressly provides that we cannot require that dollars loaned by the bank be spent in this country even though the dollars are raised in this country; isn't that correct?

MR. CROWLEY. There is a great advantage to us having something of our own." [84]

When the Administration terminated Lend-Lease on August 21, 1945, other pieces started falling into place. The British saw their worst fears becoming realities. From the start of Anglo-American commercial and financial discussions they had sought to convince their ally that the transition period would bring great dangers to England. Lord Keynes came one more time to Washington in hopes of obtaining a six billion dollar grant in aid or at least an interest-free loan. In the talks that followed, Keynes found that England did have a "war debt"; the United States was determined not to grant any monies until it was paid in full by formal commitment to American trade ideas. These were so stringent that although the British Lend-Lease "debt" was all but forgiven, two American bankers of no little prominence, Winthrop Aldrich and Russell Leffingwell, commented to Navy Secretary Forrestal that England's obligations under the terms of the loan made it "of dubious value." [85]

In return for a 3.75 billion dollar loan, Keynes pledged that his government would: (1) pay for imports with dollars or gold after 1947, (2) spend a 930 million dollar credit entirely in the United States, (3) refuse all loans from Commonwealth nations on more favorable terms than the United States had granted, and (4) establish the same quotas on goods coming from the Empire as on those coming from the United States.[86]

Even then the loan ran into some opposition in the United States. It seemed that every measure the Administration proposed was absolutely essential to American prosperity, said dubious opponents. Harry Dexter White reminded them that the postwar boom, then just beginning, would not last. They dare not hesitate now: "Our solution is international co-operation, but our point of view is as purely American as that of the most rugged economic isolationist . . . . You have already indicated your overwhelming support for the World Fund and World Bank, and the Export-Import Bank. The next step is the British loan." [87]

Using such speeches as this one of White's at Macon, Georgia, the Administration guided the business community once more into accepting its postwar program. Their successes were reflected in a letter from isolationist Robert Wood to Assistant Secretary of State Will Clayton: "If you succeed in doing away with the Empire Preference and opening up the Empire to United States commerce, it may well be that we can afford to pay a couple of billion dollars for the privilege." [88]

The drive to open up the British Empire was proceeding on all fronts. At early organization meetings of the International Monetary Fund, "Keynes ran squarely into the question of who would do the managing. The American Government made it plain that it intended to assert its power as provider. American wishes would be most influential if not dominant . . . . To make the issue still graver, Keynes perceived that the Americans thought that the Fund should exact severe censorship over the monetary policies of its members." [89]

As an Executive Director of the IMF in 1946, Harry Dexter White was also concerned. The political questions, somewhat submerged earlier, were now bubbling angrily near the surface. There were severe temptations to capitalize on the voting power evident at the Savannah organization meetings. "The chances for achieving success are likely to be inverse to the amount of voting necessary to arrive at decisions," he predicted. "Because of the universal character of voting, it resembles much too closely the operation of power politics rather than of international cooperation—except that the power employed is financial instead of military and political." [90]

White's doubts were soon confirmed with the onset of the Cold War. In its earliest stages, international cooperation in the IMF and the IBRD suffered, and more and more the United States turned to unilateral aid programs such as envisaged in the Truman Doctrine for Greece and Turkey and the Marshall Plan for most of Western Europe.

In America the boom times kept on; the dire predictions of those who had warned of a new depression seemed humorous in retrospect. At least for a time they did, but recurrent recessions starting in

1947–48, while not impairing the upward progress of the economy for any sustained period, did cause a great deal of worry. A few agreed with White that the economy rested upon a poor foundation: "Our economy is now geared to a foreign market which cannot be maintained beyond the next few years if that long." [91]

Whether American postwar planning would have succeeded without the military stimulus of the Cold War is an intriguing speculation; but even with that stimulus, by the 1960's the United States was plagued with a chronic outflow of gold, and ironically, its Allies and friends suggested Washington look to the IMF for relief. This was only one indication that the United States was being challenged not only by Soviet Russia but also by a resurgent Europe. The constant drain on American dollar and gold supplies and the growth of the Common Market loomed as the most challenging problems in international economics for the New Frontier. Anxious to find a way to solve them, the Administration asked for and received a new trade bill allowing the President far greater authority to act on trade matters than Cordell Hull had ever secured for President Roosevelt in 1934.

I still recognize the difficulty and am still convinced of the importance of a change in Russian attitude toward individual liberty but I have come to the conclusion that it would not be possible to use our possession of the atomic bomb as a direct lever to produce the change. I have become convinced that any demand by us for an internal change in Russia as a condition of sharing in the atomic weapon would be so resented that it would make the objective we have in view less probable.

Henry L. Stimson to President Harry
S. Truman, September 11, 1945

As long as we can outproduce the world, can control the sea and can strike inland with the atomic bomb, we can assume certain risks otherwise unacceptable in an effort to restore world trade, to restore the balance of power—military power—and to eliminate some of the conditions which breed war.

James C. Forrestal, 1947

14 · Russia's Opposition to America's Open World

"We simply cannot organize the world between Britain and ourselves without bringing in Russia as an equal partner," concluded Harry Hopkins in 1942; yet within three years, at the time of the United Nations Organization Conference, President Harry S. Truman had some hard thoughts about doing exactly that—excluding a recalcitrant Russia from the world organization, unless Foreign Minister V. M. Molotov came around to the American understanding of the Yalta decisions on Poland and then began working in team with Secretary Stettinius and Foreign Minister Eden.[1]

How quickly, then, had the never strong rope of Soviet-American understanding split as each strand frayed and pulled apart! Many said that Russia had cut it on purpose. To stop there may be soothing and even satisfying, but, to paraphrase Karl Marx's famous dictum, this answer is the same kind of opium which satiates both the masses and the intellectuals. At a somewhat less deadening level, it is often suggested that the rope parted as the natural result of continued abrasive contacts between two gigantic superpowers. Here also, however, one is swept along through batches of superficial evidence to an over-simplified conclusion.

Though it has been downgraded, the communist-capitalist antipathy since 1917 (including on the one side the activities of the Comintern and on the other the policy of the Cordon Sanitaire) was like an acid, bottled up during the war, but broken and spilled at its end all over the rope of alliance. "Violent social revolution anywhere in the world is disadvantageous to us," wrote one State Department aide just before American entrance into World War II. "We must contribute, if the chance exists, to an orderly social program." This statement still characterizes American foreign policy, and the split between East and West. It also points up the fact that the communist-capitalist split has a well-developed superstructure of ideas, as Marx would put it.[2]

Turning the argument around, Soviet leaders have complained of capitalist encirclement and have just as fervently insisted that fascism was the natural end of modern industrial capitalism.

After Germany's invasion of Russia in 1941 brought that nation into military alliance with the Western Allies, great hopes were expressed that the two systems could work out a mutually satisfactory peace. But as the Allies approached each other geographically, they were moving away from each other ideologically. Treasury Secretary Morgenthau, for example, who always wanted a liberal Lend-Lease policy towards Russia and who also wanted a harsh policy towards Germany to preserve Allied unity, told an aide: "Now I want to do a job where somebody says 'Thank you, I think the United States is wonderful' not the way we did in Italy, where they look to Russia as their friend . . . . I would like to see the American flag on the home of a few Italians instead of just a sickle and a hammer." [3]

Morgenthau was never among that group of men who had asserted that cooperation with the Soviet Union was impossible. He and many others had assumed that there would be room enough for Russia in the open world they were building, and they positively desired Moscow's participation in this effort. Not all of them believed that Russia could as yet be an "equal partner," as Hopkins had put it, and many abandoned the idea at the first sign of serious disagreement with the Soviets in 1945.[4]

It would be unwise to forget also that not a few who held on to this idea for some time were not liberals but dollar-a-year-men or conservatives.

In Europe, as in the Middle East and Asia, Russian security policy was based upon the spheres-of-influence approach. Put simply, they wanted to divide up the world. Roosevelt's idea of the "Big Four Policemen" was the closest thing in American policy to the Russian view. If the President had left American security plans at this point, Soviet domination of Eastern Europe *might* have been tolerated or accepted as inevitable, but Roosevelt had moved away from that concept by the time of the Teheran Conference.

The Soviet Union said it would go along, albeit reluctantly, with the new United Nations Organization which Roosevelt first outlined at that Conference in Iran, but Russia's main interest was in preserving Big Three unanimity. At Yalta, Stalin kept repeating, said James Byrnes, "If the three of us stick together, we can maintain the peace of the world." But as Senator Burton K. Wheeler, who heard this report, remarked (and he was certainly not alone in Washington even in February, 1945), Stalin only "meant we would have to agree with him, and he had his way at the Yalta Conference." [5]

Wheeler exaggerated American concessions and compromises at Yalta, but the growing bitterness in Allied relations made every agreement taste like appeasement. The Polish question symbolized this feeling and indicated that Moscow would not accept the Open Door Policy in Eastern Europe. It was especially meaningful to both sides, since President Roosevelt and his successor and Prime Minister Churchill seemed willing to go quite far to satisfy Russian desires in that country. True enough, the presence of the Red Army in Poland made any other policy but accommodation of doubtful expediency if not impossible short of war; yet the dispute embittered both sides and was an ominous sign portending much worse things to come.

Further doubts that Russia would join in Anglo-American planning for European recovery soon rose to the surface. The State Department had tried to devise programs which the Soviet state-controlled economy could participate in, and Russia was invited to the International Civil Aviation Conference, the International Labor Organization, the Bretton Woods Conference, and others. (On the other hand, Moscow was not welcomed to the scramble for oil concessions in Iran, nor was it asked to participate in Anglo-American discussions on Middle Eastern oil in general.) The Soviets eventually turned down most of these invitations and later took their satellites out of them also.

This attitude begot a multitude of antagonisms in the United States:

Aside from Washington's specific interests in Eastern Europe, the Soviets thus frustrated, as Denna Frank Fleming points out, many potential European recovery programs which were postulated upon the premise that "west Europe could recover durably only if a large measure of East-West trade were restored." President Truman had focused attention on such aspirations at the Potsdam Conference with his proposal for internationalizing central European waterways: "I wanted to see a Europe that would make Russia, England, France, and all the other countries in it secure, prosperous, and happy, and with which the United States could trade and be happy as well as prosperous." [6]

When American policy makers could no longer perceive that vista in Russian-American relations, the crucial matters for them to decide then were what should be done about reconstruction aid to the Soviet Union, and what should be done about international control of atomic energy.

Having reached a decision on each question, these founders of the "American Century" patched up any conservative-liberal divisions within the Truman Administration and set out to make the open world work, one way or another, with or without the Soviet Union.

RUSSIAN SECURITY DEMANDS AND THE SECOND FRONT

If the United States had gone to the Pacific first, suggested a participant in American policy-making and later author of several books on wartime diplomacy, the conquered peoples of Europe "might have thought us indifferent, and more of them than did might have cause to regard the Soviet Union as their one great liberating friend. This is in itself, I think, the basic political justification for our strategy." As Herbert Feis says, this was a justification after the fact, for the military consideration that Germany should be dealt with first was more important at the time. Within that decision, moreover, it was Churchill and not Roosevelt who was most widely known for his political maneuverings or admired for his statesman-like foresight because of his proposal to strike at Europe's soft underbelly in the Balkans rather than at the French snout. But even if American leaders rejected Churchill's grand scheme because it was too obviously political or too unappealing to American military thinkers, it remains true that the question of the Second Front in a larger sense had political ramifications from the beginning. [7]

Stalin himself always tied political considerations to the anti-German military alliance Russia negotiated and finally signed with England in 1942. And he would have liked the same kind of understanding with the United States. Conversely, the United States stayed out of just such an alliance with Russia primarily for the political freedom of action it had always cherished—and used.

It would hardly be too much to say that Anglo-American policy toward Russia was a long sustained reaction to the Russian Premier's letter to Churchill of November 8, 1941: "I agree with you that we need clarity, which at the moment is lacking in relations between the U.S.S.R. and Great Britain. The unclarity is due to two circumstances: first, there is no definite understanding between our two countries concerning war aims; secondly, there is no treaty between the U.S.S.R. and Great Britain on mutual military aid in Europe against Hitler." [8]

Faced with this opening, the United States and Great Britain adopted different replies: Washington wanted so much to delay political decisions that it eventually gave a premature promise of a second front to ease Russian problems in the east and thereby satisfy Stalin's desire for mutual military aid. London wanted to go the other way and grant Stalin some of his war aims, though the British wanted a say, certainly, in how these were to be accomplished.

Stalin's message reput the issue that had divided England and France from Russia in the late 1930's. Tripartite security talks had failed then largely because the two Western powers refused to give Moscow a free hand in Eastern Europe. Even at the time of the Munich Conference, many English and French leaders regarded Stalin as the more dangerous dictator in Europe. And then they assumed that they had been partially right, at least, when the Russian leaders signed the 1939 Nazi-Soviet Pact to provide their country with a breathing space or, some argued, a permanent settlement of Eastern European questions. As it turned out, even though Russia laid claim to parts of Poland, advanced into the Baltic countries of Estonia, Latvia, and Lithuania, and finally declared war on Finland, Hitler was the one who decided it would only be a breathing spell rather than a permanent settlement and marched into the East in June of 1941. This development did not put down fears that Russia would move out again, perhaps still farther west, all in the name of defense.[9]

When Germany attacked Russia, England pushed these fears to the background and concentrated on keeping the Soviets in the war, a feat not considered likely to be accomplished. But the horror of another separate Russo-German peace, which would turn almost all of Europe's resources against the United Kingdom, was so great that the British were ready to compromise past differences with the Russians. Stalin wryly reminded Churchill of this later on in the war when both were sitting more comfortably: "I cannot agree with you that Britain could easily have made a separate peace with Germany, largely at the expense of the U.S.S.R. and without serious loss to the British Empire. I think that was said rashly, for I recall statements of a different nature made by you. I recall, for example, that when Great Britain was in difficulties, before the Soviet Union became involved in the war against Germany, you believed that the British Government might have to move to Canada and fight Germany across the ocean." [10]

This was Stalin's big advantage, and he had very few others in the summer of 1941, when British representatives came to Moscow to talk about an Anglo-Russian treaty. A few days after the German invasion of Russia, President Roosevelt wrote to Admiral Leahy, then Ambassador to Vichy France, that speculative fears of future Russian domination of Eastern Europe were very much premature. The State Department took a somewhat different view, even at the time when Hitler's mechanized divisions were sweeping away all Russian opposition before them: It was anxious to learn what was being said in Moscow, what promises were being made, and what territorial divisions were being laid out. On July 10, 1941, Sumner Welles inquired closely of the British Ambassador about possible secret provisions connected with an Anglo-Russian draft treaty of mutual assistance. Two months later, Adolf Berle repeated the question and learned to his chagrin that apparently there had been at least some half-promises which, if fulfilled, would bring the "Russian system considerably west of Vienna." [11]

But nothing was settled that summer—hence Stalin's November 8th message to Churchill urging new negotiations to achieve clarity in Anglo-Russian relations. So Foreign Minister Eden left for Moscow. By this time, however, the United States had made itself an ally of England by virtue of the Atlantic Charter, and had also made known in that same document its opposition to bilateral deals among the Allies. Washington reiterated this opposition in a telegram sent to London on December 5, 1941, which the Administration had intended would bolster Eden's protests against "arrangements which would make the Soviet Union the dominating power of Eastern Europe if not of the whole Continent." This was indeed striking intervention when it is remembered that this telegram left Washington two days before Pearl Harbor.[12]

Eden used American attitudes to counter Stalin's strong representations, but the Russian leader turned the blade and pinned Eden on it. "As regards your repeated references to the necessity for His Majesty's Government to consult the United States Government, I must confess that I had overlooked this fact and believed your Government to have more freedom of action in these matters." The British Foreign Minister extricated himself, and even agreed to be the Soviet Union's advocate before the British cabinet. Moreover, he promised a favorable decision before Russian troops could win their way back to the areas Stalin had been claiming.[13]

Convincing a Washington jury with this brief turned out to be an altogether different matter. When Lord Halifax first delivered his government's arguments on behalf of Russia's demand for its 1941 frontiers, Sumner Welles responded so strongly that he almost left behind the requirements of diplomatic language. This crisis, he declared, placed the United States and Great Britain at a crossroads. What Russia was actually demanding was a return to the kind of "shoddy, inherently vicious, kind of patchwork world order which the European powers had attempted to construct during the years 1919 and 1939." Roosevelt was equally adamant, commenting that the Soviet proposal was "provincial" and that he would talk personally with Stalin about it. For the moment, Roosevelt suggested simply that there were other ways to give the Soviet Union security assurances.[14]

The search for this substitute or even something approaching one puzzled American policy makers for some time. American officials in England, especially Ambassador Winant and the visiting Harry Hopkins, came to have more sympathy for the British predicament— and to conclude that there was a certain logic to British arguments that postwar cooperation from the Soviet Union would be more likely if Russian territorial desires were at least partially met in 1942. Hopkins even championed this point of view in a conversation with the President in early March, 1942. Roosevelt then tested it against the thoughts of another adviser, William Bullitt, who had just as forcefully argued the State Department's position that "if we make a single commitment regarding the peace we have lost the chance of being free agents." The acid test of "our good faith" to Russia should instead be the prompt delivery of the supplies "we promise." [15]

Bullitt later wrote that even before America's entrance into the war, he had urged the President to obtain the reverse of Stalin's demands; in other words, the United States should be the country to have written "pledges" from Stalin. "The threat to the vital interests of the American people covered by *our Atlantic Doctrine and our Open Door doctrine* [emphasis added] might come . . . from one vast dictatorship from the Pacific to Western Europe."

"Bill, I don't dispute your facts, they are accurate," responded the President, as Bullitt recalled. "I don't dispute the logic of your reasoning. I just have a hunch that Stalin is not that kind of man. Harry says he's not and that he doesn't want anything but security for his country, and I think that if I give him everything I possibly can and ask nothing from him in return, *noblesse oblige,* he won't try to annex anything and will work with me for a world of democracy and peace." [16]

One can hardly believe that Roosevelt was quite so naïve as Bullitt's rephrasing of the President's language would indicate. The Secretary of Agriculture recorded about this time that Roosevelt told a Cabinet meeting that he had encouraged Churchill not to yield to Russian demands for the Baltic States, for then England would be faced with even greater demands—even up to half of Poland. Admittedly, though, this was an uncertain time, when minds were changing and adjusting to meet war conditions. Sumner Welles recalled some time afterward that he had had some long second thoughts on this problem: perhaps it would have been wiser after all to settle territorial issues in 1942 when American influence was at its height; moreover, he had decided a hard rejection of Russian claims "might cause a breakdown in Allied cooperation." Such considerations evidently caused Roosevelt to suggest a much milder policy than before. Russia should be willing to guarantee that plebicites be held in the Baltic countries to confirm their desire to join the Soviet Union, he said. [17]

On April 1, 1942, Roosevelt and Welles decided upon an alternative that neither liked very much but which seemed the best available given the pressures Russia was putting upon England. The Undersecretary conveyed to Ambassador Halifax that the United States would like to see some clause in the Anglo-Russian Treaty permitting reciprocal exchanges of population, thereby allowing chances for the disgruntled to leave a Russian-dominated area. Immediately his proposal came under attack from Adolf Berle, who charged that it was tantamount to surrender. Others, including the semi-official Advisory Committee on Post-War Foreign Policy, then meeting at the State Department, agreed with Berle.[18]

Happily for all American planners, the possibilities of a more satisfactory alternative in connection with a military Second Front were then increasing in talks General George C. Marshall and Harry Hopkins were having with British military chiefs and Prime Minister Churchill. The Americans came away from these meetings with the optimistic impression that their Ally had consented to a joint attack on the Continent sometime after September, 1942, to be followed up by a major invasion in early 1943.[19]

Had Roosevelt (and others) not been so anxious to defer the political problem, perhaps he would not have taken this information and used it for the basis of a dubious letter to Stalin on April 12: "I have in mind a very important military proposal involving the utilization of our armed forces in a manner to relieve your critical Western Front. This objective carries great weight with me." Could Foreign Minister Molotov be sent on to Washington after his visit to London to talk over this matter? [20]

Now it should be added that Harry Hopkins had told the British that Roosevelt, having made the somewhat unpopular decision to go after Germany first, was under pressure to bring American armed forces into contact with Nazi troops as soon as possible; but Moscow's direct pressure on London was surely just as important, as the following discussions, which took place in London and Washington, disclosed.[21]

As Molotov renewed his talks with British officials in London, American representatives were near: Ambassador Winant was instructed to express Washington's opposition to any treaty containing political arrangements. Impressed by Anglo-American unity, Molotov accepted a short treaty on May 26, 1942, pledging the two nations to aid one another against their common foe. Molotov then left for Washington to hear the rest of the bargain which had been so clearly intimated.[22]

After sitting through a broad review of the Pacific War and also hearing Roosevelt's vague suggestions about Big Four Police powers over the disarmament of the aggressor nations, Molotov brought the conversations abruptly to his main interest: Was the President familiar with the Anglo-Soviet Treaty? Roosevelt said that he was, and that he was also "glad" that the frontier problem had not been mentioned in it. Molotov remarked that his country had a very different view, but had deferred to the British and the Americans. The President then asked his guest to present Russian strategic thinking on the war against Germany.

As expected, the Russian Foreign Minister offered the argument that an immediate opening of a second front would draw off forty or more German divisions from the Eastern front and thus lead to an Allied victory in 1942 or 1943. When Molotov finished, the President turned to General Marshall and asked if the Foreign Minister's ideas seemed feasible in 1942, at least to the extent that the United States could take part in an assault upon the Continent? Marshall replied affirmatively and the President turned back to the Russian and told him to report to Moscow that the United States expected the formation of a Second Front to be accomplished in 1942.[23]

After Molotov returned to Moscow, he advised the British Ambassador that the test of their treaty "lay in a second front . . . and the United States Government must understand that." American Ambassador William Standley agreed that even the public communiqués from the Molotov-Roosevelt conversations left one with the logical assumption that Russia had given up nearly vital frontier questions in exchange for the promise of a second front.[24]

But it was not to be—not in 1942, nor even in 1943. Severe British military reverses in the African campaign against the Desert Fox, General Rommel, were part of the reason, but when the Prime Minister came to Washington in June, his first argument against even a limited assault was that the British Chiefs of Staff had been unable to come up with any plan which would not end in disaster. "Had the American staffs devised such a plan?" he challenged.[25]

With the second front up in the air, Roosevelt's position became precarious indeed: Having taken up a stake in Anglo-Russian talks on Europe's future, he was obliged to show his openers. On July 15, 1942, he sent Hopkins and Marshall back to London with orders that American "ground forces had to be put into position to fight ground forces somewhere in 1942." The British would only consider a North African campaign which had been given the code name TORCH.[26]

Churchill accepted the burden of carrying the unpleasant news to Stalin. Roosevelt tried to ease the situation, writing to Moscow: "We are coming as quickly and as strongly to your assistance as we possibly can and I hope that you will believe me when I tell you this." [27]

Russian leaders scoffed bitterly; they saw dark political motives lurking behind the change in strategy and the parallel curtailment of ship convoys from the United Kingdom and the United States. The premature promise of a second front had been a disastrous political move, and Roosevelt tried to rectify it with new promises of aid, and by sending General Patrick Hurley to survey Russian needs and to go over the "most significant aspects of our present world strategy," and finally by inviting Premier Stalin to join an Anglo-American strategy conference at Casablanca in January, 1943. On this last, Roosevelt advised the Russian leader (using all his political skill) that there were, in addition to proposed military discussions, "other matters relating to future policies about North Africa and the Far East which cannot be discussed by our military people alone." [28]

Military affairs expert Hanson Baldwin later wrote of the Casablanca Conference that even Roosevelt's famed "Unconditional Surrender" declaration was dictated by the President's desire to convince Russia that the United States would not fail to pursue the war to ultimate and complete victory! [29]

However that may be, the President's invitation to Stalin and his words to Ambassador Harriman at the First Quebec Conference later that year showed that the President was just as adept at intermixing military and political strategy as Churchill or Stalin. He told Harriman at Quebec that he wanted above all to assure the Soviets of future collective security, of an equal place at the peace table, and of the dismemberment of Germany; in exchange he hoped to convince Moscow to abstain from reaching out to take Central and Eastern Europe.[30]

And though the United States had opposed political clauses in the Anglo-Russian Treaty, Roosevelt was even prepared to go part way to meet Moscow's territorial demands.

ATTEMPTS AT ACCOMMODATION ON POLAND

Besides the Unconditional Surrender statement which Roosevelt gave reporters, the Casablanca Conference produced a new Anglo-American promise of an invasion of Continental Europe in the fall of 1943. Once again it could not be managed. Finally, at Teheran at the end of 1943, the three world leaders met and agreed on operation OVERLORD for the spring of 1944. Russian attitudes towards its western Allies improved at once.

Another reason for the détente was Churchill's initiation of discussions on Poland's future boundaries. Using matchsticks at one of the dinner meetings, the Prime Minister sketched out the possibility that Poland might be moved westward into East Germany. Roosevelt, too, made a gesture indicating his interest in this matter by asking Stalin to meet with him alone on December 1, 1943. Although the President said that internal American politics prevented him from taking part "in any such arrangement" as his two Allies seemingly were working out on Poland, he assured the Premier that when the Red armies re-occupied the three Baltic countries, "he did not intend to go to war with the Soviet Union on this point." All he desired was some sort of referendum or expression of the people's will. Stalin answered that there would be plenty of opportunities for such expressions.[31]

At this point, Roosevelt apparently had decided to go back to the once-abandoned idea of April 1, 1942. American policy was ambiguous, and that peculiar quality was the only certain thing about it. It is highly doubtful that Roosevelt ever meant to give Stalin a green light for all of Eastern Europe, but American representatives such as Arthur Bliss Lane who were later assigned there traced back their problems to the Teheran exchanges—or ones which followed Teheran. It is also true that Roosevelt suspected English motives in Eastern Europe as much as Russian motives, and many of his pro-Russian actions may have been taken in the name of the balance of power. Yet in refusing Churchill's Mediterranean-Balkan military plans, Roosevelt warned his military men that he felt it was "unwise to plan military strategy based on a gamble as to political results." [32]

Secretary of War Stimson reiterated Roosevelt's advice, but said it in such a way as to put political considerations in a proper perspective. Roosevelt probably meant what the Secretary said. "In the light of the post-war problems we shall face," he advised Roosevelt, the British attitude that the war could be won "by a series of attritions" in Italy, the Mediterranean, Greece, and Rumania "seems terribly dangerous." Russians would see through it in an instant and would denounce it as a crude attempt to fool them "into the belief that we have kept" the second front pledge.[33]

Within the group of Roosevelt's closest advisers, the most immediately concerned about the implications of the Teheran exchanges was Secretary Hull. He feared that American policy was drifting away from its principles and its determination to "establish the rule that there could be no acquisition by force." He had listened to alarming Russian statements at the Moscow Foreign Ministers Conference (just before the

Teheran meetings) that Poland was responsible for Europe's agony and should therefore be made to live in a smaller area; he had read newspaper reports that Russia was going to demand the Curzon Line as the new boundary between the two countries; and he knew generally what had happened at Teheran.[34]

Hull described these fears to Secretary Stimson, who was much less upset, reminding his colleague that before World War I Russia had owned *all* of Poland "running as far as Germany and that she was not asking for restitution of that . . . ." [35]

The Secretary of State was not calmed, and a few months later he had a chance to express himself. As the Allies steadily reduced Germany's crumbling empire in the second half of 1944, the British decided that it was time to settle the Balkan question. Ambassador Halifax gently probed the State Department for its reaction, and was startled perhaps by Hull's blunt statement that an Anglo-Russian deal "could not but derogate from the over-all authority of the international security organization which I expected would come into being." Here, of course, was a chance, which Hull took, to demonstrate the need for a United Nations in maintaining an open world.[36]

The Prime Minister came back with a telegram to Roosevelt explaining that the proposed arrangement pertained only to military matters. On June 10, 1944, the President sent him a reply drafted by the State Department which countered that military arrangements would probably "extend into the political and economic fields." But after further importunings from London, centering around the strong contention that someone had to play the hand and the promise that the arrangement would be limited to three months, Roosevelt consented to a watered-down version of the original proposal.[37]

In October the Prime Minister reopened the Balkan problem, asserting that a more permanent division of influence in Southeastern Europe should be established. He most particularly desired a Big Three Conference in order to acquaint his American Ally with the question and, better yet, to commit him to such a settlement. This posed a dilemma for American policy makers: The President could not attend such a conference before the national elections of 1944. Yet if no American were present, the European leaders might assume, as one State Department official pointed out to Harry Hopkins, that Roosevelt had washed his hands of European political problems. At the same time, if Ambassador Harriman attended the meetings, his presence would give unwarranted support to Churchill's position.[38]

Still thinking in the framework of the temporary arrangement, the President allowed a vague message to be prepared for the conferees, but Harry Hopkins intervened, stopped it, and persuaded Roosevelt that it did not safeguard American interests. Hopkins' redraft and Roosevelt's additional instructions to Ambassador Harriman placed much more emphasis upon United States concern for all the subjects before the two Allies. They made it clear that any settlement could only be "preliminary to a conference of the three of us." "It is important that I retain complete freedom of action after this conference is over." [39]

"I was somewhat puzzled by your message of October 5," wrote Stalin. "I had imagined that Mr. Churchill was coming to Moscow in keeping with an agreement reached with you at Quebec. It appears, however, that my supposition is at variance with reality." Even so, Stalin and Churchill went ahead to divide influence in the Balkans. England was to have the lead in Greece; Stalin, in Rumania and Bulgaria; and each was to have a share in the control of the other nations.[40]

But Polish questions now boiled up that were not capable of such a settlement even on a bilateral basis. Stalin began initiating unilateral actions in that country which badly upset his Allies. Since 1943, when the Soviet Union had broken diplomatic relations with the Polish government in exile in London over the Katyn Forest Massacre, Great Britain and the United States had feared that Moscow would set up a puppet government and place it in power as soon as the Red Army re-entered the country. As witnessed by his efforts at Teheran, Churchill did everything possible to prevent that from happening. He brought strong pressure indeed upon the London Poles to accept the Curzon Line and to accept compensations in the west.[41]

To Russia this Polish émigré government was a stench in its nostrils, and the feeling was returned in kind. Moscow viewed the exiles as no better than the reactionaries all through Europe who had unleashed Hitler's terror. Not only were they the cause of Europe's agony, but their representatives were fomenting their own terroristic acts against the Red Army. The Poles saw no difference between the Russian communists and their czarist predecessors: all were imperialists. The famous Warsaw uprising against the German garrison in that city brought feelings to a head on each side. The Polish government in exile insisted that they were betrayed by the Russians, while Moscow claimed that the slaughter of the Poles had started as a dark plot to discredit the Soviet Union.[42] Against this background, Russia created the Polish Committee of National Liberation as the provisional government of Poland. Thus far, Moscow had not antagonized London and Washington beyond repair. Roosevelt, for example, told Arthur Bliss Lane on November 20, 1944, that Stalin's concern not to allow the resurrection of the anti-Bolshevik Cordon Sainitaire was certainly "understandable." Lane was then instructed to stay in Washington until the exiles accepted the Curzon Line.[43]

Similarly, Thomas Lamont wrote to a liberal friend that although they both disliked Stalin's methods in Poland, he could put himself in Russian shoes: "In the light of history I should certainly advise a frontier as far west as the so-called Curzon Line; and Poland, having been partitioned three times within a century and a half and up to 1919 having no independent existence of its own, ought not to be too sticky at achieving her full aims." [44]

Stalin wanted his Allies to travel the second mile, however, and recognize the Lublin Committee as the *de facto* provisional government of Poland, as he was going to do. The United States refused. On January 5, 1945, the Soviet Union went ahead with its plan, and there the situation stood at the time of the Yalta Conference. The coming test with Russia in Poland then appeared to American policy makers to be a very critical example of how postwar relations would take shape.

COMPROMISE IS IMPOSSIBLE

At first, Roosevelt believed that the ensuing Yalta Conference decisions on Poland were a happy settlement for all sides. Appearing before Congress on March 1, he described the accord as the best possible solution of the composition of the Polish government and of the territory over which it should rule. The Big Three had agreed that a Tripartite Commission should supervise the construction of a new Polish government "organized on a broader democratic basis with the inclusion of democratic leaders from Poland itself and from Poles abroad." The Curzon Line was to be the boundary in the east, and the determination of the western frontier would be made at the peace conference ending World War II.

Unfortunately, the Commission soon fell to quarreling over the proper interpretation of the Yalta accord. On April 1 Roosevelt tried to break the impasse and show his displeasure over the lack of progress by a letter to Stalin: "Your Government appears to take the position that the new Polish provisional Government of National Unity which we agreed should be formed should be little more than a continuation of the present Warsaw Government. I cannot reconcile this either with our agreement or our discussions."

Stalin answered that the Anglo-American members of the Commission "hold that reconstruction of the Provisional Government should be understood in terms of its abolition and the establishment of an entirely new government. Things have gone so far that Mr. Harriman declared in the Moscow Commission that it might be that not a single member of the Provisional Government would be included in the Polish Government of National Unity." [45]

Roosevelt had also mentioned in his April 1 letter the apparent Soviet disregard of the Yalta Declaration on Liberated Countries. Yet another indication that Poland was to be the symbol of Allied disagreement or Russian intransigency in Eastern and Central Europe, this theme received many reworkings in the spring of 1945. Ambassador Lane wrote Secretary of State Stettinius that he thought the Polish experience was going to be repeated in Bulgaria, Rumania, and Yugoslavia, where already United States officials could not obtain information or take "legitimate steps to protect American interests . . . ." On April 23 the new American President of eleven days met Foreign Minister Molotov for the first time and confronted him with all these charges.

Earlier that day, President Truman had called together the special War Cabinet to ask each of them for an opinion about his "laying it on the line with Molotov." He looked first to Secretary Stimson: The Secretary of War "held back" for a moment and then, as he noted in his diary, said, "I was very troubled by it . . . . I said that in my opinion we ought to be very careful and see whether we couldn't get ironed out on the situation without getting into a head on collision. He was evidently disappointed at my caution and advice and passed along the circle coming on to Forrestal." The Navy Secretary felt with Truman: "We might as well meet the issue now as later on." [46]

The War Cabinet departed and Molotov came in a few hours later. Truman started right in "plain talking" to the Russian foreign minister. An agreement had been reached on Poland at Yalta, said Truman bluntly, and it only needed "to be carried out by the Soviet Government." After Truman clearly intimated that he would go ahead with the San Francisco Conference without Russia if necessary, the foreign minister defended his country's actions and concluded afterwards that he had "never been talked to like that" in all his life.[47]

Truman's lecture to Molotov did not shake Stalin's resolve to strengthen the Lublin Committee's hold on Poland, for he went ahead and granted it administrative control in western territories taken from Germany, a problem supposedly reserved for the peace conference. Two more months passed before the Tripartite Commission made any real progress.

The bluntness of Truman's opening relations with the Russians set Stimson to wondering. "Some Americans," he told an aide, "are anxious to hang on to exaggerated views of the Monroe Doctrine and at the same time butt into every question that comes up in Central Europe." Perhaps the new President was not fully aware that Churchill's ideas of "grand policy in Central Europe" differed from Roosevelt's policy. A group of liberal Congressmen had followed much the same thought process and had written Secretary Stettinius that "we had allowed ourselves to become involved in the Polish matter in exactly that sort of Anglo-American 'front' against Russia which Mr. Roosevelt had consistently striven to avoid" and had compounded that mistake "by also getting involved in what appeared to be a Western Hemisphere 'front' directed both against Russia and the idea of an effective general security organization." [48]

But for all his worry, Stimson looked the hardest for "some way of persuading Russia to play ball" in the reconstruction of Europe. So did most liberals. As early as March, President Roosevelt had considered bargaining the promised "allocation of certain warships to the Soviet Union" in exchange for Moscow's letting down "the bars for American businessmen to enter Rumania." [49]

Roosevelt had decided that the difficulties in Rumania were not a sufficient test of how well the Allies would get on together in the postwar period, but to Truman and Churchill it was sufficiently important to be raised at the Potsdam Conference. American companies had owned more than 85 per cent of the Rumanian oil, and the wish to restore their claims became part of the general desire to maintain inviolate the Anglo-American "social and economic system in East Europe." [50]

Between May 1 and 15, Truman heard from at least three key sources that American interests were effectively and rapidly being pushed out of Eastern Europe by the Russian steamroller. From Prime Minister Churchill: "There seems little doubt that the whole of the regions east of the line Lubeck-Trieste-Corfu will soon be completely in their hands."

From American officials in Bulgaria and Rumania: "If the Soviets . . . get away with their program in those countries [they will] be encouraged to try the same game in every other country in Europe as far as they [can] penetrate."

From the American Embassy in Moscow: "The procedure used by Soviet Russia in Poland, Rumania, Bulgaria, and Hungary [will] be adopted, so far as the Soviets are permitted to do so, in the case of Austria and Czechoslovakia . . . ." [51]

The President assured Ambassador Lane that these reports "would be the fundamental subject which he intended to discuss at the Big Three meeting." He left Lane with no doubts "as to his intention to insist on the eventual removal of the Soviet blackout in the countries mentioned." But Truman wanted to hear first from Harry Hopkins, then in Moscow, before deciding exactly what to say to Stalin.[52]

Hopkins' discussions with Stalin on the Far Eastern Open Door Policy have already been mentioned. Their natural connection to European matters was understood by all the parties. Hopkins made this very point in his first review of the situation, commenting that "Poland per se was not so important as the fact it had become a symbol of our ability to work out problems with the Soviet Union." Surprisingly, the Russian Premier admitted that the unilateral actions in that country might better have been left undone, but he contended also that he had met with no understanding from the Western Allies. After swiping at British attempts to "stabilize" Greece, he offered to take into the Warsaw government four Poles from other democratic groups.[53]

At another meeting, Hopkins tried to have Stalin commit himself even more firmly to tripartite cooperation in re-establishing the Polish provisional government and in preparing for future free elections. Stalin entered several caveats to these principles of democracy Hopkins was reciting, but said that he generally agreed.[54]

During Hopkins' visit, the Soviet government decided to test London and Washington on diplomatic recognition of the new governments in Bulgaria and Rumania, linking it to the less controversial matter of recognizing Finland's new government. An exchange of messages took place, which Truman brought to an end by insisting that the topic should be discussed at Potsdam.[55]

The State Department had prepared a stockpile of policy memorandums on this subject which Truman could turn to if he desired. Their firm advice was that no recognition should be given until the United States could "obtain equality of opportunity for U.S. business interests in these areas, and an agreement protecting the rights of U.S. property owners." In Rumania, for example, if Soviet economic agreements were consummated, they would "have the effect of making Rumania economically dependent on the U.S.S.R., without economic contact with other countries outside eastern Europe. Under these conditions it will probably be impossible for American interests to engage in trade with Rumania or to carry on business in that country."

"This kind of exclusive economic penetration," read still another paper, "is at variance with the general commercial policy of this Government, which looks toward the expansion of trade and investment on a multilateral, non-discriminatory basis." The United States had a "strong interest" in Eastern European trade, not only for itself but also for the "position of other countries which were importers to, and exporters from, Eastern Europe before the war."[56]

As he had indicated he would do, Truman spoke out at the first Plenary Meeting at Potsdam on the need to implement the Yalta Declaration on Liberated Europe. Then he proposed reorganizing the Rumanian and Bulgarian governments by adding representatives of all democratic elements. Diplomatic recognition could be granted then, and, finally, peace treaties could be concluded with these nations. Stalin protested that diplomatic recognition should be given to these governments as they were, just as it had been given to the new Italian government, but the President (backed by the knowledge of the atomic bomb on this day) shut off the debate: "When these countries were established on a proper basis, the United States would recognize them and not before."[57]

Actually the Russians had offered some amended working procedures for the Allied Control Commissions in the former German satellites just as the Potsdam Meetings opened, but as the American representatives in Rumania had explained in their notations on the new policies, the crux of the trouble had been and was still the lack of "goodwill on the part of the Soviet Executive" on the Commission. And James Byrnes reported the fate of these changes or concessions some time later: "Stalin also agreed to revise some control procedures in Rumania, Bulgaria, and Hungary to meet our objections—but did not live up to his agreement." [58]

THE OPEN DOOR IN POLAND

Acting upon Ambassador Harriman's reports that the Warsaw government had been broadened as the result of the inclusion of several Poles from abroad during a series of meetings between June 17 and 21, the United States accorded diplomatic recognition to the provisional government on July 5. So that question had been momentarily put aside at Potsdam, except for the matter of the western boundary.

Harriman had cabled Washington on June 28 that while he was not entirely satisfied, he believed the stage was "set as well as can be done at the present time and that if we continue to take a sympathetic interest in Polish affairs and are reasonably generous in our economic relations there is a fair chance that things will work out satisfactorily from our standpoint." This was the opening of a new campaign to restore the Open Door Policy in Poland and Eastern Europe.[59]

The State Department's policy memorandum on Poland prepared for the Potsdam Conference expanded on these aspirations: Free elections should be planned right away; Polish participation in international agencies should be encouraged; and the American Red Cross should continue its work there. "In assisting through credits and otherwise in the physical reconstruction of Polish economy, we should insist on the acceptance by Poland of a policy of equal opportunity for us in trade, investment and access to sources of information." [60]

On July 12, Washington made Ambassador Lane aware of its several ideas for Polish recovery. The Ambassador was to tell the provisional government that the United States fully supported the United Nations Relief and Reconstruction Administration's intention to distribute nearly a million tons of supplies in the next six months; it being understood also that UNRRA would appoint an American as permanent chief of its mission in Poland.

In anticipation of Export-Import Bank credits, the Polish government should be encouraged to prepare a full statement of its needs "as well as present financial resources, trade prospects and other relevant material."

The United States would also welcome proposals to facilitate payments in dollar exchange for exports. Plans were being made to provide Poland with one thousand surplus army trucks on dollar credit terms. America wanted to re-establish private trade "as soon as mechanical limitations and facilities permit." Stepped up Red Cross aid was under consideration, provided that the aid could be distributed in accordance with the organization's principles.

And to help transform these suggestions into realities, Washington said that an exchange of technical and economic specialists would be welcomed.[61]

The Ambassador took these offerings to President Boleslaw Bierut on August 2, 1945. This was their first meeting, and it was hoped that the American ideas would make it an auspicious one. But from the United States' point of view there arose difficulties right away. For one thing, the Polish government insisted upon distributing UNRRA aid itself; worse yet, a Russian official had been appointed head of the mission there. Russian suspicions had been aroused that UNRRA was a second Hoover Relief Commission. The Bolsheviks remembered that Hoover had made use of food to stop their advances and to encourage their enemies in Russia. Herbert Hoover had used food supplies to turn back 'the tide of Communism in all those countries." "He could . . . pretty well lay down the law to the applicant countries," Stimson recalled in May, 1945, when the former President had himself resurrected the idea for a new anticommunist relief mission, "and, if there was any issue between him and them, he could go at once to Paris and get his position backed up by the heads of the four governments there." [62]

A discussion of possible Export-Import Bank credits went better, but when Lane referred to the resurrection of private trade, Polish officials objected to attempts to shield property holdings behind the 1931 Treaty of Commerce and Friendship between the two countries. A few days later, Ambassador Lane saw the Minister of Industry and advised him that credits would be available when Poland accepted Article VII of the Lend-Lease Master Agreement: "I determined to take advantage of the eagerness of the Polish Government for economic assistance and to use it as a lever by which we would obtain fulfillment of Polish commitments under the Yalta and Potsdam decisions, as well as an improvement of the situation of imprisoned American citizens." [63]

But Polish "eagerness" for American aid did not solve these differences, which had arisen even in the first conversation Lane had with President Bierut. And when a Polish minister visited Washington in the fall of 1945, a State Department officer explained how difficult it was "for us to give credits to a regime whose foreign economic policy was so contrary to ours." The minister, Stanislaw Mikolajczyk, eventually convinced President Truman that limited credits for specific needs would encourage the Polish people and would not unduly bolster the present regime—with which he did not totally sympathize either. "Our thought here," Lane was advised, "is that since Mickey thinks we can help him, we ought to go ahead and extend credits according to his plan." [64]

Lane was much less hopeful, and he became totally despondent in January, 1946, when the Polish government issued a series of expropriation orders against foreign property holders. In April he opposed giving Poland any more aid, including a then-planned credit of 90 million dollars, until truly free elections were held. The Department assured him that the Polish government had promised to pay compensations, hold free elections within a year, and enter into American plans for the "expansion of world trade and employment." [65]

When Ambassador Lane resigned in a few months, he was convinced that he had witnessed the betrayal of Poland to the Russians. Hope that Eastern Europe could be brought into political and economic postwar plans was gone.

ECONOMIC AID TO RUSSIA?

European security problems naturally overlapped with economic problems and the question of economic aid for Russian rehabilitation after the war. "If a system of security removes mistrust and fear," Lauchlin Currie wrote to Harry Hopkins at the end of 1943, "the United States should be able to send a billion dollars worth of exports yearly to the USSR in the first five years of peace. This is the time when the USSR will most need imports. It is also the time when the U.S. will be reconverting and will have surplus plant and equipment." [66]

Such notions floated in and out of Administration offices, and undoubtedly Currie's message to Hopkins or ones like it formed the basis for his brief discussion of Russian-American economic potentials in the January, 1944, *American Magazine.* Currie's boss, Leo Crowley, indulged himself in similar prophecies: "Industrial development and reconstruction in China, Russia, and in other countries will open up vast new markets." [67]

At this time Donald M. Nelson and Eric Johnston were trying to change these potentials into realities through direct conversations with Premier Stalin concerning the "wish of American industry to do business with the Soviet Union." [68]

The fundamental "if" clause in Currie's original postulate was, however, far from being fulfilled. Two increasingly antagonistic security systems were struggling for the most of Europe at the end of World War II, and this had everything to do with the waning of the United States desire to aid Russian recovery. And even if Russian aspirations had not then overreached security requirements, it is doubtful that economic agreements could have been reached.

By July, 1945, the moment had passed when the two countries could have easily reversed the decline in their relations. This was especially true of one issue which had many economic as well as political ramifications. The Russians had linked reparations from Germany in a loose sort of ratio to the economic aid they expected from the United States. In the summer of 1945 the Russians were already levying heavy reparations upon Germany and were demanding a total of ten billion dollars. Secretary of War Stimson's reaction was typical: "The Russian policy on booty in eastern Germany, if it is as I have heard it reported, is rather oriental. It is bound to force us to preserve the economy in Western Germany in close cooperation with the British, so as to avoid conditions in our areas which, in the last analysis, neither Britain nor American public opinion would long tolerate." [69]

The problem was complicated because the Soviet Union had formally requested aid in January, 1945—and nothing had been done about it. It might well have been, then, that their "oriental" policy in Eastern Europe had some relation at least to the blunt occidental attitude then prevalent in Washington.

Back as far as 1943 Cordell Hull had given serious thought to the question of postwar aid to Russia, and even then he had expressed concern to Foreign Minister Anthony Eden that it would be difficult to prevail upon the American people to aid Russia unless greater cooperation were forthcoming from Moscow. Perhaps amused at Hull's fall back to American public opinion, Eden remarked laconically that, after all, the Russians *had* been destroying Germans. "We all know this, of course," the Secretary answered without a pause. "But the people who are dissatisfied with the failure of Russia to show any interest or concern about future joint efforts to promote peace and economic rehabilitation based on liberal commercial policies find that nothing would be gained thereby except that Russia and Great Britain will have succeeded in eliminating Germany." [70]

After less than satisfactory responses some months later at the Moscow Foreign Ministers Conference, Hull and his colleagues decided that the "Russians might make more of an effort to find ways of cooperating with his trade program if their chances of obtaining American loans depended upon it." [71]

This attitude touched all American thinking on the question thereafter. Roosevelt mentioned economic aid to Russian leaders at Teheran, but the first real initiative came from Foreign Minister Molotov a few weeks later when he asked Ambassador Harriman to forward Moscow's application for a billion dollar Lend-Lease credit. This project received a hearing in Washington in the spring of 1944, but aside from easing restrictions on the use of Lend-Lease supplies for the post-European war period, the response left the credit request in limbo.[72]

Near the end of 1944 the Treasury Department prepared some proposals of its own for aiding the Soviet Union. On the first day of 1945, Morgenthau wrote to the President pointing out that the Second Quebec Conference had provided an opportunity to begin reconstruction planning with England; would it not now be wise to make an equivalent gesture to Russia? It might well result in clearing up many current differences on other subjects.[73]

In conversations with Admiral Leahy, the Secretary added some more arguments for his proposal. Extending credits to Russia would divert trade into American channels which could become competitive if left to develop outside of any American interest or direction. Morgenthau gathered all his thoughts together in another memorandum of January 10. A ten billion dollar credit at 2 per cent interest for thirty-five years, he suggested, would allow the United States to obtain commitments from Russia for guaranteed access to strategic raw materials and would open up several possibilities for economic relations with Russia, and finally, it would constitute a "major step in your [Roosevelt's] program to provide 60 million jobs in the post-war period." [74]

The week before this last memo, Moscow had presented its own proposal for a 6 billion dollar credit, urging upon Ambassador Harriman that "Soviet-American relations must have certain vistas . . . and rest upon a solid economic basis." The American Ambassador reacted favorably but cautiously, noting in his report to Washington that the U.S.S.R. should be given "to understand that our willingness to co-operate wholeheartedly with them in their vast reconstruction problems will depend upon their behavior in international matters." In any event, Harriman, Leo Crowley, and Assistant Secretary of State Will Clayton all thought that the Treasury's suggestions were too generous and maintained further that aid must be employed as a diplomatic tool.[75]

At a later meeting in the White House, Ambassador Harriman deprecated the other supposed advantages of Morgenthau's program by commenting that "our basic interest might be better served by increasing our trade with other parts of the world rather than giving preference to the Soviet Union as a source of supply." [76]

With each side unsure, probing here and there, waiting for the war to end and pull away the curtain between them, which was at once a cover and a protection against direct confrontations, Washington feared to move too boldly one way or another. Hence a *New York Times* correspondent was advised during a purely off-the-record consultation in the State Department, and in a purely friendly way, to go slow in any columns on the Russian request.[77]

The previously flexible attitude on Lend-Lease stiffened somewhat as early as February and March, 1945—an indication of the way policy makers seemed to be going. A Soviet request for a 300 million dollar supply of industrial equipment, to be repaid out of a long-term credit rather than from the original Lend-Lease Act's terms, kept the issue in the foreground.[78]

Then Lend-Lease shipments were ended abruptly on May 8, 1945. This was a blow to both Russia and England, but Administration leaders worried principally about its effect on the Soviets. A Lend-Lease administrator asked for a White House appointment in order to assure himself that the President stood behind the decision, since "we would be having difficulty with the Russians and he did not want them running all over town looking for help." Naturally, the burden of such problems fell to the State Department. An aide-mémoire circulated from that Department pleased Stimson because it seemed to him a long-needed reform and let the Russians know "that we could no longer give them everything they wanted and they must apply and justify their needs in the same way others did." Lend-Lease administrators were also working on a press release which "did not seem to bring the Russians in directly." This was being done to satisfy Acting Secretary of State Grew, who admonished the Lend-Lease people that the "whole thing is full of dynamite." [79]

President Truman approved this press release, remarking as he did that the Administration would just have to face up to the Russian slashback.[80]

It was argued then and later that this cut-off, especially since it was amended shortly thereafter to allow some shipments until the end of the Japanese war, was not a political maneuver but only a legal necessity. Yet it was impossible to ignore the political concern it gave the Administration in the doing of it, or to deny that most American policy makers wanted to use further financial or economic aid as a diplomatic tool (after all, Washington was doing that very thing with its much closer Ally, England), or to avoid consideration of the developing "peculiar mood," as a Russian diplomat described it, that was in the Washington air that summer. Herbert Feis spoke for many officials certainly when he wrote in July that there were good reasons for granting aid to the Soviet Union, but then cautioned his readers that while America would permit Russia to lead in Eastern Europe, the nation "cannot happily accept Russian dictation of their policies and way of life; nor could it happily accept the exclusion of American economic enterprises." [81]

Underlining Feis's thoughts, a short time after the Lend-Lease cut-off the Acting Secretary of State answered one inquiry about Russian-American relations by noting that the moment did not seem propitious for undertaking negotiations for a treaty of friendship and commerce. Grew had good reasons for this reply: On May 16, Secretary Stimson had asked the State Department to provide protection for Singer Sewing Machine Company properties in the Soviet zone of Germany, "one of the oldest and most outstanding of our American industries known all over the world for many decades." "Perhaps the time has arrived," read a memo prepared by one of Stimson's assistants, "when the claims of American citizens against the Soviet government may be asserted, particularly if any future aid in the nature of Lend-Lease or loans to Russia is in contemplation." The State Department replied affirmatively: "We shall try not to overlook anything possible we might do to protect this legitimate American interest." [82]

Moving from the specific to the general, a special committee of the

National Foreign Trade Council looked into the question of economic aid to Russia and concluded exactly as the Administration had. Before any more aid could be offered, Moscow needed to clarify its position on these four points:

1. The portion of Soviet production which would continue to be devoted to armaments should be made public.
2. The terms of trade treaties between Russia and the East European countries should be disclosed.
3. American businessmen, journalists, and airplanes should have the opportunity to travel more freely in Russia.
4. American property rights in Eastern Europe should be protected as well as the right to distribute books, papers, and other information items.[83]

Not all leading Americans thought that Russia should be the only one of the Allies to give guaranties. An influential friend of Henry Stimson's wrote a very frank letter to President Truman on June 2 on this subject.

Now that Russia has regained self-confidence and military strength, is it surprising that without firm promises of aid from the United States, either directly or under the proposed San Francisco Charter, she should seek other methods of self-protection? I do not think so. On the contrary, it is inevitable and natural. This might have been mitigated if months ago we had made a treaty with Russia, corresponding to the Anglo-Russian and Franco-Russian treaties, or if we had proposed a general international organization of a sort that would have ensured our help in case of a resurgence by Germany. But we did neither, we made no such treaty.[84]

Reviewing this debate in the summer of 1945, the alternatives posed by the National Foreign Trade Council and by Mr. Grenville Clark's letter seem fairly accurate representations of the short-lived split in the Truman Administration. There evolved a division between those who demanded good deeds from Russia first and those who argued that the good deeds had to come from America at the same time; between those who would offer economic aid as a carrot and those who would brandish it as a stick; and finally (one must say most crucially), between those who would approach the Russians on international control of atomic energy and those who were tempted to wield it as a diplomatic hammer as long as possible.

RUSSIA AND THE CONTROL OF ATOMIC ENERGY

The simple fact that Russia had not originally been taken into Anglo-American confidences on the development of "Tube Alloys," "S-1," "X," or the "Manhattan Project," as the atomic bomb was variously known in London and Washington, was both an advantage and a disadvantage. It was certainly not difficult to comprehend the reason in the first years of research why Russia was not invited to join in its development—the Soviets were still linked to Nazi Germany in the Ribbentrop-Molotov Pact. The advantage to having such a powerful weapon in any circumstance is obvious, though the disadvantage to having developed it in secret, from the viewpoint of an Ally, was that it made relations after the war all the more difficult. It posed a tricky situation under the best of circumstances, presented a temptation in uncertain times, and finally helped to bring on a tragic ending to the war and the Grand Alliance. Neither side was endowed with what was needed to cope with this new weapon—almost superhuman reason and understanding.

After the Nazi invasion of Russia in 1941, for example, the simple explanation that the Soviet Union was a military enemy will no longer do, and one must fall back to the heritage of mistrust which began in 1917. And even this becomes inadequate when discussing the period from July to September, 1945, when at least two avenues became clearly identifiable to Anglo-American leaders when approaching even a suspected Ally.

One added note at this point: The drive for secrecy surrounding the development of atomic energy supplied its own inertial force. This no doubt prevented a clear presentation of the possible ultimate ends of each of the alternatives. Henry L. Stimson was one of the few to pause and follow out in his mind the logical conclusion of each. The military director of the Manhattan Project has told us recently that security precautions were directed from the beginning primarily against Soviet espionage. In this atmosphere it was difficult to give each alternative equal consideration.[85]

Stimson did not always feel that a direct and open approach should be made to the Russians. In December, 1942, the Secretary of War became aware of and was alarmed about an Anglo-Russian agreement to share knowledge on new weapons and their development. Not only might this include British work on S-1, but Ambassador Winant was already on his way home "to urge that we should go into such an agreement with Russia . . . ." Much to Stimson's relief, President Roosevelt "agreed with me that it would be very bad policy to go into such an agreement." [86]

Fears that the British would share their knowledge with the Soviets were unwarranted, for, as the Prime Minister remarked the following July, his country was "vitally concerned with being able to maintain her future independence in the face of the international blackmail that the Russians might eventually be able to employ." [87]

A year later, August, 1944, Stimson jotted down some notes for a talk with the President on the postwar world. These were more in the vein of Stimson's earlier career as Secretary of State. Among his thoughts was the notation that S-1 might be of use in bringing Russia "into the fold of Christian Civilization." Did Stimson mean by revealing the weapon to Russia or by making a direct approach later? His memo does not give much further explanation except that in a later section he notes under "Steps towards Disarmament" the "Impossibility of Disclosure—(S-1)." [88]

On December 31 the Secretary of War talked with the President on atomic energy once again. They discussed the coming Yalta Conference and Russia's demand for a sphere of influence in Eastern Europe. Stimson reverted to the "future of S-1 in connection with Russia . . . . I believed that it was essential not to take them into our confidence until we were sure to get a real quid pro quo from our frankness . . . . He said he thought he agreed with me." [89]

After President Roosevelt's death, President Truman appointed an Interim Committee to decide the question how to use the new weapon and the closely related problem of whether fission methods should be revealed to the Soviet Union. The committee spent a great deal of time discussing this latter question. Among the members were Stimson, Secretary of State Byrnes, George L. Harrison of the New York Life Insurance Company, and Assistant Secretary of State for Economic Affairs Will Clayton. Byrnes recalled of their meetings that although everyone recognized in the Soviet Union the nation most likely to become unfriendly to the United States, "No one seemed too alarmed at the prospect, because it appeared that in seven years we should be far ahead in this field; and, of course, in 1945 we could not believe that after their terrible sacrifices, the Russians would think of making war for many years to come." [90]

Other participants noted a different emphasis. J. Robert Oppenheimer remembered that in the June 1 meeting the talk "revolved around the question raised by Secretary Stimson as to whether there was any hope at all of using this development to get less barbarous relations with the Russians." Leo Szilard also recalled that Byrnes seemed at times more concerned with the bomb as a way of making "Russia more manageable in Europe," than as a weapon against Japan. To go back a little, on May 15 Stimson had written down that he felt that S-1 would be dominant over the tangled diplomatic problems at Potsdam.[91]

And on a different front, during the last days of the European War special army intelligence teams in the ALSOS Project and OPERATION HARBORAGE were seeking out German atomic scientists and information, first to see how far Hitler had gotten on the atomic bomb, and then to prevent either from falling into the hands of the Russians. One German scientist, his bag packed, remarked to the Americans: "I have been expecting you." [92]

On June 6 Stimson gave President Truman a report of the Interim Committee's findings. It began by recommending that no revelation should be made "to Russia or anyone else" until the first bomb had been dropped on Japan. If the Soviets should ask about the weapon at Potsdam—Truman interrupted the Secretary at this point to say that he had postponed the meeting until July 15, "to give us more time"—the President should say, "We are not quite ready to do it." As to future controls, the Committee could only suggest as yet that each nation should promise to make public all work that was being done on this subject and that an international control committee should be given full powers to inspect all countries to see whether this pledge was being carried out. If Russia did not assent to this condition, "we were far enough ahead of the game to be able to accumulate enough material to serve as insurance against being caught helpless." Stimson then branched off into another discussion with the President about the sort of *quid pro quo* which should be obtained for taking the Russians into atomic partnership. "He said he had been thinking of that and mentioned the same things that I was thinking of, namely the settlement of the Polish, Rumanian, Yugoslavian and Manchurian problems." [93]

When news of the successful atomic bomb test reached Truman and

Stimson at Potsdam on July 18, the President was, as Stimson described his mood, "tremendously pleased," "confident of sustaining the Open Door policy," and "very greatly reinforced." But it was at this time that Stimson began that rethinking process which was to lead him to oppose the President's atomic policy in the next few months. Peace was uncertain between Russia and the United States, "and the development of S1 is bringing it to a focus." Churchill shared Truman's more elated feelings. He told a military adviser that the atomic bomb altered the balance of power which would have resulted from the defeat of Germany. Once again Great Britain could say to the strongest power on the Continent, Russia, "If you insist on doing this or that, well . . . . And then where are the Russians!" [94]

Stimson gave the President some of his ideas on the growing difficulties with the Soviet Union and their relationship to the atom bomb a few days after the Potsdam meetings opened. Stable international relations could not be maintained between two such different systems of government. "After careful reflection I am of the belief that *no* world organization containing as one of its dominant members a nation whose people are not possessed of free speech but whose governmental action is controlled by the autocratic machinery of a secret political police, cannot [can] give effective control of this new agency with its devasting possibilities." Consequently, before sharing atomic information with Russia, Stimson would insist upon guaranteed free speech in the Soviet Union and a move towards a more democratic system. "We must go slowly in any disclosures or agreeing to any Russian participation whatever and constantly explore the question of how our head start in __ X __ and the Russian desire to participate can be used to bring us near to the removal of the basic difficulties which I have emphasized." [95]

Truman and Byrnes decided that Stalin should be told only of the development of a powerful new weapon which the United States intended to use against Japan. As a result of this oblique approach, the Americans were never quite sure thereafter whether Stalin's nonchalant answer was also one of innocence, the product of secret information, or simply a failure to grasp Truman's full meaning. Whatever the reason, this sort of difficulty—oblique questions and answers—plagued many later efforts to work out an international atomic policy.[96]

On the way back from the Conference, Truman informed the officers' mess on the U.S.S. *Augusta* that it did not matter if the Russians had been tough at the meetings "because the United States now had developed an entirely new weapon of such force and nature that we did not need the Russians—or any other nation." [97]

Secretary Stimson was not so sure. After having spoken so forcefully at Potsdam, and even before, the Secretary of War and his assistant, John J. McCloy, retreated to the former's hideaway in Virginia to do some rethinking. The two had become alarmed at Byrnes's inclination not to make any approach at all to the Russians on international controls. "He was on the point of departing for the foreign ministers' meeting and wished to have the implied threat of the bomb in his pocket during the conference." But for his part, Byrnes readily agreed that Stimson should talk with the President on the possibilities of an approach to the Russians. On September 5, Stimson did see the President and frankly told him that he thought Byrnes was on the wrong path and "tending to revert to power politics." The State Department was even opposing a Congressional bill for "domestic control of the production and use of atomic energy," since it brought up the point of international control also.[98]

Reaching Truman again on September 11, the long-time government servant, Stimson, gave him his final memorandum on the subject of atomic energy and Russian relations. He began by affirming the obvious: The atom bomb had changed all political considerations on the globe. "In many quarters," he continued, "it has been interpreted as a substantial offset to the growth of Russian influence on the continent." Undoubtedly Soviet leaders sensed this, and would seek to acquire the bomb as soon as possible. Therefore, Stimson concluded that the Russians would be more apt to respond favorably to a direct United States approach, "rather than through an international organization, or in our peace negotiations." His greatest fear was that the United States might continue negotiating, as if nothing had happened, but always "having this weapon rather ostentatiously on our hip . . . ." As Truman read this memorandum, the Secretary of War noted that "step by step" he expressed accord with each point. "He thought that we must take Russia into our confidence." Within a few days, however, Stimson discovered that the President was leaning back more and more to the other alternative of proven guaranties before international control.[99]

During November, 1945, President Truman joined Britain and Canada in a key joint policy statement on atomic energy. This was the first hint that some effort would soon be made for international control. The three nations proposed the creation of a United Nations commission to render to the world specific conclusions on the control of atomic energy. Unlike the Stimson memorandum, the commission called for successive stages, each dependent upon the successful completion of the one before it. Initially the Soviets would be expected not only to prove their trustworthiness but to make available information on their own atomic research progress and facilities, and to reveal "full knowledge concerning natural resources of raw materials," including uranium and titanium. After these stages had been passed, the Soviet Union would be granted information on "the practical industrial application of atomic energy." [100]

This kernel became the Baruch Plan for international control of atomic energy. As its sponsors contended, it was perhaps the first time that a nation had voluntarily offered to share knowledge of such a weapon with the entire world. But it was such an extraordinary weapon that perhaps the more extraordinary thinking of Stimson was actually the more realistic, namely that if the same suspicions in reverse which had prompted Truman to reject Stimson's way did not also prompt Moscow to reject the Baruch Plan outright in favor of their own nationalistic development, and if Russian national pride was not enough itself, then those in the Kremlin who argued against accepting the Baruch Plan could cite Truman's speech of October 27, shortly before the joint statement on atomic control. Speaking at the dedication of the new supercarrier, the U.S.S. *Franklin D. Roosevelt,* Truman had begun with the assertion that "we shall not give our approval to any compromise with evil," nor would the United States recognize any government imposed by force. "In some cases it may be impossible to prevent its imposition but we will not recognize it." The President then reviewed American interest in "free access" to internationalized rivers and waterways, equal access to trade and raw materials, and economic collaboration between the nations of the Western Hemisphere without any outside interference.[101]

Truman's phrasing and tone were very like the prewar anti-German atmosphere in Washington. There was a similar mood in the Kremlin. Within months foreign communist parties would receive instructions that the days of the Grand Alliance were over and that Russia must once again prepare to fight the capitalist nations. So soon, so startlingly soon, then, had the two supernations started attacking one another as *the enemy*.

When the American-backed Baruch Plan was formally presented in 1946, Cold War positions were already frozen. Within four years Russian-American relations had risen from passive distrust and suspicion through peaks of military alliance and plunged downward again into dangerous antagonism. America wanted a general security system; Russia depended upon spheres of influence. Washington intensely disliked being shut out of Eastern Europe; Moscow feared a resurrection of the Cordon Sanitaire. The United States met the challenge of the postwar world with offers of aid, military alliances, and gradualism; the Soviet Union demanded reparations, lowered an iron curtain, and encouraged revolution.

These issues were enough to make the United States hold back economic aid to the Soviet Union and even to hold over the Soviet Union the hammer of atomic diplomacy before making an approach to international control. The moment for settlement passed (if it was ever there), and thus the two nations fearfully and balefully watched each other across an impassible thermonuclear abyss.

He was a progressive of the nineteenth century in economic matters. And it was in economics that our troubles lay. For their solution his progressivism, his new deal, was pathetically insufficient, which is why in 1944 he wanted it to be forgot.

Rexford Tugwell, *The Stricken Land,* 1947

15 · Some Concluding Thoughts

"I like to feel that we have really accomplished marvels," wrote Franklin Roosevelt to Senator Claude Pepper three days before he died. The greatest marvel was that "the point of view of a lot of people" had been altered "toward more liberal trends, not only here but throughout the world." [1]

As always, Roosevelt's warmth and optimism burst through his words, especially in these days as the United States headed the Grand Alliance and led it to final victory over the Axis powers. Some were even more confident than Roosevelt that liberalism would triumph everywhere: The United Nations would give men of good will the best chance they ever had to defeat any future disciples of Mars. At home, the New Deal, while not perfect, represented the finest traditions of American pragmatism and would be a faithful guide to future political and social action in American life. Such have been the contentions of Roosevelt's most enthusiastic disciples.

Unfortunately this liberal faith soon grew into an outsize legend, zealously protected against any attacks from the right or the left. If the world had not turned out the way it was supposed to after 1945, that was the result of allowing the sacred fire of liberalism to go out and/or the attacks of Russian barbarians upon the civilized world. Any incongruities which turned up in the legend of the New Deal were carefully tucked away in chapters called "Behind the Mask," where human errors and failings all became a part of the "enigma" that was Franklin Roosevelt. Like the doctor in one of Nathaniel Hawthorne's tales, however, protectors who have thus removed any splotches from the New Deal have destroyed its reality. They have wrapped it in a mysticism which prevents an honest evaluation of Roosevelt's achievements just as surely as it hampers an evaluation of his failings, in both domestic and foreign policy.

326

Perhaps this study seems too one-dimensional or too "realistic." If so, it is because I have pulled too hard to free New Deal diplomacy and have fallen over the other way, and not because of a lack of sympathy with American policy makers and their problems. Naturally, the perspective of several years allows one to see how various alternatives chosen in 1933 or 1945 have worked out. I cannot deny that advantage or that it has colored my treatment of various questions. Granting that to the relativist position, my intention has been to restore the New Deal to its place between the years before 1933 and those following World War II. I have tried to demonstrate that New Deal foreign policy was not unique, did not magically or morally climb from isolation to world leadership, and does not give us a guidebook to the future. Perhaps the weakest expression of contemporary American liberalism is of those who talk about restoring the Good Neighbor Policy in Latin America. The simple fact is that Latin America has advanced beyond anything the original Good Neighbor Policy or its later modifications could comprehend or perhaps even tolerate. If one means an attitude of mind, the possibilities of success are somewhat greater, but even then it would be better to rethink our assumptions rather than to fall back to past attitudes no matter how updated they may be.

Roosevelt's liberalism was not the only liberalism at work in New Deal foreign policy formulation. Cordell Hull's nineteenth-century formula—as John Maynard Keynes called it bitterly in 1941 when he was trying to persuade the United States to abandon the most-favored-nation principle—or international laissez-faire or simply freer trade—as others referred to it—was there from the beginning. Hull has been known as a weak Secretary of State because Roosevelt failed to take him to Big Three wartime conferences and acted as his own Secretary of State on these occasions. Somewhat paradoxically, some liberals are ready to blame Hull for everything that went wrong in New Deal diplomacy. It cannot be both ways. Actually it is probably more accurate to say that Roosevelt provided the framework, and often the design, of New Deal diplomacy. Yet the number of times that Secretary Hull changed the President's mind is indeed striking. Perhaps the first time was also the most important one. In 1933 and 1934 the President was unsure about the trade policy that the United States ought to adopt. George Peek and his supporters were pulling him towards bilateralism and barter; Hull and his aides marshaled their best arguments and finally won the battle.

Their victory influenced New Deal foreign policy from then on and put it right back in the mainstream of past policies. Much legislation in the 1930's dealing with foreign policy was in support of the Reciprocal Trade Agreements Act. It was John Foster Dulles, for example, who pointed out that the Export-Import Bank was a substitute for the private loans of the 1920's. Even the neutrality debate turned into a discussion of ways and means to secure neutral rights.

Both Roosevelt and Hull defended the Open Door Policy in the Far East, but it was the Secretary who took the lead in the 1941 negotiations with Japan and who recommended that Roosevelt not meet with Prince Konoye until the Japanese accepted the tenets of the Policy. Roosevelt was always concerned about the military threat Hitler held over Europe and the world. He wanted disarmament very badly, yet the State Department was also determined to make Germany conform to its trade policies as well. And during the war Hull helped to shape the President's mind on both the postwar organization of the peace and the proper policy to adopt towards Germany.

Partly because of the liberal legend about the New Deal, economic factors in American foreign policy from 1933 to 1945 have been deemphasized. Labels such as "isolationism," "interventionism," and "internationalism" have been supplied to give us substitutes for careful analysis. Both Roosevelt's supporters and his antagonists have too willingly accepted this battleground for their disputes.

But the formulators of the Good Neighbor Policy always pointed out that their ideas were the only practicable way to restore lost trade in Latin America. From the time of Hull's report to the President on the Montevideo Conference to the 1945 Mexico City Conference, economic considerations were fundamental to hemispheric planning. Although the Great China Market never materialized, many American leaders in the New Deal period (just as their predecessors did) *acted upon the assumption* that it would, and this gave them reason enough to oppose Japan's forward movement in Asia. If that were not enough, the fear that the loss of China might mean the loss of all the Far East to Japanese hegemony stimulated others to action, for those who might shrug off the former possibility could not stand by and allow the latter.

During the war, a great deal of attention was devoted to Anglo-American economic planning, as well as to general economic policies, which were, as Harley Notter pointed out in *Postwar Foreign Policy Preparation,* the logical extension of economic foreign policy of the

1930's. He might also have said that such planning revolved around a system of ideas connected with the Open Door Policy. In Manchuria (before, during, and after the war), in the Middle East, in Latin America, in fact nearly everywhere, the United States wanted the Open Door Policy and an open world. Russia did not. And therein was the struggle which developed into Cold War.

If these things be recognized about New Deal diplomacy, perhaps the United States can formulate a policy to meet the challenge of the 1960's.

Reference Matter

Abbreviations Used in the Notes

Arabian Oil Hearings — Senate Special Committee Investigating the National Defense Program, *Hearings,* Part 41, *Petroleum Arrangements with Saudi Arabia,* 80 Cong., 1 sess. (Washington, 1948).

Batterson MSS — The William L. Batterson Collection, Sterling Memorial Library, Yale University.

China White Paper — Department of State, *United States Relations with China: with Special Reference to the Period 1942–1949* (Washington, 1949).

Cronon, *Daniels in Mexico* — E. David Cronon, *Josephus Daniels in Mexico* (Madison, Wisconsin, 1960).

Daniels MSS — The Papers of Josephus Daniels, Library of Congress.

Davis MSS — The Papers of Norman H. Davis, Library of Congress.

Documents on German Foreign Policy — Department of State, *Documents on German Foreign Policy: 1918–1945* (Washington, 1949——).

FAQ — *Foreign Affairs Quarterly.*

FCW — Department of Commerce, *Foreign Commerce Weekly.*

FR — Department of State, *Foreign Relations of the United States* (Washington, various dates).

Grew MSS — The Papers of Joseph Grew, Houghton Library, Harvard University.

Hopkins MSS — The Papers of Harry L. Hopkins, Franklin D. Roosevelt Library, Hyde Park, New York.

Hull, *Memoirs* — Cordell Hull, *The Memoirs of Cordell Hull* (2 vols.; New York, 1948).

Ickes, *Secret Diary* — Harold Ickes, *The Secret Diary of Harold Ickes* (3 vols.; New York, 1950–53).

Ickes MSS	The Papers of Harold Ickes, Library of Congress.
Lane MSS	The Papers of Arthur Bliss Lane, Sterling Memorial Library, Yale University.
Leahy MSS	The Diary of William D. Leahy, photocopy in State Historical Society of Wisconsin, Madison.
Milton MSS	The Papers of George Fort Milton, Library of Congress.
Moffat MSS	The Papers of J. Pierrepont Moffat, Houghton Library, Harvard University.
Morgenthau Diaries	John M. Blum and Henry Morgenthau, *From the Morgenthau Diaries: Years of Crisis, 1928–1938* (Boston, 1959).
NA	National Archives of the United States, Washington, D.C.
NFTC *Proceedings*	National Foreign Trade Council, *Proceedings of the National Foreign Trade Convention* (New York, various dates).
Peace and War	Department of State, *Peace and War: United States Foreign Policy, 1931–1941* (Washington, 1943).
Pearl Harbor Attack	Joint Committee on the Investigation of the Pearl Harbor Attack, *Hearings,* 79 Cong., 1 sess. (39 parts; Washington, 1948).
Potsdam Papers	Department of State, *Foreign Relations of the United States: The Conference at Potsdam, 1945* (2 vols.; Washington, 1960).
Rogers MSS	The Papers of James Harvey Rogers, Sterling Memorial Library, Yale University.
Roosevelt, *Letters*	Elliott Roosevelt, ed., *F.D.R.: His Personal Letters, 1928–1945* (2 vols.; New York, 1950).
Roosevelt MSS	The Papers of Franklin D. Roosevelt, Franklin D. Roosevelt Library, Hyde Park, New York.
OF	President's Official File
PPF	President's Personal File
PSF	President's Secretary's File
Roosevelt, *Public Papers*	*The Public Papers and Addresses of Franklin D. Roosevelt,* Samuel I. Rosenman, ed. (13 vols.; New York, 1938–50).
SDB	Department of State, *Bulletin.*
Stalin, *Correspondence*	Ministry of Foreign Affairs of the USSR, *Correspondence Between the Chairman of the Council of Ministers of the USSR and the*

Stimson MSS

Taussig MSS

Teheran Papers

Truman, *Memoirs*

Villard MSS

White MSS

Yalta Papers

Presidents of the USA and the Prime Ministers of Great Britain During the Great Patriotic War of 1941–1945 (2 vols.; Moscow, 1957).

The Papers of Henry L. Stimson, Sterling Memorial Library, Yale University.

The Papers of Charles Taussig, Franklin D. Roosevelt Library, Hyde Park, New York.

Department of State, *Foreign Relations of the United States: The Conferences at Cairo and Teheran, 1943* (Washington, 1961).

Harry S. Truman, *Memoirs*, Vol. I: *Year of Decisions* (New York, 1955).

The Papers of Oswald Garrison Villard, Houghton Library, Harvard University.

The Papers of Harry Dexter White, Firestone Library, Princeton University.

Department of State, *Foreign Relations of the United States: The Conferences at Malta and Yalta, 1945* (Washington, 1955).

Notes

Works listed in the Bibliographical Essay are cited in shortened form in the Notes. All other works are cited in full in the first reference to them in each chapter.

Chapter 1

1 Thomas Lamont, "Our Universities in an Unsettled World," speech given at New York University, November 16, 1932, Stimson MSS.

2 For the early impulse and development of nationalistic planners see Charles Forcey, *The Crossroads of Liberalism* (New York, 1961). New Deal planning is discussed at length in Broadus Mitchell, *Depression Decade* (New York, 1947). Specific recollections are in Raymond Moley, *After Seven Years* (New York, 1939), and Rexford Tugwell, *The Democratic Roosevelt* (New York, 1957).

3 William Allen White to Oswald Garrison Villard, September 4, 1930, Villard MSS.

4 Frederick Jackson Turner, "The Problem of the West," *Atlantic Monthly,* LXXVII (September, 1896), 289–97. An offprint with Turner's notes on it is in the Papers of Frederick Jackson Turner, Houghton Library, Harvard University.

5 *Nation,* CXXXV (July 27, 1932), 81.

6 Henry Steele Commager, "Twelve Years of Roosevelt," an article reprinted in Edwin C. Rozwenc, ed., *The New Deal: Revolution or Evolution* (Boston, 1949), pp. 25–33.

7 Henry L. Stimson, Diary, February 8 and 14, 1933, Stimson MSS.

8 Reprinted in Willard Thorp and others, eds., *American Issues: the Social Record* (New York, 1955), pp. 982–85.

9 Herbert Hoover, "World Economic Recovery," Department of State, *Press Releases,* VIII (February 18, 1933), 117.

10 Julius Klein to James Harvey Rogers, June 16, 1928, Rogers MSS.

11 Max Lerner, *America as a Civilization* (New York, 1957), p. 890.

12 Hamlin Garland, *Back-Trailers from the Middle Border* (New York, 1928), p. 47.

13 Hoover, Department of State, *Press Releases,* VIII, 117.

14 Quoted in Joseph Dorfman, *The Economic Mind in American Civilization* (5 vols.; New York, 1946–59), V, 632.

15 Charles A. Beard, *The Open Door at Home* (New York, 1934), p. 235 *et passim.* See also his *The Idea of National Interest* (New York, 1934).

16 Hoover, Department of State, *Press Releases,* VIII, 117.

17 Herbert M. Bratter, "The Committee for the Nation: A Case History in Monetary Propaganda," *Journal of Political Economy,* XLIX (August, 1941), 531–53.

18 Stimson, Diary, January 5, 1933, Stimson MSS.

19 Draft letter, Stimson to Paul Claudel, December 7, 1932, *ibid.*

20 Stimson to William E. Borah, September 8, 1932, *ibid.*

21 Stimson, Diary, November 11, 1932, *ibid.*

22 J. Pierrepont Moffat, Diary, January 21 and 22, 1933, Moffat MSS; memorandum of a conversation with Sir Ronald Lindsay, January 23, 1933, Stimson MSS; memorandum of a conversation with Franklin D. Roosevelt, February 17, 1933, Stimson MSS.

23 Memorandum of a conversation with President Hoover, April 10, 1931, Stimson MSS; Moffat, Diary, January 6, 1933, Moffat MSS; Robert Divine, *The Illusion of Neutrality* (Chicago, 1962), p. 33.

24 Norman H. Davis to Thomas P. Lamont, April 20, 1932, Davis MSS.

25 Roosevelt, *Public Papers,* (1928–32 vol.), pp. 673–75, 677.

26 *New York Times,* September 20, 1932.

27 Moley, *After Seven Years,* pp. 48 *et passim;* Arthur M. Schlesinger, Jr., *The Coming of the New Deal* (Boston, 1959), p. 72. See also Rexford Tugwell, *The Battle for Democracy* (New York, 1935), pp. 75, 94.

28 Tugwell, "The New Deal: The Available Instruments of Governmental Power," *Western Political Quarterly,* II (December, 1949), 545–80, and "The New Deal: The Rise of Business, Part II," *ibid.,* V (September, 1952) 483–503.

29 Adolf A. Berle, Jr., "Ready Money," *Survey Graphic,* XXIII (April 14, 1934), 171–72, and "What's Behind the Recovery Laws," *Scribner's Magazine,* XCIV (September, 1933), 129–35.

30 Adolf A. Berle to J. H. Rogers, February 7, 1933, Rogers MSS.

31 Moley, *After Seven Years,* p. 48; Herbert M. Bratter, "The Silver Episode: I," *Journal of Political Economy,* XLVI (October, 1938), 609–52.

32 Daniel R. Fusfield, *The Economic Thought of Franklin D. Roosevelt and the Origins of the New Deal* (New York, 1956), pp. 220–21.

33 Adolf A. Berle, Jr., "Private Business and Public Opinion," *Scribner's Magazine,* XCV (February, 1934), 81–87.

34 Ernest K. Lindley, *The Roosevelt Revolution* (New York, 1933), pp. 57–58, 129, 178.

35 Hull, *Memoirs* I, 81; *Congressional Record* (January 3, 1929), 70 Cong., 2 sess., LXX, 1071–73.

36 Charles C. Griffin, "Welles to Roosevelt: A Memorandum on Inter-

American Relations," *Hispanic-American Historical Review,* XXXIV (May, 1954), 190–92.

37 Sumner Welles to Arthur Bliss Lane, April 12 and May 22, 1934, Lane MSS.

38 Herbert Feis to Rogers, January 9 and March 23, 1933, Rogers MSS. See also his memo on antidepression measures, August 25, 1933, *ibid.*

39 Stanley Hornbeck to William Phillips, July 17, 1922, NA, Dept. State 611.003/1378.

40 Stanley K. Hornbeck, *Principles of American Policy in Relation to the Far East* (Washington, 1934), p. 5; memorandum, January 3, 1935, *FR, 1935,* III, 829–37.

41 Burton K. Wheeler to Villard, June 9, 1932, Villard MSS.

42 As quoted in John T. Flynn, *Country Squire in the White House* (New York, 1940), p. 18.

43 Speech before the Brooklyn Chamber of Commerce, February 1, 1920, quoted in *ibid.,* p. 21; Franklin D. Roosevelt, "Shall We Trust Japan?" *Far East Review,* XIX (August, 1923), 505–8.

44 *New York Times,* October 3, 1928. Charles A. Beard gives a lengthy treatment of Roosevelt's pre-presidential ideas on foreign policy in *American Foreign Policy in the Making: 1932–1940* (New Haven, 1946).

45 Roosevelt to Davis, October 8, 1928, Davis MSS; Fusfield, *Economic Thought of Franklin D. Roosevelt,* p. 113.

46 Roosevelt to William I. Sirovich, May 14, 1930, Roosevelt, *Letters,* I, 119. See also Dorfman, *Economic Mind,* V, 654–55.

47 Gertrude Almy Slichter, "Franklin D. Roosevelt and the Farm Problem, 1929–1932," *Mississippi Valley Historical Review,* XLIII (September, 1956), 238–58; Rexford Tugwell, "The Preparation of a President," *Western Political Quarterly,* I (June, 1948), 131–53, and "The New Deal in Retrospect," *ibid.,* I (December, 1948), 373–85.

48 Ickes, *Secret Diary* II, 240–41 *et passim.*

49 Ernest K. Lindley, *Roosevelt Revolution,* pp. 186–90, and *Half Way with Roosevelt* (New York, 1936), p. 292. See also Charles A. Beard and Mary R. Beard, *America in Midpassage* (New York, 1939), p. 166.

50 Davis to Stimson, December 28, 1932, Stimson MSS.

51 *Commercial and Financial Chronicle,* November 26, 1932.

52 Stimson, Diary, July 11, 1932, Stimson MSS.

53 Stimson, Diary, January 15, 1933, *ibid.*

54 *New York Times,* January 18, 1933; Moley, *After Seven Years,* p. 94.

55 Memo of a message from Franklin Roosevelt, December 23, 1932, and Hoover to Stimson, January 15, 1933, Stimson MSS.

56 Draft letter by Stimson, January 20, 1933, *ibid.*

57 *Congressional Record* (April 7 and May 29, 1933), 73 Cong., 1 sess., LXXVII, 1394, 4484.

58 As quoted in Beard, *American Foreign Policy,* p. 75.

Chapter 2

1 Cordell Hull to Roosevelt, February 14, 1935, Roosevelt MSS, PPF, 1820; Moffat, Diary, September 11, 1934, Moffat MSS.
2 George N. Peek and Samuel Crowther, *Why Quit Our Own?* (New York, 1936), p. 107.
3 Edgar W. Smith to Villard, September 25, 1936, Villard MSS.
4 Moffat, Diary, March 28, 1933, Moffat MSS.
5 Leon Trotsky, "Nationalism and Economic Life," *FAQ,* XII (April, 1934), 395–402. The most interesting thing about this article is that the editors, who were certainly not Marxists or Marxist sympathizers, thought it important enough and challenging enough to print. Basil Rauch, *Roosevelt: From Munich to Pearl Harbor* (New York, 1950), p. 7.
6 For indications of internationalism in the campaign, see Herbert M. Bratter, "The Silver Episode: I," *Journal of Political Economy,* XLVI (October, 1938), 609–52; Rauch, *Roosevelt,* pp. 18–19; Jeannette P. Nichols, "Roosevelt's Monetary Diplomacy in 1933," *American Historical Review,* LVI (January, 1951), 295–317.
7 Memorandum of a telephone conversation with Sir John Simon, July 25, 1932, Davis MSS; Harvey Bundy to Stimson, enclosing draft reply to a British note, undated [February/March, 1933], Stimson MSS. See also a draft by Stimson and Ogden Mills of a letter to Franklin Roosevelt, undated [December, 1932/January, 1933], Stimson MSS.
8 Memorandum for the Secretary of State, January 16, 1933, Stimson MSS.
9 Feis, quoted in Bundy to Stimson, undated [February/March, 1933], *ibid.;* memorandum of a telephone conversation with Roosevelt, January 15, 1933, *ibid.;* Nichols, *American Historical Review,* LVI (January, 1951), 295–317.
10 Rexford Tugwell, *The Democratic Roosevelt* (New York, 1957), p. 291; *Morgenthau Diaries,* pp. 65–66; Stimson, Diary, April 18, 1933, Stimson MSS.
11 Moley is quoted by Shepard Stone in "Anglo-American Economic Issues," *Current History,* XXXVIII (July, 1933), 399–405.
12 Hull to R. G. Atherton, April 28, 1933, *FR, 1933,* I, 578–80; memoranda of conversations with Ramsay MacDonald, March 30, 1933, 10 A.M. to 11 A.M. and 4 P.M. to 5 P.M., Davis MSS.
13 Davis to Hull, May 3, 1933, *FR, 1933,* I, 586–87; Moffat, Diary, May 4, 1933, Moffat MSS.
14 Memorandum of a trans-Atlantic conversation, May 6, 1933, *FR, 1933,* I, 587–91; Davis to Hull, May 9, 1933, and Roosevelt to MacDonald, May 23, 1933, *ibid.,* I, 597–600, 611; Nichols, "Roosevelt's Monetary Diplomacy," pp. 295–317.
15 Memorandum, December 16, 1933, Roosevelt, *Letters,* I, 376.

16 Department of State, *Press Releases,* VIII (June 17, 1933), 444; Joe R. Wilkinson, *Politics and Trade Policy* (Washington, 1960), pp. 2–4.

17 Roosevelt to Hull, July 1 and 2, 1933, *FR, 1933,* I, 669–70, 673–74.

18 Memorandum of a trans-Atlantic conversation, July 5, 1933, *FR, 1933,* I, 689; Hull to Roosevelt, July 2, 1933, and Roosevelt to Hull, July 4, 1933, *ibid.,* 676–78.

19 Moffat, Diary, July 6, 7, 12, Moffat MSS.

20 *Morgenthau Diaries,* p. 66; Herbert M. Bratter, "The Committee for the Nation: A Case History in Monetary Propaganda," *Journal of Political Economy,* XLIX (August, 1941), 531–53; George F. Warren to Rogers, March 8, 1932, Rogers MSS.

21 James Harvey Rogers, "Federal Reserve Policy in World Monetary Chaos," *American Economic Review,* Special Supplement, XXIII (March, 1933), 119–29, and "Gold, International Credits and Depression," *Journal of the American Statistical Association,* XXVII (September, 1932), 237–50; Joseph Dorfman, *The Economic Mind in American Civilization* (5 vols.; New York, 1946–59), V, 688–89.

22 Dorfman, *Economic Mind,* V, 688–89; Graeme K. Howard to Rogers, May 17, 1932, Rogers MSS. In this context see Roosevelt's comments at Press Conferences 10 and 31, April 7 and July 5, 1933, Roosevelt, *Public Papers* (1933 vol.), pp. 118–21, 269.

23 Henry A. Wallace, *New Frontiers* (New York, 1934), pp. 173–91; Ickes, *Secret Diary* I, 110.

24 Wallace, *New Frontiers,* p. 95; Arthur M. Schlesinger, Jr., *The Coming of the New Deal* (Boston, 1959), p. 253; Stimson, Diary, October 27, 1933, Stimson MSS. See also Herbert M. Bratter, "The Silver Episode: II," *Journal of Political Economy,* XLVI (December, 1938), 802–37.

25 Bratter, *Journal of Political Economy,* XLVI (December, 1938), 802–37; Davis to Key Pittman, March 18, 1931, and Pittman to Davis, March 20, 1931, Davis MSS; Allan Seymour Everest, *Morgenthau, the New Deal and Silver* (New York, 1950), pp. 13, 101.

26 Moley, quoted in *Congressional Record* (January 8, 1934), 73 Cong., 2 sess., LXXVIII, 188.

27 Press Conference 88, January 15, 1934, Roosevelt, *Public Papers* (1934 vol.), p. 49; Everest, *Morgenthau, the New Deal and Silver,* p. 36.

28 *Morgenthau Diaries,* pp. 123–24. See also Rogers to Roosevelt, November 26, 1935, Rogers MSS: "Anything the United States Government can do in assisting the Gold Bloc countries to make their devaluation as conservative as possible will minimize the jolt to our own rapidly recovering economy."

29 Memorandum of a conversation with Roosevelt, January 9, 1933, Stimson MSS; *Morgenthau Diaries,* p. 54.

30 *Review of Reviews and World's Week,* XLVIII (May, 1933), 48–49.

31 William Castle to Fred Eberhardt, March 3, 1933, *FR, 1933,* II, 780–82.

32 Howard to Rogers, May 17, 1932, and W. D. Sullivan to Rogers, June 24, 1932, Rogers MSS.

33 *New York Times*, January 10, 1933; William E. Dodd, *Ambassador Dodd's Diary* (New York, 1941), p. 74.

34 William Appleman Williams, *Russian-American Relations, 1781–1947* (New York, 1952), p. 236; Benjamin H. Williams, *Foreign Loan Policy of the United States Since 1933* (New York, 1939), pp. 23–24; Moffat, Diary, September 8, 1933, Moffat MSS.

35 *Congressional Record* (April 12, 1933), 73 Cong., 1 sess., LXXVII, 1538; Wallace to Roosevelt, November 7, 1933, NA, Dept. State 711.61/322; William Appleman Williams, *Russian-American Relations*, p. 239; *Morgenthau Diaries*, p. 56.

36 James A. Farley, *Jim Farley's Story* (New York, 1948), p. 44.

37 John Foster Dulles, "The Securities Act and Foreign Lending," *FAQ*, XII (October, 1933), 33–45.

38 Roosevelt to R. Walton Moore, August 31, 1934, NA, Dept. State 861.51/2662 1/2.

39 Hull to Roosevelt, September 21, 1933, *FR: The Soviet Union 1933–1939*, pp. 12–13; Villard to George Messersmith, August 27, 1934, Villard MSS; William C. Bullitt to Acting Secretary of State, January 4, 1934, and Bullitt to Hull, March 15, 1934, *FR: The Soviet Union, 1933–1939*, pp. 55–62, 66–67.

40 Bullitt to Hull, April 8, 1934, *FR: The Soviet Union, 1933–1939*, pp. 79–81.

41 Bullitt to Hull, April 20, 1936, *ibid.*, pp. 291–96.

42 William Appleman Williams, *Russian-American Relations*, p. 247.

43 William C. Bullitt, "How We Won the War and Lost the Peace," *Life*, XXV (August 30, 1948), 82–84, (September 6, 1948), 86–88.

44 Export Managers to Hull, February 20, 1934, NA, 811.516 Ex-IB/8; Roosevelt, *Public Papers* (1934 vol.), pp. 80–81; Roosevelt to George N. Peek, July 17, 1935, Roosevelt, *Letters*, I, 494–95.

45 Dan Roper to Roosevelt, August 24, 1936, Roosevelt MSS, PSF, 17; Hugh Thomas, *The Spanish Civil War* (New York, 1961), p. 210 *et passim*.

46 F. A. Southard, "American Industry Abroad Since 1929," *Journal of Political Economy*, XLI (August, 1933), 530–47; Hal B. Lary, *The United States in the World Economy* (Washington, 1943), pp. 62 ff., 103 ff.

47 Fred Greene, "The Military View of American Policy," *American Historical Review*, LXVI (January, 1961), 354–77; Mahan is quoted in William Appleman Williams, *The Shaping of American Diplomacy* (Chicago, 1956), pp. 424–27.

48 William H. Standley and Arthur Agerton, *Admiral Ambassador to Russia* (Chicago, 1955), p. 31; Hull, *Memoirs*, I, 288; memorandum of a conversation with Mr. Migone, February 5, 1934, Moffat MSS.

49 Memorandum of a conversation, September 26, 1934, Davis, MSS.

50 Nancy Harvison Hooker, ed., *The Moffat Papers* (Cambridge, Mass., 1956), p. 115.

51 David H. Popper, "The End of Naval Disarmament," *Foreign Policy Reports*, XI (October 23, 1935), 202–12.

52 George Fort Milton to Will Clayton, February 27, 1938, Milton MSS.

53 Eliot Wadsworth to Roosevelt, November 22, 1935, Roosevelt MSS, PPF, 1335; Edward M. House, "Some Foreign Problems of the Next Administration," *FAQ*, XI (January, 1933), 211–19; Henry A. Wallace, *America Must Choose* (Boston, 1934), pp. 10–11; Treasury Department to Marvin H. McIntyre, September 18, 1934, Roosevelt MSS, PSF.

54 Department of State, *Press Releases*, X (June 11, 1934), 387–89; Francis Sayre, *America Must Act* (Boston, 1936), pp. 7–10, and *The Way Forward* (New York, 1939); Henry L. Stimson and MacGeorge Bundy, *On Active Duty in Peace and War* (New York, 1948), p. 299.

55 Charles Evans Hughes to American Diplomatic Officers, August 18, 1923, quoted in Ruhl J. Bartlett, ed., *The Record of American Diplomacy* (3rd ed.; New York, 1954), p. 503; William S. Culbertson to Wallace McClure, May 3, 1933, Davis MSS.

56 William S. Culbertson, *Reciprocity* (New York, 1937), pp. 154–63.

57 *Ibid.,* pp. 238–43.

58 Peek and Crowther, *Why Quit Our Own?*, p. 40.

59 *Ibid.,* p. 11.

60 Department of State, *Press Releases,* IX (December 16, 1933), 340–43.

61 Hull to William Phillips, December 7, 1933, and Phillips to Hull, December 8, 1933, *FR, 1933,* IV, 161, 168; Phillips to Hull, December 12, 1933, *ibid.,* I, 930; Moffat, Diary, February 27, 1934, Moffat MSS.

62 For a good brief description of the RTA Act see Charles A. Beard and Mary R. Beard, *America in Midpassage* (New York, 1939), p. 247.

63 American Manufacturers Export Association to Roosevelt, December 16, 1933, Roosevelt MSS, OF, 614A; Charles Taussig to Hull, November 7, 1934, Taussig MSS.

64 Roosevelt to Hull, November 19, 1934, Roosevelt MSS, OF, 20; Hull to Roosevelt, November 28, 1934, Roosevelt MSS, PSF.

65 Sayre to Marvin McIntyre, November 24, 1934, and Sayre to Roosevelt, November 28, 1934, Roosevelt MSS, PSF.

66 *Ibid.;* Hull to Roosevelt, November 28, 1934, *ibid.*

67 Rexford Tugwell, "The Preparation of a President," *Western Political Quarterly,* I (June, 1948), 131–53; Peek and Crowther, *Why Quit Our Own?,* pp. 129, 159.

68 Peek and Crowther, *Why Quit Our Own?,* p. 256.

69 Memorandum of a conversation, October 22, 1936, *FR, 1936,* I, 689.

70 William K. Hancock, *Survey of British Commonwealth Affairs* (2 vols.; Oxford, 1937), II, Part 1, 51–52.

71 Newton Baker to Davis, July 8, 1935, Davis MSS.

72 Page 84.

Chapter 3

1 For the background of the Good Neighbor Policy see Laurence Duggan, *The Americas* (New York, 1949); Sumner Welles, *Naboth's Vineyard* (New York, 1928); and Bryce Wood, *The Making of the Good Neighbor Policy* (New York, 1961).

2 Quoted in Wood, *Making of the Good Neighbor Policy,* p. 76.

3 Stimson, Diary, November 11, 1932, Stimson MSS; Walter C. Thurston to Stimson, July 15 and 22, 1932, William S. Culbertson to Stimson, June 4 and 5, 1932, and Fred M. Dearing to Stimson, September 10, 1932, *FR, 1932,* V, 397–99, 405–6, 430–31, 433–34, 962; Stimson, Diary, February 20, 1933, Stimson MSS; Moffat, Diary, February 7, 1933, Moffat MSS.

4 Duggan, *The Americas,* p. 56.

5 Donald Dozer, *Are We Good Neighbors?* (Gainesville, Florida, 1959), p. 11; Wood, *Making of the Good Neighbor Policy,* pp. 44–45; William Allen White to Villard, July 31, 1930, Villard MSS.

6 Memorandum of a conversation with officials of the Standard Fruit and Steamship Company, April 21, 1931, Stimson MSS; Wood, *Making of the Good Neighbor Policy,* p. 46.

7 Memorandum of a conversation with W. W. Lancaster of National City Bank of New York, March 7, 1932, Stimson MSS.

8 Edwin Lieuwen, *Arms and Politics in Latin America* (New York, 1960), p. 188; Duggan, *The Americas,* pp. 55–56.

9 Thomas P. Lamont to James E. Sobind, January 9, 1928, Villard MSS.

10 As reported in the *Commercial and Financial Chronicle,* November 26, 1932.

11 Memorandum by Sumner Welles, February 27, 1922, NA, Dept. State 710.11/568; Charles C. Griffin, "Welles to Roosevelt: A Memorandum on Inter-American Relations," *Hispanic-American Historical Review,* XXXIV (May, 1954), 190–92.

12 Stimson, Diary, January 9, 1933, Stimson MSS; Felix Frankfurter to Stimson, April 18, 1933, and memorandum of a conversation with Roosevelt, March 28, 1933, *ibid.*

13 Carleton Beals, "A New Code for Latin America," *Scribner's Magazine,* XCV (January, 1934), 27–34; Nelson T. Johnson to Arthur B. Lane, April 15, 1935, Lane MSS; Hull, quoted in *Congressional Record* (February 10, 1934), 73 Cong., 2 sess., LXXVIII, 2374.

14 Howard J. Trueblood, "Trade Rivalries in Latin America," *Foreign Policy Reports,* XIII (September 15, 1937), 154–64; NFTC *Proceedings, 1935,* pp. 55–57; Willy Feurlein and Elizabeth Hannan, *Dollars in Latin America* (New York, 1941), p. 6 *et passim.*

15 Adolf A. Berle, Jr., "Peace without Empire," *Survey Graphic,* XXX (March, 1941), 102–8; Carleton Beals, *Pan America* (New York, 1940), p. 361.

16 Roosevelt to Frank Murphy, November 26, 1941, Roosevelt MSS, PPF, 1662.

17 Interview with Berle, December 9, 1959.

18 Stimson, Diary, October 26, 1933, and November 13, 1931, Stimson MSS. Absolutely essential to an understanding of Cuban-American relations in this period are Robert F. Smith, *The United States and Cuba: Business and Diplomacy, 1917–1960* (New York, 1961), pp. 113–36, and Wood, *Making of the Good Neighbor Policy,* pp. 55–57.

19 Stimson, Diary, January 9 and 10, 1933, Stimson MSS.

20 *Congressional Record* (April 18, 1933), 73 Cong., 1 sess., LXXVII, 1900–1901; Smith, *United States and Cuba,* p. 145.

21 Welles to State Department, May 13, 1933, Taussig MSS; Smith, *United States and Cuba,* p. 146; Charles Taussig to Roosevelt, May 18, 1933, Roosevelt MSS, OF, 470.

22 Welles to Roosevelt, May 18, 1933, Roosevelt MSS, OF, 470.

23 Cuban Chamber of Commerce in the United States to Roosevelt, April 4, 1933, Roosevelt MSS, OF, 159; Wayne Johnson to Hull, May 26, 1933, *ibid.*

24 Laurence Duggan to Taussig, May 25, 1933, Taussig MSS; William Phillips to Roosevelt, July 21, 1933, Roosevelt MSS, OF, 159.

25 Press Conference 42, August 9, 1933, Roosevelt MSS, PPF-1P; Smith, *United States and Cuba,* pp. 148–50.

26 Navy cables, September 8 and 18, 1933, Roosevelt MSS, OF, 159; Wood, *Making of the Good Neighbor Policy,* pp. 71–72, 80; Smith, *United States and Cuba,* p. 152.

27 Roosevelt to Wallace, September 13, 1933, and W. H. Moran to Louis M. Howe, October 16, 1933, Roosevelt MSS, OF, 159.

28 Smith, *United States and Cuba,* pp. 152–60; Wood, *Making of the Good Neighbor Policy,* pp. 87–96.

29 Navy cable, December 11, 1933, Roosevelt MSS, OF, 159.

30 Stimson, Diary, October 26, 1933, Stimson MSS; William Phillips and Welles to Roosevelt, November 22, 1933, Roosevelt MSS, OF, 159.

31 See Wood's excellent account of this contradiction, *Making of the Good Neighbor Policy,* pp. 84–85.

32 Smith, *United States and Cuba,* p. 156.

33 Welles to Roosevelt, March 12, 1934, Roosevelt MSS, OF, 159.

34 Hull to Roosevelt, June 29, 1934, *ibid.;* Roosevelt to George Norris, September 21, 1943, Roosevelt MSS, PPF, 880; Josephus Daniels, Diary, April 2, 1934, Daniels MSS; Stimson, Diary, October 29, 1934, Stimson MSS.

35 George Messersmith to Roosevelt, May 23, 1941, Roosevelt MSS, PSF; Messersmith to Moffat, August 24, 1940, Moffat MSS.

36 Hull to Roosevelt and State Department to Roosevelt, April 16, 1934, Roosevelt MSS, PSF; Welles to Arthur Bliss Lane, April 12, 1934, Lane MSS; Stimson, Diary, October 28, 1933, Stimson MSS; Duggan, *The Americas,* p. 63.

37 Duggan, *The Americas*, p. 63; Lane to Daniels, October 15, 1933, Daniels MSS. A good presentation of this critical period is in E. David Cronon, "Interpreting the Good Neighbor Policy," *Hispanic-American Historical Review*, XXXIX (November, 1959), 538–68.

38 Daniels, Diary, January 21, 1934, Daniels MSS; Duggan, *The Americas*, p. 64.

39 Hull to Roosevelt, February 15, 1935, Roosevelt MSS, PSF.

40 Moffat, Diary, September 8 and 9, 1934, Moffat MSS.

41 Memorandum by Herbert Feis, October 29, 1934, Rogers MSS; Moffat, Diary, December 14, 1934, Moffat MSS.

42 Senate Committee on Banking and Currency, *Study of the Export-Import Bank and World Bank*, 83 Cong., 2 sess. (Washington, 1954), Part 1, pp. 36–37; George N. Peek to Francis Sayre, April 12, 1935, Rogers MSS.

43 William S. Culbertson, *Reciprocity* (New York, 1937), p. 80; the Chargé in Brazil to the Secretary of State, July 31, 1935, *FR, 1935*, IV, 381–82.

44 *FR, 1936*, V, 250, 260–61; Trueblood, *Foreign Policy Reports*, XIII (September 15, 1937), 154–64; NFTC *Proceedings, 1937*, p. 339; Moffat, Diary, July 21, 1937, Moffat MSS.

45 Hull, *Memoirs*, I, 496; Fred M. Dearing to Roosevelt, March 10, 1936, Roosevelt MSS, PSF; Rogers to Roosevelt, December 13, 1938, Rogers MSS; NFTC *Proceedings, 1936*, pp. 440–41.

46 Forrest K. Davis and Ernest K. Lindley, *How War Came: An American White Paper* (New York, 1942), p. 27; Daniels to Roosevelt, November 2, 1936, Roosevelt MSS, PPF, 86.

47 Langman (Montevideo) to Berlin, April 21, 1938, Von Schoen (Santiago) to Berlin, May 7, 1938, and Ritter (Rio de Janeiro) to Berlin, March 30, 1938—*Documents on German Foreign Policy*, Series D (1937–45), V, 831, 835–36, 824–26; Percy Bidwell, "Latin America, Germany and the Hull Program," *FAQ*, XVII (January, 1939), 374–90.

48 Dozer, *Are We Good Neighbors?*, p. 26; Daniels to Roosevelt, April 5, 1935, Roosevelt MSS, PPF, 86; Feurlein and Hannan, *Dollars in Latin America*, p. 6; Wood, *Making of the Good Neighbor Policy*, p. 153.

49 *SDB*, IV (June 28, 1941), 756–61.

50 Stimson to Pierre Jay, March 26, 1933, and Jay to Stimson, March 23, 1933, Stimson MSS.

51 A copy is in Roosevelt MSS, OF, 4194; Welles to Daniels, April 24, 1936, Daniels MSS.

52 The fullest account of the Pan American empire is in Matthew Josephson, *Empire of the Air* (New York, 1944), pp. 43, 45, 74.

53 *Ibid.*, pp. 122, 135, 18–19; *Congressional Record* (January 8, 1939), 75 Cong., 3 sess., LXXXIII, 222; *FCW*, I (November 30, 1940), 383.

54 NFTC *Proceedings, 1936*, p. 244; NFTC *Proceedings, 1938*, pp. 71–77.

55 As quoted in James Fred Rippy, *Globe and Hemisphere* (Chicago, 1958), p. 195.

Chapter 4

1 Adolf A. Berle to Stimson, February 27, 1940, Stimson MSS.
2 Stimson to Walter Lippmann, October 4, 1932, *ibid.*
3 Stimson, "Special Features of American Foreign Policy in the Far East," p. 32 (a memorandum in the Stimson MSS).
4 Joseph Grew, "Relations with Japan as Observed by the American Embassy in Tokyo, 1932–1937" (unpublished manuscript in the University of Chicago Library, Chicago, Illinois), p. 63.
5 Allan Seymour Everest, *Morgenthau, the New Deal and Silver* (New York, 1950), pp. 115–18; editorial, *United States Naval Institute Proceedings*, LIX (August, 1933), 1208; Ethel B. Dietrich, *The Far Eastern Trade of the United States* (New York, 1940), p. 34; NFTC *Proceedings, 1935*, pp. 104, 112.
6 Nelson Johnson to Stimson, September 7, 1940, Stimson MSS.
7 Joseph Grew, memorandum of a conversation with H. Togo, November 10, 1941, "A Report on Japanese-American Relations," p. 245 (unpublished manuscript in the University of Chicago Library, Chicago, Illinois).
8 Austin Tappan Wright, *Islandia* (2nd ed.; New York, 1958), p. 13.
9 As quoted in Charles C. Tansill, *Back Door to War* (Chicago, 1952), pp. 56–58.
10 Thomas P. Lamont, "Preliminary Report of Negotiations, 1920" (copy in Davis MSS).
11 Charles Evans Hughes, "Some Aspects of Our Foreign Policy," an address before the American Historical Association, December 29, 1922, New Haven, Connecticut (copy in Stimson MSS).
12 Memorandum on the Open Door Policy, February 22, 1932, NA, Dept. State 693.001/323.
13 Hughes, "Some Aspects," Stimson MSS; C. Walter Young, *The International Relations of Manchuria* (Chicago, 1929), p. 242.
14 Memorandum of a conversation, April 22, 1929, Stimson MSS.
15 Grew, "Relations with Japan," p. 5.
16 Editorial, *Nation*, CXXXV (July 6, 1932), 2.
17 Stimson, Diary, May 19 and 22, 1932, Stimson MSS.
18 A copy of this report is in Stimson MSS.
19 Memorandum of a conversation with the Chinese Minister, January 7, 1932, and memorandum of a conversation, June 2, 1932, *ibid.*
20 Stimson to Lippmann, October 4, 1932, Stimson MSS; Stimson, Diary, October 5 and December 30, 1932, *ibid.*
21 See both references in note 20 above.
22 Memorandum, March 2, 1933, "Accomplishments in Major Policy in American Foreign Relations with the Countries of the Far East from

March 4, 1929 to date," pp. 17–18, Stimson MSS. See also Henry L. Stimson, *The Far Eastern Crisis* (New York, 1936), pp. 89–90. For a list of American trade interests in the Far East at this time see Dietrich, *Far Eastern Trade,* pp. 6–9.

23 Pages 89–90.

24 Stimson–McGeorge Bundy conversations, 1947 Stimson MSS; Stimson, Diary, January 15, 1933, *ibid.;* Hull, *Memoirs,* I, 277; Senate Committee on Naval Affairs, *Hearings on Appropriations, 1936,* 74 Cong., 2 sess. (Washington, 1936), p. 58.

25 Stimson, Diary, April 27–May 25, 1933, and March 17, 1934, Stimson MSS.

26 Stanley K. Hornbeck to William Phillips, April 6, 1933, *FR, 1933,* III, 668; memorandum of a conversation, August 8, 1933, *ibid.,* III, 643–45.

27 Nelson Johnson to Secretary of State, June 26, 1934, and Phillips to Johnson, October 3, 1934, NA, Dept. State 893.60/31.

28 Hull to Joseph Grew, October 6, 1933, *FR: Japan, 1931–1941,* I, 125–26; memorandum of a conversation, May 16, 1934, *Peace and War,* pp. 220–22.

29 F. S. Fales to Hull, April 4, 1933, NA, Dept. State 893.6363/Manchuria/1; Hull to Grew, July 5, 1934, *FR, 1934,* III, 714–15; Grew to Hull, August 6, 1934, NA, Dept. State 893.6363/Manchuria/39; Phillips to Grew, October 31, 1934, and Grew to Hull, November 27, 1934, *FR, 1934,* III, 752, 768.

30 Hull to Grew, April 24, 1935, *FR, 1935,* III, 906–7; Moffat to Davis, November 3, 1934, Davis MSS.

31 *Morgenthau Diaries,* p. 205; Everest, *Morgenthau, the New Deal and Silver,* pp. 108–18; Treasury Department memo to Roosevelt, undated, Roosevelt MSS, PSF.

32 Roosevelt to Morgenthau, December 6, 1934, Roosevelt MSS, OF, 150; *Morgenthau Diaries,* pp. 207–28.

33 Grew to Hull, August 9, 1934, and Phillips to Robert W. Bingham, September 10, 1934, NA, Dept. State 893.6363/Manchuria/39.

34 Davis to Roosevelt, December 14, 1934, Davis MSS.

35 Moffat, Diary, October 24, 1934, Moffat MSS; William E. Dodd, *Ambassador Dodd's Diary* (New York, 1941), p. 208; Nancy Harvison Hooker, ed., *The Moffat Papers,* (Cambridge, Mass., 1956), pp. 118–19; William H. Standley and Arthur Agerton, *Admiral Ambassador to Russia* (Chicago, 1955), p. 37.

36 Captain Shimomura to Standley, August 6, 1934, and Standley to Shimomura, August 9, 1934, Davis MSS. See also Louis Morton, "War Plan ORANGE: Evolution of a Strategy," *World Politics,* XI (January, 1959), 221–50; Moffat, Diary, November 3 and 4, 1934, Moffat MSS.

37 Johnson to Hull, August 23, 1934, NA, Dept. State 893.6363/Manchuria/51.

38 David H. Popper, "The End of Naval Disarmament," *Foreign Policy Reports,* XI (October 23, 1935), 202–12; Davis to Hull, October 31, 1934, Davis MSS.

39 Hooker, *Moffat Papers,* pp. 118–19.

40 Grew to State Department, January 19, 1935, Roosevelt MSS, PSF; Grew, "Relations with Japan," pp. 63, 90–95; Hull to Roosevelt, March 16, 1935, Roosevelt MSS, PSF.

41 NFTC *Proceedings, 1935,* pp. 104, 112; memorandum by Stanley K. Hornbeck, July 25, 1935, *FR, 1935,* III, 607–9.

42 Grew, "Relations with Japan," p. 63.

43 Dietrich, *Far Eastern Trade,* p. 12.

44 Everest, *Morgenthau, the New Deal and Silver,* p. 59; Phillips to Roosevelt, March 2, 1935, *FR, 1935,* III, 547–50; Phillips to American Embassy in London, March 2, 1935, Dept. State NA, 893.51/5430; Hornbeck to Hull, May 18, 1934, NA, Dept. State 893.51/5894; memorandum by Hornbeck, June 11, 1934, and Hornbeck to Hull, June 12, 1934, *FR, 1934,* III, 388–90, 390–91.

45 Memorandum by Hornbeck, June 11, 1934, *FR, 1934,* III, 388–90; memorandum by Hornbeck, July 25, 1935, *FR, 1935,* III, 607–9.

46 Thomas Lamont to Hornbeck, June 13, 1934, NA, Dept. State 893.51/5900.

47 Hornbeck to Lamont, June 15, 1934, *ibid.;* memorandum by Hornbeck, June 18, 1934, NA, Dept. State 893.51/5903; memorandum of a conversation, September 19, 1934, and Lamont to Hornbeck, October 11, 1934, *FR, 1934,* III, 412–17, 420–21.

48 Memorandum by Herbert Feis, January 11, 1936, NA, Dept. State 893.51/6070; memorandum by Hornbeck, January 11, 1936, NA, Dept. State 893.51/6060; memorandum by Hornbeck, March 26, 1936, *FR, 1936,* IV, 469–72; Hull to the American Embassy in London, April 1, 1936, NA, Dept. State 893.51/6118.

49 Johnson to Hull, September 7, 1937, Davis MSS; memorandum of a conversation, December 29, 1936, *FR, 1936,* IV, 502–3; J. P. Morgan and Company to State Department, January 22, 1937, NA, Dept. State 893.51/6280; memorandum by Hornbeck, January 28, 1937, NA, Dept. State 893.51/6284; R. G. Atherton to Secretay of State, February 10, 1937, *FR, 1937,* IV, 568–69; Roosevelt to Hull, March 11, 1937, Roosevelt MSS, OF, 150; Bingham to Hull, March 15, 1937, Lamont to State Department, May 5, 1937, and memorandum by Hornbeck, November 9, 1937, *FR, 1937,* 576–77, 586–88, 624–25.

50 Memorandum of a conversation, July 12, 1937, *Peace and War,* pp. 368–70.

51 Ickes, *Secret Diary,* II, 192–93; Moffat, Diary, September 7, 1937, Moffat MSS.

52 Everest, *Morgenthau, the New Deal and Silver,* pp. 110–24.

53 H. H. Kung to Roosevelt, July 13, 1937, and Roosevelt to Kung, August

2, 1937, Roosevelt MSS, PSF; American Chamber of Commerce to Department of State, June 29, 1937, NA Dept. State 893.51/6408.

54 Sumner Welles, *Seven Decisions That Shaped History* (New York, 1951), p. 71.

55 Moffat, Diary, October 5, 1937, Moffat MSS; Roosevelt to Stimson, November 24, 1937, Stimson MSS; Dodd, *Ambassador Dodd's Diary*, p. 428; Department of State to British Embassy, October 19, 1937, *FR, 1937*, IV, 92.

56 Memorandum of a conversation with Roosevelt, October 20, 1937, Davis MSS.

57 Yoshida to Davis, December 3, 1937, Davis MSS; two memoranda of conversations, October 29, 1937, *ibid.;* memorandum of a conversation, November 2, 1937, *ibid.;* Moffat, Diary, November 20, 1937, Moffat MSS.

58 Moffat, Diary, November 20, 1937, Moffat MSS.

59 Memoranda of conversations, November 4, 5, and 8, 1937, Davis MSS.

60 Moffat, Diary, November 3, 1937, Moffat MSS.

61 Memoranda of conversations, November 15 and 22, 1937, Davis MSS.

62 Davis to Roosevelt, December 8, 1937, *ibid.*

63 Feis to Stimson, November 23, 1937, Stimson MSS.

64 Quoted in A. L. P. Dennis, *Adventures in American Diplomacy: 1895–1905* (New York, 1928), p. 234.

Chapter 5

1 Moffat, Diary, March 20, 1933, Moffat MSS.

2 Roosevelt to Villard, August 4, 1936, Villard MSS.

3 *Ibid.;* Joseph Davies, *Mission to Moscow* (New York, 1941), p. 146.

4 Hull, *Memoirs*, I, 520.

5 Moffat, Diary, August 27, 1937, Moffat MSS; Sumner Welles, *Seven Decisions That Shaped History* (New York, 1951), p. 12.

6 Allan Nevins, *The New Deal and World Affairs* (New Haven, 1950), p. 62.

7 Stimson, Diary, January 15, 1933, Stimson MSS; Roosevelt to Adolf A. Berle, June 26, 1941, Roosevelt MSS, PSF.

8 Moffat, Diary, March 17–20, 1933, Moffat MSS; *FR, 1933*, I, 31–34.

9 Davis to Thomas P. Lamont, February 23, 1933, Davis MSS; Moffat, Diary, April 17, 1933, Moffat MSS.

10 *Documents on German Foreign Policy*, Series C, I, 173–75; Moffat, Diary, May 3 and 8, 1933, Moffat MSS; Hull to Bingham, May 8, 1933, *FR, 1933*, I, 130–31; Robert Divine, *The Illusion of Neutrality* (Chicago, 1962), pp. 46–48; F. P. Walters, *A History of the League of Nations* (2nd ed.; London, 1960), pp. 242–45.

11 Walters, *History of the League of Nations*, p. 544; Moffat, Diary, May 11, 1933, Moffat MSS.

12 Moffat, Diary, May 13, 1933, Moffat MSS; Stimson, Diary, April 27 and

May 25, 1933, Stimson MSS; Walters, *History of the League of Nations,* p. 538; Robert Divine, "Roosevelt and Collective Security, 1933," *Mississippi Valley Historical Review,* XLVIII (June, 1961), 42–59; Davis to Hull, May 23, 1933, *FR, 1933,* I, 166–68.

13 Divine, *Mississippi Valley Historical Review,* XLVIII (June, 1961), 42–59; Moffat, Diary, August 17, 1933, Moffat MSS.

14 Moffat, Diary, August 17, 1933, Moffat MSS.

15 Memorandum of a conversation with Paul Boncour, September 19, 1933, Davis MSS; Roosevelt to Ramsay MacDonald, August 30, 1933, *FR, 1933,* I, 210–11; memorandum of a conversation with MacDonald, September 18, 1933, Davis MSS; Moffat, Diary, October 14 and 15, 1933, Moffat MSS.

16 Memorandum of a conversation with MacDonald, September 18, 1933, Davis MSS.

17 Memoranda of conversations with Boncour and Sir John Simon, September 22 and 23, 1933, *ibid.*

18 Memorandum of a conversation with Constantine von Neurath, September 25, 1933, *ibid.*

19 Walters, *History of the League of Nations,* pp. 548–49; Moffat, Diary, October 15, 1933, Moffat MSS.

20 Memorandum of a trans-Atlantic conversation, October 10, 1933, *FR, 1933,* I, 273–76.

21 Memorandum of a conversation with Roosevelt, April 28, 1934, Davis MSS; Moffat, Diary, May 28, 1934, Moffat MSS; memorandum by the Undersecretary of State, May 25, 1934, *FR, 1934,* I, 70–71.

22 Memorandum of a conversation with Louis Barthou, May 26, 1934, Davis MSS.

23 Davis to William Dodd, June 5 and 21, 1934, *ibid.;* report on the London Naval Conference by Norman Davis to the Council on Foreign Relations, April 16, 1936, *ibid.*

24 Moffat to Davis, July 5, 1934, Davis MSS.

25 Hugh Wilson to Davis, July 5, 1934, *ibid.*

26 Raymond Leslie Buell, *Isolated America* (New York, 1940), p. 65.

27 James A. Farley, *Jim Farley's Story* (New York, 1948), p. 56; some of these trade stimulants listed in *FCW,* X (January 23, 1943) 5, and XIX (May 12, 1945), 42–43; quoted in Ernest K. Lindley, *Half Way with Roosevelt* (New York, 1936), p. 350; Joe Wilkinson, *Politics and Trade Policy* (Washington, 1960), pp. 12–13.

28 Moffat, Diary, October 1, 1937, Moffat MSS.

29 Frank P. Chambers, Christina Phelps Harris, and Charles C. Bayley, *This Age of Conflict* (rev. ed.; New York, 1950), p. 598.

30 *Morgenthau Diaries,* pp. 134–49.

31 Wayne S. Cole, "Senator Key Pittman and American Neutrality Policies," *Mississippi Valley Historical Review,* XLVI (March, 1960), 644–62; Hull, *Memoirs,* I, 408–9.

32 Divine, *Illusion of Neutrality,* pp. 121–49.

33 Walter Lippmann, *Interpretations, 1933–1935,* ed. Allan Nevins (New York, 1936), p. 331.

34 Villard to Hull, August 5, 1936, Villard MSS.

35 Henry A. Wallace, *America Must Choose* (Boston, 1934), p. 2.

36 Henry A. Wallace, "Beard: The Planner," *New Republic,* LXXXI (January 2, 1935), 225–26.

37 Lippmann, *Interpretations,* pp. 340, 345.

38 Franklin D. Roosevelt, *Roosevelt's Foreign Policy* (New York, 1942), p. 103.

39 Cole, *Mississippi Valley Historical Review,* XLVI (March, 1960), 644–62. Whitney H. Shepardson and William O. Scroggs, eds., *The United States in World Affairs, 1937* (New York, 1938), p. 51; Divine, *Illusion of Neutrality,* pp. 194, 162, 165, 184.

40 Francis B. Sayre, *The Protection of American Export Trade* (Chicago, 1940), p. 17; George Messersmith to William Phillips, June 26, 1933, *Peace and War,* pp. 191–92.

41 Hull, *Memoirs,* I, 170.

42 Moffat, Diary, November 3, 1938, Moffat MSS; memorandum by Rudolf Schoenfield, February 3, 1936, *FR, 1936,* II, 213.

43 Hull, *Memoirs,* I, 373–75; Moffat, Diary, June 6, 1934, Moffat MSS.

44 Charles C. Tansill, *Back Door to War* (Chicago, 1952), p. 283.

45 William E. Dodd, *Ambassador Dodd's Diary* (New York, 1941), pp. 5–6, 8–9; Moffat to Phillips, June 22, 1933, Moffat MSS; Hull, *Memoirs,* I, 236–39.

46 Hull to Acting Secretary of State, June 13, 1933, *FR, 1933,* II, 440–41; E. H. Carr, *German-Soviet Relations Between the Two World Wars, 1919–1939* (Baltimore, 1951), pp. 78–79, 112–13.

47 Messersmith to Phillips, April 21, 1934, *Peace and War,* pp. 211–14; Dodd, *Ambassador Dodd's Diary,* p. 80; Moffat, Diary, January 18 and 19, and March 28, 1934, Moffat MSS.

48 Moffat, Diary, June 1, 4, and 6, 1934, Moffat MSS; Moffat to Roosevelt, June 2, 1934, *ibid.* See also all references in note 47 above.

49 Memorandum by the Assistant Economic Adviser, April 26, 1934, *FR, 1934,* II, 421–23.

50 Moffat to Roosevelt, enclosing Messersmith's letter, June 2, 1934, Moffat MSS.

51 Dodd to Davis, June 13, 1934, Davis MSS; Dodd, *Ambassador Dodd's Diary,* p. 110; Dodd to Hull, July 14, 1934, cited in Tansill, *Back Door to War,* p. 291; memoranda by the Assistant Secretary of State, April 12 and August 13, 1934, *FR, 1934,* II, 420–21, 435–37; Foreign Ministry to Embassy in the United States, May 22, 1934; Chargé to Foreign Ministry, June 28, 1934, *Documents on German Foreign Policy,* Series C, II, 830–38, and III, 100–101.

52 Moffat, Diary, July 11, 12, and 19, 1934, Moffat MSS; Hull to Dodd, July 7, 1934, *FR, 1934,* II, 377.

53 Dodd, *Ambassador Dodd's Diary,* p. 151; Moffat, Diary, August 30 and September 14 and 17, 1934, Moffat MSS.

54 Memorandum by a Special State Department Committee, October 12, 1934, *FR, 1934,* II, 448–53.

55 Moffat, Diary, October 12, 13, and 14, 1934, Moffat MSS; memorandum by Herbert Feis, November 21, 1934, *FR, 1934,* II, 326–27; Moffat, Diary, December 28, 1934, Moffat MSS.

56 Hull, *Memoirs,* I, 373; Moffat, Diary, December 14, 1934, Moffat MSS; Gilbert Fite, *George N. Peek and the Fight for Farm Parity* (Norman, Oklahoma, 1954), pp. 276–77.

57 Hull, *Memoirs,* I, 374.

58 Memorandum by Moffat, April 30, 1935, *FR, 1935,* II, 444–45; memorandum of a conversation, November 24, 1936, *FR, 1936,* II, 252–54; memorandum by Moffat, April 4, 1935, *FR, 1935,* II, 441–42.

59 Hull to the German Ambassador, June 28, 1935, *FR, 1935,* II, 432–37; memorandum by the Secretary of State, October 1, 1935, *ibid.,* II, 464–66.

60 Memorandum by the Secretary of State, May 4, 1936, *FR, 1936,* II, 225–27.

61 Hull, *Memoirs,* I, 472; *Morgenthau Diaries,* pp. 149–51.

62 Dodd, *Ambassador Dodd's Diary,* p. 381; Messersmith to Villard, January 26, 1937, Villard MSS.

63 Dorothy Thompson, *Let the Record Speak* (Boston, 1939), pp. 120–30.

64 Welles, *Seven Decisions,* pp. 16–18; William L. Langer and S. Everett Gleason, *The Challenge to Isolation* (New York, 1952), pp. 22–27.

65 Welles, *Seven Decisions,* pp. 16–18.

66 Davies, *Mission to Moscow,* p. 255.

67 Hull, *Memoirs,* I, 365; memorandum by the Secretary of State, July 20, 1936, and memorandum by Francis Sayre, December 19, 1936, *FR, 1936,* I, 677, 704.

68 Memorandum by the Secretary of State, January 18, 1937, *FR, 1937,* II, 2–3.

69 Memorandum by the Assistant Secretary of State, January 26, 1937, and Davis to Hull, April 10, 1937, *FR, 1937,* II, 6–8, 72–74; Davis to Neville Chamberlain, undated (1937), Roosevelt MSS, PSF.

70 Robert W. Bingham to Hull, July 6, 1937 (sent on to Roosevelt), Roosevelt MSS, PSF.

71 Joseph P. Kennedy to Hull, October 18, 1938, *FR, 1938,* II, 65–66; Chamberlan to Roosevelt, September 28, 1937, Roosevelt MSS, PSF. See also memorandum by the Secretary of State, August 9, 1937, *FR, 1937,* II, 65–66.

72 Memorandum by the Assistant Secretary of State, September 9, 1938, *FR, 1938,* II, 53–55.

73 *Morgenthau Diaries,* pp. 166–67; White to Morgenthau, September 6, 1938, and Herman Oliphant to Morgenthau, October 20, 1938, White MSS.

74 Oliphant to Morgenthau, October 20, 1938, White MSS; State Department, *Reciprocal Trade Agreement with the United Kingdom* (Washington, 1938), pp. 7 ff.

Chapter 6

1 Press Conference 614-A, January 12, 1940, Roosevelt MSS, PPF-1P.

2 Memorandum, March 17, 1939, NA, Dept. State 710/118, cited in Bryce Wood, *The Making of the Good Neighbor Policy* (New York, 1961), p. 415.

3 James Fred Rippy, *Globe and Hemisphere* (Chicago, 1958), pp. 117, 122, 256.

4 Carleton Beals, "Colombia: Again the Good Neighbor," *Current History*, L (March, 1939), 20–23; D. M. Phelps, ed., *Economic Relations with Latin America*, Michigan Business Papers, No. 6 (Ann Arbor, Michigan, 1940), p. 31.

5 Department of State, *Press Releases*, XX (January 14, 1939), 33–34; Donald M. Dozer, *Are We Good Neighbors?* (Gainesville, Florida, 1959), pp. 53–54; Carleton Beals, *Pan America* (New York, 1940), p. 361.

6 Memorandum of a conversation with Roosevelt and Hull, January 14, 1939, Daniels MSS.

7 Frank Knox to Roosevelt, October 14, 1939, Roosevelt MSS, PPF; Phelps, *Economic Relations*, p. 48.

8 Frank Page to Harry Hopkins, June 18, 1941, Hopkins MSS.

9 Wood, *Making of the Good Neighbor Policy*, p. 334.

10 *Ibid.*, pp. 185–95.

11 Frederick Hausermann, "Latin American Oil in War and Peace," *FAQ*, XXI (January, 1943), 354–61.

12 Charlton Ogden to Hull and Roosevelt, June 14, 1938, Roosevelt MSS, PPF, 3794.

13 R. Walton Moore to Daniels, November 23, 1936, and Moore to Daniels, December 10, 1936, cited in Cronon, *Daniels in Mexico*, pp. 122–27; Daniels to Hull, August 18, 1936 [not sent], Daniels MSS; Rogers to Roosevelt, October 7, 1937, Rogers MSS.

14 Roosevelt to Moore, January 16, 1937, and Hull to Roosevelt, March 26, 1937, Cronon, *Daniels in Mexico*, pp. 145–47.

15 *Ibid.*, pp. 159–63; Hull to Daniels, August 31, 1937, Daniels MSS; Daniels, Diary, September 11, 1937, Daniels MSS; Daniels to Roosevelt, September 14, 1937, Daniels MSS.

16 Daniels, Diary, November 6 and December 23, 1937, and January 22, 1938, Daniels MSS; Hull to Daniels, November 17, 1937, *ibid.*; Allan Seymour Everest, *Morgenthau, the New Deal and Silver* (New York, 1950), pp. 86–88; Cronon, *Daniels in Mexico*, pp. 176–78.

17 Daniels, Diary, March 19, 1938, Daniels MSS.

18 New York *Journal of Commerce*, September 14, 1938; James W. Gerard to Roosevelt, July 27, 1939, Roosevelt MSS, PPF, 977.

19 Interview with Adolf Berle, December 9, 1959; memorandum of a conversation, March 21, 1938, *FR, 1938*, V, 729–33.

20 Daniels to Roosevelt, March 22, 1938, and draft letter, Daniels to Roosevelt, July 30, 1938, Daniels MSS.

21 Morgenthau to Roosevelt, March 25, 1938, Roosevelt MSS, OF, 146; memorandum by Herbert Feis, March 24, 1938, NA, Dept. State 812.515 Silver Purchase/736, cited in Cronon, *Daniels in Mexico*, pp. 190–92.

22 Morgenthau to Roosevelt, March 25, 1938, Roosevelt MSS, OF, 146; D. Graham Hutton, "The New-Old Crisis in Mexico," *FAQ*, XVI (July, 1938), 626–39.

23 William O. Scroggs, "Mexican Oil in World Politics," *FAQ*, XVII (October, 1938), 172–75; Wood, *Making of the Good Neighbor Policy*, p. 405; Daniels to Roosevelt, March 29, 1938, Daniels MSS; Cronon, *Daniels in Mexico*, pp. 207–9, 247.

24 Press Conference 447, April 1, 1938, Roosevelt MSS, PPF-1P.

25 Memorandum of a conversation with the Mexican Ambassador, April 2, 1938, and memorandum by Laurence Duggan, May 31, 1938, *FR, 1938*, V, 740, 754.

26 Daniels, Diary, July 23, 1938, Daniels MSS; Welles to Najera, June 29, 1938, *ibid.*; Everest, *Morgenthau, the New Deal and Silver*, p. 91.

27 *Morgenthau Diaries*, pp. 493–97; White to Morgenthau, October 10, 1938, White MSS.

28 Everest, *Morgenthau, the New Deal and Silver*, pp. 91–93.

29 *Morgenthau Diaries*, p. 497; Daniels to Roosevelt, September 15 and October 29, 1938, Daniels MSS; Daniels, Diary, August 22, 1938, Daniels MSS; Daniels to Roosevelt, August 20, 1938, Roosevelt MSS, PSF.

30 See all references in note 29 above.

31 Daniels, Diary, October 29, 1938, Daniels MSS; Josephus Daniels, *Shirt-sleeve Diplomat* (Chapel Hill, North Carolina, 1947), pp. 248–49.

32 Memoranda of conversations, January 13 and 14, 1939, Daniels MSS.

33 Roosevelt to Daniels, February 15, 1939, Roosevelt MSS, OF, 146; Daniels, Diary, March 6 and 30, 1939, Daniels MSS.

34 Special handwritten diary kept by Josephus Daniels for the days May 16 to June 16, 1940, Daniels MSS; Hull to Frank Knox, October 14, 1940, cited in Cronon, *Daniels in Mexico*, pp. 240–46; I. F. Stone, "The Squeeze on Mexico," *Nation*, CLI (November 30, 1940), 523–24; Willy Feurlein and Elizabeth Hannan, *Dollars in Latin America* (New York, 1941), pp. 8–9; memorandum of a conversation with Lázaro Cárdenas, February 25, 1939, Daniels MSS; *SDB*, II (April 13 and May 4, 1940), 380–83, 470–73.

35 Page 229.

36 NFTC *Proceedings, 1938*, 382–86.

37 Daniels to Hull, August 22, 1938, Daniels MSS; Daniels, Diary, November 19, 1938, and February 27, 1939, *ibid.*

38 Daniels, Diary, November 12, 1940, *ibid.; Documents on German Foreign Policy*, Series D, V, 828.

39 Moffat, Diary, August 24, 1938, Moffat MSS.

40 Daniels, Diary, June 16, 1940, Daniels MSS; Roper to Roosevelt, May 28, 1941, Roosevelt MSS, PPF, 1023; Daniels, Diary, June 19, 1941,

356 · *Notes to Pages 122–128*

Daniels MSS; Cronon, *Daniels in Mexico,* p. 259; Castillo Nájera to Secretary of State, February 27, 1941, *FR, 1941,* VII, 371–83.

41 Hull, *Memoirs,* II, 1141; Everest, *Morgenthau, the New Deal and Silver,* p. 86; Cronon, *Daniels in Mexico,* pp. 263–64, 265; Daniels, *Shirtsleeve Diplomat,* p. 267.

42 Wood, *Making of the Good Neighbor Policy,* p. 257.

43 Special conference with the Senate Military Affairs Committee, January 31, 1939, Roosevelt MSS, PPF-1P.

44 William L. Langer and S. Everett Gleason, *The Challenge to Isolation* (New York, 1952), p. 132.

45 Bernard Baruch, *My Own Story: The Public Years* (New York, 1960), p. 275; Senate Special Committee Investigating the National Defense Program, *Hearings,* 77 Cong., 1 sess. (Washington, 1942), p. 4506.

46 Stetson Conn and Byron Fairchild, *The Framework of Hemisphere Defense,* in *United States Army in World War II* (Washington, 1960), pp. 173–75.

47 *Ibid.;* Edwin Lieuwen, *Arms and Politics in Latin America* (New York, 1959), p. 191.

48 Morgenthau to Harry L. Hopkins, January 16, 1939, and Hopkins to Morgenthau, January 21, 1939, Hopkins MSS.

49 Press Conference 652-A, June 14, 1940, Roosevelt MSS, PPF-1P.

50 David H. Popper, "Policies and Problems of the U.S. Navy," *Foreign Policy Reports,* XVII (May 1, 1941), 38–48; Senate Committee on Foreign Relations, *Hearings on S. 275,* 77 Cong., 1 sess. (Washington, 1941), Part 1, p. 131; Dozer, *Are We Good Neighbors?,* p. 74.

51 Carleton Beals, "Totalitarian Inroads in Latin America," *FAQ,* XVII (October, 1938), 78–89; Stimson, Diary, August 27, 1940, Stimson MSS.

52 Conn and Fairchild, *Framework of Hemisphere Defense,* pp. 243–44; Senate Special Committee Investigating the National Defense Program, *Hearings,* 77 Cong., 1 sess. (Washington, 1942), pp. 4510–12; Matthew Josephson, *Empire of the Air* (New York, 1944), p. 161.

53 Josephson, *Empire of the Air,* p. 161; Stimson, Diary, August 27, 1940, Stimson MSS.

54 *FCW,* XVIII (December 30, 1944), 15; memorandum by Stimson, September 13, 1940, Stimson MSS; *FCW,* I (November 30, 1940), 383.

55 Dozer, *Are We Good Neighbors?,* p. 78; Conn and Fairchild, *Framework of Hemisphere Defense,* p. 196; Daniels, Diary, March 4, 1941, Daniels MSS.

56 Press Conference 614-A, January 12, 1940, Roosevelt MSS, PPF-1P.

57 Press Conference 6, June 2, 1939, Hopkins MSS; *Daily Proceedings of the Second Constitutional Convention of the Congress of Industrial Organizations* (San Francisco, 1939), p. 270–72.

58 Feurlein and Hannan, *Dollars in Latin America,* pp. 40–41; *FCW,* XI (May 22, 1943), 39; *SDB,* I (November 18, 1939), 566.

59 Edward Noble to Roosevelt, November 27, 1939, Roosevelt MSS.

60 Minutes of a Business Advisory Council Meeting, September 15, 1939, Hopkins MSS; White memorandum on aid to Latin America [1939?], White MSS; Hansen to White, March 27, 1940, *ibid.*

61 Phelps, *Economic Relations with Latin America*, p. 23.

62 Juan T. Trippe, "The Business Future—Southward," *Survey Graphic*, XXX (March, 1941), 136–39.

63 Rockefeller to Roosevelt, November 6, 1940, Roosevelt MSS, PPF, 6035; Adolf Berle to Roosevelt, July 15 and 18, 1940, Roosevelt MSS, PSF.

64 Memorandum by the Assistant Secretary of State to the Undersecretary of State, May 24, 1940, *FR, 1940*, V, 353–54; confidential statement to the Inter-American Financial and Economic Advisory Committee, July 11, 1940, *ibid.*, V, 371–73; memorandum by George Messersmith, January 8, 1941, *FR, 1941*, VII, 127–33.

65 Jesse Jones, *Fifty Billion Dollars* (New York, 1951), p. 223; *SDB*, XI (December 3, 1944), 669; "X," "Export-Import Bank Loans to Latin America," *Foreign Policy Reports*, XVII (June 15, 1941), 82–92; memorandum by Herbert Feis, January 22, 1940, and memorandum, April 11, 1940, *FR, 1940*, V, 600–601, 602–3.

66 Jefferson Caffery to Hull, May 22, 1940, and Hull to Caffery, May 31, 1940, *FR, 1940*, V, 605–6, 607; Caffery to Hull, July 8 and September 5, 1940, *ibid.*, V, 608, 610; Senate Committee on Banking and Currency, *Study of the Export-Import Bank and World Bank*, 83 Cong., 2 sess. (Washington, 1954), Part 1, pp. 98–99; *SDB*, V (July, 1941), 19.

67 *FCW*, XI (June 26, 1943), 3 ff.

68 Minutes of Business Advisory Council meetings, October 5 and November 3, 1939, and January 16, 1940, Hopkins MSS.

69 *FCW*, II (January 25, 1941), 135 ff.; Bureau of Foreign and Domestic Commerce to Hopkins, November 11, 1940, Hopkins MSS.

70 *FCW*, II (February 15, 1941), 269 ff.; James Fred Rippy, *Latin America and the Industrial Age* (New York, 1947), p. 257 *et passim.*

Chapter 7

1 Joseph Grew, "Manuscript on Japan: A Survey of the Record as Known to the Embassy in Tokyo at the Closing Period of My Mission to Japan" (unpublished manuscript in the University of Chicago Library, Chicago, Illinois), pp. 12–15; Roosevelt to Grew, January 21, 1941, *FR, 1941*, IV, 7.

2 Admiral Harold Stark to Admiral Thomas Hart, September 22, 1941, Pearl Harbor Attack, Part 5, p. 2118.

3 Memorandum by Hull, September 7, 1939, *FR: Japan, 1931–41* (2 vols.; Washington, 1943), II, 9–15.

4 The best defense of American policy is in Herbert Feis, *The Road to Pearl Harbor* (Princeton, 1950).

5 On the other side see Paul Schroeder, *The Axis Alliance and Japanese-American Relations, 1941* (Ithaca, New York, 1958).

6 Feis, *Road to Pearl Harbor,* p. 204; address to the National Press Club, March 17, 1938, *Peace and War,* p. 411.

7 Forrest K. Davis and Ernest K. Lindley, *How War Came* (New York, 1942), p. 210.

8 Carl H. Boehringer (Osaka) to State Department, July 25, 1940, NA, Dept. State 694.0031/13.

9 Harry Hawkins to Joseph Ballantine, November 10, 1941, *FR, 1941,* IV, 576–79.

10 Feis, *Road to Pearl Harbor,* p. 216.

11 Department of State, *Press Releases,* XVIII (January 15, 1938), 104.

12 Memoranda of conversations, March 4, 1937, November 28, 1937, December 28, 1937, May 17, 1938, and July 4, 1938, Grew MSS.

13 William D. Leahy to Roosevelt, January 6, 1938, Roosevelt MSS, PSF; Senate Committee on Naval Affairs, *Hearings on H.R. 9218,* 75 Cong., 3 sess. (Washington, 1938), pp. 59–60.

14 *Congressional Record* (April 19, 1938), 75 Cong., 3 sess., LXXXIII, 5523.

15 Stark to the Secretary of the Navy, November 12, 1940, Roosevelt MSS, Tully Safe File.

16 Note by Maxwell M. Hamilton on a message from Nelson T. Johnson to the State Department, July 1, 1938, NA, Dept. State 893.51/6638; memorandum of a conversation, July 15, 1938, *FR, 1938,* III, 538–40; Morgenthau to Roosevelt, November 11, 1938, Roosevelt MSS, PSF.

17 Hull to Grew, November 20, 1938, NA, Dept. State 693.001/399.

18 Committee to Rogers, March 16, 1939, Rogers MSS; E. C. Carter to Stimson, February 18, 1940, Stimson MSS.

19 W. Cameron Forbes to Stimson, February 10, 1940, Stimson MSS.

20 Nathaniel Peffer, "Would Japan Shut the Open Door in China?" *FAQ* XVII (October, 1938), 37–50.

21 Grew to Hull, November 30, 1938, NA, Dept. State 693.001/430.

22 Memorandum to the Treasury and the President, November 14, 1938, Roosevelt MSS, PSF.

23 Morgenthau to Roosevelt, November 11, 1938, *ibid.;* Jesse Jones to Morgenthau, October 24, 1938, *ibid.*

24 Hull to Roosevelt, May 8, 1936, *ibid.*

25 Memorandum to the Treasury and the President, November 14, 1938, *ibid.*

26 Memorandum by Hull, January 12, 1939, NA, Dept. State 611.9431/170.

27 Johnson to Hull, March 30, 1938, NA, Dept. State 893.5151/434.

28 Hornbeck and Feis memoranda, cited in Charles C. Tansill, *Back Door to War* (Chicago, 1952), pp. 502–4; Adolf Berle is quoted by William L. Langer and S. Everett Gleason, *The Challenge to Isolation* (New York, 1952), p. 158.

29 Feis, *Road to Pearl Harbor,* p. 22; memorandum of a conversation, July 20, 1939, Roosevelt MSS, PSF.

30 Roosevelt to Grew, November 30, 1939, *ibid.*
31 New York *Daily News,* January 11, 1940, clipping in Stimson MSS.
32 Grew to Department of State, March 28, 1940, NA, Dept. State 611.9431/198.
33 Hull to Grew, July 4, 1940, *FR, 1940,* IV, 381–87.
34 Hull to Roosevelt, September 13, 1940, Roosevelt MSS, PSF.
35 Paul Schroeder, *The Axis Alliance and Japanese-American Relations, 1941* (Ithaca, 1958), pp. 103 ff.
36 Speech reprinted in *FR: Japan, 1931–41,* II, 113 ff.
37 Stimson, Diary, September 27, October 2 and 4, 1940, Stimson MSS.
38 Pearl Harbor Attack, Part 1, pp. 266–305; Stimson, Diary, October 12, 1940, Stimson MSS.
39 Davis and Lindley, *How War Came,* p. 157.
40 Roosevelt to Welles, November 22, 1940, Roosevelt MSS, PSF; "The China Lobby—Part One," in Max Ascoli, ed., *Our Times: The Best from the Reporter Magazine* (New York, 1960), pp. 6–24; Chiang Kai-shek to Roosevelt, May 17, 1940, Roosevelt MSS, PSF.
41 Feis, *Road to Pearl Harbor,* pp. 101–3.
42 State Department to Roosevelt, December 10, 1940, Roosevelt MSS, PSF.
43 Memorandum of a conversation, February 14, 1941, *FR: Japan, 1931–41,* II, 387–88.
44 Hull, *Memoirs,* I, 277.
45 Reprinted in Feis, *Road to Pearl Harbor,* p. 178.
46 See Robert J. C. Butow, "The Hull-Nomura Conversations: A Fundamental Misconception," *American Historical Review,* LXV (July, 1960), 822–37.
47 Grew, "Manuscript on Japan," pp. 50–51, 141.
48 Memorandum on Japanese-American Relations, April 9, 1941, NA, Dept. State 694.119/3611; Schroeder, *Axis Alliance,* p. 79.
49 Butow, *American Historical Review,* LXV (July, 1960), 822–37.
50 Feis, *Road to Pearl Harbor,* p. 241 *et passim;* Pearl Harbor Attack, Part 2, p. 421; press release, July 24, 1941, *FR: Japan, 1931–41,* II, 316–17.
51 Richard M. Leighton and Robert W. Coakely, *Global Logistics and Strategy, 1940–1943,* in *United States Army in World War II* (Washington, 1955), p. 129; Maurice Matloff and Edwin M. Snell, *Strategic Planning for Coalition Warfare,* in *United States Army in World War II,* (Washington, 1953), p. 63; Welles to Wakasugi, July 23, 1941, *FR: Japan, 1931–41,* II, 522–26; William L. Langer and S. Everett Gleason, *The Undeclared War* (New York, 1953), p. 659.
52 Memorandum of a conversation, July 24, 1941, *FR: Japan, 1931–41,* II, 529; Schroeder, *Axis Alliance,* pp. 175 ff.; Grew, "Manuscript on Japan," pp. 50–51; Pearl Harbor Attack, Part 2, p. 424; Stimson, Diary, August 9 and 10, 1941, Stimson MSS.
53 Stimson, Diary, October 6, 1941, Stimson MSS.

54 Feis, *Road to Pearl Harbor*, p. 299.
55 Memorandum of a conversation with Toyada, August 22, 1941; Grew, "Manuscript on Japan," p. 161; Japanese government to Department of State, August 28, 1941, *Peace and War*, p. 722.
56 Stimson, Diary, October 28, 1941, Stimson MSS.
57 Kichisaburo Nomura to Tokyo, October 17, 1941, Pearl Harbor Attack, Part 12, p. 77; Hull, *Memoirs*, II, 1058–59.
58 Stimson, Diary for November 11, 1941, Pearl Harbor Attack, Part 11, p. 5431.
59 Roosevelt to Hull, *ca.* November 20, 1941, and Churchill to Roosevelt, November 26, 1941, *FR, 1941*, IV, 626, 665; memorandum for Roosevelt from Stimson, November 27, 1941, Pearl Harbor Attack, Part 19, pp. 3517–19; Ickes, *Secret Diary*, III, 655; Stimson, Diary, November 26, 1941, Stimson MSS.
60 Stimson, Diary, November 25, 1941, Stimson MSS.
61 Pearl Harbor Attack, Part 2, p. 499.
62 Cited in Robert E. Sherwood, *Roosevelt and Hopkins: An Intimate History* (2nd ed.; New York, 1950), pp. 428–29.

Chapter 8

1 For samples of the kind of evidence used by revisionists to show that Roosevelt took the nation into the war because of an inability to overcome the depression, see *Morgenthau Diaries*, pp. 391–92; William E. Dodd, *Ambassador Dodd's Diary* (New York, 1941), p. 426; Ickes, *Secret Diary*, II, 240–41; Basil Rauch, *Roosevelt: From Munich to Pearl Harbor*, (New York, 1950), p. 89; T. S. Eliot, *The Idea of a Christian Society* (New York, 1940), pp. 58–59. Eliot continues: "What is more depressing still is the thought that only fear or jealousy of foreign success can alarm us about the health of our own Nation; that only through this anxiety can we see such things as depopulation, malnutrition, moral deterioration, the decay of agriculture as evils at all."
2 Stimson, Diary, March 28, 1938, Stimson MSS.
3 State Department to Roosevelt, undated [1937], Roosevelt MSS, PSF; Ickes, *Secret Diary*, II, 342–43.
4 "The U.S. Frontier," *Fortune*, XXI (February, 1940), 97–104, 145.
5 Department of State, *Press Releases*, XIII (July 6, 1935), 33.
6 Howard J. Trueblood, "Gold: An American Dilemma," *Foreign Policy Reports*, XV (September 1, 1939), 142–52; Stuart Chase, *Tomorrow's Trade* (New York, 1945), p. 63.
7 Thomas Lamont, "Trade is a Two-Way Street," *Collier's*, CV (March 9, 1940), 22, 61; Carleton Beals, *Pan America* (New York, 1940), p. 280.
8 Herbert Feis, *The Spanish Story* (New York, 1948), pp. 4, 11.
9 *Ibid.*, p. 12; Moffat, Diary, December 30, 1937, Moffat MSS.
10 Moffat, Diary, March 9, May 19, and May 26, 1939, Moffat MSS; Feis, *Spanish Story*, pp. 14–16.

11 Moffat, Diary, March 29, 1939, Moffat MSS.

12 Moffat, Diary, April 3 and July 25, 1939, *ibid.*

13 Moffat, Diary, July 24, 25, 29, and 30, 1939, *ibid.;* Feis, *Spanish Story,* p. 16.

14 Moffat, Diary, May 1, 1940, Moffat MSS.

15 Harold G. Moulton *et al., Capital Expansion, Employment, and Stability* (Washington, 1940), pp. 41–42, 334–35; David Lynch, *The Concentration of Economic Power* (New York, 1946), pp. 21–25.

16 Press Conference 439, March 4, 1938, Roosevelt, *Public Papers* (1938 vol.), p. 133; Lynch, *Concentration,* pp. 21–25.

17 Lynch, *Concentration,* pp. 21–25.

18 Robert E. Sherwood, *Roosevelt and Hopkins: An Intimate History* 2nd ed.; New York, 1950), pp. 95–103; Senate Committee on Commerce, *Hearings on the Nomination of Harry L. Hopkins to be Secretary of Commerce,* 76 Cong., 1 sess. (Washington, 1939), p. 8; minutes of press conference, March 8, 1939, Hopkins MSS.

19 Sherwood, *Roosevelt and Hopkins,* p. 102.

20 Press Conference 6, June 2, 1939, Hopkins MSS.

21 Undated speech draft [1939?], *ibid.*

22 Moulton, *Capital Expansion,* p. 164; Adolf Berle to Roosevelt, August 16, 1938, Roosevelt MSS, PSF.

23 Moffat, Diary, October 26, 1938, Moffat MSS; Franklin D. Roosevelt, *Roosevelt's Foreign Policy* (New York, 1942), p. 158.

24 Joseph Alsop and Robert Kintner, *American White Paper* (New York, 1940), p. 16.

25 Adolf A. Berle quoted in William L. Langer and S. Everett Gleason, *The Challenge to Isolation* (New York, 1952), p. 202–3.

26 Berle to Stimson, March 20, 1940, Stimson MSS; Moffat, Diary, April 30, May 4 and 5, 1940, Moffat MSS; Forrest K. Davis and Ernest K. Lindley, *How War Came* (New York, 1942), pp. 126–27.

27 Moffat, Diary, October 15 and 16, 1938, Moffat MSS; NFTC *Proceedings,* 1938 p. 443; NFTC *Proceedings, 1937,* p. 137.

28 Moffat, Diary, January 22, 23, and 24, 1938, Moffat MSS; George Messersmith to Hull, February 18, 1938, *FR, 1938,* I, 17–24.

29 NFTC *Proceedings, 1938,* p. 354; Milton to Harper Sibley, February 3, 1938, and Milton to D. B. Evans, March 4, 1938, Milton MSS. See also Wayne C. Taylor's remarks in *FCW,* III (May 3, 1941), 183; memorandum, November 13, 1939, White MSS.

30 Page 141.

31 Hull, *Memoirs,* I, 747; Ickes, *Secret Diary,* III, 161; Robert Divine, *The Illusion of Neutrality* (Chicago, 1962), pp. 263, 282; Joe Wilkinson, *Politics and Trade Policy* (Washington, 1960), p. 16; Roosevelt, *Public Papers* (1941 vol.), p. 184.

32 *New York Times,* March 26, 1940.

33 Charles A. Beard, *President Roosevelt and the Coming of the War, 1941* (New Haven, 1948), p. 153.

34 "Fortune Forum of Executive Opinion," *Fortune,* XXII (September, 1940), 73; "A.D. 1939," *ibid.*, XXI (January, 1940), 29–31, 93; Russell Davenport to Roosevelt, March 9, 1939, Roosevelt MSS, OF, 3618; Divine, *Illusion of Neutrality,* p. 293.

35 Thomas Lamont to Davis, May 7, 1940, Davis MSS; Bernard M. Baruch, *My Story: Public Years* (New York, 1957), p. 260. Wendell Willkie, quoted in Charles A. Beard, *American Foreign Policy in the Making, 1932–1940* (New Haven, 1946), p. 273; W. Averell Harriman to Roosevelt, September 1, 1939, Roosevelt MSS, PPF, 6207.

36 Moffat, Diary, September 21, 1939, Moffat MSS; Langer and Gleason, *Challenge to Isolation,* p. 227.

37 Stimson, War Diary, Part 1, Stimson MSS.

38 Business Advisory Council report, January 12, 1940, Hopkins MSS.

39 Karl Schriftgiesser, *Business Comes of Age* (New York, 1960), pp. 11, 117; Burton K. Wheeler to Villard, September 21, 1940, Villard MSS.

40 Stimson, Diary, December 3, 1940, and August 29, 1941, Stimson MSS.

41 Stimson, Diary, December 18, 1940, Stimson MSS; Bruce Catton, *The War Lords of Washington* (New York, 1948), p. 24.

42 Copy of the speech (October 4, 1940) in Batterson MSS.

43 Letter reprinted in Whitney H. Shepardson and William O. Scroggs, eds., *The United States in World Affairs, 1937* (New York, 1938), p. 271.

44 Rauch, *Roosevelt,* pp. 59–64; Senate Committee on Naval Affairs, *Hearings on H.R. 9218,* 75 Cong., 3 sess. (Washington, 1938), pp. 59–60.

45 Rauch, *Roosevelt,* pp. 59–64; Moffat, Diary, January 27 and 31, 1938, Moffat MSS.

46 *Congressional Record* (January 6, 1938). 75 Cong., 3 sess., LXXXIII, 87, 88, 95.

47 *Ibid.,* pp. 5707, 5788.

48 *Ibid.*

49 *Ibid.,* pp. 5518, 5520. See also Ernest Lundeen's rebuttal, *ibid.,* p. 5519, and Gerald Nye's further rejoinder, *ibid.,* p. 5571.

50 Roosevelt to James Couzens, September 17, 1936, Roosevelt, *Letters,* I, 616–17.

51 *FCW,* V (October 11, 1941), 2, 3–5, 41–43; Senate Subcommittee on Foreign Trade and Shipping of the Special Committee on Post-War Economic Policy and Planning, *Hearings,* 78 Cong., 2 sess., and 79 Cong., 1 sess., (Washington, 1945), Part 4, p. 617.

52 *Congressional Record* (May 10, 1938), 75 Cong., 3 sess., LXXXIII, 6549.

53 Speech for Newtown Rally, May 22, 1941, Batterson MSS; *FCW,* V (October 11, 1941), 43.

54 Langer and Gleason, *Challenge to Isolation,* pp. 33–34; *Peace and War,* p. 430; Moffat, Diary, September 30, 1938, Moffat MSS.

55 Moffat, Diary, November 9, 1938, and May 23, 1939, Moffat MSS;

Moffat to Hull, May 19, 1939, *ibid.*; memorandum by the Acting Secretary of State, March 17, 1939, *FR, 1939,* II, 567–68; Chargé in Washington to the Foreign Ministry, September 12, 1938, *Documents on German Foreign Policy,* Series D, V, 726–32.

56 Langer and Gleason, *Challenge to Isolation,* pp. 48–50; Alsop and Kintner, *American White Paper,* pp. 30–31.

57 Alsop and Kintner, *American White Paper,* p. 41. For a similar expression by Roosevelt see Langer and Gleason, *Challenge to Isolation,* pp. 138–39, 202–3.

58 *Documents on German Foreign Policy,* Series D, VI, 243–45; Hugh Gibson, ed., *The Ciano Diaries: 1939–1943* (New York, 1945), p. 66.

59 Stimson, Diary, May 8, 1940, Stimson MSS; Moffat, Diary, April 26 and May 3, 1940, Moffat MSS; report by the Undersecretary of State on his Special Mission to Europe, *FR, 1940,* I, 21–117; memorandum by the Economic Policy Department, March 13, 1940, *Documents on German Foreign Policy,* Series D, VIII, 915; Roosevelt to Mussolini, May 30, 1940, *FR. 1940,* II, 713.

60 Davis and Lindley, *How War Came,* pp. 119–20; William L. Langer and S. Everett Gleason, *The Undeclared War,* (New York, 1950), pp. 228–42.

61 Senate Committee on Foreign Relations, *Hearings on S. 275,* 77 Cong., 1 sess. (Washington, 1941), Part 1, p. 178.

62 Notes by John J. McCloy for Stimson's use, January 29 and 30, 1941; notes on an off-the-record talk with senators on Lend-Lease Bill, March 2, 1941, Stimson MSS.

63 Notes for talk with War Department officials, March 17, 1941, Stimson MSS; Jan Ciechanowski, *Defeat in Victory* (New York, 1947), pp. 1–5, 6; Langer and Gleason, *Undeclared War,* pp. 284 ff.

64 Stimson, Diary, April 24, May 23 and 24, 1941, Stimson MSS.

65 Roosevelt, *Public Papers* (1941 vol.), pp. 386–87.

66 Hoover to Hull, March 27, 1941, Stimson MSS. On Hoover's relationship to Woodrow Wilson see Herbert Hoover, *Ordeal of Woodrow Wilson* (New York, 1958), pp. 102–3 *et passim.*

67 Moffat, Diary, Septmeber 12 and November 2, 1939, and February 2, 1940, Moffat MSS. See also Herbert Feis, *Seen from E. A.* (New York, 1947), pp. 42–43.

68 Stimson, Diary, May 12, 1940, Stimson MSS; Henry Grady to American Consul at Nairobi, March 13, 1940, *FR, 1940,* III, 119–20, 120–21. France was expected to give American trade equal rights, too. Welles to Hull, March 11, 1940, *FR, 1940,* I, 16.

69 Cabinet report, April 4, 1940, Hopkins MSS.

70 Moffat, Diary, March 31 and September 24, 1941, Moffat MSS.

71 Sumner Welles, *Where Are We Heading?* (New York, 1946), p. 6; memorandum of a conversation with Lord Halifax, August 20, 1941, Moffat MSS.

72 Roosevelt to Churchill, July 14, 1941, and memorandum of a con-

versation by Sumner Welles, *FR, 1941,* I, 342, 182. This subject will be discussed at length in Chapters 13 and 14. See also Berle to Hull, September 15, 1941, Hull to John G. Winant, December 5, 1941, and Hull to Thurston, December 5, 1941, *FR, 1941,* I, 188, 194, 196.

73 "And What Shall We Do Then?," *Fortune,* XXIV (October, 1941), 102 ff.

Chapter 9

1 *Fortune,* XXV (May, 1942), 59–63; Robert E. Sherwood, *Roosevelt and Hopkins: An Intimate History* (2nd ed.; New York, 1950), p. 921; Jacob Viner, "American Interest in the Colonial Problem," in Percy Bidwell, ed., *The United States in a Multi-National Economy* (New York, 1945), pp. 2 ff.

2 Sherwood, *Roosevelt and Hopkins,* p. 921.

3 *Ibid.,* p. 507; Don Lohbeck, *Patrick J. Hurley* (Chicago, 1956), p. 219; Rexford Tugwell, *The Democratic Roosevelt* (New York, 1957), pp. 591–92; Edgar Snow, *Journey to the Beginning* (New York, 1959), pp. 254–56; Ickes, *Secret Diary,* I, 242.

4 Patrick Hurley to Harry Truman, November 26, 1945, China White Paper, p. 581.

5 Maurice Matloff and Edwin M. Snell, *Strategic Planning for Coalition Warfare,* in *United States Army in World War II* (Washington, 1955), p. 10; Hull, *Memoirs,* II, 1599.

6 Stimson to Hoover, January 3, 1933, Stimson MSS.

7 Hurley to Hoover, December 22, 1932, Stimson MSS; Lohbeck, *Patrick J. Hurley,* p. 223.

8 H. B. Hawes to Stimson, January 26, 1940, Stimson MSS.

9 Roosevelt, *Public Papers* (1934 vol.), pp. 118–19; Garel Grunder and William E. Livezey, *The Philippines and the United States* (Norman, Oklahoma, 1951), p. 222; Hull to Roosevelt, March 17, 1935, Roosevelt MSS, PSF.

10 Roosevelt, *Public Papers,* (1934 vol.), pp. 266–68; William Phillips to Roosevelt, November 8, 1934, Roosevelt MSS, PSF; Shirley Jenkins, *American Economic Policy Towards the Philippines* (Stanford, 1954), p. 38; Ethel B. Dietrich, *The Far Eastern Trade of the United States* (New York, 1940), pp. 52–56.

11 Jenkins, *American Economic Policy,* p. 38.

12 Henry A. Wallace to Roosevelt, December 11, 1937, Roosevelt MSS, PPF, 3702.

13 Stephen Early to Roosevelt, March 16, 1938, Roosevelt MSS, PSF; Francis Sayre, *Glad Adventure* (New York, 1957), p. 199.

14 Henry L. Stimson and McGeorge Bundy, *On Active Duty in Peace and War* (New York, 1948), pp. 298, 397–99, 403; Douglas MacArthur to Adams, January 28, 1942, MacArthur to Marshall, February 8, 1942, and Marshall to MacArthur, February 9, 1942, *FR, 1942,* I, 888–97.

15 Minutes of a telephone conversation between Stimson and Millard Tydings, September 27, 1943, Stimson MSS; Sherwood, *Roosevelt and Hopkins,* p. 792.

16 Minutes of a telephone conversation with J. W. Wadsworth, June 13, 1944, Stimson MSS.

17 Cited in Jenkins, *American Economic Policy* p. 57.

18 *New York Times,* January 17, 1960.

19 Snow, *Journey to the Beginning,* pp. 254–55.

20 Reginald Coupland, *The Cripps Mission to India* (London, 1942), pp. 19–20.

21 Hull, *Memoirs,* II, 1482–83.

22 Roosevelt to Hull, December 27, 1941, and memorandum of a telephone conversation, December 30, 1941, *FR, 1942,* I, 13, 23–24; Winston S. Churchill, *The Hinge of Fate* (Boston, 1950), pp. 209 ff.; memorandum by the Assistant Secretary of State, February 17, 1942, and W. Averell Harriman to Roosevelt, February 26, 1942, *FR, 1942,* I, 603, 608.

23 Roosevelt to Churchill, March 10, 1942, *FR, 1942,* I, 615–16; Churchill, *Hinge of Fate,* pp. 212–17; Welles to Wilson, March 11, 1942, *FR, 1942,* I, 617–18.

24 Churchill, *Hinge of Fate,* pp. 216–18; Sherwood, *Roosevelt and Hopkins,* p. 524; Louis Johnson to Hull, April 9 and 11, 1942, *FR, 1942,* I, 630–32.

25 Johnson to Hull, April 9 and 11, 1942, *FR, 1942,* I, 630–32.

26 Churchill, *Hinge of Fate,* pp. 217–21.

27 *New York Times,* May 17, 1942.

28 Minutes of a press conference between Louis Johnson and Indian newsmen, April 22, 1942, Roosevelt MSS, OF, 48-H. See also Johnson to Hull, May 4, 1942, *FR, 1942,* I, 648–50.

29 Louis Fischer to Roosevelt, August 7, 1942, Roosevelt MSS, PSF; Gandhi to Roosevelt, July 1, 1942, and Roosevelt to Gandhi, August 1, 1942, *FR, 1942,* I, 677, 703; Hull, *Memoirs,* II, 1489–90.

30 Ickes to Roosevelt, August 10, 1942, and Roosevelt to Ickes, August 12, 1942, Roosevelt MSS, PPF, 3650.

31 Hull to John G. Winant, November 20, 1942, *FR, 1942,* I, 746; William Phillips, *Ventures in Diplomacy* (Boston, 1952), pp. 343, 354–94; Hull, *Memoirs,* II, 1490–91; Roosevelt to Hopkins, March 19, 1943, Roosevelt, *Letters,* II, 1414.

32 Arthur H. Vandenberg, Jr., ed., *The Private Papers of Senator Vandenberg* (New York, 1952), pp. 52–53.

33 W. D. Pawley to Roosevelt, October 15, 1944, Roosevelt MSS, OF, 48-H.

34 Churchill to Roosevelt, January 14, 1942, Roosevelt MSS, PSF.

35 Speech to the Royal Empire Society, July 29, 1942 (copy in Taussig MSS).

36 Roosevelt to Hull, January 11, 1941, *FR, 1941,* III, 2–4; Nancy

Harvison Hooker, ed., *The Moffat Papers* (Cambridge, Mass., 1956), pp. 352–53.

37 "What Victory Will Bring Us," *American Magazine,* CXXXVIII (January, 1944), 20–21, 87–89.

38 Moffat, Diary, July 23 and 26, 1937, February 8, 16 and April 11, 1938, Moffat MSS; Roosevelt to Hull, April 12, 1938, Roosevelt MSS, PSF; memoranda of conversations, April 18, June 15, and November 14, 1939, *FR, 1939,* II, 315–17, 319.

39 Stimson, War Diary, August 19, 1940, Stimson MSS. See also Stimson, Diary, November 20, 1944, Stimson MSS.

40 Elliott Roosevelt, *As He Saw It* (New York, 1946), pp. 75–76. Although this book is apparently based only upon recollections and impressions, the number of times Elliott's father spoke to him and to others about the economic disadvantages of colonialism to the United States as well as its moral wrongs is indeed striking. Eleanor Roosevelt, *This I Remember* (New York, 1949), p. 281; Roosevelt, *Public Papers* (1944–45 vol.), pp. 68–70, 127–28.

41 Hull, *Memoirs,* II, 1595; William L. Langer, *Our Vichy Gamble* (New York, 1947), p. 97; William D. Leahy, *I Was There* (New York, 1950), pp. 9, 44–45, 54–55.

42 Leahy, *I Was There,* pp. 9, 44–45, 54–55.

43 Roosevelt to Leahy, January 20, 1942, Roosevelt, *Letters,* II, 1275; Roosevelt, *Public Papers* (1942 vol.), pp. 455–56, 472, 479–80.

44 Leahy, *I Was There,* p. 188; Stettinius to Roosevelt, October 29, 1943, Roosevelt MSS, PSF; Elliott Roosevelt, *As He Saw It,* pp. 114–15; Edward R. Stettinius to Wallace Murray, November 5, 1943, *Teheran Papers,* pp. 155–56; minutes of a meeting with the Joint Chiefs of Staff, November 15, 1943, *Teheran Papers,* pp. 194–95.

45 Chinese minutes of a Roosevelt-Chiang meeting, November 23, 1943, *Teheran Papers,* pp. 323–25; Charles Bohlen minutes of a Roosevelt-Stalin meeting, November 28, 1943, *ibid.,* pp. 483–86; Edward R. Stettinius, *Roosevelt and the Russians* (New York, 1949), pp. 236–38.

46 Roosevelt to Hull, January 24, 1944, *Teheran Papers,* pp. 872–73.

47 State Department to Roosevelt, July 4, 1944, Roosevelt MSS, PSF; Roosevelt to Hull, August 18, 1944, *ibid.,* OF, 4752; Bohlen notes of Roosevelt-Stalin meeting, February 8, 1945, *Yalta Papers,* p. 770; Roosevelt, *Public Papers* (1944–45 vol.), pp. 562–63; Leahy, *I Was There,* p. 410; memorandum to the President's Naval Aide, undated, 1945, *Potsdam Papers,* I, 915–25.

48 For the postwar struggle in Indo-China see Virginia Thompson, *French Indo-China* (Stanford, 1954), and Ellen Hammer, *The Struggle for Indo-China* (Stanford, 1954).

49 Leahy, Diary, December 6, 1945, Leahy MSS; Hull, *Memoirs,* II, 1600; Roosevelt, *Public Papers* (1944–45 vol.), pp. 563–64; Cleona Lewis, *The United States and Foreign Investment Problems* (New York, 1948), pp. 209–11.

50 Sumner Welles, *Where Are We Heading?* (New York, 1946), pp. 288–89.
51 Sherwood, *Roosevelt and Hopkins,* pp. 572–73; Roosevelt to Jan Christian Smuts, November 24, 1942, Roosevelt, *Letters,* II, 1371–72.
52 Hull to Roosevelt, March 17, 1943, Harley Notter, ed., *Postwar Foreign Policy Preparation* (Washington, 1954), p. 471; Stimson, Diary, November 30, 1943, Stimson MSS; Hull, *Memoirs,* II, 1600.
53 "On Our Economic Relations with Britain," *FAQ,* XXI (April, 1943), 462–75; Hull, *Memoirs,* II, 1697
54 Francis Sayre, *Dependent Peoples and World Order* (Denver, 1948), pp. 15–19.
55 Stettinius to Forrestal, December 30, 1944, Notter, *Postwar Foreign Policy Preparation,* p. 660.
56 Joseph Grew to Roosevelt, January 13, 1945, Roosevelt MSS, OF, 4630.
57 Stettinius, *Roosevelt and the Russians,* pp. 44–45; *Yalta Papers,* pp. 92, 569–70.
58 Stettinius, *Roosevelt and the Russians,* p. 238; James F. Byrnes, *Speaking Frankly* (New York, 1947), p. x; Leahy, *I Was There,* pp. 313–14; Bohlen minutes, February 9, 1945, and Alger Hiss notes, February 9, 1945, *Yalta Papers,* pp. 844, 858. Churchill reacted the same way to a proposed declaration on Eastern Europe, asking that it be made plain that it did not refer to the British Empire, *Yalta Papers,* p. 848.
59 Notter, *Postwar Foreign Policy Preparation,* p. 387; memorandum of a conversation, November 15, 1944, *Yalta Papers,* p. 57; Hull, *Memoirs,* II, 1599; Roosevelt, *Public Papers* (1944–45 vol.), p. 225.
60 Walter Millis, ed., *The Forrestal Diaries* (New York, 1951), p. 33; Leahy, *I Was There,* p. 258; James F. Byrnes to Roosevelt, March 23, 1945, Roosevelt MSS, PSF; Stimson and Bundy, *On Active Duty,* pp. 599–603; Stimson, Diary, March 30, 1945, Stimson MSS; Roosevelt, *Public Papers* (1944–45 vol.), p. 610.
61 *Congressional Record,* (April 12, 1945), 79 Cong., 1 sess., XCI, A1706; memorandum of a conversation with the President, April 18, 1945, Stimson MSS.
62 Draft statement on trusteeships, September 24, 1945, Taussig MSS; Sayre, *Dependent Peoples,* pp. 14–15.
63 United Nations Information Organization, *Documents of the United Nations Conference on International Organization* (16 vols.; New York and London, 1945), X, May 12 to June 16, 1945, pp. 433–44, 544–46. See also Edward R. Stettinius, *Report to the President* (Washington, 1945).

Chapter 10

1 American Assembly, *The United States and Latin America* (New York, 1959), p. 157.
2 Speech to members of the Canadian Society, February 16, 1935, *Peace and War,* p. 252.

3   Spruille Braden, "Latin American Industrialization and Foreign Trade," in Lloyd J. Hughlett, ed., *The Industrialization of Latin America* (New York, 1946), p. 486. For an interesting view of Adam Smith, and one which can be applied to this chapter, see R. Koebner, "Adam Smith and the Industrial Revolution," *Economic History Review,* 2nd series, XI (April, 1959), 381–91.

4   *SDB,* III (October 26 and November 2, 1940), 345, 374–81; Laurence Duggan, *The Americas* (New York, 1949), p. 97.

5   *SDB,* X (May 13, 1944), 427.

6   NFTC *Proceedings, 1943,* pp. 400–402. See also *FCW,* XIV (January 15, 1944), 13.

7   *FCW,* XVIII (February 10, 1945), 7–9; Koebner, *Economic History Review,* 2nd series, XI (April, 1959), 381–91; Senate Subcommittee on Foreign Trade and Shipping of the Special Committee on Post-War Economic Policy and Planning, *Hearings,* 78 Cong., 2 sess., and 79 Cong., 1 sess. (Washington, 1945), Part 4, p. 711.

8   Koebner, *Economic History Review,* 2nd series, XI (April, 1959), 381–91.

9   University of Chicago Round Table (radio program), No. 8, May 9, 1943; James Fred Rippy, *Globe and Hemisphere* (Chicago, 1958), pp. 25–26.

10 Wendell C. Gordon, *International Trade* (New York, 1958), p. 48; Gunnar Myrdal, *Economic Theory and Under-Developed Regions* (London, 1957), pp. 141–46. See also A. J. Brown, *Introduction to the World Economy* (London, 1959), pp. 111–12.

11 See C. Reiser, "Latin America: Pains of Growth," *Fortune,* LVII (February, 1958), 112–19; Rippy, *Globe and Hemisphere,* pp. 50–51.

12 Carl Parrini, "The Export-Import Bank and United States Government Foreign Investment" (unpublished Master of Science essay, University of Wisconsin, 1957), pp. 16–17; *FCW,* XV (May 27, 1944), 10; *FCW,* XI (June 26, 1943), 3 ff.

13 *FCW,* XV (May 27, 1944), 10.

14 Senate Committee on Banking and Currency, *Study of the Export-Import Bank and World Bank,* 83 Cong., 2 sess. (Washington, 1954), Part 1, pp. 18, 61, 100; Roosevelt to Warren Lee Pierson, March 28, 1945, Roosevelt MSS, OF, 971.

15 Duggan, *The Americas,* p. 103; *FCW,* XIII (November 27, 1943), 9; Inter-American Economic and Financial Advisory Committee, *Handbook* (Washington, 1943), pp. 91–92.

16 Duggan, *The Americas,* pp. 84, 91; Donald M. Dozer, *Are We Good Neighbors?* (Gainesville, Florida, 1959), p. 129.

17 *New York Times,* January 13, 1960.

18 Notes on a trip to Winnipeg, May 23, 1941, Moffat MSS.

19 Joseph C. Rovensky to Taussig, October 23, 1944, Taussig MSS.

20 Harley Notter, ed., *Postwar Foreign Policy Preparation* (Washington, 1954), p. 70; Arthur P. Whitaker, ed., *Inter-American Affairs: 1942* (New York, 1943), p. 14.

21 Duggan, *The Americas,* pp. 88–91; Welles to Hull, January 19, *FR, 1942,* V, 30–32; Hull, *Memoirs,* II, 1379–80.
22 Hull, *Memoirs,* II, 1379–80; *FR, 1942,* V, 332 ff.
23 Duggan, *The Americas,* pp. 90–91; Dozer, *Are We Good Neighbors?,* p. 137; Stimson, Diary, October 20, 1942, Stimson MSS.
24 Sumner Welles, *Where Are We Heading?* (New York, 1946), p. 199, and *The Time for Decision* (New York, 1944), pp. 238–41; Duggan, *The Americas,* p. 91; Dozer, *Are We Good Neighbors?,* pp. 138–40.
25 Duggan, *The Americas,* p. 91.
26 Dozer, *Are We Good Neighbors?,* p. 140; Edwin Lieuwen, *Arms and Politics in Latin America* (New York, 1959), p. 193; Welles, *Time for Decision,* p. 237; notes of a secret meeting at the State Department, January 4, 1944, Stimson MSS.
27 Welles, *Time for Decision,* p. 239.
28 Stimson, Diary, June 23, 1944, Stimson MSS.
29 Cited in Dozer, *Are We Good Neighbors?,* p. 141.
30 Duggan, *The Americas,* p. 115.
31 Interview with Adolf Berle, December 9, 1959.
32 Cited in Dozer, *Are We Good Neighbors?,* p. 213; Grew to Hull, May 3, 1945, Grew MSS.
33 Arthur P. Whitaker, ed., *Inter-American Affairs: 1945* (Washington, 1946), p. 46; Dozer, *Are We Good Neighbors?,* p. 219.
34 *Globe and Hemisphere,* pp. 2, 47.
35 Forrestal to Hopkins, January 1, 1944, Hopkins MSS.
36 *Ibid.*
37 *SDB,* IX (July 17, 1943), 46.
38 Ickes to Roosevelt, October 8 and December 8, 1941, Ickes MSS; Roosevelt to Ickes, February 28, 1942, Roosevelt MSS, OF, 56.
39 Ickes to Roosevelt, April 17, 1942, and Roosevelt to Ickes, May 4, 1942, Roosevelt MSS, OF, 4435.
40 State Department to George Messersmith, August 6, 1942 (copy in Ickes MSS).
41 Roosevelt to Hull, November 23 and December 7, 1942, Roosevelt MSS, OF, 4435.
42 Hull to Roosevelt, December 14, 1942, Roosevelt to Welles, February 16, 1943, Welles to Roosevelt, February 17, 1943, and Roosevelt to Welles, February 19, 1943, Roosevelt MSS, OF, 4435.
43 Ickes to Roosevelt, December 21, 1943, Ickes MSS; Hull to Roosevelt, July 4, 1944, and Roosevelt to Hull, July 19, 1944, Roosevelt MSS, OF, 5528.
44 Whitaker, *Inter-American Affairs: 1942,* pp. 63–64; Stimson, Diary, June 3, 1943, Stimson MSS; memorandum of a conversation with Frank Page, December 21, 1944, Grew MSS; Edward R. Stettinius to Roosevelt, December 30, 1944, Roosevelt MSS, OF, 971.
45 Raymond Mikesell, *Foreign Investment in Latin America* (Washington, 1955), p. 66; *Fortune,* XXXI (January, 1945), 231, and XXXI (May, 1945), p. 272.

46 Roosevelt to I. Medina, September 14, 1942, Roosevelt MSS, OF, 535.

47 Welles to Roosevelt, December 30, 1942, Roosevelt to Ickes, November 4 and December 31, 1943, and Ickes to Roosevelt, April 10, 1945, Roosevelt MSS, OF, 535.

48 Duggan to Lane, November 13, 1942, and Hull to Ickes, January 19, 1943, Lane MSS.

49 James H. Wright to Lane, January 21, 1943, ibid.

50 Frank Hausermann, "Latin American Oil in War and Peace," FAQ, XXI (January, 1943), 354–61.

51 Carleton Beals, "Inside the Good Neighbor Policy," Harpers, CLXXXVII (August, 1943), 213–21.

52 I. F. Stone, "Did Hull and Welles Tell the Truth?" Nation, CLVI (January 9, 1943), 42–44.

53 Ibid.

54 Beals, Harpers, CLXXXVII (August, 1943), 213–21; Rippy, Globe and Hemisphere.

55 New York Times, October 16, 1959.

56 Cooke to Miguel Alvario Ozario de Almeida, June 30, 1943, The Papers of Morris L. Cooke, Franklin D. Roosevelt Library, Hyde Park, New York.

57 James H. Causey to Cooke, September 17, 1942, ibid.

58 Frank Oram to Alex Tennant, October 15, 1942, ibid.; memorandum of a conversation with Adolf Berle, June 26, 1941, Moffat MSS.

59 Press release, December 1, 1942, and Cooke to State Department, June 1, 1943, Cooke Papers; interview with Adolf Berle, December 9, 1959.

60 Memoranda of conversations with President Truman, Ambassador Martins, and Mr. Chalmers, June 13, 1945, Grew MSS.

61 Dozer, Are We Good Neighbors?, p. 242.

62 Mikesell, Foreign Investments in Latin America, pp. 110–17.

63 "Decline of the Good Neighbor," Time, XLIV (October 9, 1943), 18–19; memorandum of a conversation, January 8, 1945, Yalta Papers, p. 67; Duggan, The Americas, p. 78; SDB, XII (January 21, 1945), 94–95.

64 Whitaker, Inter-American Affairs: 1945, pp. 13, 116; SDB, XII (April 8, 1945), 627; Olive Holmes, "American Nations Seek Common Ground in Postwar Planning," Foreign Policy Bulletin, XXIV (March 23, 1945), 1–2; Duggan, The Americas, p. 78.

65 Congressional Record (March 12, 1945), 79 Cong., 1 sess., XCI, 2027.

66 Leahy, Diary, March 29, September 6, 12, 1945, Leahy MSS.

67 S. F. Bonsal to Lane, December 9, 1943, and January 7, 1944, Lane MSS.

68 Lane to Paul Daniels, November 20, 1944, ibid.; Stimson, Diary, April 26, 1945, Stimson MSS; memorandum of a conversation with John J. McCloy, May 8, 1945, ibid.

69 Stimson, Diary, June 26–30, 1945, Stimson MSS; Lieuwen, Arms in Latin America, pp. 223–24, 237–38.

70 Louis Halle, "Whom Does the Cavalry Support?" *New Republic,* CXLII (May, 1960), 13–14.

Chapter 11

1 John A. Loftus, "Petroleum in International Relations," *SDB,* XIII (August 5, 1945), 173–77.

2 Memorandum by the Acting Chief of the Division of African Affairs, July 6, 1945, *Potsdam Papers,* I, 997–98. See also *SDB,* IX (August 21, 1943), 103–10.

3 Elihu Root to Henry White, November 28, 1905, *FR, 1905,* pp. 678–79.

4 Bainbridge Colby to American Minister in Persia, August 16, 1920, cited in William Appleman Williams, *America and the Middle East* (New York, 1958), p. 35. See also Herbert Feis, *Petroleum and American Foreign Policy* (Stanford, 1944), pp. 4–6.

5 Henry L. Stimson, "Important Accomplishments in the Countries of the Near East," pp. 1–7, special memorandum in Stimson MSS; John W. Frey and H. Chandler Ide, *A History of the Petroleum Administration for War, 1941–1945* (Washington, 1946), pp. 281–85; Harvey O'Connor, *The Empire of Oil* (New York, 1956), p. 271 ff.

6 *SDB,* IX (August 21, 1943), 103–10.

7 Stimson, Diary, October 29, 1933, Stimson MSS. For examples of the effort to protect the Open Door Policy in the Near East and Africa in the 1930's, see memorandum to William Phillips, May 22, 1934, Moffat MSS; Hull to Robert W. Bingham, October 23, 1936, *FR, 1936,* I, 734–35; R. Walton Moore to William Bullitt, January 25, 1940, *FR, 1940,* III, 928–30.

8 *FCW,* VI (March 14, 1942), 5.

9 Alexander Kirk to Hull, May 12, 1941, Adolf A. Berle to Kirk, September 5, 1941, Kirk to Hull, October 15, 1941, and Hull to Kirk, October 25 and December 10, 1941, *FR, 1941,* III, 304, 313–14, 316; memorandum of a conversation, July 9, 1945, and memorandum relating to aviation matters, July 9, 1945, Grew MSS; *Congressional Record* (February 10, 1945), 79 Cong., 1 sess., XCI, 1222–23.

10 Memorandum of a conversation, April 14, 1941, Wallace Murray to L. Dreyfus, January 28, 1941, and Dreyfus to Hull, July 5, 1941, *FR, 1941,* III, 194–95, 255–57, 260–61; memorandum by Murray, February 13, 1941, and Near Eastern Affairs to Welles, October 14, 1941, *ibid.,* II, 258–60, 446–47.

11 H. F. Matthews to Leahy, December 10, 1942, Leahy MSS; Leahy, Diary, February 10, 1943, *ibid.;* Roosevelt to Dwight D. Eisenhower, June 17, 1943, *ibid.;* Hull, *Memoirs,* II, 1500.

12 Press Conference 879, February 12, 1943, Roosevelt MSS, PPF-1P; Welles to Roosevelt, March 5, 1943, and Roosevelt to Welles, March 8, 1943, Roosevelt MSS, PSF.

13 "Cairo Questionaire," *Time,* XLII (October 18, 1943), 20.

14 James M. Landis, "Anglo-American Cooperation in the Middle East,"

Vital Speeches, XI (May 1, 1945), 428–32; *Congressional Record* (February 10, 1945), 79 Cong., 1 sess., XCI, 1222–23.

15 Roosevelt to Acting Secretary of State, February 12, 1944, Roosevelt MSS, OF, 4117.

16 Roosevelt to James M. Landis, January 11, 1945, Roosevelt MSS, OF, 423.

17 *SDB,* X (February 26, 1944), 204; *FCW,* XV (April 1, 1944), 3, 37–38.

18 *SDB,* XI (December 10, 1944), 720–22; *SDB,* XII (January 21, 1945), 81; Hull to Roosevelt, July 20, 1944, Roosevelt MSS, OF, 5572.

19 Hull to Roosevelt, July 20, 1944, Roosevelt MSS, OF, 5572.

20 *SDB,* XII (February 25, 1945), 299–300.

21 *Congressional Record* (February 10, 1945), 79 Cong., 1 sess., XCI, 1225–28.

22 Memorandum of a conversation, March 10, 1945, Grew MSS.

23 Welles to Roosevelt, September 1, 1942, Roosevelt MSS, OF, 2418; Charles de Gaulle, *Memoirs, Unity, 1942–1944* (New York, 1959), 22–26.

24 Edward R. Stettinius to Roosevelt, October 30 and November 1, 1943, Roosevelt MSS, PSF; Roosevelt to Hull, January 24 and February 8, 1944, Roosevelt, *Letters,* II, 1490, 1493.

25 Stettinius to Roosevelt, August 9, 1944, Roosevelt MSS, OF, 2418; Hull, *Memoirs,* II, 1546; S. Kuwaitly to Roosevelt, September 19, 1944, Roosevelt MSS, OF, 2418.

26 Charles Eade, comp., *Victory: War Speeches by the Right Hon. Winston S. Churchill* (Boston, 1946), pp. 80–81.

27 Memorandum of a conversation, March 10, 1945, Grew MSS; Kuwaitly to Roosevelt, April 2, 1945, Roosevelt MSS, OF, 2418; memorandum of a conversation, May 19, 1945, Grew MSS; *Potsdam Papers,* I, 959; William D. Leahy, *I Was There* (New York, 1950), p. 373; Winston S. Churchill, *Triumph and Tragedy* (Boston, 1953), pp. 561–66; memorandum of a conversation with Dr. Costi K. Zurayk, May 31, 1945, Grew MSS; Draft message from the President to General de Gaulle, May 29(?), 1945, Grew MSS.

28 Memorandum of a conversation with the President, June 1, 1945, and Grew to Stettinius, June 18, 1945, Grew MSS; *Potsdam Papers,* I, 959–60; Department of State minutes, July 23, 1945, *Potsdam Papers,* II, 299–308.

29 Department of State minutes, July 23, 1945, *Potsdam Papers,* II, 299–308.

30 Memorandum by George V. Allen, July 24, 1945, *ibid.,* II, 317–19; Herbert Feis, *Between War and Peace: The Potsdam Conference* (Princeton, 1960), pp. 291–95; *Potsdam Papers,* I, 1010–14.

31 *Potsdam Papers,* I, 1028–54; Feis, *Between War and Peace,* pp. 294–99; Thompson minutes, July 22, 1945, and Department of State minutes, July 23, 1945, *Potsdam Papers,* II, 244–60, 300–311.

32 *Potsdam Papers,* II, 527, 577, 1434, 1437; Feis, *Between War and Peace,* pp. 299–301.

33 Feis, *Between War and Peace,* pp. 306–8; James F. Byrnes, *Speaking Frankly* (New York, 1947), pp. 76, 94–96; Walter Millis, ed., *The Forrestal Diaries* (New York, 1951), p. 103; Sumner Welles, *Where Are We Heading?* (New York, 1946), p. 68.

34 Arthur C. Millspaugh, *Americans in Persia* (Washington, 1947), p. 236; Welles, *Where Are We Heading?,* pp. 262–63; Don Lohbeck, *Patrick J. Hurley* (Chicago, 1956), p. 238.

35 Memorandum of a conversation, October 10, 1941, and memorandum by the Chief of the Division of Near Eastern Affairs, November 5, 1941, *FR, 1941,* III, 374–76, 373. See also *ibid.,* III, 377, 378–79, 381–82.

36 Memorandum of a conversation, January 13, 1942, cited in T. H. Vail Motter, *The Persian Gulf Corridor and Aid to Russia,* in *United States Army in World War II* (Washington, 1952), pp. 288–90.

37 *Ibid.*

38 *Ibid.,* pp. 162–63; Millspaugh, *Americans in Persia,* pp. 47–48, 222.

39 Robert E. Sherwood, *Roosevelt and Hopkins: An Intimate History* (2nd ed.; New York, 1950), pp. 558–59; Vail Motter, *Persian Gulf Corridor,* pp. 156–57, 170.

40 Lohbeck, *Patrick J. Hurley,* pp. 195–96; Hull, *Memoirs,* II, 1503–4. See also Arabian Oil Hearings, p. 25430.

41 Stettinius to Roosevelt, October 29, 1943, Roosevelt MSS, PSF.

42 Vail Motter, *Persian Gulf Corridor,* pp. 442–47; Lohbeck, *Patrick J. Hurley,* pp. 221–28; Millspaugh, *Americans in Persia,* p. 8.

43 Edward R. Stettinius, *Roosevelt and the Russians* (New York, 1949), pp. 180–81; Roosevelt to Mrs. L. Stuyvesant Chandler, January 12, 1944, Roosevelt MSS, OF, 4678.

44 Vail Motter, *Persian Gulf Corridor,* pp. 445–46, 471–75; *SDB,* X (February 12, 1944), 181; Roosevelt to Patrick Hurley, March 25, 1944, Roosevelt, *Letters,* II, 1503; Leahy, *I Was There,* p. 226.

45 Millspaugh, *Americans in Persia,* p. 233; *SDB,* XI (July 23, 1944), 90–92.

46 Herbert Feis, *Seen from E. A.* (New York, 1947), pp. 175–78.

47 *Fortune,* XXXI (January, 1945), 231.

48 W. Averell Harriman to Stettinius, December 28, 1944, *Yalta Papers,* p. 65.

49 Stettinius to Roosevelt, January 18, 1945, *ibid.,* p. 43; Stettinius, *Roosevelt and the Russians,* pp. 65–66.

50 Memorandum of a conversation, January 31, 1945, Grew MSS; minutes of a Foreign Ministers meeting, February 1, 1945, *Yalta Papers,* p. 501.

51 Stettinius, *Roosevelt and the Russians,* pp. 171–81; Welles, *Where Are We Heading?,* p. 258; Charles Bohlen minutes of fourth Plenary Meet-

ing, February 7, 1945, and minutes of Foreign Ministers meeting, February 8, 1945, *Yalta Papers,* pp. 715, 739–40.

52 Feis, *Between War and Peace,* pp. 302–4; Millspaugh, *Americans in Persia,* p. 228; J. C. Hurewitz, *Middle East Dilemmas* (New York, 1953), p. 29; Halford L. Hoskins, *Middle East Oil in United States Foreign Policy* (Washington, 1950), p. 60.

53 Hoskins, *Middle East Oil,* p. 60.

54 Memoranda of conversations, May 28 and 29, 1945, Grew MSS; *New York Times,* December 5, 1959.

55 "Mr. Ickes' Arabian Nights," *Fortune,* XXIX (June, 1944), 123 ff.

56 Hull to Roosevelt, June 30, 1939, Roosevelt MSS, OF, 3500; Welles, *Where Are We Heading?,* p. 262; Benjamin Shwadran, *The Middle East, Oil, and the Great Powers* (New York, 1955), p. 290.

57 Hull to Roosevelt, June 30, 1939, Roosevelt MSS, OF, 3500.

58 Arabian Oil Hearings, pp. 24170, 24724, 24741, 24805, 24813.

59 *Ibid.*

60 *Ibid.,* pp. 24715, 24724, 24725, 24813, 24744, 25415, 25371.

61 *Ibid.*

62 *Ibid.,* pp. 24805, 24814, 24860, 25232–34.

63 *Ibid.*

64 Roosevelt to Stettinius, February 18, 1943, and Hull to Roosevelt, March 30, 1943, Roosevelt MSS, OF, 3500.

65 Byrnes to Roosevelt, October 4, 1943, Roosevelt MSS, OF, 56; Frey and Ide, *Petroleum Administration for War,* p. 276; Stimson, Diary, June 8, 1943, Stimson MSS.

66 Arabian Oil Hearings, pp. 25240–41; Leahy, *I Was There,* p. 184; Stimson, Diary, June 4, 9, 11, and 15, 1943, Stimson MSS; memorandum for the Secretary of War, June 11, 1943, Stimson MSS; Feis, *Seen from E. A.,* pp. 117–18.

67 Welles, *Where Are We Heading?,* p. 262; Arabian Oil Hearings, pp. 25243–44, 25275; Feis, *Seen From E. A.,* pp. 143, 148.

68 Frye and Ide, *Petroleum Administration for War,* pp. 278–79; Orville Harden to Ickes, November 5, 1943, Ickes MSS. See also James F. Byrnes to Roosevelt, January 17, 1944, Roosevelt MSS, OF, 3500; Feis, *Petroleum and American Foreign Policy,* p. 45.

69 Arabian Oil Hearings, pp. 24846, 25209; Stettinius to Roosevelt, October 30, 1943, Roosevelt MSS, OF, 56; Hull, *Memoirs,* II, 1521–22.

70 Ickes to Roosevelt, August 7, 1944, Roosevelt MSS, OF, 5588.

71 Hopkins to Roosevelt, August 5, 1944, Hopkins MSS; Frey and Ide, *Petroleum Administration for War,* pp. 281–86.

Chapter 12

1 China White Paper, pp. 34–37.

2 George Kennan, *Russia and the West under Lenin and Stalin* (Boston, 1961), p. 374 *et passim.* See also George Kennan, *American Foreign*

Policy Since 1900 (Chicago, 1951); Sumner Welles, *Where Are We Heading?* (New York, 1946), pp. 299–300; Herbert Feis, *The China Tangle* (Princeton, 1953), p. 252.

3 *Washington Post*, April 7, 1942; "The Time Is Now," *Fortune*, XXIV (September, 1941), 42–43.

4 James Roosevelt to Hopkins, August 22, 1941, Roosevelt MSS, PSF; Roosevelt to Morgenthau, December 6, 1934, *ibid.;* Robert E. Sherwood, *Roosevelt and Hopkins: An Intimate History* (2nd ed.; New York, 1950), p. 578.

5 Joseph Stilwell to Stimson, June 27, 1942, Stimson MSS.

6 See Feis, *China Tangle*, p. 137.

7 Richard M. Leighton and Robert W. Coakely, *Global Logistics and Strategy, 1940–1943*, in *United States Army in World War II*, p. 525.

8 Charles F. Romanus and Riley Sunderland, *Stilwell's Mission to China*, in *United States Army in World War II* (Washington, 1953), pp. 62, 85; memorandum of a conversation, January 21, 1942, and Roosevelt to Chiang Kai-shek, March 11, 1942, *FR: China, 1942*, pp. 7, 29.

9 Theodore White, ed., *The Stilwell Papers*, (New York, 1948), pp. 204–5; Romanus and Sunderland, *Stilwell's Mission to China*, p. 279; Sumner Welles, *Seven Decisions That Shaped History* (New York, 1951), p. 150.

10 Maurice Matloff and Edwin M. Snell, *Strategic Planning for Coalition Warfare*, in *United States Army in World War II* (Washington, 1955), p. 205; Chiang Kai-shek to T. V. Soong, April 19, 1942, *FR: China, 1942*, pp. 33–34; Romanus and Sunderland, *Stilwell's Mission to China*, pp. 171, 175.

11 Romanus and Sunderland, *Stilwell's Mission to China*, pp. 171, 175; Soong to Hopkins, May 13, 1943, Roosevelt MSS, OF, 56.

12 Don Lohbeck, *Patrick J. Hurley* (Chicago, 1956), pp. 291–93. See also White, *Stilwell Papers*, for the events which led up to this interview.

13 *Yalta Papers*, p. 589.

14 Sherwood, *Roosevelt and Hopkins*, pp. 716–17.

15 The best account of these developments is in Wesley R. Fishel, *The End of Extra-territoriality in China* (Berkeley, 1952), p. 219 *et passim.*

16 *Ibid.*, p. 193; memorandum by Walter Adams, March 19, 1942, *FR: China, 1942*, pp. 270–71.

17 Hull to John G. Winant, August 27 and September 1, 1942, *FR: China, 1942*, pp. 282, 287–88. See also Feis, *China Tangle*, p. 62; Hull, *Memoirs*, II, 1583.

18 *FR: China, 1942*, pp. 312, 334–35; *American Journal of International Law*, XXXVII (April, 1943), 286–89; Jesse Jones to Roosevelt, October 18, 1943, Roosevelt MSS, OF, 172-B.

19 NFTC *Proceedings, 1944*, pp. 194–95, 215.

20 Memorandum of a conversation by the Secretary of State, February 25, 1943, *FR: China, 1943*, pp. 11–12.

21 Sherwood, *Roosevelt and Hopkins,* pp. 718–19; Edward Frederick Lindley Wood, "FDR Wanted George VI to Give Hong-Kong to China," *Ladies Home Journal,* LXXIV (March, 1957), 31–44; Sumner Welles, "Roosevelt and the Far East: II," *Harpers,* CCII (March, 1951), 70–80; White, *Stilwell Papers,* pp. 252–54.

22 William D. Leahy, *I Was There* (New York, 1950), p. 314.

23 Stimson, Diary, November 30, 1943, Stimson MSS; Hull, *Memoirs,* II, 1257; Roosevelt to Hull, October 28, 1943, *Teheran Papers,* p. 49.

24 Minutes of a meeting with the Joint Chiefs of Staff, November 19, 1943, *Teheran Papers,* p. 257; minutes of a meeting with the Combined Chiefs of Staff, November 24, 1943, *ibid.,* pp. 323–24.

25 Charles E. Bohlen minutes of second Roosevelt-Stalin meeting, November 29, 1943, *ibid.,* p. 532; Chinese notes of Roosevelt-Chiang meeting, November 23, 1943, *ibid.,* pp. 323–24.

26 *Ibid.,* p. 401; Hopkins memorandum on Russian interests in China, November 29, 1943, *ibid.,* p. 376; minutes of Pacific War Council meeting, January 12, 1944, *ibid.,* p. 869. See also Patrick Hurley to Roosevelt, November 20, 1943, *ibid.,* pp. 102–3; minutes of Tripartite Luncheons, November 30 and December 1, 1943, *ibid.,* pp. 567, 589.

27 Memorandum of a conversation by the Secretary of State, June 28, 1943, *FR: China, 1943,* pp. 65–67; R. G. Atherton to Secretary of State, May 28, 1943, *ibid.,* pp. 57–59.

28 Clarence Gauss to Hull, January 8, 1942, Hull to Morgenthau, January 10, 1942, and memorandum of a conversation, January 30, 1942, China White Paper, pp. 473–76.

29 *Ibid.*

30 Morgenthau to Roosevelt, December 11, 1943, *ibid.,* pp. 488–89; Gauss to Hull, December 9, 1943, *FR: China, 1943,* pp. 476–79.

31 Gauss to Hull, December 9, 1943, *FR: China, 1943,* pp. 476–79.

32 *Ibid.*

33 State Department memorandum, December 27, 1943, *ibid.,* pp. 484–89; Feis, *China Tangle,* pp. 121–23.

34 Feis, *China Tangle,* pp. 121–23. See also *FR: China, 1943,* pp. 180–82.

35 Welles, *Where Are We Heading?,* pp. 300–301.

36 Harry L. Hopkins, "What Victory Will Bring Us," *American Magazine,* CXXXVIII (January, 1944), 20–21, 87–89.

37 Francis Sayre, "Freedom Comes to the Philippines," *Atlantic Monthly,* CLXXV (March, 1945), 82–88.

38 Senate Committee on Foreign Relations, *Hearings on Nominations—Department of State,* 78 Cong., 2 sess. (Washington, 1944), p. 74; *SDB,* XII (March 11, 1945), 404.

39 Theodore White, "China's Postwar Plans," *Fortune,* XXVIII (October, 1943), 150 ff.

40 Draft telegram, Richard Patterson to Henry A. Wallace, July 7, 1944,

Grew MSS; NFTC *Proceedings, 1944,* pp. 189, 222–23; Charles H. Behre and Kung-Ping Wang, "China's Mineral Wealth," *FAQ,* XXIII (October, 1944), 130–39.

41 Grew to Gauss, August 16, 1944, Grew MSS; Stimson, Diary, June 23, 1944, Stimson MSS.
42 Feis, *China Tangle,* p. 157; notes by John Carter Vincent, June 21, 1944, China White Paper, pp. 549–51.
43 Roosevelt to Donald M. Nelson, August 18, 1944, Roosevelt, *Letters,* II, 1529–30; Chiang Kai-shek to Roosevelt, December 1, 1944, Roosevelt MSS, PPF, 7308; Nelson to Roosevelt, March 19, 1945, Roosevelt MSS.
44 Grew to Nelson, January 15, 1945, Grew MSS; Bruce Catton, *The War Lords of Washington* (New York, 1948), pp. 284–86.
45 Henry Grady to Roosevelt, December 9, 1944, and Roosevelt to Grady, December 16, 1944, Roosevelt MSS, PPF, 3658.
46 Feis, *China Tangle,* pp. 261–62, 202, 232–33.
47 *Yalta Papers,* pp. 352–57.
48 Bohlen notes, February 8, 1945, *ibid.,* pp. 769 ff.
49 Stimson, Diary, March 8, 1945, Stimson MSS; Feis, *China Tangle,* p. 280; Stettinius to Hurley, April 23, 1945, Feis, *China Tangle,* p. 288; Tien fong-Cheng, *A History of Sino-Russian Relations* (Washington, 1957), p. 258; Harold M. Vinacke, *The United States and the Far East, 1945–1951* (Stanford, 1952).
50 Department of Defense, *The Entry of the Soviet Union into the War against Japan: Military Plans 1941–1945* (Washington, 1955), p. 67.
51 *Ibid.; Fortune,* XXXI (April, 1945), 109 ff.
52 Memorandum of a conversation with Stettinius, McCloy, and Harriman, May 12, 1945, Grew MSS; Grew to Stimson, May 12, 1945, *Entry of the Soviet Union into the War against Japan,* pp. 69–70. See also memorandum of a conversation with the President, May 15, 1945, Grew MSS.
53 Stimson, Diary, May 13 and 15, 1945, Stimson MSS.
54 Herbert Hoover to Stimson, May 15, 1945, *ibid.*
55 Stimson to John J. McCloy, May 19, 1945, *ibid.;* Stimson to Grew, May 21, 1945, Grew MSS; Feis, *China Tangle,* p. 307.
56 Grew to McCloy, May 21, 1945, Grew MSS.
57 Memorandum of a conversation by Bohlen, May 28, 1945, *Potsdam Papers,* I, 42–43; Hopkins to President Truman, May 29, 1945, *Entry of the Soviet Union into the War against Japan,* p. 73; Feis, *China Tangle,* p. 310.
58 Grew to Hopkins, June 6, 1945, Grew MSS; memorandum of a talk with the President, June 6, 1945, Stimson MSS.
59 Memorandum of a conversation with President Truman and Dr. T. V. Soong, June 9, 1945, Grew MSS; Leahy, Diary, June 9, 1945, Leahy MSS; memorandum of a conversation with Soong, June 11, 1945, and

memorandum of a conversation with Bohlen, Soong, and the President, June 14, 1945, Grew MSS. See also memorandum of a conversation, June 6, 1945, *Potsdam Papers,* I, 176.

60   Feis, *China Tangle,* p. 320; Harriman to Truman, July 8, 1945, *Potsdam Papers,* I, 234.

61   Minutes of a meeting held at the White House, June 18, 1945, *Potsdam Papers,* I, 903–10; *ibid.,* I, 858–60; Truman to Stalin, July 31, 1945, *ibid.,* II, 1333–34; *ibid.,* I, 858–72.

62   See all references in note 61 above.

63   Stimson, Diary, July 15, 1945, Stimson MSS; Stimson to Byrnes, July 16, 1945, *Potsdam Papers,* II, 1223–24, 631, 1265–66, 1322–23.

64   Memorandum by Special Assistant to the Secretary of State, March 28, 1960, *Potsdam Papers,* II, 1582–87; Stimson, Diary, July 17, 1945, Stimson MSS; Leahy, Diary, July 17, 1945, Leahy MSS; Feis, *China Tangle,* pp. 328–29; Harrison to Stimson, July 17, 1945, *Potsdam Papers,* II, 1360–65; Stimson, Diary, July 18, 1945, Stimson MSS.

65   Truman to Hurley, July 23, 1945, *Potsdam Papers,* II, 1244; John Carter Vincent to Dunn, July 23, 1945, *ibid.,* II, 1241–43; Stimson, Diary, July 23, 1945, Stimson MSS; James Byrnes, *All in One Lifetime* (New York, 1959), p. 291; Walter Millis, ed., *The Forrestal Diaries* (New York, 1951), p. 78; Byrnes-Churchill conversation, July 23, 1945, *Potsdam Papers,* II, 276.

66   Millis, *Forrestal Diaries,* p. 78.

67   Stimson, Diary, June 24, 1945, Stimson MSS.

68   Byrnes, *All in One Lifetime,* p. 304; Feis, *China Tangle,* p. 330, 342–44; Truman, *Memoirs,* I, 423–27; Byrnes to Harriman, August 22, 1945, China White Paper, p. 119; Truman, *Memoirs,* I, 447–50.

69   Leahy, Diary, September 11 and October 24, 1945, Leahy MSS.

70   Grew to Barrett Wendell, November 16, 1945, Grew MSS; Arthur Bryant, *Triumph in the West* (New York, 1960), p. 389; Feis, *China Tangle,* p. 418.

71   Cited in William Appleman Williams, *The Shaping of American Diplomacy* (Chicago, 1956), pp. 1104–5.

72   Everett F. Drumwright to Alfred Kohlberg, September 3, 1946, Villard MSS.

Chapter 13

1   *New York Times,* March 15, 1962.

2   Bullitt to Hull, January 17, 1938, Davis MSS; William C. Bullitt, *The Great Globe Itself* (New York, 1946), p. 121.

3   See Richard N. Gardner, *Sterling-Dollar Diplomacy* (Oxford, 1956).

4   Gilbert Fite, *George N. Peek and the Fight for Farm Parity* (Norman, Oklahoma, 1954), p. 298.

5   Harley Notter, ed., *Postwar Foreign Policy Preparation* (Washington, 1954), pp. 355–56; Herbert Feis, "Economics and Peace," *Foreign Policy Reports,* XX (April, 1944), 14–19.

6 Will Clayton to Hopkins, November 18, 1944, and Hopkins to Clayton, November 20, 1944, Hopkins MSS.

7 Harry L. Hopkins, "What Victory Will Bring Us," *American Magazine,* CXXXVIII (January, 1944), 20–21, 87–89.

8 Rexford Tugwell, "The Compromising Roosevelt," *Western Political Quarterly,* VI (June, 1953), 320–41; New York *Herald Tribune,* May 20, 1944.

9 Robert E. Sherwood, *Roosevelt and Hopkins: An Intimate History* (2nd ed.; New York, 1950), pp. 359–60, 572–73.

10 *Ibid.,* pp. 711–18.

11 *Ibid.*

12 Memorandum of a conference between the Secretary of War, the Secretary of State, and the Secretary of the Navy, May 11, 1943, Stimson MSS; Hull, *Memoirs,* II, 1644–66.

13 Hull, *Memoirs,* II, 1644–66.

14 Charles E. Bohlen minutes of Roosevelt-Stalin meeting, November 29, 1943, *Teheran Papers,* pp. 529–33; William D. Leahy, *I Was There* (New York, 1950), p. 208–9, 265–66.

15 Sherwood, *Roosevelt and Hopkins,* pp. 832–34.

16 *Potsdam Papers,* I, 256–66; Senate Special Committee on Post-War Economic Policy and Planning, *Problems of Foreign Trade and Shipping,* 79 Cong., 1 sess. (Washington, 1945), Part 4, pp. 774–75.

17 Hull, *Memoirs,* II, 1265–66, 1286–87; Stimson, Diary, December 18, 1943; Stimson MSS.

18 Walter Millis, ed., *The Forrestal Diaries* (New York, 1951), p. 10.

19 Memorandum of a conversation with Anthony Eden, John G. Winant, and Henry Morgenthau, August 13, 1944, White MSS.

20 Copies in White MSS and Stimson MSS, September 7 and 8, 1944.

21 Stimson, Diary, September 5, 1944, Stimson MSS; Stimson to Roosevelt, September 15, 1944, *ibid.*

22 Notes by Assistant Secretary McCloy, September 20, 1944, *ibid.;* Stimson, Diary, September 27, 1944, *ibid.;* Hull, *Memoirs,* II, 1615–21.

23 Hull, *Memoirs,* II, 1606–14.

24 Sherwood, *Roosevelt and Hopkins,* pp. 818–19; undated Briefing Book paper, *Potsdam Papers,* I, 435–50.

25 Department of State minutes, July 21, 1945, *Potsdam Papers,* I, 203–15.

26 Matthew Josephson, *Empire of the Air* (New York, 1944), pp. 3, 202–3; Henry Wallace, *Sixty Million Jobs* (New York, 1945), p. 138.

27 Feis, *Foreign Policy Reports,* XX (April, 1944), 14–19.

28 J. Parker Van Zandt, *Civil Aviation and Peace* (Washington, 1944), p. 15; "Logic of the Air," *Fortune,* XXVII (April, 1943), 70–74, 188–90, 192, 194; Ickes, *Secret Diary,* III, 459–60.

29 Senate Subcommittee of the Committee on Appropriations, *Hearings on Treasury and Post Office Departments Appropriation Bill, 1942,* 77 Cong., 1 sess. (Washington, 1941), pp. 64, 115.

30 *Ibid.,* pp. 117–28.

31 Leahy, Diary, August 31, 1942, Leahy MSS; Josephson, *Empire of the Air,* p. 219; Adolf Berle to Roosevelt, October 29, 1943, Roosevelt MSS, PSF.

32 House Committee on Foreign Affairs, *Hearings on Extension of the Lend-Lease Act, 1943,* 78 Cong., 1 sess. (Washington, 1943), p. 123.

33 Josephson, *Empire of the Air,* p. 11; *New York Times,* March 21, 1943.

34 Hopkins, *American Magazine,* CXXXVIII (January, 1944), 20–21, 87–89.

35 Leahy, Diary, August 31, 1943, Leahy MSS; Josephson, *Empire of the Air,* p. 11.

36 *New York Times,* October 2, 1943; memorandum of a conversation, November 11, 1943, *Teheran Papers,* pp. 177–79; Roosevelt to Hull, May 20, 1944, Roosevelt, *Letters,* II, 1511–12.

37 House Committee on Foreign Affairs, *Extension of the Lend-Lease Act, 1943,* pp. 204, 210, 215–16, 228–29.

38 Department of State, *Proceedings of the International Civil Aviation Conference* (2 vols.; Washington, 1949), I, 462, 55–62.

39 Leahy, *I Was There,* p. 280.

40 Department of State, *International Civil Aviation Conference,* I, 501–2; Sumner Welles, *The Time for Decision* (New York, 1944), p. 410.

41 Department of State, *International Civil Aviation Conference,* I, 4, 494–96; *FCW,* XVIII (February 17, 1945), 36; Millis, *Forrestal Diaries,* p. 19; memorandum of a conversation with President Truman, June 5, 1945, Grew MSS; Truman, *Memoirs,* I, 440–41; memorandum of a conversation with the President and William L. Clayton, May 7, 1945, Grew MSS.

42 Memorandum of a conversation with the President and Clayton, May 7, 1945, Grew MSS; interview with Berle, December 9, 1959.

43 Stimson, Diary, November 5, 1943, Stimson MSS.

44 Speech before the Merchants Association of New York, January 28, 1941 (copy in Davis MSS).

45 Nancy Harvison Hooker, ed. *The Moffat Papers* (Cambridge, Mass., 1956), pp. 350–53.

46 Lord Halifax to Hull, enclosing Keynes's memorandum of May 23, 1941, Roosevelt MSS, OF, 48.

47 Roosevelt to E. M. Watson, May 26, 1941, Roosevelt MSS, OF, 48; memorandum of a conversation, June 20, 1941, Roosevelt MSS, PSF; Berle to Roosevelt, June 21, 1941, and Roosevelt to Berle, June 26, 1941, Roosevelt MSS, PSF.

48 Memorandum by the Assistant Secretary of State, July 28, 1941, *FR, 1941,* III, 10–12; Gardner, *Sterling-Dollar Diplomacy,* pp. 41–42, 56–57.

49 See all references in note 48 above.

50 Maynard Keynes to Acheson, July 29, 1941, and Harry Hawkins to Acheson, August 1, 1941, *FR, 1941,* III, 16–17, 19–22.

51 Hull to Halifax, May 21, 1941, *ibid.*, III, 121.
52 Memorandum of a conversation, August 9, 1941, *ibid.*, I, 353.
53 See Gardner, *Sterling-Dollar Diplomacy*, pp. 43–47.
54 *Ibid.*, p. 46; Moffat, Diary, September 4, 1941, Moffat MSS.
55 Gardner, *Sterling-Dollar Diplomacy*, pp. 61–62.
56 *Ibid.*
57 Hull, *Memoirs*, II, 1152–53; Hull to Winant, January 30, 1942, *FR, 1942*, I, 525–27.
58 Hull to Winant, January 30, 1942, *FR, 1942*, I, 525–37.
59 Hull, *Memoirs*, II, 1153.
60 Herbert Feis, "Restoring Trade After the War," *FAQ*, XX (January, 1942), 282–92; House Committee on Foreign Affairs, *Extension of the Lend-Lease Act, 1943*, p. 109
61 Copy enclosed in letter to Roosevelt, September 15, 1943, Roosevelt MSS, PPF, 1483.
62 Gardner, *Sterling-Dollar Diplomacy*, pp. 101–9; copy of Council pamphlet, Hopkins MSS; Thomas Balogh, "The League of Nations on Post-War Foreign Trade Problems," *Economic Journal*, LIV (June 1944), 256–61.
63 Memorandum of a conversation, November 17, 1943, and Bucknell to Hull, May 13, 1944, White MSS.
64 Bucknell to Hull, May 13, 1944, *ibid.*
65 Howard P. Whidden, "Reaching a Lend-Lease Settlement," *Foreign Policy Reports*, XX (April 15, 1944), 22–31.
66 C. Hartley Gratton and George R. Leighton, "The Future of Foreign Trade," *Harpers*, CLXXXIX (August, 1944), 193–202; Senate Special Committee on Post-War Economic Policy and Planning, *Economic Problems of the Transition Period*, 78 Cong., 2 sess., and 79 Cong., 1 sess. (Washington, 1945), pp. 497–514.
67 Senate Special Committee, *Economic Problems of the Transition Period*, p. 1082.
68 Roosevelt to Leo Crowley, September 28, 1944, Roosevelt MSS, OF, 5430.
69 Gunnar Myrdal, "Is American Business Deluding Itself?" *Atlantic Monthly*, CLXXIV (November, 1944), 51–58.
70 Sherwood, *Roosevelt and Hopkins*, p. 817; memorandum of a conversation, September 20, 1944, *Yalta Papers*, p. 135.
71 Stettinius to Roosevelt, February 10, 1945, *Yalta Papers*, p. 962; memorandum of a conversation with the Earl of Halifax, February 16, 1945, Grew MSS; John Biggs-Davison, *The Uncertain Ally* (London, 1955).
72 Gardner, *Sterling-Dollar Diplomacy*, pp. 145–62.
73 *Congressional Record* (March 16, 1945), 79 Cong., 1 sess., XCI, Part 11, A 1656–58, and Part 6, 7557.
74 The original plans can be compared in "Discussions Regarding Postwar Economic and Financial Arrangements," *FR, 1942*, I, 163–242;

and a detailed commentary is in Gardner, *Sterling-Dollar Diplomacy,* Chapter 5. See also a Treasury comparison of the plans, dated October 19, 1942, White MSS.

75 Memorandum of a conversation by the Assistant Secretary of State, October 6, 1942, *FR, 1942,* I, 224–25.

76 Gardner, *Sterling-Dollar Diplomacy,* pp. 112, 120–21, 125.

77 *Ibid.,* pp. 131–37

78 Herbert Feis, *The Sinews of Peace* (New York, 1944), p. 90, and "Economics and Peace," *Foreign Policy Reports,* XX (April, 1944), 14–19.

79 Roosevelt to Conference, June 29, 1944, Roosevelt MSS, OF, 5544.

80 "The Bretton Woods Proposals," undated memorandum, Roosevelt MSS, OF, 5544.

81 Gardner, *Sterling-Dollar Diplomacy,* p. 137.

82 House Committee on Banking and Currency, *Bretton Woods Agreements Act,* 79 Cong., 1 sess. (Washington, 1945), p. 48.

83 Karl Schriftgeisser, *Business Comes of Age* (New York, 1960), pp. 65, 125; David S. McLellan and Charles E. Woodhouse, "The Business Elite and Foreign Policy," *Western Political Quarterly,* XIII (March, 1960), 172–90.

84 Senate Committee on Banking and Currency, *Study of the Export-Import Bank and World Bank,* 83 Cong., 2 sess. (Washington, 1954), Part 1, pp. 20–21.

85 Gardner, *Sterling-Dollar Diplomacy,* Chapter 11; Biggs-Davison, *Uncertain Ally,* pp. 106–7; Millis, *Forrestal Diaries,* p. 246.

86 Biggs-Davison, *Uncertain Ally,* pp. 106–7.

87 Speech draft, April 4, 1946, White MSS.

88 Cited in Gardner, *Sterling-Dollar Diplomacy,* p. 197.

89 Herbert Feis, "Keynes in Retrospect," *FAQ,* XXIX (July, 1951), 564–77.

90 Some notes on the Articles of Agreement of the International Monetary Fund, May, 1946, White MSS.

91 Undated speech draft, White MSS.

Chapter 14

1 Robert E. Sherwood, *Roosevelt and Hopkins: An Intimate History* (2nd ed.; New York, 1950), p. 578; William D. Leahy, *I Was There* (New York, 1950), pp. 351–52; Leahy, Diary, April 23, 1945, Leahy MSS.

2 Herbert Feis, *The Changing Pattern of International Affairs* (New York, 1940), p. 91. See also Moffat, Diary, September 3, 1939, Moffat MSS.

3 Notes of a meeting in Morgenthau's office, July 26, 1944, White MSS.

4 Among those who apparently thought that cooperation with the Soviets was possible were Donald M. Nelson, Leo Crowley, Thomas Lamont,

and Ambassador Harriman. Hence Hopkins' criticism that dollar-a-year men led the opposition to Russia needs to be qualified. For this criticism see Rexford Tugwell, *The Stricken Land* (New York, 1947), p. 179.

5 Burton K. Wheeler to Villard, February 21, 1945, Villard MSS.

6 Denna Frank Fleming, *The Cold War and Its Origins* (2 vols.; New York, 1961), I, 259; Truman, *Memoirs*, I, 377.

7 Herbert Feis, *Churchill, Roosevelt, Stalin: The War They Waged and the Peace They Sought* (Princeton, 1957), p. 46.

8 Stalin to Churchill, November 8, 1941, Stalin, *Correspondence*, I, 33–34.

9 A good summary of this period is in Frederick L. Schuman, *Russia Since 1917* (New York, 1957), pp. 251–77.

10 Stalin to Churchill, January 29, 1944, Stalin, *Correspondence*, I, 191–92.

11 Roosevelt to Leahy, June 26, 1941, Leahy MSS; memorandum of a conversation by Sumner Welles, July 10, 1941, and Adolf Berle to Hull, September 15, 1941, *FR, 1941*, I, 182, 188.

12 For an account of American diplomacy on this issue at this time see Hull to Roosevelt, February 4, 1942, *FR, 1942*, III, 504–12.

13 John G. Winant to Hull, January 19, 1942, *ibid.*, III, 494–503.

14 Memoranda of conversations, February 18 and 20, 1942, *ibid.*, 512–24.

15 Notes on visit to Washington, March 2, 3, and 4, 1942, Moffat MSS; William Bullitt, "How We Won the War and Lost the Peace," *Life*, XXV (August 30, 1948), 82–97.

16 Bullitt, *Life*, XXV (August 30, 1948), 82–97.

17 Dean Albertson, *Roosevelt's Farmer* (New York, 1961), pp. 267–68; Sumner Welles, *Seven Decisions That Shaped History* (New York, 1951), pp. 124–39; memorandum by the Acting Secretary of State, April 1, 1942, *FR, 1942*, III, 538–39.

18 Berle to Welles, April 3, 1942, *FR, 1942*, III, 539–40; Harley Notter, ed., *Postwar Foreign Policy Preparation* (Washington, 1954), p. 187.

19 Winston S. Churchill, *The Hinge of Fate* (Boston, 1950), pp. 316–25.

20 Roosevelt to Stalin, received April 12, 1942, Stalin, *Correspondence*, I, 22–23.

21 Sherwood, *Roosevelt and Hopkins*, pp. 536–38.

22 Churchill, *Hinge of Fate*, pp. 326–29; Winant to Hull, May 24, 1942, *FR, 1942*, III, 558–63.

23 Memorandum of a conference held at the White House, May 29 and 30, 1942, *FR, 1942*, III, 566–76; Sherwood, *Roosevelt and Hopkins*, pp. 560–65.

24 William Standley to Hull, July 22, 1942, and Winant to Hull, July 10, 1942, *FR, 1942*, III, 612–13, 608–9.

25 Sherwood, *Roosevelt and Hopkins*, pp. 588–91.

26 *Ibid.*, pp. 603–5.

27 Roosevelt to Stalin, received August 19, 1942, Stalin, *Correspondence,* I, 32–33.
28 Roosevelt to Stalin, December 8, 1942, *ibid.,* I, 43.
29 Hanson Baldwin, *Great Mistakes of the War* (New York, 1950), pp. 24–25.
30 Feis, *Churchill, Roosevelt, Stalin,* pp. 174–75.
31 Notes of a Roosevelt-Stalin Meeting, December 1, 1943, *Teheran Papers,* pp. 594–95.
32 Maurice Matloff, *Strategic Planning for Coalition Warfare, 1943–1944,* in *United States Army in World War II* (Washington, 1959), pp. 215, 342, 491.
33 Stimson, Diary, December 6, 1943, Stimson MSS.
34 Feis, *Churchill, Roosevelt, Stalin,* p. 196; memorandum of a meeting at the State Department, January 11, 1944, Stimson MSS.
35 Memorandum of a meeting at the State Department, January 11, 1944, Stimson MSS.
36 Hull, *Memoirs,* II, 1451–55.
37 *Ibid.*
38 Sherwood, *Roosevelt and Hopkins,* pp. 832–34.
39 *Ibid.*
40 Stalin to Roosevelt, October 8, 1944, Stalin, *Correspondence,* I, 163; Winston S. Churchill, *Triumph and Tragedy* (Boston, 1953), pp. 227–28.
41 Charles E. Bohlen minutes of Tripartite Political Meeting, December 1, 1943, *Teheran Papers,* pp. 596–99.
42 Feis, *Churchill, Roosevelt, Stalin,* pp. 378–89.
43 Arthur Bliss Lane, *I Saw Poland Betrayed* (Indianapolis, 1948), p. 66.
44 Thomas Lamont to Villard, December 7, 1944, Villard MSS.
45 Roosevelt to Stalin, April 1, 1945, and Stalin to Roosevelt, April 7, 1945, Stalin, *Correspondence,* I, 201–4, 211–13.
46 Feis, *Churchill, Roosevelt, Stalin,* pp. 577–78; Leahy, *I Was There,* pp. 351–52; Stimson, Diary, April 23, 1945, Stimson MSS.
47 Stimson, Diary, April 23, 1945, Stimson MSS.
48 Stimson, Diary, April 26 and 30, 1945, Stimson MSS; Congressmen to Secretary of State, May 18, 1945, Grew MSS.
49 Stimson, Diary, May 26, 1945, Stimson MSS; memorandum of a conversation with the President, March 2, 1945, Franklin Roosevelt Memorial Foundation Papers (Roosevelt Library Group 21), Franklin D. Roosevelt Library, Hyde Park, New York.
50 Truman, *Memoirs,* I, 360–61; Fleming, *The Cold War,* I, 205, 258; Winant to Grew, July 13, 1945, *Potsdam Papers,* I, 408–10.
51 Churchill to Truman, May 12, 1945, *Potsdam Papers,* I, 9; memoranda of conversations with the President, May 2 and 10, 1945, Grew MSS.
52 Memorandum of a conversation with the President, June 4, 1945, Grew MSS.
53 Memorandum by the Assistant to the Secretary of State, May 27, 1945,

and Grew to W. Averell Harriman, June 29, 1945, *Potsdam Papers,* I, 31–41, 398.

54 Memorandum by the Assistant to the Secretary of State, May 30, 1945, *ibid.,* I, 53–57.

55 The Acting Secretary of State to Harriman, June 18, 1945, *ibid.,* I, 182.

56 The Acting Secretary of State to the President, June 11, 1945, *Potsdam Papers,* I, 178–82; Staff Committee paper, June 22, 1945, Briefing Book papers, June 29 and July 5, 1945, and Briefing Book paper, undated, *ibid.,* I, 186–91, 357–62, 370–74, 420–23; Grew to Harriman, June 29, 1945, *ibid.,* I, 423–26.

57 L. R. Thompson minutes of first Plenary Meeting, July 17, 1945, *Potsdam Papers,* II, 52–59; proposal by the United States Delegation, July 17, 1945, *ibid.,* II, 643–44; Department of State minutes of fifth Plenary Meeting, July 21, 1945, and Thompson minutes of eighth Plenary Meeting, July 24, 1945, *ibid.,* II, 203–15, 357–68.

58 Melbourne to the Secretary of State and Grew to Rudolf Schoenfield, July 17, 1945, *ibid.,* II, 690–92; James F. Byrnes, *All in One Lifetime* (New York, 1959), pp. 302–3; Grew to Forrest Davis, August 15, 1945, Grew MSS.

59 Harriman to Grew, June 28, 1945, *Potsdam Papers,* I, 727–28.

60 Briefing Book paper, June 29, 1945, *ibid.,* I, 714–15.

61 Grew to Lane, July 12, 1945, *ibid.,* I, 788–89.

62 Lane, *I Saw Poland Betrayed,* pp. 142–46; memorandum of a talk with Herbert Hoover, May 13, 1945, Stimson MSS; Stimson, Diary, May 29, 1945, Stimson MSS.

63 Lane, *I Saw Poland Betrayed,* pp. 142–46, 226–27.

64 Lane to Elbridge Durbrow, November 5, 1945, and Durbrow to Lane, November 29, 1945, Lane MSS.

65 Lane, *I Saw Poland Betrayed,* pp. 232–39.

66 Lauchlin Currie to Hopkins, December 31, 1943, Hopkins MSS.

67 Harry L. Hopkins, "What Victory Will Bring Us," *American Magazine,* CXXXVIII (January, 1944), 20–21, 87–89; *FCW,* VI (February 5, 1944), 29.

68 Feis, *Churchill, Roosevelt, Stalin,* pp. 641, 644.

69 William Appleman Williams, *Russian-American Relations, 1781–1947* (New York, 1952), pp. 274 ff.; memorandum for the President, July 22, 1945, Stimson MSS; Briefing Book paper, June 29, 1945, *Potsdam Papers,* I, 456–61; *Potsdam Papers,* II, 831–49.

70 Hull, *Memoirs,* II, 1248.

71 Feis, *Churchill, Roosevelt, Stalin,* p. 642. See also Herbert Feis, *The Sinews of Peace* (New York, 1944), pp. 31–32.

72 Roosevelt to Harriman, December 1, 1943, Roosevelt MSS, OF, 220; Feis, *Churchill, Roosevelt, Stalin,* pp. 643–44.

73 Morgenthau to Roosevelt, January 1, 1945, *Yalta Papers,* pp. 309–10.

74 Leahy, Diary, January 10, 1945, Leahy MSS; Treasury memorandum to Roosevelt, January 10, 1945, White MSS.

75 Feis, *Churchill, Roosevelt, Stalin,* pp. 646–47.

76 William Appleman Williams, *American-Russian Relations,* p. 275.

77 Memorandum of a conversation with James B. Reston, January 24, 1945, Grew MSS.

78 Memorandum of a conversation with Mr. Novikov, February 20, 1945, Grew MSS; memoranda of conversations with Andrei A. Gromyko, February 27 and March 3, 1945, *ibid.*

79 Memorandum of a conversation with Leo Crowley, May 11, 1945, Grew MSS; Stimson, Diary, May 11, 1945, Stimson MSS; memorandum of a conversation with Stettinius, McCloy, and Harriman, May 12, 1945, Grew MSS.

80 Memorandum of a conversation with Stettinius, McCloy, and Harriman, May 12, 1945, Grew MSS.

81 John Biggs-Davison, *The Uncertain Ally* (London, 1955), p. 101; Herbert Feis, "Political Aspects of Foreign Loans," *FAQ,* XXIII (July, 1945), 609–19.

82 Grew to Mr. Mason, May 15, 1945, Grew MSS; memorandum, May 14, 1945, and Stimson to Grew, May 16, 1945, Stimson MSS; Grew to Stimson, May 18, 1945, Grew MSS.

83 NFTC *Proceedings, 1945,* p. 47.

84 Grenville Clark to Harry S. Truman, June 2, 1945, Stimson MSS.

85 Leslie R. Groves, *Now It Can Be Told* (New York, 1962), p. 141.

86 Stimson, Diary, December 27, 1942, Stimson MSS.

87 Groves, *Now It Can Be Told,* p. 132.

88 Stimson, Diary, August 23 and December 31, 1944, Stimson MSS.

89 *Ibid.*

90 Fletcher Knebel and Charles W. Bailey, *No High Ground* (New York, 1960), pp. 70, 103; Byrnes, *All in One Lifetime,* pp. 283–84.

91 Louis Morton, "The Decision to Use the Atomic Bomb," *FAQ,* XXXV (January, 1957), 334–53; Stimson, Diary, May 14 and 15, 1945, Stimson MSS.

92 Groves, *Now It Can Be Told,* pp. 234–42.

93 Memorandum of top secret talk with Truman, June 6, 1945, Stimson MSS; *Potsdam Papers,* I, 941–42.

94 Notes for Diary, July 15–24, 1945, Stimson MSS; Knebel and Bailey, *No High Ground,* pp. 119, 120, 255; Arthur Bryant, *Triumph in the West* (New York, 1960), pp. 363–64.

95 Stimson to Truman, July 22, 1945, *Potsdam Papers,* I, 1155–57.

96 Byrnes, *All in One Lifetime,* p. 300.

97 Knebel and Bailey, *No High Ground,* pp. 2–3.

98 Stimson, Diary, August 12 to September 5, 1945, Stimson MSS; George L. Harrison to Stimson, September 11, 1945, *ibid.*

99 Henry L. Stimson and McGeorge Bundy, *On Active Duty in Peace and War* (New York, 1948), pp. 641–48; Stimson, Diary, September 12 and 21, 1945, Stimson MSS.

100 Fleming, *The Cold War,* I, 326–27.
101 Copy of speech is in Leahy MSS.

Chapter 15

1 Roosevelt to Pepper, April 9, 1945, Roosevelt MSS, PSF.

Bibliographical Essay

The first place to look for primary materials on any phase of the New Deal is, of course, the Franklin D. Roosevelt Library in Hyde Park, New York. The Roosevelt Papers for the 1932–45 period are subdivided into three main categories: the President's Secretary's File, the President's Official File, and the President's Personal File. The first of these is the most important to the student, just as it was to the President, for many of the most significant and pressing papers were kept in this file. This is not to say that the other files do not contain large quantities of materials of interest to the student of New Deal foreign policy. OF, 159, contains much material on American-Cuban relations in 1933, for example, and OF, 48-H, contains some valuable documents on United States policy towards Indian nationalism. The single most important PPF would probably be PPF-1P, the stenographic records of President Roosevelt's press conferences.

Other collections at Hyde Park include the Harry L. Hopkins Papers, the Charles Taussig Papers, and the Morris L. Cooke Papers. The first of these has not often been used, and many of the papers belonging to Hopkins had not been released when I used them. The documents in this collection are particularly rich in material pertaining to the period when Hopkins was Secretary of Commerce at the end of the 1930's. Press conferences, speech drafts, minutes of the Business Advisory Council meetings, and some correspondence during World War II, make up the bulk of the available manuscripts. Of course, many of Hopkins' papers were printed by Robert Sherwood in *Roosevelt and Hopkins: An Intimate History* (2nd ed.; New York, 1950). This work contains an amazing number of documents and excerpts from documents for the World War II era. The Taussig Papers and the Cooke Papers are primarily of use for Latin American relations and will be discussed later.

At Sterling Memorial Library, Yale University, are the Henry L. Stimson Papers. Stimson's Diary contains a wealth of material not only for the New Deal period, but also for the years when he was Secretary of State (1928–32). Of special interest are Stimson's summaries of his achievements

389

in foreign relations for those years. These long memoranda dated only a few days before he left the Department of State to Cordell Hull are extremely useful for Middle Eastern and Far Eastern relations. Letters to Stimson from men like Herbert Hoover, Grenville Clark, Frank Knox, Joseph Stilwell, and many others make this a collection second in importance only to the Roosevelt Papers. Also in the Sterling Library are the James Harvey Rogers Papers. Rogers advised Roosevelt to try inflation, but the papers also contain documentation of his interest in an expanding foreign trade.

Houghton Library, Harvard University, holds the J. Pierrepont Moffat Papers, the Joseph Grew Papers, and the Oswald Garrison Villard Papers. The former are particularly important to an understanding of European relations; Moffat was Chief of the Western European Division during these years, then Minister to Australia, and finally Minister to Canada in the early 1940's. Nancy Harvison Hooker has edited a few of these papers in *The Moffat Papers* (Cambridge, 1956), but the larger part of the materials remains unpublished. Moffat was a sophisticated and articulate diplomat who recorded Department proceedings day by day in his multivolumed diary. The Grew Papers contain a great deal of material on Far Eastern relations and some significant documents from the period when Grew was acting Secretary of State for long periods in the first half of 1945. Villard's papers are filled with correspondence with liberal leaders like William Allen White and Burton K. Wheeler.

In the Library of Congress are several collections of particular interest to the student of New Deal diplomacy. The most important, the Cordell Hull Papers, are still restricted for the period after 1928, but the Norman H. Davis Papers, the Harold Ickes Papers, the Josephus Daniels Papers, and others may be consulted. The Davis Papers are important for their records of international conferences during the 1930's. Davis was the chief delegate to the Geneva World Disarmament Conference, the London Naval Conference of 1936, and the Brussels Nine-Power Conference of 1937. The memoranda of conversations at this last conference are unmatched for a quick look into the dilemmas of the 1930's in the Far East. The Ickes Papers are mainly of interest for World War II oil negotiations, since the manuscript diary is not yet open to scholars. The Daniels Collection is the most complete record available of any New Deal Ambassador's mission. Daniels' records of the strained relations between the United States and Mexico in the late 1930's are obligatory reading.

The published volumes of the State Department Archives, *Foreign Relations of the United States* (Washington, various dates), are the most important published source for the student of foreign policy. Although some important documents are not printed, the volumes are generally well done. Even better than the yearly volumes are the special editions of the *Yalta Papers* (*The Conferences at Malta and Yalta, 1945*), the *Teheran Papers* (*The Conferences at Cairo and Teheran*), and the two volumes of *Potsdam Papers* (*The Conference at Potsdam*).

For economic diplomacy the published proceedings of the National Foreign Trade Council, *Proceedings of the National Foreign Trade Convention* (New York, various dates) are significant not only because they contain speeches and remarks by men primarily interested in foreign trade operations, but also speeches by members of the State and Commerce departments which broaden and deepen one's understanding of the documents printed in such places as *Foreign Relations*.

At the head of the list of published personal papers are the Samuel I. Rosenman, ed., *Public Papers and Addresses of Franklin D. Roosevelt* (13 vols.; New York, 1938–50). Unfortunately not all the public papers are printed in this edition, and the greatest weakness of these volumes probably is that they reproduce so few press conferences. Elliott Roosevelt's collection of his father's letters, *F.D.R.: His Personal Letters, 1928–1945* (2 vols.; New York, 1950) add only a small number of documents on any one subject.

Cordell Hull's *Memoirs* (2 vols.; New York, 1948) do not suffer much from his biases, and, indeed, are most valuable for Hull's recollection of his attitudes and outlook on various key issues. His reminiscences about the Moscow Foreign Minister's Conference of 1943 alone make the volumes worth reading. Henry Morgenthau's diaries, in John M. Blum, *From the Morgenthau Diaries: Years of Crisis, 1928–1938* (Boston, 1959), and Allan Seymour Everest's *Morgenthau, the New Deal and Silver* (New York, 1950) contain much material on Morgenthau's attitudes on such issues as German-American relations, the Silver Purchase Act, the problems of the Mexican silver purchase agreement, and the impact of American financial policies in the 1930's upon China.

The Secret Diary of Harold Ickes (3 vols.; New York, 1950–53) reveals only a few incidences in foreign policy that are not treated somewhere else. State Department *Press Releases* (until 1939), the State Department *Bulletin,* and the Commerce Department's *Foreign Commerce Weekly* are of value primarily because they reprint large numbers of speeches made by Department officers at various places at various times.

Books and articles by New Deal participants, such as Rexford Tugwell's *The Democratic Roosevelt* (New York, 1957) and his articles in the *Western Political Quarterly* from 1948 to 1952, Henry A. Wallace's *America Must Choose* (Boston, 1934), Adolf Berle's articles in *Survey Graphic* and *Scribner's* magazines, Raymond Moley's *After Seven Years* (New York, 1939), and George N. Peek and Sanford Crowther's *Why Quit Our Own?* (New York, 1936), all present a point of view but all provide material and insight for subsequent study. Peek's treatment of the Hull trade agreement program is particularly interesting whether one agrees with it or not.

The single best work on American relations with Europe during the "neutrality years" is Robert Divine's *The Illusion of Neutrality* (Chicago, 1962). Based upon many manuscript sources including some records of the Senate Committees involved, Divine's work brings us a far more accurate picture of Roosevelt's mind than either Basil Rauch's *Roosevelt: From*

Munich to Pearl Harbor (New York, 1950) or Charles Beard's *American Foreign Policy in the Making, 1932–1940* (New Haven, 1946). William S. Culbertson's, *Reciprocity* (New York, 1937) contains an appendix with documents on the development of America's reciprocal trade agreements program since the time of McKinley's Administration, and even before. Culbertson himself had not a little to do with the direction of American economic foreign policy. On the German side, see Department of State, *Documents on German Foreign Policy: 1918–1945,* Series C and D (Washington, 1949——).

For the years when America was deciding to accept political involvement, Sumner Welles, *Seven Decisions That Shaped History* (New York, 1951), William L. Langer and S. Everett Gleason, *The Challenge to Isolation* (New York, 1952) and *The Undeclared War* (New York, 1953), Joseph Alsop and Robert Kintner, *American White Paper* (New York, 1940), Forrest K. Davis and Ernest K. Lindley, *How War Came* (New York, 1942) are the most valuable. The revisionist studies, while raising some key questions, center too much in Roosevelt's personal character. Charles Tansill's *Back Door to War* (Chicago, 1952), is heavily documented in some key areas, but in general is unsatisfactory in demonstrating its conclusions. Charles A. Beard's *President Roosevelt and the Coming of the War* (New Haven, 1948) tries to deal with the larger implications of Roosevelt's handling of foreign policy, and should be read even if one does not agree with its conclusions.

Articles include Wayne S. Cole, "Senator Key Pittman and American Neutrality Policies," *Mississippi Valley Historical Review,* XLVI (March, 1960), 644–62, and Robert Divine, "Roosevelt and Collective Security, 1933," *Mississippi Valley Historical Review,* XLVIII (June, 1961), 42–59.

LATIN AMERICA

Manuscript collections used in the Latin American chapters include, in addition to the Roosevelt Papers, the Daniels Papers, the Cooke Papers, the Taussig Papers, the Arthur Bliss Lane Papers, and the Harry Dexter White Papers. The Lane Papers are in the Sterling Memorial Library, and although they contain few documents of significance, there are some important communications with the State Department and individual Department officers for the period when Lane was Minister to various Central American nations and later when he was American Minister to Colombia during World War II. The White Papers are in the Firestone Library, Princeton University. There are copies of several memoranda that Treasury Department officials sent to Secretary Morgenthau, which apparently influenced him in regard to Latin American affairs from 1938 to 1941.

On the background of the Good Neighbor Policy, and its development, there are several indispensable secondary works. Laurence Duggan's *The Americas* (New York, 1949) is the single most honest, well-balanced, and informative discussion written by a policy maker in the New Deal years. Bryce Woods' *Making of the Good Neighbor Policy* (New York, 1961),

Donald Dozer's *Are We Good Neighbors?* (Gainesville, Fla., 1959), and Edwin Lieuwen's *Arms and Politics in Latin America* (New York, 1960) are among the best of the new books on United States relations with Latin America. Particularly impressive is Wood's discussion of how the United States met the problem of Bolivian and Mexican oil expropriations after 1937. A very important document is edited by Charles C. Griffin in "Welles to Roosevelt: A Memorandum on Inter-American Relations," *Hispanic-American Historical Review*, XXXIV (May, 1954), 190–92.

James Fred Rippy's *Latin America and the Industrial Age* (New York, 1947) and his *Globe and Hemisphere* (Chicago, 1958) are particularly important as studies of American economic relations with Latin America as are Carleton Beals's *Pan America* (New York, 1940) and Willy Feurlein and Elizabeth Hannan's *Dollars in Latin America* (New York, 1941). On the activities of the Export-Import Bank, and the changes in the Good Neighbor Policy's attitude after 1938 towards positive help to industrialization projects, see Senate Committee on Banking and Currency, *Study of the Export-Import Bank and World Bank,* 83rd Congress, 2nd Session (Washington, 1954). American relations with troublesome nations in Latin America during World War II are reflected in the yearbook, *Inter-American Affairs,* Arthur P. Whitaker, ed. (New York, various dates).

Specific topics are well treated in Robert F. Smith, *The United States and Cuba: Business and Diplomacy, 1917–1960* (New York, 1961), and E. David Cronon, "Interpreting the Good Neighbor Policy," *Hispanic-American Historical Review,* XXXIX (November 1959), 538–68. Smith has documented his work with archival sources and other primary materials to show the development of American economic policy towards Cuba while Cronon has given us a picture of the dilemma the Cuban Revolution of 1933 created for the young Good Neighbor Policy.

Cronon's book, *Josephus Daniels in Mexico* (Madison, 1960), is particularly welcome as the first full-scale attempt to discuss the Mexican oil expropriation crisis and Daniels' role in preventing a breakdown in Mexican-American relations. Unfortunately Cronon has not followed up this book with a sequel to show how much of Daniels' work was undone in later years.

Matthew Josephson's *Empire of the Air* (New York, 1944) gives us the story of Pan-American Airways' impact on Latin America and on American foreign policy, and secondly how Pan American was used to further the aims of policy makers after 1938.

THE FAR EAST

Of special interest for Far Eastern affairs are the Joseph Grew Papers, the Norman Davis Papers, and the Henry L. Stimson's Papers. The State Department archives on Manchurian questions and the attempt to revitalize the Second China Consortium go beyond the printed documents in the *Foreign Relations* series.

William Standley and Arthur Agerton's *Admiral Ambassador to Russia* (Chicago, 1955) gives some of Standley's experiences at naval conferences and discussions, though more of this material can be found in the Davis Papers.

A good selection of Hull's speeches are printed in the State Department's *Peace and War: United States Foreign Policy, 1931–1941* (Washington, 1943). In addition there are the special *Foreign Relations* volumes on *Japan: 1931–41* (2 vols.; Washington, 1943).

The Congressional investigations of the Pearl Harbor Attack, Joint Committee on the Investigation of the Pearl Harbor Attack, *Hearings,* 79th Congress, 1st Session (39 parts; Washington, 1948), contain much information, none more valuable than copies of the Japanese Ambassador's correspondence with Tokyo.

Herbert Feis's *The Road to Pearl Harbor* (Princeton, 1950) and Paul Schroeder's *The Axis Alliance and Japanese-American Relations* (Ithaca, 1958) are the two best secondary works on the 1941 conversations and Japanese policy. Not to be overlooked is Robert J. C. Butow's fine article, "The Hull-Nomura Conversations: A Fundamental Misconception," *American Historical Review,* LXV (July, 1960), 822–37.

For relations with China the beginning point is the Department of State, *United States Relations with China: with Special Rereference to the Period 1942–1949* (Washington, 1949). The Teheran and Yalta Papers supplement the China White Paper. Theodore White's collection of *The Stilwell Papers* (New York, 1948) and Charles Romanus and Riley Sunderland's *Stilwell's Mission to China,* in *United States Army in World War II* (Washington, 1953) demonstrate the difficulties with even the concept of the "China Theater."

On the end of extra-territoriality see Wesley R. Fishel, *The End of Extra-territoriality in China* (Berkeley, 1952). The breakdown of China and American frustrations in dealing with it are discussed in Herbert Feis, *The China Tangle* (Princeton, 1953). For the kind of false hopes that were raised once more about China during World War II see Theodore White's revealing article "China's Postwar Plans," in *Fortune,* XXVIII (October, 1943) 150 ff.

On American decisions to encourage Russia to enter the war in the Far East and then the agonizing second appraisal, see Department of Defense, *The Entry of the Soviet Union into the War Against Japan: Military Plans 1941–1945* (Washington, 1955).

The discussions at Potsdam over Russia's entry into the Far Eastern war can be found in the *Potsdam Papers,* James Byrnes, *All in One Lifetime* (New York, 1959), Walter Millis, ed., *The Forrestal Diaries* (New York, 1951), and Harry S. Truman, *Memoirs,* Vol. I: *Year of Decisions* (New York, 1955).

THE COLONIAL WORLD AND THE MIDDLE EAST

A photostatic copy of William D. Leahy's Diary in the State Historical Society of Wisconsin, Madison, does not contain much material not in his printed memoirs, *I Was There* (New York, 1950). Both are particularly good for American relations with the French colonial empire. Charles Taussig's Papers are of value because Taussig was a member of the Anglo-American Caribbean Commission.

Philippine relations are discussed in Garel Grunder and William E. Livezey, *The Philippines and the United States* (Norman, Oklahoma, 1951), Shirley Jenkins, *American Economic Policy Towards the Philippines* (Stanford, 1954), Ethel B. Dietrich, *The Far Eastern Trade of the United States* (New York, 1940), and Francis Sayre, *Glad Adventure* (New York, 1957).

On India, see Winston Churchill, *The Hinge of Fate* (Boston, 1950), and William Phillips, *Ventures in Diplomacy* (Boston, 1952).

American anti-colonialism can be followed in Don Lohbeck, *Patrick J. Hurley* (Chicago, 1956), the Hull *Memoirs*, Sherwood, *Roosevelt and Hopkins*, Elliott Roosevelt, *As He Saw It* (New York, 1946), and Edward R. Stettinius, *Roosevelt and the Russians* (New York, 1949).

American plans for a trusteeship system are presented in the Hull *Memoirs* and Francis Sayre's *Dependent Peoples and World Order* (Denver, 1948). Also see Sayre's article, "Freedom Comes to the Philippines," *Atlantic Monthly*, CLXXV (March, 1945), 82–88.

Other significant articles include Herbert Feis, "On Our Economic Relations with Britain," *Foreign Affairs Quarterly*, XXI (April, 1943), 462–75, and Harry Hopkins, "What Victory Will Bring Us," *American Magazine*, CXXXVIII (January, 1944), 20 ff.

The Stimson Papers are rich in materials on American interest in Middle Eastern oil both in the 1920's and during World War II. The Senate Special Committee Investigating the National Defense Program's *Hearings,* Part 41, *Petroleum Arrangements with Saudi Arabia,* 80th Congress, 1st Session (Washington, 1948), are the single best source for that subject. Loaded with documentation from the National Archives is T. H. Vail Motter's, *The Persian Gulf Corridor and Aid to Russia,* in *United States Army in World War II* (Washington, 1952). An American adviser to Iran during World War II, Arthur C. Millspaugh, has written of his frustrations and the difficulties of American policy in *Americans in Persia* (Washington, 1947). See also Sumner Welles, *Where Are We Heading?* (New York, 1946).

American recognition policies in the Levant are discussed in Leahy, *I Was There,* Herbert Feis, *Between War and Peace: The Potsdam Conference* (Princeton, 1960), and *Potsdam Papers.*

The Anglo-American oil agreement and its background are discussed in Herbert Feis, *Seen From E. A.* (New York, 1947) and Halford L. Hopkins, *Middle East Oil in United States Foreign Policy* (Washington, 1950). Important also is John W. Frey and H. Chandler Ide, *A History of the Petroleum Administration for War, 1941–1945* (Washington, 1946).

Specifically on Ickes' role, there are some documents in his Papers and in the Roosevelt Papers. In addition the article, "Mr. Ickes' Arabian Nights," *Fortune,* XXIX (June, 1944), 123–28, should be consulted.

Landis sums up his mission in "Anglo-American Cooperation in the Middle East," *Vital Speeches,* XI (May 1, 1945), 428–32.

POSTWAR PLANNING

The financial and economic negotiations which led to the Bretton Woods proposals are detailed in the Harry Dexter White Papers. A pioneer study on economic diplomacy is Richard N. Gardner's *Sterling-Dollar Diplomacy* (Oxford, 1956). Gardner makes use of the White Papers and also some of the William L. Clayton Papers. There is an important exchange between Clayton and Harry Hopkins on the importance of postwar foreign trade in the Hopkins Papers. Harley Notter has edited the State Department's *Postwar Foreign Policy Preparation* (Washington, 1954), which has a great deal of material on economic policy. Hull's *Memoirs* have, of course, a great deal of material on economic policy also.

On air power Josephson's *Empire of the Air*, Henry Wallace's *Sixty-Million Jobs* (New York, 1945), and J. Parker Van Zandt's *Civil Aviation and Peace* (Washington, 1944), are the best secondary works. The Department of State's *Proceedings of the International Civil Aviation Conference* (2 vols.; Washington, 1949), are worthwhile, but much material around the time of this Conference can be found in Leahy's *I Was There* and in the Leahy Diary.

Articles include, "The Logic of the Air," *Fortune*, XXVII (April, 1943), 70 ff., and Herbert Feis's "Economics and Peace," *Foreign Policy Reports*, XX (April, 1944), 14–19.

Discussions of Lend-Lease repayment are in Gardner, *Sterling-Dollar Diplomacy, The Yalta Papers, The Stimson Papers*, the Hull *Memoirs, The Moffat Papers*, and Herbert Feis's article, "Restoring Trade After the War," *Foreign Affairs Quarterly*, XX (January, 1942), 282–92.

American fears for the postwar period fill hundreds of pages of testimony, as in the Special Committee on Post-War Economic Policy and Planning's *Economic Problems of the Transition Period*, 78th Congress, 2nd Session, and 79th Congress, 1st Session (Washington, 1945). Secondary works include Herbert Feis's *The Sinews of Peace* (New York, 1944), Karl Schriftgeisser's *Business Comes of Age* (New York, 1960), and the article by David S. McLellan and Charles E. Woodhouse, "The Business Elite and Foreign Policy," *Western Political Quarterly*, XIII (March, 1960), 172–90. See also Herbert Feis's "Keynes in Retrospect," *Foreign Affairs Quarterly*, XXIX, (July, 1951), 564–77.

RUSSIA'S OPPOSITION

The special *Foreign Relations* volumes on the Teheran, Yalta, and Potsdam conferences are the first place to look for information on this subject. The Roosevelt Papers and the Grew Papers for the crucial period in early 1945 should be consulted. On economic aid the White Papers and the Leahy Diary are valuable. On atomic policy the Stimson Papers and the autobiographical *On Active Duty in Peace and War* (New York, 1948), by Stimson and McGeorge Bundy must be read. *The Forrestal Diaries*, edited by Millis, contain much material sent by Ambassador Harriman to Washington in 1945.

Secondary works on the background of the Cold War include Herbert Feis, *Churchill, Roosevelt, Stalin: The War They Waged and the Peace They Sought* (Princeton, 1957), Denna Frank Flemming, *The Cold War and Its Origins* (2 vols.; New York, 1961), and William Appleman Williams, *Russian-American Relations, 1781–1947* (New York, 1952). And see especially the article by William C. Bullitt, "How We Won the War and Lost the Peace," *Life,* XXV (August 30, 1948), 82–97.

On the Polish question the Arthur Bliss Lane Papers and his book, *I Saw Poland Betrayed* (Indianapolis, 1948), and the *Teheran, Yalta, and Potsdam Papers* are the best sources. For the Russian side, both on the question of the second front and Eastern Europe, see Ministry of Foreign Affairs of the USSR, *Correspondence Between the Chairman of the Council of Ministers of the USSR and the Presidents of the USA and the Prime Ministers of Great Britain during the Great Patriotic War of 1941–1945* (2 vols.; Moscow, 1957).

Other important articles include Herbert Feis's "Political Aspects of Foreign Loans," *Foreign Affairs Quarterly,* XXIII (July, 1945), 609–19, and Louis Morton's "The Decision to Use the Atomic Bomb," *Foreign Affairs Quarterly,* XXXV (January, 1957), 334–53.

Secondary works on atomic policy that are useful include Leslie Groves, *Now It Can Be Told* (New York, 1962) and Fletcher Knebel and Charles W. Bailey, *No High Ground* (New York, 1960).

Index

Hawes-Cutting Bill for Philippine Independence, 178
Hitler, Adolf, 152, 163. *See also* Germany
Hoover, Herbert C.: Farewell Address, 7–10 *passim;* early career, 8; arms sales and the depression, 11; on European war debts and the depression, 22; letter to Stimson in 1941 on U.S. postwar relations with Great Britain, 172; attitude on Philippine independence in 1932, 178; letter to Stimson on European policy, 254; on Eastern European policy after World War I, 312
Hopkins, Harry L.: fears Axis takeover in Latin America, 124; on Japanese-American relations, 150; as Commerce Secretary, 158–59; on U.S. trade policy towards U.K., 172–73; on British imperialism, 176–77; on need for bases in Philippines, 181; on bases in West Indies, 185–86; supports strong Middle Eastern policy, 221; on Lend-Lease to Saudi Arabia, 233; comments on the Anglo-American oil agreement, 236; on postwar aid to China, 248; mission to Moscow, 255–56; and Will Clayton on foreign trade, 263; on protecting foreign investments, 263–64; on commercial airbases, 273; on Russia in postwar world, 292; note to Roosevelt on Anglo-American economic planning, 283; on Anglo-Russian relations, 298; advises Roosevelt against Anglo-Russian settlement of Balkan issues, 305; discusses Polish issues with Stalin, 309–10; on postwar trade with Russia, 313–14
Hornbeck, Stanley K.: policy adviser in the State Department, 16; on the Nine Power Treaty, 68–69; Second China Consortium, 78–80; on military opposition to Japan, 142; and extra-territoriality in China, 243
Hughes, Charles E., 8, 40–41, 68–69
Hull, Cordell: and New Deal trade policy, 15, 24; at London Economic Conference, 25, 28, 29–30; on recog-

nition of the Soviet Union, 35–36; on naval re-armament, 38; and most-favored-nation trade policy, 44
— Latin American policies: 1933 Cuban Revolution, 48; Montevideo Conference, 50, 58; Lima Foreign Ministers Conference, 110; on land expropriations, 113; intervenes in Mexican oil dispute, 114; Mexican oil crisis, 119, 121; Mexican oil settlement, 122; 1935 speech on Good Neighbor Policy, 194; relations with Argentina, 202–3; Mexican oil in World War II, 207–8; Colombian oil, 210
— Far Eastern policies: on Japanese forward movement, 70–71, 73–74, 79–80, 134; restatement of U.S. policy, 1938, 137; opposes direct aid to China, 140; on Far Eastern trade, 141; allows 1911 Japanese-American Commercial Treaty to lapse, 142; further appeals to Japan, 143; last-ditch talks with Nomura, 145-51 *passim;* freezes Japanese assets, 147; opposes Roosevelt-Konoye meeting, 148; and extra-territoriality in China, 243–44; Moscow Declaration, 245; hopes and fears for China, 245–46
— European policies: outline of, 85, 86; opposes barter with Germany, 99, 100, 101; opposes bilateral trade deal with Germany, 103, 104; opposes Armistice Day Conference, 105; efforts to persuade British to accept American trade policy, 106; German threat to U.S. trade policies, 154, 169; opposes Big Four regional planning for postwar security, 265–66; opposes Morgenthau Plan, 269; pushes for Article VII of the Lend-Lease Agreement 280; worries about Teheran, 304; economic planning with the Soviet Union, 314–15
— policies towards colonial and underdeveloped areas: India, 182; State Department Trusteeship planning, 190; support for Culbertson Mission to the Middle East, 222; favors expansion of policy in Iran, 227–28;